HUMAN BEHAVIOR IN ORGANIZATIONS:
Three Levels of Behavior

Charles R. Milton

University of South Carolina

PRENTICE-HALL, INC., Englewood Cliffs, N.J. 07632

Library of Congress Cataloging in Publication Data

MILTON, CHARLES R
   Human behavior in organizations.

   Includes index.
   1. Organizational behavior. 2. Organizational
behavior—Case studies. I. Title.
HM133.M515   302.3'5   80-24762
ISBN 0-13-444596-1

To my wife, Fay, who has given constant assistance and support.

Editorial/production supervision and interior
design by Richard C. Laveglia
Cover design by Miriam Recio
Manufacturing buyer: Gordon Osbourne

Printed in the United States of America

10 9 8 7 6 5 4 3 2 1

Prentice-Hall International, Inc., *London*
Prentice-Hall of Australia Pty. Limited, *Sydney*
Prentice-Hall of Canada, Ltd., *Toronto*
Prentice-Hall of India Private Limited, *New Delhi*
Prentice-Hall of Japan, Inc., *Tokyo*
Prentice-Hall of Southeast Asia Pte. Ltd., *Singapore*
Whitehall Books Limited, *Wellington, New Zealand*

CONTENTS

Preface

This book is about human behavior in organizations and is relevant for anyone—student, manager or non-manager—who wishes to understand, predict and influence organizational behavior. It provides the background beginning students will need to analyze behavioral situations and respond more appropriately.

An introductory principles of management course, while helpful, is not a prerequisite for understanding this book. Whatever one's background, the author feels simply memorizing theories, concepts, and models is not sufficient to produce understanding. New insights must be tested through experience. Consequently, cases, carefully tailored to each chapter, are provided to give the student an opportunity to apply new insights and make them meaningful and relevant.

Many books on organizational behavior have significantly overlapped principles of management, personnel management, and organization theory. The author has avoided such duplication and confined the content of this text to individual, group, and organizational levels of behavior. A model of organizational behavior has been utilized as a vehicle to achieve this purpose.

The author wishes to express his gratitude to the following people who reviewed the original manuscript and whose suggestions, critiques, and encouragement helped to shape the final draft of the manuscript. Prof. John P. Alexander, *Burlington County College;* Prof. Hrach Bedrosian, *New York University;* Prof. Louis Desfosses, *State University of New York at Brockport;* Prof. Cecil D. Green, *Riverside Community College;* Dr. John E. Logan, *University of South Carolina;* Prof. Robert H. Madden, *Southwestern College;* Prof. C.W. Millard, *Iowa State University;* Prof. John D. Minch, *Cabrillo College;* Prof. Edward J. Morrison, *University of Colorado;* Prof. Milo C. Pierce, *Corpus Christi State University;* Prof. John W. Seybolt, *The University of Utah;* Mr. John W. Stockman, *Consultant;* Prof. Arthur B. Sweney, *Wichita State University.*

Finally, the author has sought to provide a text that covers the relevant topics of organizational behavior in an interesting and readable manner.

CHAPTER 1

ORGANIZATIONAL BEHAVIOR

The primary purpose of this book is to develop an understanding of behavior in organizations. If you have been involved in an organization, even in a limited way, you may have had occasion to wonder what was happening, or failing to happen, and why. Whether you are studying to be a manager or have no aspirations along such lines, everyone needs to know as much about organizational behavior as possible. All of us are, or will be, involved with one or more organizations in our lifetimes.

However, merely understanding organizational behavior is not sufficient. One must also be able to use such understanding to predict what is likely to happen and subsequently to influence or control organizational events. The total effort is illustrated as follows.

Understanding ⟶ Prediction ⟶ Influence

For a manager who must make things happen and whose success is measured by his or her ability to do so, the importance of being able to understand, predict, and influence events and situations is obvious. It may be less apparent that understanding organizational behavior is also important to the nonmanager. Episodes such as the following ones take place every day in organizations, whatever their nature.

TWO FACETS OF THE NEED TO KNOW

As Jim Walton was driving home from work, his mind turned to the events of the day. Why was the boss so steamed when he learned that a scheduled order could not possibly get out on time? Jim thought, "I resented the implication that my section was dragging its heels and not performing as well as it could. I tried to explain how things were going, but this only made him more irritable. He seemed to resent my effort. To top it all off, some of the guys have been acting funny. Not talking, joking, or kidding around as usual. Is it pressure to get the order out? Do they resent my effort to stand up for the group? Many more days like this and I'll be looking for another job. Besides, the work has become too routine. Do I want this the rest of my life? I'm sure glad that there's a cold beer in the refrigerator."

Dan Weber, supervisor, was driving home after the day's work. What a day! Did anything go right? To top it all off, an important order wasn't going to be completed on time. The boss had stressed this one. A good job delivered on time could lead to a new contract that the firm needed badly to offset a slump in business. Why couldn't the guys see this and come through? Dan thought, "How will this affect my performance evaluation next week? Promotion? Imagine Jim Walton trying to make excuses for the crew! What does he know? Who does he think he is anyway? Should I crack down? Push them harder? One sure thing, things can't go on as they have today."

In these interrelated events, both supervisor and employee are perplexed about what is taking place. The supervisor, Dan Weber, needs to understand what is happening in his work group. The men may not really appreciate the importance of the job, or they may be up against something beyond their control. Such understanding will help Dan Weber predict or anticipate what is likely to happen if things continue as they are now or if he pushes harder. His job will be made easier if he can anticipate the consequences of possible corrective changes, especially the effect on morale and productivity. Finally, Dan Weber can use his understanding to develop a plan of action to implement the change he decides upon.

Jim Walton, employee, also needs to understand what is happening to him. His feeling of security and adjustment, like his supervisor's, is affected by his lack of understanding of what has happened. Jim Walton needs to predict or anticipate how his behavior will affect his co-workers or his boss. Also, it is helpful to be able to anticipate how he may be influenced by other employees and organizational activities. Finally, Jim Walton, like most people, is not passive but seeks to influence others and the flow of work events.

Both manager and nonmanager would be helped by an understanding of human behavior in an organizational setting.

THE STUDY OF ORGANIZATION BEHAVIOR

Organizations exist to product goods or services, health care, recreation, protection, religious affiliation, and so on. Whatever the organization's objective, people must be employed and utilized as individuals and as groups. This leads us to the following definition: Organization behavior is the study of individuals and groups within organizations.[1]

However, organizations also develop patterns of action and reaction as they respond to environmental changes and utilize individuals and groups. These develop as an organization seeks to integrate the human variables (abilities, needs) and organization variables (goals, tasks, technologies). Characteristic patterns of leadership, conflict, adjustment, and coping with change become established and permeate the organization. The organization develops its own "personality," its own way of doing things that affects individuals and groups. Consequently, our study of organizational behavior will consist of examining behavior at three levels —individual, group, and organizational.

AN OVERVIEW OF ORGANIZATIONAL BEHAVIOR

Each of the three levels of behavior can be presented as a *model* of behavior. Such a model can identify some of the key variables and show how these are related. Models permit us to simplify reality so that we can focus on some of its primary characteristics and seek to understand them.

Behavior at the Individual Level

The model for developing our understanding of organizational behavior begins with behavior at the individual level. In Figure 1-1 we see four factors that make the individual what he or she is and influence his or her behavior: perceptions, attitudes, values, and motivations. These same factors can affect an individual's effectiveness or performance. Finally, individual effectiveness, job satisfaction, and motivation are affected by job design, that is, by the structuring of job tasks and duties.

Figure 1-1

A Model of Behavior at the Individual Level

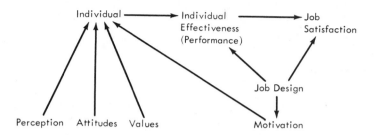

Behavior at the Group Level

The next building block in our model of organizational behavior is the group as shown in Figure 1-2. Since the individual interacts with other persons in his or her work group, interpersonal behavior links people with one another. Personal interactions between two or more persons are influenced by one's personal system, self-concept, needs, and interpersonal orientations.

Next, work group behavior is looked at from the standpoint of the background factors (technology, management practices, economic influences, etc.), required behaviors, and emergent behaviors. The results of group behavior are seen in terms of productivity, satisfaction, and individual development.

However, most work groups do not operate in isolation; rather, they must interact with other groups to attain an organization's objectives. Intergroup relations are influenced by power, goals, and values of the groups.

Figure 1-2

A Model of Behavior at the Group Level

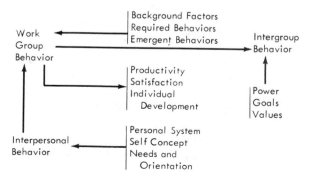

4

Behavior at the Organizational Level

The third part of our model is behavior at the organizational level as presented in Figure 1-3. Behavior at this level is greatly influenced by those who manage or direct an organization, and leadership plays a central role in shaping behavior at the individual, group, and organizational levels. Leadership also determines the attention given to communication, which ties the organization together.

Figure 1-3

A Model of Behavior at the Organizational Level

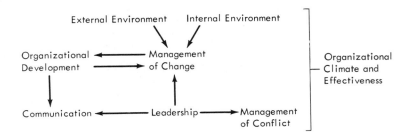

The management of change is a response that may be initiated from an external or internal source. Organizational development is an approach for changing appropriate factors (people, tasks, structures, and technologies) at the individual, group, and organizational levels of behavior. The last variable at the organizational level deals with the management of conflict. Organizational climate and effectiveness are considered outputs of behavior at the third, or organizational, level.

The Complete Model and Organization of the Book

The completed model showing several linkages between the behavioral levels appears in Figure 1-4. The model emphasizes the three levels of behavior, key variables and linkages between variables.

The chapters that follow move through each of the levels of behavior. The next five chapters focus upon individual behavior. Chapters 2 and 3 develop the topic of internal human processes basic to understanding the individual: perceptions, attitudes, values, and motivations. Effectiveness of the individual in an organizational context is considered in Chapters 4 and 5, which emphasize the work environment, job strain, and job design as

5

Figure 1-4

A Three-Level Model of Organizational Behavior

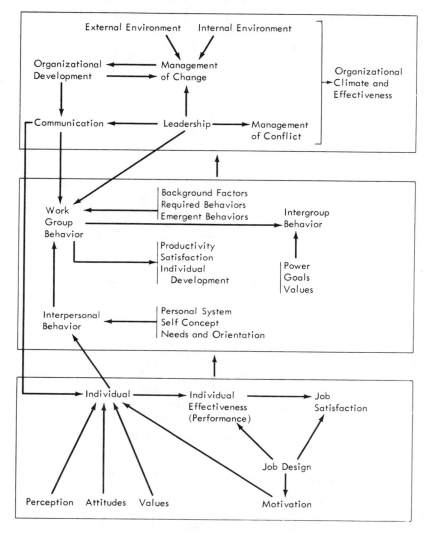

causal factors. Chapter 6 examines the concept of job satisfaction and measures to increase the quality of life on the job.

The second portion of the text, Chapters 7–9, considers group and intergroup behavior. Chapter 7, "Interpersonal Behavior," serves as a linking topic between the individual and the group as a focus of analysis. Personal interactions between two or more persons and the dynamics that structure such interactions are the primary concerns in this chapter. The results of interpersonal interactions are examined from a cost–benefit perspective. In Chapter 8, the work group is examined as it is affected by factors that range from external social and economic factors to required job interactions. Intergroup behaviors are examined in Chapter 9 from the standpoint of antecedents to cooperation and conflict and how these may be managed. This chapter also examines a special kind of intergroup relation: union and management. The dynamics of this association are related to intergroup variables.

The final section of the text considers behaviors related to the total organization as an entity. Chapter 10 explores the ramifications of leadership and the contingency implications of this function; leadership styles and the organization context of leadership are examined. Chapter 11 focuses on the organization-wide implications of communication and its management. Chapters 12 and 13 examine the dynamics of change and the contribution of organization development as an emerging behavioral discipline to intelligent change management.

Chapter 14 deals with conflict management. Following the presentation of conflict models, various approaches to the resolution of conflict at different levels of organizational behavior are presented. Chapter 15 explores the important, but complicated, areas of organizational climate and organizational effectiveness.

THREE BASIC VIEWPOINTS OF ORGANIZATIONAL BEHAVIOR

The model of organizational behavior as shown in Figure 1-4 indicates the complexity of this area of study. One needs all the assistance available when embarking on such a task. While there are numerous approaches to examining organizational behavior, three will be used to guide our study: systems theory, behavioral viewpoints, and contingency approach to problem analysis.

Systems Theory

The term ''system'' is not a new one. Everyone is familiar with the idea of a solar system, a nervous system, or a registration system. All systems have the following characteristics:[2]

1. There are a number of parts, and
2. The parts are related to one another in an interdependent manner.

Consequently, a system is defined as a set of elements or parts in mutual interaction.

Open and closed systems

There are two kinds of systems: closed and open. A closed system is one that responds to nothing outside itself. There are no exchanges with the environment that would permit the inflow of energy of any kind. Consequently, a closed system cannot restore itself, and, like the so-called perpetual motion machine, it "runs down."

In contrast, an open system admits inputs that are transformed or changed in some manner to become outputs as follows:

Inputs ⟶ Transformation ⟶ Outputs

All open systems exist in an environment that is more or less complex. Both humans and organizations have the characteristics of an open system. For example, an individual has sensory mechanisms that regulate inputs from the environment: sight, sound, touch, taste, and smell. These inputs are processed by the central nervous system; the output is some kind of behavior.

Equilibrium and growth responses of systems

In addition to being comprised of mutually interacting and interdependent parts, open systems have two additional characteristics. Systems return to their original state—equilibrium—after being disturbed. After being upset or disrupted, adjustive and corrective activities are set into motion that return the system to a stable condition. For example, if a copying machine breaks down in the reproducing section of an organization, every effort will be made to repair the machine and get operations back to normal. If your hand becomes infected, the white corpuscles in the bloodstream rally to restore affected areas to their previous healthy condition.

In addition to returning to equilibrium, open systems have a tendency to learn or grow.[3] Changing environmental pressures require that a system adopt new patterns of behavior, that is, learn, if it is to survive. Organizations offer new products and services to meet changes in consumer tastes and preferences; to do otherwise invites stagnation and decline. An individual must learn, acquire new skills, and develop additional abilities to avoid becoming obsolete and losing material and psychological rewards.

An open system requires both equilibrium and growth to perform well over a period of time. However, a balance must be maintained between the two actions. Growth and learning require movement away from the existing equilibrium, that is, change. For example, a work group comfortable with the present way of operating may resist an attempt to introduce more efficient work procedures. Moreover, if a change is introduced too rapidly, an individual or group may not learn the new behaviors adequately, and operations become badly disorganized. For this reason, many changes are introduced step by step over a period of time. In this manner a new equilibrium is sought, but the necessary growth is not disruptive.

An organization as a system

An organization as an open system is shown in Figure 1-5. Various inputs from the environment—for example, human, material, monetary, energy, and informational—are permitted to enter the organization. Within the organization the inputs are subjected to transformation by various subsystems. The parts of a system have ordered patterns of activity for using the inputs and for achieving the organization's purposes. The outputs have both material and social characteristics, that is, productivity, satisfaction, and individual development. The lines at the bottom of Figure 1-5 reflect feedback information as to the status of the outputs. Such feedback may signal that the outputs are appropriate or that adjustments are needed in the transformation process and/or in the inputs. In both instances, the feedback serves to bring the system back to equilibrium.

In summary, the systems viewpoint is a reminder that external as well as internal factors may be involved in a situation. Furthermore, there are tendencies for both equilibrium and growth in most human and organizational systems. These properties represent opposite characteristics that must be considered when a change is made in a system. Finally, the systems viewpoint alerts us to the interdependence and interaction of the parts

Figure 1-5

An Organization as an Open System

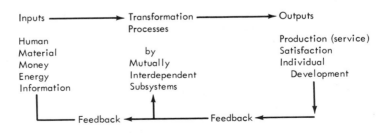

of a system. A change in one subsystem may affect other parts of the system; a total systems perspective is necessary.

Behavioral Viewpoints

The influence of the behavioral sciences—psychology, sociology, and anthropology—on the study of organizational behavior has been significant over the past thirty years. Figure 1-6 shows some of the topics examined by each science and their association with different levels of behavior.

From Figure 1-6 we see that psychology has provided insights into individual behavior by studying perception, learning, personality, and motivation. Sociology has revealed the dynamics of group behavior by investigating norms, roles, status, and power. Social psychology is the study of individual behavior within a group that draws upon both psychology and sociology. Topics of concern in social psychology are group affiliation,

Figure 1-6

Some Topics of Study Found in the Behavioral Sciences and the Level of Behavior Illuminated

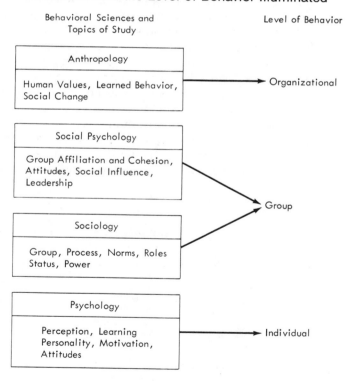

group cohesion, attitudes, communication, social influence, and leadership. Anthropology has been concerned with peoples' learned behaviors and values as influenced by their culture. An organization is affected by the predominant values existing in its environment and brought into the organization by its employees.

Collectively, these scientific disciplines are providing a body of knowledge pertaining to how people behave, why they behave as they do, and the relationship between human behavior and the total environment.[4] From these disciplines we also become oriented to the basic viewpoint that behavior is caused. It is not arbitrary or random but is a definite response to the situation. Furthermore, behavior is caused by multiple factors. This helps us to overcome the tendency to think that behavior has a single cause. Planning or action based upon single-cause thinking is likely to be completely erroneous or, at best, superficial.

Our understanding also is enhanced by knowing that behavior may be functional, dysfunctional, or both for a system.[5] Behavior is functional if it supports or facilitates something; it is dysfunctional if it impairs or obstructs. For example, if a supervisor pushes and drives his or her workers, this can be functional for increasing output in the short run but dysfunctional for job satisfaction and morale. Furthermore, because systems are interrelated, a change in one subsystem can be functional, dysfunctional, or both for other subsystems. A change in work procedures in one section of an organization may be completely disruptive for another interrelated unit using different procedures. One needs to examine the potential nature of the impact for all implicated systems.

Finally, we gain an appreciation from the behavioral sciences that behavior has intended and unintended consequences. Punishment is intended to prevent offensive behavior, but it may drive the behavior "underground," where it assumes more subtle forms of expression. Likewise, a coffee break is intended for relaxation, for "getting away from it all"; however, work problems are frequently addressed and resolved during this time. One must be sensitive to the intended as well as the potentially unintended consequences of behavior.

Contingency Approach

The basic idea of the contingency approach is that there is no one best solution to problems. Each problem must be analyzed in light of all its unique complexities and a solution based upon existing factors and their interrelationships with each other. Over the past decade, there has been a movement away from universal principles of management and behavioral solutions that are considered appropriate under any set of conditions. For a long time advocates of human relations were prescribing democratic or participative leadership without regard to people, tasks, or technology. Now participative management is considered in terms of when it is and is not effective.

While each situation is unique, there are often discernible similarities from one problem setting to another. Such similarities, if put in the context of the total problem, will provide insights, suggest cause-and-effect relationships, and point to tentative solutions or guidelines for dealing with the new problem. For example, people are notable for their individual differences, but their similarities also facilitate understanding behavior.

The contingency approach calls for one to study the situation, identify the key factors involved, use theories and concepts to explain what is happening, and then take appropriate action.

Figure 1-7 gives an overall framework for the contingency approach. First, an analysis must be made of the situation. Key internal factors such as task, technology, people, and the like and their importance and interaction must be considered.[6] Because an organization is an open system, the external factors that are relevant to the situation also must be examined. Interaction between external and internal factors must also be evaluated; this is shown by an arrow between both factors.

However, an understanding of internal and external factors does not complete the contingency approach. Relevant theories, concepts, and models of organizational behavior and management are applied to gain additional insight into what is happening. This not only helps one to understand the situation but it also suggests promising courses of action and helps one to select the most promising alternative to effect a change in the situation. By using the contingency approach, one can make a decision or take a course of action that is dependent on the unique characteristics of the situation.

Figure 1-7

A Contingency Approach to Problem Analysis

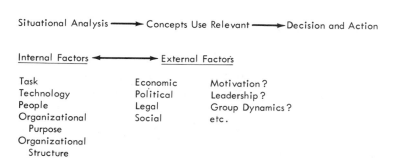

The contingency approach facilitates our understanding by encouraging the identification of key variables and their interaction in a situation. Also, it is a reminder that behavioral and other concepts and ideas are available that can help us to understand what is happening and guide our decisions and actions.[7] Above all, the contingency approach prevents simple overgeneralizations from one situation to another and the application of "universal" solutions.

SUMMARY

Both the manager and non-manager need to understand, predict, and influence organizational behavior. To facilitate this objective, human behavior at the individual, group, and organizational levels are the focus of our study. An overall model of organization behavior was presented that included these three levels and provides the framework for the book.

Three basic viewpoints will guide our study and give significant, but interdependent, insights for understanding organizational behavior.

Systems theory reminds us of external and internal influences, interaction, and the tendencies for both equilibrium and growth in human organizational behavior

The behavioral sciences provide concepts for understanding individual, group, and organizational behavior. Understanding is also aided by the realization that behavior may be functional, dysfunctional, or both for an organizational system.

Finally, the contingency approach gives us an appreciation of the unique factors in each situation and helps avoid the use of universal solutions. An identification of key internal and external variables, their interaction, and the use of relevant concepts provide a flexible framework for decision making and action.

QUESTIONS FOR STUDY AND DISCUSSION

1. Do you agree that nonmanagers need to be able to understand, predict, and influence organizational behavior? Why?

2. What are the characteristics of an open system?

3. How are the levels of study (individual, group, and organizational) related to the behavioral sciences? To the concept of systems?

4. Can you give any examples from your personal experience that demonstrate the way in which organizations develop consistent patterns of action and reaction?

5. What is equilibrium? How is it achieved?

6. What is meant when we say that behavior may be functional, dysfunctional, or both for a system? Can you give an example of this?

7. What is the contingency approach? How does this help in the study of organizational behavior?

8. Do you have any objectives you wish to achieve in your study of organizational behavior? If so, what are they?

NOTES

[1]Cummings, L. L., "Towards Organizational Behavior," *The Academy of Management Review* 3, (January 1978), p. 91.

[2]Lundberg, Craig, "Toward Understanding Behavioral Science by Administrators," *California Management Review* 6, (Fall 1963), pp. 43–52.

[3]Clark, James V., "A Healthy Organization," in William T. Greenwood, ed., *Management and Organization Behavior Theories* (Cincinnati: South-Western Publishing, 1965), p. 572.

[4]Wadia, Moneck S., "Management, Education and the Behavioral Sciences," *Advanced Management* 31, (September 1961), pp. 7–10.

[5]Seiler, John A., *Systems Analysis in Organization Behavior* (Homewood, Ill.: Richard D. Irwin, 1967), pp. 18–20.

[6]Carlisle, Howard M., *Situational Management* (New York: AMACOM, 1973), pp. 19–27.

[7]Luthans, Fred and Steward, Todd I., "A General Contingency Theory of Management," *The Academy of Management Review*, Vol. 2, No. 2, April 1977, pp. 181–195.

cases cases cases

Case Study: Look Busy or Else

Woodwork Manufacturing Company is a furniture producer that specializes in curio cases and small tables. In past years it has experienced rapid sales growth and an expansion of physical facilities. Regardless of the firm's rapid growth, however, management still operates in many respects as if it were still a small operation. For example, the president walks through the plant and corrects workers who are "goofing off" or doing something wrong on the spot. On one occasion when there was nothing coming down the conveyor into the packing department, the workers were lying down next to the conveyor with their foreman, Howard Scott, when the president arrived. He gave Scott an angry dressing down before the men and said that another such incident would result in Scott's being fired. As a result, Scott required his men to be standing at all times, even when there was no work to be done.

THE SHIPPING DEPARTMENT

Ben Shelly has been foreman of the Shipping Department for a good many years. He is generally looked up to by the men of his department and is regarded as fair, a man that can be trusted. Shelly stays in his office working on shipping schedules.

The assistant foreman, John Wiley, is a young man who has been at Woodwork about four years. He is well liked by the men and really isn't considered a supervisor in the official sense of the word (see the organizational chart below). He is respected because of his skill at getting his work done.

The work of the Shipping Department consists mainly of lifting heavy boxes and moving them from the storage to the loading area where they are to be loaded onto a truck for transport throughout the country. The variety of furniture styles is wide, and it is up to the foreman and his assistant to determine how many of each style should be sent to each truck. The pattern of work is as follows. Two men, the pushers, are stationed at the end of a

Figure 1

A Partial Organization Chart for the Woodwork Manufacturing Company

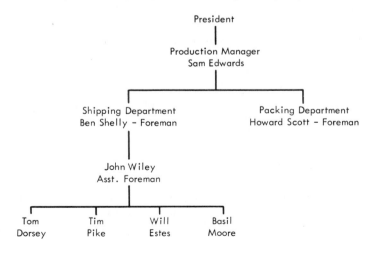

conveyor located in the packing department. They take turns loading up carts with as many boxes as possible. While one man pushes his cart back into the storage areas, the other loads up his cart. By the time the second worker finishes, the first pusher is back with an empty cart. The conveyor does not deliver boxes at an even flow. At times these two men have their hands full keeping up with the conveyor; at other times nothing comes down the line.

Two of the pushers are Tom Dorsey and Jim Pike. When Tom and Jim take their carts into storage, they are met by the "stacker," Will Estes, who has finished unloading a cart that he trades for the loaded one. He then stacks the boxes into the area reserved for that style of furniture. The work requires considerable physical strength and skill. The stacker must sometimes stack the heavy boxes twenty-five feet high to save storage space. He must do this without dropping the boxes or permitting them to fall. The boxes have a wide range of sizes and weights. Also, the pace of this job varies, depending on the flow from the conveyor. Tom, Will, and Jim work independently of other men in the department.

CONFLICT

One of the regular workers, Basil Moore, is a source of trouble. Although in his early fifties, Moore is strong and has no trouble with his work. Moore had been a foreman in another furniture factory but he had been dismissed for continually coming to work drunk. Moore does not get along with the other men because he still considers himself a manager and tries to boss the workers. The workers suspect Moore of reporting on them to the plant manager. The men often criticize Moore to his face and cut him off from their socializing. Sometimes they hide his tools. Even this group pressure, however, fails to affect Moore. He continues to come into conflict with the other men, especially the pushers. The storage areas are marked by yellow lines on the floor. Just enough room is allowed between the areas to enable the pushers to move their carts through. Since Moore has the responsibility of arranging the boxes to provide maximum available space, he often stacks boxes beyond the yellow line. This results in the pushers' running into the stacks since their carts are loaded so high that they cannot see over them. The pushers then move the boxes that were over the yellow line into storage areas where they do not belong.

This conflict has caused one of the stackers to complain to the assistant foreman, John Wiley, who has promised to correct Moore the next time that boxes are stacked over the line. But, when it happened again, the foreman put off correcting Moore. Moore, however, went to Mr. Edwards, production manager, who said that Moore could stack over the line since storage space was limited. As a result the pushers have given up moving the boxes, and the foreman and assistant foreman have said nothing further about the matter.

The production manager, Sam Edwards, is well known among the men for firing workers "on the spot." When Edwards walks through the plant, he is usually preceded by warnings such as "Sam's coming!" When the men want to put someone down they call him "Sam" or "Sam, Jr." This name is often applied to Basil Moore, who is suspected of spying for Edwards. The pushers and stacker have developed a way of avoiding Edwards when there is a slack period in the number of boxes coming down the conveyor. Since the boxes are stacked so high in the storage areas, there are many places among the boxes that afford hiding space. When slack time occurs, the stacker and pushers climb up among the boxes, out of sight, and remain there for as long as thirty minutes. The workers resent Sam's moving around to check on them. They feel that during slack time they have earned a rest, especially since there is nothing to do except try to look busy. Consequently, during a slack period the men take elaborate precautions to avoid Sam Edwards.

Most of the men in the department get along well. They talk and joke often. At lunch they eat on a covered truck ramp. None of the eating groups are rigid in makeup, and usually they sit at random. One group includes Ben Shelly, John Wiley, Howard Scott, and Basil Moore. The men play cards each day as they eat. The other men often watch and join in the conversation. A second card-playing group usually forms, but its makeup varies. The men have a half hour for lunch and a ten-minute break in the morning and in the afternoon.

QUESTIONS

1. Pick one level of behavior—individual, group, or organizational—and answer the following questions.
   a. What is happening?
   b. Why is it happening?
   c. Are there any functional or dysfunctional behaviors?
   d. Is there a problem? If so, state the problem.
   e. If there is a problem, do the following:
      (1) Give two proposed solutions for solving the problem.
      (2) Project the consequences or results of implementing each solution, both favorable and unfavorable.
      (3) Select the best solution.
      (4) Develop a step-by-step plan of action for implementing the best solution.

2. Look at the topics of study in behavioral sciences as shown in Figure 1-6. Do any of the topics hold a promise of helping to understand what is happening in this case? Which ones?

3. Are there any systems implications in the case? If so, what are they?

PART 1

INDIVIDUAL BEHAVIOR

CHApTER 2

PERCEPTION, ATTITUdES, ANd VALUES

LEARNING OBJECTIVES

When you have finished this chapter, you should be able to:

Describe the factors affecting the perceptual process and the shortcuts used to evaluate others.

Cite the components and characteristics of an attitude.

State the functions of attitudes and four approaches to attitude change.

Explain what values are and how they may influence behavior.

Chapters 2 and 3 examine some of the psychological processes that influence individual behavior. A simple model will help you to understand how these processes are part of the total situation.[1]

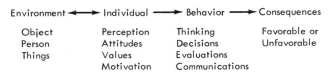

Environment	Individual	Behavior	Consequences
Object	Perception	Thinking	Favorable or
Person	Attitudes	Decisions	Unfavorable
Things	Values	Evaluations	
	Motivation	Communications	

The environment consists of varied stimuli that surround the individual: objects, persons, and things. Since the individual responds to some environmental stimuli and excludes others, the arrow between environment and individual points in both directions. In other words, an individual is not a passive recipient of stimuli; rather, the individual's perceptions, attitudes, values, and motivations (needs) influence his or her sensitivity. These factors also affect behaviors such as thinking, decision making, evaluations, communication, and the like.

Finally, the model shows that behavior results in some kind of consequence for the individual. The consequences of behavior may be favorable or unfavorable to the individual. Behavior followed by favorable or pleasing consequences is likely to be repeated again. On the other hand, if the consequences are unpleasant, the individual will try new behaviors.

As the following psychological factors—perceptions, attitudes, values, and motivations—are discussed, it will be helpful to keep the overall behavioral context in mind.

PERCEPTION

The Perceptual Process

We see the same things differently. All of us have become aware of this whether by comparing descriptions of cloud patterns or by evaluating some current event. Since we perceive things, objects, or events differently, our response will vary in thought or overt behavior. Sometimes this process is called filtering, looking through rose-colored glasses, or perception. Perception is the process of selection, organization, and interpretation of stimuli from the environment.

The selection of stimuli occurs because, at any moment in time, we are subjected to many diverse sights, sounds, persons, and so on. However, we are not aware of all the stimuli that could impinge on our consciousness. If it were otherwise, at times we would be confused or overwhelmed. Perceptual selection prevents such confusions so that one's surroundings become meaningful and manageable.

The organization and interpretation of environmental stimuli is influenced by learning from past experiences. Consistent characteristics are attributed to objects, persons, and things. In this manner each person creates his or her own world of reality, which is as different as the varied backgrounds and experiences of each individual. Given the same setting or environment, what is important to one person is not likely to have the same relevance for another. The meaning and significance assigned to various aspects of the surroundings are built up through past experiences and are not necessarily inherent in the stimuli itself.

Since adaptive behavior is necessary for adjusting to life's varied situations, perceptions are learned in terms of what is important and useful.[2] For example, if an employee has experienced only tough, autocratic supervisors who could be related to successfully only by doing exactly as told and adopting a subservient attitude, that employee is quite likely to see a new boss as an autocrat and behave as he or she has in the past. The employee's perception and subsequent behavior have been strongly influenced by past experiences.

The Person Perceived

Everyone attempts to analyze the behavior of other people, but frequently we are not aware of the variables that significantly affect such evaluations. The perceptual process is influenced by the status of the other person, which in turn may have an effect on the judgment made about his or her behavior.

For example, in an organization, peoples' positions or roles differ from another. In a committee meeting, the comments of the production official may be perceived differently from those of the sales manager even though both are saying the same thing. More importance is attached to the remarks of the person having the higher status.

The visibility of individual traits also influences the accuracy of our perception. Supervisors have frequently been asked to rate their employees on loyalty, which provides few if any cues for observation. Since the situation demands an evaluation, the decision may be based on a highly individualized reaction such as punctuality or friendliness.

The Situation

Situational aspects are also relevant to the perceptual process. One's position or job in an organization influences what is seen and the importance attached to perceived behavior. The production official perceives and evaluates through "production eyes." Problems are more likely to be seen as production problems or have production implications. The sales official and personnel manager likewise view troublesome issues from their own unique viewpoints.[3] The rank-and-file employee is quite likely to perceive change, or any problem, in a different manner from his or her supervisor. Managers are inclined to see change as a challenge, whereas employees are likely to feel threatened. Each will be influenced by his or her position and individual needs; each will perceive a situation differently.

The Perceiver

Perception is not simply a reaction to events, people, or things; it is influenced by conditions within the individual. One of the most persuasive internal factors affecting perception is our needs; we tend to see whatever serves our needs. For example, a member of management and a member of labor have the same set of economic data before them, yet divergent conclusions are drawn about appropriate wage levels. Why? Because each has different needs and objectives, the information is interpreted differently.

However, internal needs are not the only factors that influence perception. One's perception is also affected by other contemporary factors such as fatigue and anxiety. Such factors influence which environmental conditions are attended to and the interpretations to be made of these stimuli. Later in the chapter, the influence of attitudes and values on perception will be examined.

Self-perception

To understand human behavior in general and perception more specifically, we must examine how we perceive ourselves—the self-concept. The self-concept is how one sees himself or herself. One's self-concept is stated in terms of "I" or "me" and is the mental image of what we think we are; it answers the questions of "Who am I?" and "What am I?" For example, the central beliefs about one's self may include such beliefs as "I am a student, intelligent, competent, sociable," and so on.

The self-structure is not only unique to each individual but has a consistency that persists over time.[4] Our activities are organized and integrated in relation to the self, and, consequently, we tend to establish a relatively consistent life-style. We have a characteristic way of acting, thinking, and reacting that tends to distinguish us from everyone else. Such uniqueness and consistency is maintained because we accept those ideas and experiences that are compatible with our self-concept but reject or modify those that are in conflict with our self-concept. When confronted by situations that threaten our self-concept, feelings of uneasiness or anxiety cause us to defend ourselves. At this point, various defense mechanisms such as rationalization, compensation, projection, and displacement are used by the individual. The use of these mechanisms permits stabilization of the self-system, but it may result in single-track thinking and behavior that limits understanding and the examination of alternative behavior patterns. Consequently, it may become impossible for individuals to recognize personal shortcomings and overcome problem areas.

Self-perception and Perceiving Others

Perceiving one's self clearly is related to how accurately we evaluate others. Also our perception of other persons is influenced by our own personal characteristics.

Self-insight and Perceptual Accuracy: Knowing yourself makes it easier to see others more accurately. When we are aware of our own personal characteristics, we make fewer errors in perceiving others. People with self-insight are less likely to view others in terms of extremes but in objective terms.

If we accept ourself, we are more likely to see the favorable aspects of others. That is, if we accept ourselves as we are, we widen our range of vision in seeing others; we can look at them and be less likely to be very negative or critical. We tend to see weaknesses in other people in areas in which we ourselves are weak. Also, we are more inclined to like others who have traits that we accept in ourselves, and we are more apt to reject those who have the traits that we do not like in ourselves. Additionally, the people that we like are perceived more accurately in the ways in which they are similar to us, and we perceive them less accurately in the ways in which they are unlike us. People we do not like are seen as different from ourselves; we perceive most accurately their traits that are unlike our own, and their similar traits least accurately.[5]

Personal Characteristics and Perception: Our own characteristics affect the characteristics that we are likely to see in others. Secure people, as compared with those who are insecure, tend to see others as warm rather than cold. The extent of our own sociability influences the degree of importance that we give to the sociability of others when we form impressions of them. The relatively few categories that we use in describing others tend to be those that we use in describing ourselves. Traits in ourselves that are important to us will be used more than others when we form impressions of others. We have certain "constant tendencies" in using certain categories in judging others and the importance or weight given to these categories or traits.

Self-perception is important for those who work with and/or manage people in formal organizations. For example, anyone wanting to perceive someone else accurately must look at that person, not at himself or herself. What is seen in someone else is influenced by one's personal traits, but, if one knows his or her own traits, that person is aware of his or her frame of reference.

The question to be asked when viewing another is; Am I looking at that person and forming my impression of his or her behavior in the situation, or am I just comparing the person with myself?[6]

PERCEPTUAL PROCESSES: SHORTCUTS TO EVALUATION

How thorough and complete are we in making evaluations of others? Perhaps not as much as we would like to think because of shortcuts taken in the evaluation process. Everyone uses stereotyping, projection, expectancy, and attribution to some extent in making social judgments.

Stereotyping

Stereotyping consists of classifying persons by using labels or evaluative frameworks learned in the past. One assigns traits or behaviors to others if something is known about that person. For example, professors are absent minded; Republicans are conservative. The cues used for such classifications are derived from generalizations about race, ethnic background, and socioeconomic status. However, people are more complex than the simple cues used for classification purposes. Stereotyped behaviors and traits are economical because they permit one to short-circuit the process of evaluating others in detail. Therefore, predictions about their behavior can be made more readily. On the other hand, such evaluations are often incorrect. For example, consider the action implications if we stereotype all welfare recipients as lazy and not wanting a job as long as a dole is provided. A closer, detailed study may reveal that a large majority prefer meaningful work that provides not only a livelihood, but also independence and integrity. The problem may, in fact, be that the labor market functions imperfectly, not that people are lazy.

Many groups are subjected to stereotyping. One study found older workers were rated as harder to change, less creative, more cautious, and having less physical capacity; however their performance records were as good as those of younger employees.[7] Sex-role stereotyping, often by both sexes, holds that men are naturally superior in supervisory positions because they are dominant, aggressive, and competitive. However, research in real-life situations has failed to find differences between male and female leaders in leader behavior.[8]

Halo Effect

The halo effect is somewhat similar to stereotyping. However, with the halo effect, an impression made by a single trait, favorable or unfavorable, forms the basis for an overall evaluation of the person. One trait is generalized to include others that are never examined closely. The foreman who places a premium upon arriving at work on time might rate an employee who is prompt superior on output and quality of performance without even really examining these dimensions of performance.

Projection

Projection is to attribute our own characteristics, favorable or unfavorable, to other people. For example, intensive studies have identified a collection of traits described as the authoritarian personality.[9] Such an individual rigidly adheres to conventional middle-class values, is submissive toward the moral authorities of his or her group, condemns and rejects people who violate conventional values, is preoccupied with power and status considerations, tends to identify with powerful figures, and is generally hostile toward members of outgroups. The results of several studies have shown that the highly authoritarian-oriented person assumes that others have values like his or her own and rates others high on most of the authoritarian traits. Thus, our own characteristics can be projected or ascribed to others.

Expectancy

Expectancy is a mental set that assures us of finding what it is that we are looking for or seeking. Sometimes called the self-fulfilling prophecy, a person can make happen what he or she wishes to have happen. In one experiment, students were given intelligence tests and afterward the teachers were told some of their classes of pupils were much more intelligent than others.[10] This was an experimental ruse, however, since the researcher had actually randomized the students so that each group represented the same level of intelligence. The children that the teacher thought were more intelligent received better grades than did those whom the teachers thought were less intelligent—the teachers had seen what they expected to see.

Since assumptions affect our expectancies, it is evident that one must become more conscious of assumptions being made about others. If a supervisor assumes that his or her work crew is lazy, indolent, and unwilling to accept responsibility, his or her supervisory behavior will reflect and eventually confirm those assumptions. Direction of the work group will tend toward detailed directions, constant surveillance, and pressure for production. Such tactics produce the very kind of work behaviors assumed to exist in the first place, a self-fulfilling prophecy.

Attribution

Attribution is an inference as to the causes of another's behavior. When people do something, we tend to evaluate why they acted in such a manner. The search for causes focuses on internal or external factors.[11] For example, if a student drops out of school, is it because he or she lacked the basic abilities to succeed (internal attribution) or because he or she found the program of study dull and boring (external attribution)? Our judgment of another's behavior will differ considerably depending on whether an external or internal cause is accepted. Several studies have demonstrated that, when women are successful, their success is more likely to be attributed to luck, task ease, or effort than to skill or ability. On the other hand, success for men is more often attributed to ability.[12]

Since most causes or attributes are not directly observable, one depends on his or her perception. It is the perceived rather than the actual determinants that are used to explain behavior. Furthermore, even though a situation is the result of numerous factors, we prefer single-cause explanations. Obviously, this can lead to inaccurate evaluations of the behaviors of others.

ATTITUDES

We do not see things as they really are; rather, we view things through perceptual filters. Perception is also influenced by one's attitudes, and understanding of others and their behaviors will be increased if we understand attitudes. Attitudes are "regularities of an individual's feelings, thoughts, and predisposition to act toward some aspect of his or her environment."[13]

The Components of an Attitude

From the definition just given, it is apparent that an attitude has three components or elements. One is the *cognitive* component or the thoughts, ideas, and beliefs that a person has. Another is the *affective,* or feeling, component. The third is the *behavioral* component, that is, the tendency to act consistently with attitude. Consequently, an attitude may be considered as a way of thinking, feeling, and behaving. For example, if you have a close associate and if your thoughts about him or her are favorable, your feelings about the associate will be ones of respect and consideration and your behavior toward him or her will be that you will associate with that person frequently. Your thoughts and feelings are inner reactions, whereas your behavior is an outer reaction. Furthermore, your attitude is not likely to gyrate from positive to negative or even neutral in a short period of time; an attitude has a high degree of stability or consistency.

Figure 2-1 summarizes in graphic form what has been said about attitudes. Note that attitudes are affixed to attitude objects—persons, concepts, things, and situations. Such objects may evoke feelings, thoughts, and a tendency to act.

Characteristics of Attitudes

Additional insight into attitudes is possible if we examine their characteristics or dimensions that can vary.[14]

Attitudes vary in their intensity or strength of the feeling component. For example, the feeling that you have about environmental pollution may be very strong or very weak. The belief or cognitive component has two

Figure 2-1

Attitude and Attitude Objects

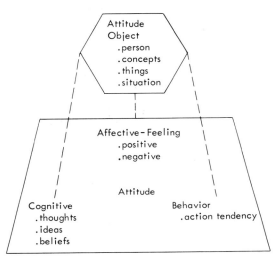

characteristics: (1) it can be specific or general and (2) it can vary in complexity. A belief component is specific if one thinks that his or her boss is autocratic but general if all managers or authority figures are thought to be autocrats. Complexity refers to the number of beliefs or cognitive elements contained in an attitude. It is generally assumed that the fewer the belief elements, the easier it is to change an attitude.

Finally, an attitude has the characteristics of centrality. Centrality refers to an attitude's role as part of a value system that is closely related to one's self-concept or how one sees one's self. The importance or centrality of an attitude will affect one's readiness to respond or change. Later material will examine more closely this characteristic of an attitude.

How Attitudes Are Acquired

Broadly speaking, our attitudes are a product of our culture. More specifically, attitudes are learned from the numerous circumstances of each person's life. One of the most significant sources of attitudes is the family that has "ready-made" attitudes toward things such as religion, politics, and minority groups. These attitudes may be adopted uncritically. Family contacts may also set the pattern for future interpersonal relations as attitudes toward one's father, mother, and siblings become generalized to personal contacts later in life. In addition, the family generally instills attitudes that are considered appropriate for its social and economic position in society. Attitudes toward work and the degree of emphasis placed on achievement are generally shaped in the family setting. Attitudes also are structured by the groups to which the individual belongs to during his or her lifetime. Such reference groups vary from those encountered in school to trade unions or professional associations and may reinforce, modify, and/or instill new attitudes.

The Function of Attitudes

Whatever the source of attitudes, they perform a function for the individual that reflects the reasons for holding specific attitudes. One study has classified the functions performed and the needs that attitudes serve as follows:[15]

Adjustive or utilitarian attitudes.

These attitudes are either the means for reaching a desired objective or the means for avoiding undesirable consequences. They are dependent on the perception of an attitude object—person, thing, or situation—having utility for achieving favorable or desirable goals. For example, a positive attitude will exist toward a foreman who is seen as instrumental in attaining one's work and economic goals.

Ego-defensive attitudes.

These attitudes help the individual avoid facing his or her personal inadequacies or the reality of dangers around him or her. Defensive behaviors enable the individual to withdraw or deny the existence of threatening situations or to distort reality by rationalization, projection, and displacement. Such actions may help the individual to live with himself or herself. For example, when we are unable to admit to ourselves that we have deep feelings of inferiority, we may project these feelings onto some convenient minority group and bolster our ego by attitudes of superiority toward this group.

Value-expressive attitudes.

These attitudes give positive expression and clarity to the individual's central values and self-concept. For example, an individual who considers himself or herself a progressive manager will hold attitudes appropriate to the type of person that the individual perceives himself or herself to be; the individual finds reward in the expression of any attribute associated with his or her self-concept.

Attitude formation is a constant process, and new experiences and influences continually suggest new attitudes important for implementing existing values. An individual will often adopt or internalize the values of a group. This is most likely to take place when four conditions exist: (1) when the values of the group are highly consistent with values that are important to the individual, (2) when the group has a clear model of what a good member should be like and indoctrinates group members in these terms, (3) when the activities of the group in attaining its goals permit the individual a genuine opportunity for participation, and (4) when the individual shares in the rewards of group activity that includes his or her own efforts. Such an experience gives clarity to the self-image and also molds the self-image closer to what one desires.

Knowledge-expressive attitudes.

These attitudes supply standards and frames of references for understanding events and structuring experiences in what would otherwise be an unorganized chaotic world. Such attitudes provide a means for interpreting what we perceive to be important. For example, developing stereotypes provides the individual with a more consistent, but less realistic, picture of ethnic groups or occupations.

Attitude Organization

Will a change in attitude lead to a change in actual behavior? The problem of attitude change and whether behavior will undergo a corresponding shift has been a pressing issue.[16] As noted previously, attitudes consist of affective, cognitive, and behavioral intentions. To change attitudes, we must understand how these elements are likely to change and under what conditions the change is likely to take place.

Cognitive Dissonance

A considerable amount of attitude research has focused on whether a person will act in accordance with his or her verbally expressed attitude. Consistency theory emphasizes that an individual's attitudes are normally consistent with each other. That is, behavior is consistent when one's attitude and behaviors also are consistent. For example, if one believes in participative management, that individual does not believe in autocratic methods. If one believes in hard work and advancement, that individual will not be "gold bricking."

Leon Festinger developed a theory of cognitive dissonance that specifies the conditions under which attitude and behavior correspond and why they do so.[17] Dissonance is created when attitudes and behavior are inconsistent. Any knowledge, opinion, belief about one's self or one's behavior, or belief about the environment is considered to be a cognitive element. Two cognitive elements are consonant with one another if one follows from the other. For example, if you believe in self-direction and self-control for your subordinates, you would seek to provide a work environment conducive to their learning and assuming more responsibility. However, if you believed in self-development and self-control but sought to rigidly specify subordinate behavior, dissonance would prevail. In this case the cognitive elements do not fit or are inconsistent with one another. The greater the divergency of two elements, the greater the dissonance. Of course many cognitive elements have nothing to do with each other; that is, they are not related in any meaningful manner.

Three conditions arise from the presence of dissonance.

1. The existence of dissonance is psychologically uncomfortable and will motivate the individual to reduce the dissonance and achieve consistency.
2. When dissonance is present, the individual also will actively avoid situations and information that will likely increase the dissonance.
3. The strength of the pressure to reduce dissonance is a function of the magnitude of dissonance.

Item 3, pressure to reduce dissonance, points to the importance of examining the total attitude structure. The magnitude of dissonance is expressed in terms of the following ratio.

$$\text{Dissonance} = \frac{\text{Importance} \times \text{number of dissonant elements}}{\text{Importance} \times \text{number of consonant elements}}$$

One or two dissonant elements or beliefs among many is not likely to produce discomfort. However, the more nearly equal the number of dissonant and consonant elements, the greater the dissonance. Equally significant is the importance that one attaches to the elements.

Three ways of reducing dissonance are as follows.

Change of a behavioral element.

When an individual realizes that his or her behavior is inconsistent with a belief, that individual may change his or her behavior. For example, if an employee realizes that his or her poor performance record is not conducive to obtaining a wage increase and eventually being promoted, that employee might decide to change his or her work habits.

Change of an environmental element.

Sometimes the behavior of a person is dissonant with some environmental factor that can be changed. In this instance a person might reduce the dissonance between his or her knowledge that poor performance leads to fewer wage increases by submitting a suggestion for changing existing work procedures to his or her foreman. Nearly everyone has observed an acquaintance who sought to reduce the dissonance between the knowledge that smoking causes cancer and his or her use of cigarettes by changing to a filter-tip brand or perhaps a pipe.

Add new elements.

One may add new cognitive elements when it is difficult to change dissonant knowledge, opinions, or beliefs. In this instance it is often possible to add new elements to outweigh the dissonant ones. For example, the cigarette smoker worried about lung cancer may tell himself or herself that smoking is relaxing and helps to keep one's weight down and therefore is beneficial to his or her health.

Attitude Change

Traditionally, efforts to change attitudes have sought to modify the behavior, thinking, and feelings of the situation.

Change behavior.

One of the most direct, but complicated, approaches to dealing with an undesirable attitude is to attempt to change the accompanying behavior. Discipline is exercised when the individual is subjected to negative reinforcement such as temporary layoff or demotion to induce a change in behavior. At best, however, one will probably change his or her behavior to the smallest degree possible to avoid punishment. Even then, the supervisor must be constantly present to monitor the individual's behavior that may have only gone underground. Furthermore, the undesirable attitude may not have changed at all and probably has become even more negative than previously. This is especially true if the disciplinary offense has been poorly handled. All too frequently, discipline is perceived by the employee as inconsistent, unfair, and a criticism of his or her personality rather than of behavior. For these reasons, dealing only with the behavioral aspects of an undesirable attitude is not usually a very effective approach.

Change ideas and beliefs.

Frequently, management has sought to change the thinking component of an attitude—the ideas and beliefs. In many cases, an undesirable attitude may be the result of insufficient or misleading information. In some instances, companies have found employees to have a neutral or negative attitude toward their fringe benefits and have sought to change what were considered mistaken ideas. Company newspapers or paycheck stuffers have frequently been used to communicate the variety of benefits received and the amount that each adds to employees' take-home pay. Also explanatory information is used to increase the acceptance of new regulations or procedures and to help prevent the development of undesirable attitudes and behavior.

For attitudes resulting primarily from the lack of facts or ideas, that is, having little or weak feelings, giving information and presenting facts will have a good chance of modifying the attitude. An attitude that has deep emotional content will probably not change by providing information or even reasoning with someone. By providing new information, management is introducing new cognitive elements that may cause dissonance within the individual. It is hoped that the dissonance generated by new information will be sufficiently strong to induce the employee to change his or her thinking about a given topic.

Change feelings.

The feeling dimension of an attitude is much more difficult to deal with than is the thinking one. The most promising approach for dealing with feelings or emotions in others involves listening. While this may sound simple and easy, it is extremely difficult for action-oriented managers. Active listening requires listening to what the other person has to say and trying to understand what it is that he or she is saying. One has to be a sympathetic listener, as the atmosphere of the interview should be an understanding, nonthreatening one in which the individual feels free to express his or her feelings, problems, and attitudes. Such an atmosphere is not created by chance and requires a great deal of time and effort. For many of us this is a difficult task requiring skills that we do not possess. However, the main purpose of the interviewer is to help the other person gain a clearer understanding of his or her own feelings and attitudes. This can best be accomplished by repeating or restating what the individual says in an abbreviated fashion. ''You feel that the company is cheap and is cheating its employees on fringe benefits.'' By responding in this manner, the listener acts as a sounding board, reflecting to the other person an accurate replay of his or her own feelings and attitudes. Understanding and acceptance of what has been said is conveyed, and the person is encouraged to continue. If a criticism or judgment is given, or perhaps a brief lecture or solution, the complaintant will probably stop communicating.

Active listening can lead to changes in attitudes and help to create a better work atmosphere. Also, it usually relieves the person of some of the tensions that he or she is experiencing. This is not only helpful but necessary for exploring courses of action that may be required for further change. Emotions can prevent the kind of thinking necessary for problem solving and for developing goal-oriented behavior.

Change situations.

One of the most common approaches to changing attitudes is to modify the situations that are the source of unfavorable attitudes. Potentially disturbing conditions are located by the use of attitude or opinion surveys that contain questions pertaining to work conditions, supervision, pay, and other organizational variables. The process of soliciting relevant information and its utilization is shown in Figure 2-2.

Figure 2-2

Job Factors That Influence Attitudes

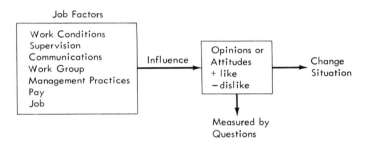

Numerous job factors are perceived by the employee and influence his or her attitude toward each aspect of the employee's work world. Questions are structured so that the employee can register his or her opinion. Several typical questions to which an employee might be asked to respond appear in the following table.

	Strongly Agree	Agree	Disagree	Strongly Disagree
We get the kind of training that permits us to do a good job				
People get along well with each other in my work group				
I have confidence in the ability of my immediate supervisor				

An individual may react by indicating that he or she strongly agrees, agrees, disagrees, or strongly disagrees with the statement and, in doing so, has given an opinion that mirrors his or her attitude.

If a high percentage of the employees register dissatisfaction with some aspect of their work life, management may attempt to change the situation if it is possible to do so. While some work situations, such as eating facilities, are relatively easy to modify, others may require policy changes or a long-term effort, if, for example inadequate supervision is a problem. Although one cannot definitely say that negative opinions will be reflected in job performance or production, the potential for this to happen is always present. Furthermore, absenteeism and turnover may also be influenced by opinions, as both represent efforts of a different kind to escape the job. However intangible the relationship of attitudes to job behaviors may be, many organizations, through a sense of social responsibility, are seeking to enhance the quality of work life by changing situations that precipitate poor attitudes. Whether such social responsibility is important in an organization depends on its value system.

VALUES

We have noted previously that an attitude can be characterized by centrality (or tie) to values associated with the self-concept and may be value expressive. At this point we need to examine values more closely to determine what they are and how they influence behavior.

Values are desirable end states or conditions that one would like to see prevail above all others.[18] Consequently, values form the basis for an individual view of the world and provide a sense of coherence and unity to living. Since values represent the individual's concept of an ideal relationship or state of affairs, they are used to assess rightness or wrongness. As such, values provide a standard that guides comparisons, evaluations, decisions, and actions.

Values and Attitudes

Values are linked to attitudes in the sense that a value can serve as an organizing theme for a number of attitudes.[19] Some attitudes are specific expressions of more general values. The interrelationships of attitudes and values are conceptualized in Figure 2-3.

The figure depicts attitudes as focused directly on objects such as ideas, things, persons, and situations, whereas a value is less situation bound, that is, less directly related to such objects. Values are more general, central, and resistant to change than are attitudes. When a value is

Figure 2-3

A Conceptualization of Values, Attitudes, and Attitude Objects

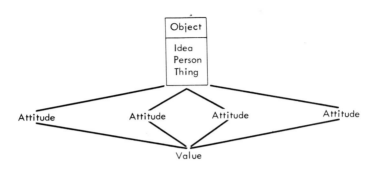

internalized, it becomes, consciously or unconsciously, a standard or criterion for developing and maintaining attitudes toward relevant objects and situations.[20]

A Measure of Values

We may learn something about our values by taking a test designed to identify the relative importance of different values. One of these tests is described in the following paragraphs.

The most widely used scale for measuring values was developed by Allport and Vernon.[21] They view values as common to all, so that one person can be compared with another. The six values are

1. The *theoretical man* most values the discovery of truth. He is empirical, critical, and rational, aiming to order and systematize his knowledge.
2. The *economic man* most values that which is useful. He is interested in practical affairs, especially those of business, judging things by their tangible utility.
3. The *aesthetic man* most values beauty and harmony. He is concerned with grace and symmetry, finding fulfillment in artistic experiences.
4. The *social man* most values altruistic and philantropic love. He is kind, sympathetic, unselfish, valuing other men as ends in themselves.
5. The *political man* most values power and influence. He seeks leadership, enjoying competition and struggle.
6. The *religious man* most values unity. He seeks communion with the cosmos, mystically relating to its wholeness.

The Allport and Vernon measure was given to high-level American executives attending the Advanced Management program at the Harvard Business School.[22] The average value profile is as follows.

Value	Score
Economic	45
Theoretical	44
Political	44
Religious	39
Aesthetic	35
Social	33

The major orientation of this group is a combination of economic, theoretical, and political values. While the economic and political orientations are consistent with our stereotypes of business executives, the theoretical orientation may come as a surprise. However, the high-level executive needs to have theories and rational approaches to his or her work to satisfy economic and political values. In working with others, the executive has to be explicit and rational. Also being removed from direct operations, the executive has to think in abstract terms when integrating human and material resources. The study also indicates the values of executives, on the average, are different from those in other professions.

Values in a University Setting

Scott conducted research over a one-year period in ten fraternities and sororities at the University of Colorado to determine the way in which personal values affected these organizations.[23] A preliminary survey indicated twelve values that appeared to be relevant to fraternities and sororities:

1. *Intellectualism:* Having strong intellectual and cultural interests, trying to learn a great deal about things, even though the knowledge may not be useful.
2. *Kindness:* Being mostly concerned about other people, doing good for them, and trying to make them happy, even if it is against one's interests.
3. *Social skills:* Being charming, popular, well mannered, and getting along with all kinds of people.
4. *Loyalty:* Being a loyal, devoted member of the group, never criticizing it to outsiders, and working hard to get it ahead of other groups.

5. *Academic achievement:* Studying a great deal and working hard to get good grades.
6. *Physical development:* Being a well-developed outdoors type who enjoys physical activity.
7. *Status:* Having strong leadership qualities, being respected by others, and gaining recognition for one's achievements.
8. *Honesty:* Always telling the truth and being completely honest, never cheating or lying, even though these might make for an easier relationship with others.
9. *Religiousness:* Being a religious person, both in belief and practice, attending church regularly, and abiding by the Bible's teachings.
10. *Self-control:* Always being patient and self-controlled, never losing one's temper, no matter what the provocation.
11. *Creativity:* Being inventive, creative, and always thinking of different ways of doing things.
12. *Independence:* Being independent, outspoken, free thinking, and unhampered by the bounds of tradition or social restraint.

For each of the above "dimensions," statements were developed; the final questionnaire consisted of sixty statements.

Scott's research confirmed the influence of values in the fraternity's and sorority's internal processes and interpersonal relations. For example:

1. Recruitment: In the recruitment of pledges to Greek organizations there is a general emphasis on interpersonal, organization-maintaining values. Organizations tend to recruit new members with values similar to those of the old members.
2. Socialization: Members' values were likely to become more heterogeneous, rather than more homogeneous, with time.
3. Maintenance of member allegiance: The degree to which a person is attracted to membership in any particular organization to which he or she belongs depends on the degree to which he or she values group loyalty in general. The most satisfied members of an organization are those whose values are compatible with the dominant group functions.
4. Status differentiation: The sociometric ratings that a person receives from others depend in part on the raters' own values. Status differentiation within these social organizations is not very clear cut.
5. Mutual friendships: Members who like one another are more likely to hold similar values than are members who dislike one another.
6. Attrition: Attrition among value deviants is most pronounced in organizations with high group cohesiveness. Attrition among new members is highest in organizations where selection processes have resulted in the poorest value match with old members.

Changes in Value System

While some investigators conclude that one's personal value system is relatively stable, there is evidence that this is not completely true of large segments of the American population. In one study, personal value interviews, one to two hours in length, were conducted with a representative selection of 1,006 college students and 2,516 noncollege students whose ages ranged from sixteen to twenty-five. Daniel Yankelovich compared these results, compiled in 1973, with the 1969 study for CBS news.[24] Table 2-1 shows how college and noncollege students compared on some traditional American values in 1973.[25]

Table 2-1
Belief in Traditional American Values, 1973

	Total Noncollege (%)	Total College (%)
Doing any job well is important	89%	84%
Business is entitled to make a profit	85	85
People should save money regularly	80	71
Commitment to a meaningful career is very important	79	81
Private property is sacred	74	67
A "strong" person can control his or her life	70	65
Competition encourages excellence	66	62
Duty comes before pleasure	66	54
Hard work will always pay off	56	44
Humans are basically good but society is corrupt	50	46
People who accept things are better off	31	15

Source: Daniel Yankelovich, *The New Morality: A Profile of American Youth in the 70's* (New York: McGraw-Hill, 1974) p. 91.

Yankelovich concludes from this data that the new set of values incubated on the nation's campuses in the 1960s has been disseminated to the entire youth generation. The wide chasm between college and noncollege values has diminished greatly and disappeared altogether for some values.

Table 2-2 shows the changes in some values for both noncollege and college groups between 1969 and 1973.[26]

Table 2-2

Belief in Traditional American Values, 1969 vs. 1973

Values	Noncollege		College	
	1973 (%)	1969 (%)	1973 (%)	1969 (%)
People should save money regularly	80	89	71	76
Private property is sacred	74	88	67	76
A "strong" person can control his or her own life	70	77	65	62
Competition encourages excellence	66	81	62	72
Hard work will always pay off	56	79	44	57

Source: Daniel Yankelovich, *The New Morality: A Profile of American Youth in the 70's* (New York: McGraw-Hill, 1974) p. 93.

The shift in the values of the noncollege group appears to have been quite dramatic but less so for the college group. Yankelovich concluded that a large majority of the people who do not attend college continue to believe in most aspects of the puritan ethic but that some erosion has occurred.

One "new value" to emerge in the Yankelovich analysis involves the vague concept of self-fulfillment that is often felt to conflict with the concern for economic security. The self-fulfillment theme is a way of saying that there must be something more to life than making a living, struggling to make ends meet, and caring for others. It also implies a greater preoccupation with self at the expense of sacrificing for family, employer, and community. The college group and increasingly the older generation do not feel the need to submerge their "real selves" in their work. These groups also feel that personal self-fulfillment and the pursuit of a successful career should be compatible. Money, security, and possessions are included in the overall scheme, partly demanded as a matter of right, but subordinate to the main goal of finding just the right life-style for expressing their psychological potential. Many noncollege youths, including those working in blue-collar jobs, have taken up the quest of the college group for a definition of success that emphasizes self-fulfillment and quality of life, as well as money and security.[27]

Additional research has supported Yankelovich's conclusions that young people have become less favorably inclined toward traditional work values. The results of a study by Taylor and Thompson indicated the younger workers valued self-expression through work, intrinsic rewards and extrinsic rewards, such as pay, more than did older workers.[28] Another study of age and work values based on a sample of 3,053 workers found that older workers attached more significance to the moral importance of work and pride in craftsmanship. Younger workers placed greater emphasis on money, the importance of friends over work, and the acceptability of welfare as an alternative to work. These results were not due to seniority, education, income, sex, or occupational status.[29]

The change to a self-fulfillment value system and the appeal of nonfinancial rewards, participation in decision making, and meaningful, as well as interesting, work will place new demands upon administrators of all kinds of organizations. Managers can no longer assume that employees hold the same values as they do, will respond to the same incentives, or accept the traditional quality of work life. The change in values noted are closely interrelated to motivation, which will be examined in the next chapter.

The Values of Managers

In a study by England into the personal value systems of American managers, he concluded that the personal value systems of individual managers influence their organization and simultaneously that their personal value systems are influenced by organization life.[30] The basic idea underlying this research is that values have different behavioral implications that are of two kinds: *nonrelevant* or *weak values* that have little or no impact on behavior and *conceived values* that are likely to be translated into behavior. However, there are three varieties of conceived values, each with a different probability of influencing behavior. These values are defined and some of the managerial values associated with each are given here.

Operative values—These values have the greatest influence on behavior and have a high probability of being translated from intentions to actual behavior. Some of the managerial values falling into this category are as follows:

High Productivity	Employees	Ambition
Industrial Leadership	Customers	Ability
Organizational Stability	Co-workers	Cooperation
Profit Maximization	Boss	Achievement
Organizational Efficiency	Managers	Job Satisfaction
Organizational Growth	Owners	Creativity

Intended values—These values are professed as important but have only a moderate probability of being translated from the intentional state into behavior because of situational factors. Managerial values in this category are as follows:

Employee Welfare	Individuality
Trust	Government
Loyalty	Property
Honor	Rational
Dignity	Religion

Adopted values—These values may be professed but do not exert much influence because they are not a significant part of the individual's personality structure and affect behavior largely because of situational factors. Managerial values in this category are as follows:

Labor Unions	Conflict
Aggressiveness	Risk
Influence	Prejudice
Power	Force
Compromise	

A Model of Value Related Behavior

The model on which this particular research is based shows how the categories of values affect behavior. Figure 2-4 illustrates how values are influential in two ways—behavior channeling and perceptual screening. Behavior channeling is shown by problem solving and decision making. For example, a manager who places a high value on honesty when confronted with a situation of questionable ethics would be channeled away from the situation because of his or her operative value. This represents a direct influence of values in behavior. On the other hand, perceptual

Figure 2-4

Theoretical Model of Value Related Behavior

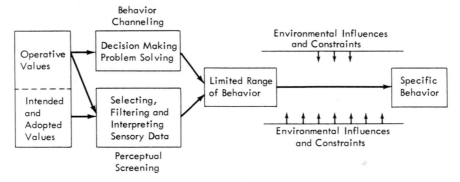

Source: Adapted from George W. England, "Personal Value Systems of American Managers," *Academy of Management Journal* 10, (March 1967), p. 55.

screening is influenced by intended, adopted, and operative values. As we have previously noted, one sees what one wants to see.

Finally, in Figure 2-4 we observe that values are only one of the factors involved in behavior. The influence of values must be considered in context of environmental influences and constraints. For example, the manager with a value of honesty may find his or her behavior limited by company policies, practices, and pressures.

Values in Conflict

During the past decade there has been a steady stream of newspaper and magazine articles that have blamed business for nearly every social ill, from pollution and racial tension to unemployment. There have been numerous reports of unethical conduct, bribes, payoffs, and illegal political contributions at home and abroad. Many people are questioning the adequacy of profit-motivated organizations for meeting society's goals. One author attributes some of these problems to the following:

> There have been important changes in the world. There have, partly as a result, also been important changes in what people expect of corporate executives. To some extent, our priorities have been re-ordered, and we now demand things from business that we used to argue were not its proper role . . . And there have been changes in what are considered acceptable standards of moral behavior, as well. Things that were countenanced as normal practice, in business no less than in politics, are now regarded as unacceptable. And there have been changes in the ways in which we hold businessmen accountable, as well as to whom they must defend their actions.[31]

This author feels that many of the difficulties of business—which are reflected in our news media—are due to the business system's unwillingness or inability to accept and adapt to a rapidly changing environment. One also might add there have also been crucial changes in the value system by which business decisions are evaluated. Business executives have failed to keep pace with the changes in the value system associated with the economic system, society, and individual welfare. Decision making must be guided by a different standard of ethics and morality if the business system is to regain public confidence.

Additional insight may be gained into this conflict of values if some values are considered more important than others in our society. Values may be conceptualized as forming a hierarchy of different levels of importance—the business firm, the economic system, society, and, finally, the ultimate value in American society, the individual.[32] Figure 2-5 outlines this value hierarchy and suggests that it may serve as a guide for management decisions.

Figure 2-5

The Value of Hierarchy
A Model for Management Decision

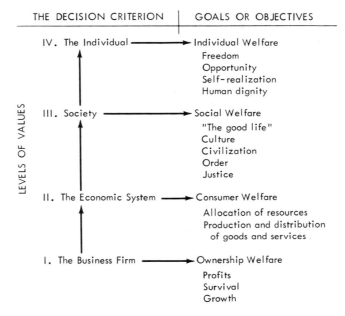

THE DECISION CRITERION | GOALS OR OBJECTIVES

LEVELS OF VALUES

IV. The Individual ⟶ Individual Welfare
Freedom
Opportunity
Self-realization
Human dignity

III. Society ⟶ Social Welfare
"The good life"
Culture
Civilization
Order
Justice

II. The Economic System ⟶ Consumer Welfare
Allocation of resources
Production and distribution
of goods and services

I. The Business Firm ⟶ Ownership Welfare
Profits
Survival
Growth

Source: Wilmar F. Bernthal, "Value Perspectives in Management Decisions," *Academy of Management Journal* 5, (December 1962), p. 196.

The ranking of values indicates that the limits in pursuing objectives at one level are set by the goals or values at higher levels. For example, the business firm in seeking its goals and objectives is restrained by values inherent in the economic system, society, and individual welfare. If these higher values are ignored or minimized, one can expect conflicts such as those already described. Responsible business management requires decisions and actions that contribute to the goals of the organization without violating higher values or goals. Decisions contain value judgments that affect others in their roles as consumers, members of society, or employees. If these decisions violate higher values, conflict may be expected.[33]

Self-understanding of Personal Values

Few of us are conscious and articulate about our values, although we feel uncomfortable when these values are violated. Everyone could benefit by paying more attention to the operation of their values.[34] One should examine his or her behavior and thoughts from time to time to uncover which values are held. The approach of comparing and contrasting behavior with the behavior of others facing similar situations and problems is very helpful. In this text, cases from real organizational settings are provided, and you may be requested to make recommendations on how the problems may be handled based upon your own analysis of the situation. Whether working individually or in groups, you may compare and contrast your analysis with those of other students and achieve some insight into your personal values. Examples of questions that may be helpful follow: (1) Are the goals of organizational efficiency or high productivity given more emphasis or weight than those of employee welfare or social welfare? (2) Are ability or ambition more significant than trust or tolerance in your analysis? Questions such as these may provide some clarification of personal values as well as those of others.

SUMMARY

Perception is extremely important for understanding organizational behavior. We may perceive the same situation differently, and our resulting behavior, whether overt or covert, may be unique. One does not react in a certain way because of what the surrounding situation actually is but because of what the individual perceives it to be. While perception is an automatic, unconscious process, it is learned, purposeful, and functional in meeting our needs. The manager must be aware of the potential effect of stereotyping, halo, projection, expectancy, and attribution upon his or her decisions and actions. The search for reliable evidence, feedback, and self-perception or insight are crucial for more objective perceptions and actions.

One's attitude conveys feelings, thoughts, and behavioral tendencies toward persons, concepts, and situations in the environment. As with perception, attitudes are learned; they meet our needs and tend to influence us in an automatic, unconscious fashion. Because attitudes have a potential behavioral component, management has frequently sought to influence personnel by communicating information or facts, altering undesirable situations, and serving as a sympathetic listener to employees with problems. Such efforts are directed toward the affective, cognitive, and behavioral components of attitudes.

Finally, we examined the nature of values that reflect our beliefs about desirable end states or conditions that we would like to see prevail above all others. Values serve as an organizing theme for attitudes that are focused on more specific objects (persons, situations, and things). The significance of values was examined in light of their influence upon the perception of situations and problems as well as upon the decisions and solutions to these problems. Lack of sensitivity to the value system of others in society was seen to have conflict potential for organizations.

QUESTIONS FOR STUDY AND DISCUSSION

1. Why is an understanding of the perceptual process important for managers?
2. What factors affect an individual's perceptual processes?
3. Why is it important to perceive ourselves accurately?
4. What are the three components of an attitude? How are the components related?
5. What purposes do attitudes have for an individual?
6. Why is an understanding of attitudes important for those who work with others? Can the components of an attitude be changed? How?
7. What are values? How do values affect behavior?
8. Do you agree with the self-fulfillment theme Yankelovich found in his survey of values? Why?
9. What values of society have changed over the last decade? Do these affect organizations? How can organizations sense such value changes? Can organizations influence societal values? How?

NOTES

[1]Maier, R.F. Norman, *Psychology in Industry,* 3rd ed. (Boston: Houghton Mifflin, 1965), p. 26.

[2]Cantril, Hadley, "Perception and Interpersonal Relations," E.P. Hollander and Raymond G. Hunt, Eds., *Current Perspectives in Social Psychology* (New York: Oxford University Press, 1963), pp. 290-298.

[3]Dearborn, Dewitt C. and Herbert A. Simon, "Selective Perception: A Note on the Departmental Identification of Executives," *Sociometry* 21, (1958): 140-144.

[4]Knowles, Henry P. and Borje O. Saxberg, *Personality and Leadership Behavior* (Reading, Mass.: Addison-Wesley, 1971): 71-86.

[5]Costello, Timothy W. and Sheldon S. Zalkind, *Psychology in Administration* (Englewood Cliffs, N.J.: Prentice-Hall, Inc., 1963), pp. 45-49.

[6]*Ibid.,* p. 46.

[7]Rosen, B. and T.H. Jerdee, "The Influence of Age Stereotypes on Managerial Decisions," *Journal of Applied Psychology* 61, (1976): 428-432.

[8]Osborn, Richard N., and William M. Vicars, "Sex Stereotypes: An Artifact in Leader Behavior and Subordinate Satisfaction Analysis," *Academy of Management Journal* 19, No. 3 (September 1976): 439-449.

[9]Secord, Paul F. and Carl W. Backman, *Social Psychology* (New York: McGraw-Hill, 1964), p. 80.

[10]Rosenthal, R., *Experimenter Effects in Behavioral Research* (New York: Appleton-Century-Crofts, 1966).

[11]Kelley, Harold H., *Attribution in Social Interaction* (Morristown, N.J.: General Learning Press, 1971).

[12]Heilman, Madeline E. and Richard A. Guzzo, "The Perceived Cause of Work Success as a Mediator of Sex Descrimination in Organizations," *Organizational Behavior and Human Performance* 21, (June, 1978): 346-357.

[13]Secord and Backman, op. cit., p. 95. Also see M. Fishbein and I. Ajzen, *Belief, Attitude, Intention, and Behavior: An Introduction to Theory and Research* (Reading, Mass.: Addison-Wesley, 1975).

[14]Katz, Daniel, "The Functional Approach to the Study of Attitudes," *The Public Opinion Quarterly* 24, (1964): 163-204.

[15]Ibid, pp. 168-172.

[16]Schuman, H. and M.P. Johnson, "Attitudes and Behavior," *Annual Review of Sociology,* ed, Alex Inkeles, (Palo Alto, Calif.: Annual Reviews, 1976): 161-207.

[17]Festinger, Leon, *A Theory of Cognitive Dissonance* (Stanford, Calif.: Stanford University Press, 1957) and Secord and Backman, op. cit., pp. 115-119.

[18]Rokeach, Milton, *The Nature of Human Values* (New York: Free Press, 1973), p. 5.

[19]Meddin, Jay, "Attitudes Values and Related Concepts: A System of Classification," *Social Science Quarterly* 55, No. 4, (March, 1975): 889-900.

[20]Rokeach, Milton, "A Theory of Organization and Change Within Value-Attitude Systems," *Journal of Social Issues* 24, (1968): 16.

[21]Allport, Gordon W., P. Vernon, and G. Lindsey, *Study of Values* (Boston: Houghton-Mifflin, 1960).

[22]Guth, William D. and Renato Tagiuri, "Personal Values and Corporate Strategy," *Harvard Business Review* 43 (September-October 1965): 123-132.

[23]Scott, William A., *Values and Organizations: A Study of Fraternities and Sororities* (Chicago: Rand McNally, 1965), pp. 24-25, 218-240.

[24]Yankelovich, Daniel, *The New Morality: A Profile of American Youth in the 70's* (New York: McGraw-Hill, 1974), p. vi and vii.

[25]*Ibid.,* p. 91.

[26]*Ibid.,* p. 93.

[27]*Ibid.,* pp. 5-6, 20-22, 28-29.

[28]Taylor, Ronald N. and Mark Thompson, "Work Value Systems of Young Workers," *Academy of Management Journal* 19, No. 4 (December 1976): 522-536.

[29]Cherrington, David J., Spencer Condie, and J. Lynn England, "Page and Work Values," *Academy of Management Journal* 22, No. 3, (September 1979): 617-623.

[30]England, George W., "Personal Value Systems of American Managers," *Academy of Management Journal* 10, No. 1 (March 1967): 53-68; G.W. England and R. Lee, "The Relationship Between Managerial Values and Managerial Success in the United States, Japan, India and Australia," *Journal of Applied Psychology* 59 (1974): 411-419.

[31]Blumenthal, M.M., "Ethics, Morality, and the Modern Corporate Executive," in *Values: A Special Report,* Reprint from Dividend, Graduate School of Admin., The University of Michigan, (Spring 1976): 4-8.

[32]Bernthal, W.F., "Values Perspectives in Management," *Academy of Management Journal* 5, No. 3 (December 1962): 196–201.

[33]Brown, Martha A., "Values—A Necessary but Neglected Ingredient of Motivation on the Job," *Academy of Management Review* 1, No. 4 (October 1976): 15-23.

[34]Guth and Tagiuri, op. cit., p. 42.

cases cases cases

Case Study: The Truth or Perception

The plant is a small operation consisting of three shifts and is located in a small town where a large percentage of the population is black. The company is quite proud of the fact that it has black employees at all levels of its hourly force—from the lowest as a utility worker to the highest as chemical operator.

One black operator has retired and another has accepted a job closer to home, so the plant manager looks to his force for a black worker with potential as chemical operator to fill one of the positions.

FIRST ASSIGNMENT: CHEMICAL OPERATOR

Plant Manager: Charlie Walcot has asked that he be considered for the job. He's only been here for about a month, and we really haven't had a chance to look at him closely.

Assistant to Plant Manager: So, are you going to give him a chance?

Plant Manager: Well, it looks like I have to. He is training with Terry on the easiest reactor now.

The three-month training period was unsuccessful for Charlie. Charlie was reassigned to the position of utility worker. Charlie agreed that he was not yet ready to be a chemical operator and was willing to be a utility worker for a while longer.

SECOND ASSIGNMENT: FORK TRUCK DRIVER

Almost a year went by before Charlie asked to be considered for another position. Charlie was promoted to fork truck driver on the third shift.

Assistant to Plant Manager: I see that Charlie has been promoted to fork truck driver on your shift.

Shift Supervisor: I guess they figured that he walked so slow, putting him on a fork truck might speed him up some.

Assistant to Plant Manager: How is he doing on the third shift?

Shift Supervisor: As well as can be expected. I have to stay on him all the time to get any work out of him. He is just slow and lets his mind wander. I tell him exactly what to do and how to do it and to report to me as soon as it is done.

49

The assistant to the plant manager then went to the plant superintendent.

Assistant to Plant Manager: I have been watching Charlie Walcot for several months now and would like your opinion of him.

Plant Superintendent: I have had several very discouraging reports concerning Charlie. I find it quite difficult to believe that anyone could be as poor a worker as the reports make him out to be. I am now trying to form my own opinion.

Assistant to Plant Manager: Did the supervisors recommend Charlie?

Plant Superintendent: Well, in a way. I had to force their opinion. They all were very reluctant to say anything good about Charlie. But I am not going to put anyone in a job unless I feel that he is qualified. As far as Charlie goes, I am going to try to see if he can be turned into a good employee.

For the next few months, there were several meetings between the plant superintendent and Charlie.

Assistant to Plant Manager: How is your work with Charlie coming along?

Plant Superintendent: Not so good. I am beginning to believe some of the reports that were first given to me by the supervisors.

Assistant Plant Manager: But I have seen you and Charlie in your office several times. What's been going on?

Plant Superintendent: I have had some heart-to-heart talks with Charlie. I've tried to show him how to prove himself a good worker, but I just don't seem to be getting through. For one week after the meetings, he's a real fireball. But then he drifts back into his old habits.

Assistant to Plant Manager: What have you suggested for him to prove himself?

Plant Superintendent: For one thing, he owes the Employee's Loan Fund $100 and is making no attempt to pay it back. I have told him that he should work overtime to get sufficient money to start a weekly payback schedule. I have even gone over a complete budget system for him since his marriage. He does not have any concept of how to handle money. We figured out how much overtime each week it would require to turn over a new leaf. One week later, it is as if we had never talked at all.

Assistant to Plant Manager: Is overtime common for fork truck drivers?

Plant Superintendent: Yes, especially on third shift. We normally operate the third shift for a six-day week.

Assistant to Plant Manager: Is Charlie working any overtime?

Plant Superintendent: No, I cannot force him. I am not sure that he is being approached right. I do not mean that he should be given an engraved invitation, but Harry, his supervisor, does not exactly like Charlie.

Assistant to Plant Manager: What is your opinion of Charlie now?

Plant Superintendent: I am quite undecided. I think that some of the trouble is with Charlie and that some is with his supervisors.

A NEW OPPORTUNITY

In November, a position became available on first shift working for the production supervisor. Charlie asked to be considered and was promoted from the third shift to the first shift. The plant superintendent wanted to talk to the production supervisor before the actual move.

Plant Superintendent: I have decided to let Charlie work for you on the first shift.

Production Supervisor: Hmmm—I have heard more bad reports about Charlie than good. Why are you letting Charlie work for me?

Plant Superintendent: I am hoping that you can do something with him. I have given up all hope that I can do anything for him. I am going to give him one more try to work for you.

Production Supervisor: I will try, but don't expect too much.

Several weeks went by with the assistant to plant manager observing Charlie's performance in his new job.

Assistant to Plant Manager: I see that Charlie is working for you now. How do you feel about this?

Production Supervisor: I have tried to keep an open mind about Charlie. I treat him like any other employee. I tell him what to do and I expect him to do it.

Assistant to Plant Manager: How is this working?

Production Supervisor: He does what I ask satisfactorily and on some occasions has even gone beyond what I expected.

Assistant to Plant Manager: Do you mean that he has made a complete turnaround?

Production Supervisor: No, not quite. After doing an excellent job today, tomorrow, he may make such a mess that I get so mad at him I cannot even talk to him.

Assistant to Plant Manager: Do you let him know how you feel when he is not working satisfactorily?

Production Supervisor: No, not always. I do not want to make a special case out of him. Besides, I have too much to do now without taking time to talk to him every time something upsets me. With our northern plant closing, I have to worry about supplying the whole East Coast with our product.

PAINTING ASSIGNMENT

Several months went by with very little change in Charlie's performance. The production supervisor was walking in front of the new personnel office when the personnel manager stopped him.

Personnel Manager: How do you feel about recommending Charlie for the painter's job that just opened up?

Production Supervisor (smiling): I would recommend him highly.

Personnel Manager: Seriously, can you recommend Charlie for a promotion based on his current job performance?

Production Supervisor: Since you put it that way, I would say that Charlie is performing satisfactorily.

Personnel Manager: That's not what I asked. Would you recommend Charlie for the promotion?

Production Supervisor: I really have to go. I'll talk with you later.

Later the production supervisor had a meeting with the plant manager to talk about Charlie and the conversation that he had had with the personnel manager. The plant manager said that this was an excellent way to get rid of the problem. He suggested that they merely transfer Charlie. The plant manager went to talk with the personnel manager.

Plant Superintendent: Charlie has more seniority than anyone else who is being considered for the job. You know that this is a very important factor when considering promotions.

Personnel Manager: I know, but even more important is his performance in his present job. How does the production supervisor feel about this?

Plant Superintendent: We both agree that Charlie is working satisfactorily.

Personnel Manager: You are both evading my question. Do you recommend Charlie for the promotion?

Plant Superintendent: No, not really. But, if we do not promote Charlie now, we have even a more difficult job of giving Charlie some concrete reasons why he is not getting the job.

Personnel Manager: Charlie does not get along with the maintenance foreman. Do you know why?

Plant Superintendent: I think that most of the problems developed when Charlie was using the fork truck and the foreman needed it for a job. He told Charlie to get off and let him have the fork truck. Charlie told him he was busy and could not stop. The foreman told him he would be in trouble if he did not get off the truck. Charlie got off and went straight to the production supervisor who straightened it out, but the maintenance department got mad at Charlie for that.

Personnel Manager: For Charlie, this would not be a very good atmosphere in which to work.

Plant Superintendent: I think you're right. But how are we going to explain to Charlie why he did not get the job?

Personnel Manager: His supervisor must explain the reasons. I want to have a meeting tomorrow with you, the production supervisor, and Charlie to settle this matter.

THE OUTCOME

The production supervisor was notified by the plant superintendent that there would be a meeting and that he would have to explain why Charlie was not being recommended for the new job. The meeting was in the plant superintendent's office.

Personnel Manager: Charlie, we have met today to tell you that you have not been promoted to painter because of your current working performance.

Production Supervisor: You are performing satisfactorily. Whenever I specifically ask for something to be done, you do it. However, rarely do you do anything on your own. For me to recommend anyone, the person must have self-motivation.

Plant Superintendent: I agree. I have worked with you for almost three years, and I do not see a great deal of improvement in your performance.

Personnel Manager: Is this a surprise to you, Charlie?

Charlie: I am not really surprised. I did not think I would get the job. The plant superintendent won't recommend me for any higher position.

Plant Superintendent: You are absolutely right. Unless you show some improvement, I will never approve a promotion.

Personnel Manager: Can you cite any specific areas in which Charlie is falling down?

Production Supervisor: For one thing, he lacks overtime.

Personnel Manager: Has Charlie ever refused overtime?

Production Supervisor: I cannot remember exactly, but, with the poor condition of the plant and his work area, Charlie shows no interest in working overtime to keep his area clean. He punches the clock at 4:30 sharp every day.

Personnel Manager: What other areas?

Production Supervisor: Just his irresponsible attitude toward his work. Charlie is improving, but not to the point of accepting the responsibility of this promotion.

Charlie: I don't think that I'll ever get a higher position here. I think the best thing for you to do now is to fire me.

CASE QUESTIONS

1. Is Charlie getting a fair deal? What evidence do you have to support your position?

2. Are any perceptual mechanisms evident in this case?

3. Is it likely that Charlie's perception of his performance differs from that of his supervisor? Why?

4. At the end of the case, how do you think Charlie sees himself?

5. How can management check on its perceptions?

6. What would you suggest that management do at the close of the case? Why?

cases cases cases

Case Study: A Rejected Report

Mrs. Jablon was called by Mrs. McDonald, the Director of Nursing Service, shortly after moving into town and was asked to meet with her concerning employment. Mrs. McDonald, a registered nurse, had been Director of Nursing Service for three years.

Mrs. Jablon was graciously received and found that Mrs. McDonald had learned, through a mutual friend, quite a bit about her previous experience as a general staff nurse, head nurse supervisor, and director of inservice education. Mrs. McDonald related that the hospital was facing a severe shortage of nurses. She felt that to attract qualified nurses they were going to have to make many improvements, one of which was to develop an inservice education department. In the course of the morning, Mrs. Jablon was introduced to many of the nursing service personnel, the hospital administrator, and some of the department heads. Mrs. Jablon was offered the job of inservice education instructor and asked to let them know her decision within a week.

Mrs. Jablon decided to accept the job if the hospital would agree to give her some secretarial help, attempt to acquire an assistant instructor and to be given at least four weeks to orient herself to the hospital, the personnel, the policies, and procedures—not only in nursing but in all departments. Mrs. McDonald responded to these requests by saying, "I'll have to see if the hospital administrator will agree." The hospital administrator readily approved saying he thought the requests to be reasonable and wise.

Mrs. Jablon began to spend some time with all departments as well as nursing units in the hospital. She spent several days in the nursing office and made a number of observations. Mrs. McDonald spent most of her time in the office but one day announced she was going to make the rounds and asked Mrs. Jablon to accompany her. During these rounds, she criticized, in public, several of the personnel about their appearance or performance using a rather loud voice. She visited several personal acquaintances or prominent people who were patients in the hospital and always asked the question: "Have you had a back-rub today?" Later she told Mrs. Jablon that she found that the best way to evaluate the quality of nursing care was to find out if patients had been given back-rubs. Mrs. Sneed, the assistant director of nursing service, spent most of her time on the telephone trying to get nurses who were not working to work part-time. The rest of her time was spent rescheduling the regular staff's time to fill the gaps. During this time Mrs. Jablon worked with the supervisors of each shift who stayed very busy but were generally helpful to the different hospital units. Mrs. McDonald left written notes for them and one supervisor remarked to another, "I'm damned if I do and damned if I don't—I'm ready to look for another job." There was only one supervisor for each shift. In the patient care sections, work loads were extremely heavy but the personnel seemed to take a personal interest in each patient.

A TROUBLED START

Mrs. Jablon realized that she would have to prove the value of inservice education by offering interesting and well-planned programs. She was very careful to put her plans into writing and gain the approval of the director before commencing a new program, feeling that by these means later problems could be avoided. She established some priority needs since it was impossible to begin everything at once. Some of these were orientation for new personnel; weekly training sessions for aides, orderlies, and ward secretaries; bi-monthly meetings for registered nurse (R.N.) groups and licensed practical nurse (L.P.N.) groups. She had to schedule repeat times for each group so that all personnel could be relieved to attend these meetings. During the first meeting she allowed informal discussion concerning areas of interest and asked for volunteers to various committees. She was rather surprised by the interest and enthusiasm expressed by each group. One group she really felt the need to "win friends and influence" was the R. N. staff group so she arranged for their meeting in the dining room where coffee was to be served. The group seemed to enjoy this since they did not often get to take a coffee break, especially on days when they had to go to a meeting. During the first few meetings this group began to air some of the problems they faced. Some problems were approached through brainstorming sessions. Several of the solutions were to plan programs of an educational nature which required administrative approvals or changes.

Mrs. Jablon wrote up some of the problems with proposed solutions and presented them at the weekly conference with the director. She was shocked when Mrs. McDonald said that she didn't like the idea of meetings being held in the dining room—that many groups abused the "coffee break" privilege anyway. She further stated that it was unwise for Mrs. Jablon to let the groups turn the meetings into "grievance" sessions and that from now on she would attend all meetings of the R.N. and L.P.N. groups. Mrs. Jablon countered Mrs. McDonald's remarks by pointing out that if inservice were to succeed she would have to have the cooperation of this group rather than their antagonism. She also indicated that she could not function unless permitted to at least try some of her ideas. With a somewhat hostile air the meeting was closed. The inservice director felt she was not given a definite answer so she proceeded with her original plans. Attractive calendars for inservice education programs were posted in every nursing unit. Attempts were made to involve the nursing personnel in these programs. The next meeting of the R.N. group was held in the dining room with coffee being served. Mrs. McDonald attended but made very few comments; however, the nurses were very reluctant to talk openly as they had done in their previous meetings. Nothing further was mentioned concerning coffee being served at these meetings and the practice continued.

A NEW PROBLEM

After the inservice program had been in operation for about two months, Mrs. McDonald called Mrs. Jablon to her office and related that at the department heads meeting that morning there had been much criticism of the ward secretaries from other departments, particularly the laboratory, pharmacy, and X-ray sections. She felt that the criticisms were unjust but she wanted inservice to give priority to improving the "training" of the ward secretaries.

Mrs. Jablon immediately began an investigation by asking for a representative from X-ray, Pharmacy, Laboratory and the Personnel Department to meet with herself, a head nurse, and a ward secretary. After several meetings they came up with these findings and proposed solutions:

Problem:

To improve the quality of performance of ward secretaries on nursing units.

Nature of the Problem:

Thirty ward secretaries are responsible for tasks directly related to patient care and almost every department in the hospital.

Problems originating with this position are due to a tremendous turnover in personnel; twenty people have been trained as ward secretaries this year.

The performance records of most ward secretaries are very poor and result in confusion, errors in patient care, and loss in revenue to the hospital.

Source of Data:

1. Personnel records—termination interviews.
2. Personal interviews with secretaries now in employment—with both long and short terms of service.
3. Observation.
4. Job description from ward secretaries.
5. Interviews with department heads to determine if problems exist in this area.

Information Obtained:

Far too many persons leaving this position for the following reasons, in order of frequency:

1. Too little training before being left alone to handle the position.
2. Salary too low. Does not attract and hold the caliber of person needed to to efficiently perform tasks outlined in job description.
3. Person being moved from one unit or shift to another without notice or explanation. Poor employee-employer communication.
4. Too many duties.

5. Staff often too busy to give assistance or guidance.
6. No distinct person having authority, everyone giving orders.

Proposed Solution:

A. Although not the primary problem, to attract a qualified person who will likely remain at the hospital, we must seriously consider a salary increase for this position. An applicant for this position must have a high school education since complex duties are required. This person is paid less than aides and orderlies who have fewer duties and a tenth-grade education level requirement.

We are creating our own problem by using a person with little or no training, and must devise and implement a formal training for this position.

B. Training Program:

From the information obtained from personnel we determined that the majority of persons hired for this position are recent high school graduates. A personnel survey showed that 19 out of 30 ward secretaries are below the age of 25 and have never been employed before their present job. These persons have no prior medical experience, although the performance of tasks in the job description require some technical knowledge in the field of health care.

The training program should be in two parts. Part I will require formal classroom work consisting of terminology, basic understanding of all duties outlined in the job description, with simulated practices in the classroom, hospital policies, work organization, and ethics. The exact amount of training time for Part I has not been established, but probably two weeks of pre-service training.

Part II—On-the-job training so that a person realizes the scope of the position and is prepared to meet the challenge and face the unexpected.

This training program should be developed by the Department of Nursing Service with Inservice Education and all other related departments cooperating in developing the curriculum in order to cover all areas thoroughly.

It is the committee's feeling that the actual training can best be done by a ward secretary now in employment. One who has a thorough basic knowledge of the job as well as an efficient approach to the actual job performance.

If possible, this person should be relieved, at least for the present time, from routine unit duty. She should be placed under inservice to conduct these classes for new ward secretaries and to up-grade the secretaries presently employed. She would teach the classroom instruction, on the job training, and serve as follow-up instructor after the secretaries have been released to work alone on units.

It might be possible to offer a certificate for completion of this course and to change the job title to ward manager. These two items could give some much needed prestige to this position.

We feel that the items listed will lessen the tremendous turnover in this position and thus provide better patient care, improved service, and lessen lost revenue due to overlooked charges.

We cannot give an exact sum in savings in dollars. However, it was found that in five days, with three new secretaries on the units, one department, the Pharmacy, lost $900.00 in charges. On any given Monday on a random audit of drug sheets, almost all units miss between $40.00 and $200.00 in charges. This totals to between $2,100.00 to $10,400.00 per year. This represents only one department.

REACTION

Mrs. McDonald told Mrs. Jablon that she did not feel the report was factual and that it reflected poorly on the nursing department. She said it would be impossible to relieve the ward secretary to help with the training of this group and that inservice and the head nurses were going to have to do a better job. Mrs. Jablon asked if she would present it to the administrator and got an emphatic "No."

QUESTIONS

1. What was Mrs. McDonald's expectations when she requested a study of the ward secretaries? Does this explain her reaction?

2. Do you share Mrs. McDonald's perception that the report is not "very factual"? Why?

3. Is Mrs. McDonald's self-concept involved? How? Does this influence her behavior or reaction to the report?

4. Evaluate Mrs. McDonald's attitude toward the report. What function does this attitude appear to serve? Will her attitude be readily changed? Why?

CHAPTER 3

MOTIVATION:
A MAINSPRING of BEHAVIOR

LEARNING OBJECTIVES

When you have finished this chapter, you should be able to:

- *Draw and explain a general model of motivation.*
- *Understand and compare four content theories of motivation.*
- *Diagram and explain two process theories of motivation.*
- *Describe motivation variables in an organizational context.*
- *Explain two different assumptions made about people that will affect efforts to motivate others.*

In this chapter, behavior at the individual level remains the focus of attention as the complicated area of motivation is examined. For a foundation, a generalized model of motivation is developed. Six theories of motivation are presented. Four of these are content theories that concern primarily the need factors that energize behavior. Two are process theories that focus on the complete motivation sequence, that is, on how behavior is started, directed, sustained, and stopped. A systems orientation inherent in the process theories notes the interaction of motivation variables.

Since motivation theories are confined to a limited number of variables, the organization context of motivation is surveyed. In addition to human needs, individual attitudes, interests, and capacities influence motivation. Numerous work environmental and job characteristics have a direct, but often intangible, influence upon motivation.

Assumptions about people or human nature affect how others are induced to perform. Two contrasting views—Theory X and Theory Y—provide insight into how attempts to motivate others are shaped by the assumptions that one holds.

The chapter closes with suggested guidelines for motivation that one may find helpful in analyzing problems of performance.

A GENERALIZED MODEL OF MOTIVATION

In general terms, motivation is a process that involves three variables: (1) energizing, (2) behavior or actions, and (3) incentive or goals.[1]

Energizing occurs when one has a need or desire for something. Needs and desires are called motives and are the "whys" for goal-directed behavior. The goal may be some object, person, or activity that satisfies the need. For example, if you are hungry (a need), you may go to a nearby restaurant for a meal (behavior). There you find food (goal) that when consumed satisfies your hunger need. The entire motivation process can be diagrammed as shown in Figure 3-1. The motivation process outlined must be expanded to appreciate its complexity.

Figure 3-1

The Motivation Process

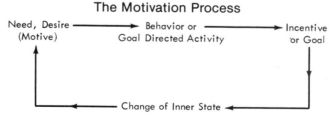

Source: Adapted from Richard M. Steers and Lyman W. Porter, *Motivation and Work Behavior* 2nd ed. (New York: McGraw-Hill, 1979), p. 7.

Energizing

The energizing force—need or desire—is the reason underlying behavior. However, one has numerous needs that compete for attention. It is the need having the greatest strength that will lead to activity. The need or desire is a condition of tension or disequilibrium that the individual will seek to eliminate or reduce.

Needs and desires are associated with an expectancy or likelihood that certain activities will alleviate the need. Past experiences, vicarious or personal, and known experiences of others shape the degree of expectancy. Unless one anticipates that certain behavior will lead to the satisfaction or reduction of a need, energizing is not likely to take place. For example, an unemployed person who has repeatedly sought a job, but without success, may simply give up the search.

Behavior

Goal-directed behavior is accompanied by cues from within the individual and/or the environment as to the appropriateness of the behavior. Such feedback may lead to the modification of the behavior or provide assurance that the behavior is adequate for achieving the intended goal. For example, an individual who feels a need for more job competence can embark on a self-study program. However, if that person concludes that such a study is of little or no value in achieving the desired level of competence, he or she may decide to enroll in an evening course at a local college.

In addition to the adjustment or learning that may occur, goal-directed behavior can also be a means of satisfying certain needs independently of attaining the goal. An employee who has a desire and goal for promotion may experience the satisfaction of several needs, namely, the needs for growth, recognition, and competence.

The Goal

When the goal or incentive is attained, there can be two different results. The intensity of some needs such as hunger or thirst are fulfilled upon gratification. Other needs may increase in intensity after the goal is reached. An increase in pay may increase the desire for more pay; an achievement may increase the desire for additional achievements; attaining competence may induce the need for higher levels of competence.

Goal attainment affects subsequent expectations of further goal attainment. One's goal can be completely achieved or varying degrees of success may be experienced. If an individual repeatedly falls short of attaining his or her goal, that individual may "lower his sights." His or her level of aspiration has been reduced. This is another way of saying that the individual's expectations have been altered. Likewise, if one success follows another, an individual will likely raise his or her level of aspiration; that is, the person's expectations of further goal attainment have been elevated.

THEORIES OF MOTIVATION

The theories of motivation to be considered in this chapter have been divided in two groups.[2] One group, designated *content theories,* is concerned with needs and factors that energize behavior. The other group, *process theories,* focuses on how behavior is started, directed, sustained, and stopped. Additionally, the interaction of major motivational variables are examined to provide a systems orientation. For example, the interrelationship of needs, choices, and incentives are studied to determine how they influence behavior.

Four content theories that examine factors that energize motivated behavior will be presented in the following section: (1) Maslow's need hierarchy theory, (2) Alderfer's E.R.G. theory, (3) Herzberg's motivation-hygiene theory, and (4) McClelland's achievement theory.

CONTENT THEORIES OF MOTIVATION

Maslow's Need Hierarchy Theory

One of the earliest and best-known theories of motivation is Maslow's need hierarchy.[3] Maslow's model is built on three basic premises.

1. People are "wanting beings"; that is, they are motivated by a desire to satisfy various needs. Unsatisfied needs influence behavior, but satisfied needs do not act as motivators.
2. A person's needs are arranged sequentially in a hierarchy of importance from the most basic (food and shelter) to the highest (self-actualization).
3. One moves from a lower level to the next level only after the lower-level needs are minimally satisfied. For example, the individual will concentrate on satisfying safety and security needs before directing his or her behavior toward satisfying social needs, the next level.

The need hierarchy consists of five need categories: (1) physiological, (2) safety and security, (3) belongingness and love, (4) esteem, and (5) self-actualization.

As seen in Figure 3-2, needs are arranged in a hierarchy from the lowest, most basic, level, physiological, to the highest, self-actualization. The individual will systematically satisfy his or her needs by starting with the most basic (physiological) and then move up the hierarchy. Furthermore, the more basic need groups will take precedence over all those above them in the hierarchy; that is, the individual's behavior is dominated and determined by the most basic group of needs that are unfulfilled. If the

Figure 3-2

Maslow's Need Hierarchy

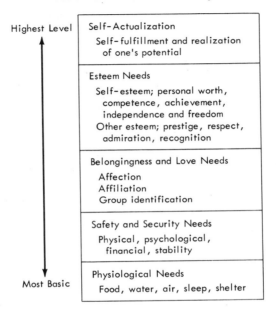

physiological needs are relatively well gratified, there then emerges a new set of needs, the safety needs. After the social needs are generally satisfied, the belongingness needs predominate, and so on up the hierarchy.

It is important to note that a need does not have to be satisfied completely before the next need emerges to influence one's behavior. Most individuals in our society are partially satisfied in all their basic needs and partially unsatisfied at the same time. By assigning arbitrary figures, Maslow states that the average person is satisfied perhaps 85 percent in his or her physiological needs, 70 percent in his or her safety needs, 50 percent in his or her belonging and love needs, 40 percent in his or her self-esteem needs, and 10 percent in his or her self-actualization needs. In other words, the individual experiences relative degrees of satisfaction and dissatisfaction in all basic needs at the same time.

Research studies have failed to support the need hierarchy concept of motivation, but several conclusions may still be drawn.[4]

1. There is some evidence to support Maslow's position that, for lower-level needs, increased satisfaction leads to decreased importance.

2. Several studies also show that lower-level workers tend to be less satisfied and/or more concerned with basic needs, whereas managers express concern for the higher-order needs such as achievement, esteem, and self-actualization.

These findings do not provide a test of the theory, and the authors conclude that Maslow's Need Hierarchy has neither been proved nor disproved.

The most persuasive evidence against the validity of Maslow's need hierarchy has been obtained by the factor analysis technique. This approach is used to test the structuring of variables and their independence. A review of six studies using factor analysis failed to show that Maslow's need categories are independent as his model indicates.[5] For example, an overlap appears between safety and several physiological needs and also between safety and some love needs. In view of this overlap, it is suggested that the need categories are erroneous.

Regardless of research findings, individual needs have been identified that are important if one is to understand behavior. Implications for managerial actions also are contained in Maslow's theory—it is beneficial to create a work environment in which employees can develop to their fullest potential.

Alderfer's E.R.G.

Seeking a more adequate understanding of motivation than Maslow's theory provided, Alderfer developed and tested his E.R.G. theory,[6] which compresses Maslow's five need categories into three core needs that people strive to meet—existence (E), relatedness (R), and growth (G).

Existence needs constitute the various physiological and material desires. Hunger, thirst, and shelter represent physiological existence needs. Pay, fringe benefits, and physical working needs are other types of existence needs associated with the work situation. These needs are comparable to Maslow's physiological and safety needs.

Relatedness needs include all the needs that involve relationships with other people—family members, supervisors, co-workers, subordinates, and friends. The exchange of acceptance, confirmation, understanding, and influence are elements of the relatedness process. These depend on a process of sharing and a mutuality of feeling. The relatedness category of needs is similar to the safety, social, and several self-esteem needs of Maslow.

Growth needs include all the needs that involve creative or personal growth. Such needs are satisfied when one becomes involved in problems that call for one to fully utilize his or her capacities or develop new ones. Within Maslow's framework, this includes self-actualization and several self-esteem needs.

E.R.G. theory is based upon several basic propositions that are outlined as follows:

1. Need frustration: (a) the less existence needs are satisfied, the more they will be desired, and (b) the less relatedness needs are satisfied, the more they will be desired. For example, if the need for pay is not being satisfied, the desire for pay will be increased; that is, frustration of the need has resulted in an increased desire.

2. Frustration regression: (a) the less relatedness needs are satisfied, the more existence will be desired, and (b) the less growth needs are satisfied, the more relatedness needs will be desired. These two propositions are based on the idea that, when a person is not satisfied in attaining less concrete ends, he or she regresses to needs that are more concrete. For example, when intangible growth needs are blocked, the individual "drops back" to relatedness needs that are more concrete and certain of attainment.

3. Satisfaction progression: (a) the more existence needs are satisfied, the more relatedness needs will be desired, and (b) the more relatedness needs are satisfied, the more growth needs will be desired. As a person fulfills the more basic desires, more energy is available to deal with the less concrete, more personal, and more uncertain aspects of living. For example, as existence needs are fulfilled, less energy is required to meet material needs.

4. The final proposition holds that the more growth needs are satisfied, the more they will be desired. In this case, there is no higher need category toward which the individual can move. Instead, the more one experiences the satisfaction of growth needs, the more he or she will seek additional growth opportunities.

The threefold division of human needs is the most apparent difference between E.R.G. theory and Maslow's theory. But two other important differences should be noted. Alderfer assumes that all needs are simultaneously active and that "prepotency" (from more basic to complex) does not play as significant a part as it does for Maslow. Both theories hold that an individual will progress to a higher-order need once a lower-order need has been satisfied (satisfaction progression). Alderfer indicates how a lack of satisfaction of higher-order needs can lead to lower-order needs becoming more important (frustration leads to regression).

Alderfer's E.R.G. theory is a relatively new, and little research has been conducted to test its validity. Several studies have shown stronger support for E.R.G. theory than for Maslow's need hierarchy.[7] However, additional research will be needed to test the implications of E.R.G. theory.

Motivation-Hygiene Theory

Whereas Maslow's need hierarchy was based upon his clinical observations, Herzberg's motivation-hygiene theory was based upon job data.[8] His research was based upon the hypothesis that factors involved in job satisfaction were separate and distinct from the factors that led to job dissatisfaction. The study began with in-depth interviews of over two hundred engineers and accountants. These interviews probed sequences of events in the work lives of respondents to determine the factors that were involved in their feeling exceptionally happy and exceptionally unhappy with their jobs.

In analyzing the data from these interviews, Herzberg concluded that two different categories of factors, essentially independent of each other, affect behavior in different ways. When the respondents felt dissatisfied with their jobs, they were concerned about specific facets of their work environment. These factors were named "hygiene" factors; that is, hygiene factors were so termed because they serve as preventatives to job dissatisfaction. When the respondents felt satisfied with their jobs, they were concerned with factors necessary for improvement in performance. These factors were labeled motivators because they seemed to be related to stimulating superior performance. The various hygiene and motivating factors are shown in Table 3-1.[9]

Table 3-1

Motivation and Hygiene Factors

Hygiene Factors	Motivation Factors
Company policy and administration	Achievement
Supervision	Recognition for accomplishment
Interpersonal relationships	The work itself
Salary	Responsibility
Working conditions	Advancement
Security, status	Growth

In summary, the hygiene factors (1) meet one's needs to avoid unpleasantness, (2) relate to how one is treated on the job, and, (3) are external to the job. On the other hand, the motivation factors (1) meet one's need for growth, (2) relate to how one is utilized on the job, and, (3) relate to the job itself. Hygiene factors are the primary cause of dissatisfaction on the job, whereas the motivation factors are the primary cause of satisfaction. These two sets of factors are not opposites of each other; rather, they represent two different dimensions. The opposite of job satisfaction is not job dissatisfaction but *no* job satisfaction; likewise, the opposite of job dissatisfaction is not job satisfaction, but *no* job dissatisfaction. The following illustrates this point:

Job satisfaction ←——————→ No job satisfaction

Job dissatisfaction ←——————→ No job dissatisfaction

For this reason, Herzberg's theory is often called a two-factor theory.

If Herzberg's theory is correct, one would expect highly satisfied people to be highly motivated and therefore more productive. Herzberg and his colleagues reviewed twenty-seven studies in which there was a quantitative relationship between job attitude and productivity.[10] Only fourteen of the studies indicated a positive relationship. That is, in thirteen studies, job attitude and productivity were not related. In a later series of twenty studies, it was found that seventeen demonstrated a positive relationship between job satisfaction and job performance.[11] The remaining three studies revealed a negative relationship.

After examining this research and other investigations, it was concluded that the same job factor could cause job satisfaction for one person and job dissatisfaction for another.[12] Studies have indicated that whether a given factor will be a source of dissatisfaction or satisfaction on the job is influenced by (1) occupational level, (2) age, sex, and education of the respondents, (3) culture, and (4) the respondent's standing in his or her group. The two investigators also concluded that intrinsic job factors are more important to both satisfying and dissatisfying job events. Finally, the reviewers concluded that the motivation–hygiene theory is an oversimplification of the relationship between motivation and satisfaction and of the sources of job satisfaction and dissatisfaction. Motivation is only one of the conditions necessary for productive work.

The motivation–hygiene theory has had a considerable impact upon managers. It has a commonsense appeal and is expressed in a language that is easily understood. Herzberg's theory has been the central focus of numerous employee motivation and job-enrichment programs. The following chapter will delve into job enrichment and demonstrate how the motivation–hygiene concept serves as the foundation for the most widely used job-enrichment programs.

Achievement Motivation Theory

McClelland hypothesized that there was a relationship between an aroused need for achievement and the amount of entrepreneurial activity and the resulting economic growth within a culture.[13] Proof for this was first sought in the less economically developed societies. It was supposed that these societies could be differentiated on their rate of economic growth by measuring the strength of their need for achievement on a societal level. The need for achievement was measured by assessing the achievement imagery found in the folk tales of the various cultures. McClelland found that the societies with a high need for achievement also had a high percentage of the population engaged in entrepreneurial activity.

Although most of McClelland's work relates the need for achievement in a society to its economic development, his approach has been extended to the study of the individual and work-related behavior. While the need for achievement was of central concern, McClelland's work has been expanded to include the need for power and affiliation. Each need is defined as follows:

1. Need for achievement—a need to excel in relation to competitive or internalized standards.
2. Need for power—a need for control and influence over others.
3. Need for affiliation—a need for warm, friendly relationships.

Basic theory.

Each person has the potential energy to behave in a variety of ways. The way in which one behaves, however, depends on the relative strength of his or her various motives and the opportunities presented by the situation. In other words,[14]

> A person's aroused motivation to behave in a particular way is said to depend on the strength of readiness of his motives and on two kinds of perceptions of the situation: his expectancies of goal-attainment and the incentive values he attaches to the goals presented.

This is summarized as follows:

$$\text{Aroused motivation} = M \times E \times I$$

Where

M = strength of the basic motive

E = expectancy of attaining the goal

I = perceived incentive value of the goal

The presence and strength of achievement, affiliation, and power motives are assessed by the Thematic Apperception Test, a series of pictures of fairly ambiguous social and work situations. The subject is asked to make up a story suggested by each picture, and the stories are analyzed for evidence of the different kinds of imagery associated with various motives. The score for an individual indicates the frequency with which he or she tends to think spontaneously in terms of achievement, affiliation, or power.

Research and application

One with a strong need for achievement exhibits definite characteristics in his or her behavior. Such a person

1. seeks and assumes a high degree of personal responsibility,
2. sets moderate achievement goals,
3. takes calculated risks, and
4. wants concrete feedback on his or her actions.

McClelland found that managers or executives scored considerably higher on the average in achievement thinking than did professionals or specialists of comparable education and background. This was true not only in the United States, but also Italy and Poland. In general, more successful managers tend to score higher on achievement than do less successful managers. Persons with a strong need for achievement also make good sales representatives, sales managers, consultants, and fund raisers.[15]

Individuals with a strong need for power seek control and influence over others by means of suggestion, opinion, and evaluation. They are seen by others as forceful, outspoken, hard-headed, and demanding. On the other hand, the use of power is determined by other needs and values. Wainer and Rubin measured the motive pattern of the chief executives of fifty-one small technical companies,[16] the results indicated that

> the highest performing companies in this sample were led by entrepreneurs who exhibited a high *n* Achievement and a moderate *n* Power. Those entrepreneurs who had a high *n* Achievement coupled with a high *n* Power performed less well than their high *n* Achievement counterparts who exhibited only a moderate level of *n* Power. Within the moderate *n* Achievement group, higher performing companies were led by entrepreneurs who had a high *n* Affiliation.

These investigations speculated that a high need for power could produce autocratic or authoritarian leadership that interfers with the effective use of talented manpower. Therefore, high *n* power could cancel out high *n* achievement and make for less effective company management. A previous study by another investigator supported this line of reasoning.[17]

McClelland has extended his work to the training of managers in the United States and several foreign countries. Since motives are learned, the achievement motive can be developed. In training sessions, achievement responses are elicited and reinforced or rewarded and subsequently extended to personal everyday life events. Such programs have had reasonable success.

Attention also can be given to motivation in the selection, hiring, and utilization of personnel.[18] First, tasks can be analyzed to determine what behavior—achievement, power, affiliation—are required for their successful performance. Second, candidates can be reviewed for behavioral and motivational patterns considered appropriate for the job. Finally, after the selection of an applicant, the work environment can be managed by arousing and reinforcing the kind of motivation that will produce appropriate job behavior.

PROCESS THEORIES OF MOTIVATION

The process theories of motivation not only seek to determine what energizes behavior but also to determine the relationship between variables constituting the motivation process. Two theories will be considered: Vroom's expectancy theory and Adams' equity, or social comparison, theory.

Expectancy Theory

Basic to the expectancy view of motivation is the idea that individuals have expectancies concerning the outcomes that are likely to occur as the result of what they do. Furthermore, individuals have different preferences for various outcomes. This means that individuals are considered as thinking and reasoning and as having anticipations concerning future events. Consequently, they may choose one course of action over another. V. H. Vroom developed a theory of work motivation that gives significant insight into this motivational process.[19] The basic variables in this process are expectancies, outcomes, instrumentalities, valences, and choices. The variables are interrelated in the following manner.

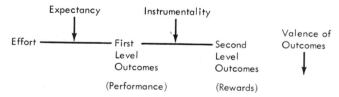

Expectancy

The effort that one exerts to obtain a first-level outcome (some aspect of performance) is influenced by his or her expectancy that the outcome will actually happen. If the chances of affecting performance are seen as low or nonexistent, little or no effort will be exerted. On the other hand, if the chances of attaining a performance goal seem high, one may "go all out." Expectancy is defined as a belief concerning the likelihood or probability that a particular act or effort will be followed by a particular outcome. Consequently, expectancy is an effort-to-performance relationship. The degree of belief, or expectancy, may vary between zero, or complete lack of belief, to 1, or complete certainty. However, expectancy is based upon the individual's perception of the situation, not on objective reality.

Instrumentality

Obtaining the first outcome or performance goal may mean nothing in and of itself to an individual. Yet it can be instrumental in achieving a desired second outcome or reward. For example, achieving production or a first-level outcome can be instrumental for obtaining pay, security, recognition, and so forth. Instrumentality is the degree of belief that the first outcome (performance) may be seen as leading to some kind of second outcome (reward). Instrumentality is a performance-to-outcome association and may vary from −1 to +1.

Valence

Finally, second-level outcomes are of varying degrees of importance or value to the individual. This attraction is called valence and is based upon the extent to which an outcome meets the needs of an individual. Valence is the strength of an individual's preference for an outcome and may be positive or negative. Valence ranges from −1 to 0, or no importance, to +1, or maximum importance. For example, an increase in production may result in an individual's being rejected by his or her work associates when group acceptance has a positive valence.

In the diagram of the motivating process, across the top are three variables. From the left to right, these are valance, instrumentality, and expectancy. These are known as VIE, the label frequently applied to this theory.

Quantifying VIE

Each of the VIE variables has a numerical range, and they may be used collectively to determine motivation or effort to perform. For example, an individual sees a probability of .8 of extra effort leading to attaining higher production or a first-level outcome. Moreover, the individual strongly believes that such performance will lead to an increase in pay and places a value of .9 on this happening. Finally, the individual highly desires an increase in pay and ascribes it a high valence of .9. When these factors are combined in a multiplicative manner (.8 × .9 × .9 = .65), one can conclude that the individual has a strong motivation to perform. What happens when expectancy or instrumentality is zero? Motivation is also zero.

Making a choice

By evaluating the VIE factors in a work situation, it becomes clearer why an individual chooses from among different levels of effort. One may choose to work hard or to provide only the effort to maintain a job, depending upon the individual's evaluation of the situation. Figure 3-3 gives an example of the process governing choices between two alternative courses of action.

Figure 3-3

The Choice between Two Courses of Action

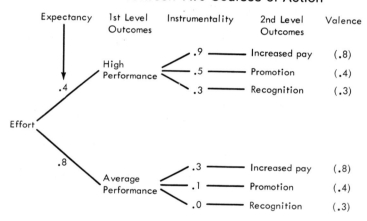

In Figure 3-3 the valence for each second-level outcome is multiplied by its instrumentality and then by the expectancy of obtaining that particular first-level outcome. The results are as follows:

$$
\begin{aligned}
V \times I \times E \\
.8 \times .9 \times .4 &= .29 \\
.4 \times .5 \times .4 &= .08 \\
.3 \times .3 \times .4 &= \underline{.04} \\
&= .51 \text{ for High Performance Alternative}
\end{aligned}
$$

$$
\begin{aligned}
V \times I \times E \\
.8 \times .3 \times .8 &= .19 \\
.4 \times .1 \times .8 &= .03 \\
.3 \times .0 \times .8 &= \underline{.00} \\
&= .22 \text{ for Average Performance Alternative}
\end{aligned}
$$

From the summary values obtained, one would predict that the individual would choose the high-performance alternative.

Influencing VIE

An individual's expectancy of achieving a first-level outcome is affected by the work situation itself, communication from others, past experiences in similar situations, and the individual's self-esteem or self-confidence.[20] However, organizations can influence the work situation and therefore motivation. For example, coaching, training, and job design will influence an employee's expectancy of attaining performance goals.

Instrumentality also can be influenced by a reward system that clearly states and links performance to second-level outcomes or rewards. This linkage is facilitated by leadership behavior and company policy relating to pay and promotion.

Although organizations can influence expectancies and instrumentalities, the value that employees place upon rewards (second-level outcomes) may vary greatly. Individual differences will influence preferences for pay, promotion, recognition, more job autonomy, and so on; consequently, organizations must place some emphasis on matching employee preferences with the rewards made available.

Expectancy theory provides a framework for understanding employees' motivation to perform and the organizational influences that may affect such behavior. The testing of expectancy theory, usually by survey questionnaire, has given excellent results in predicting employee behavior.[21]

Equity Theory

Equity theory, developed by Adams, is based upon the premise that motivation is affected by the degree of equity that an individual perceives in his or her work situation. If an employee thinks that he or she is being paid less than his or her associates for the same amount and quality of work, that employee will be dissatisfied and will seek to reduce the inequity. The degree of equity is defined in terms of the ratio of an individual's outcomes (pay) to inputs (effort) as compared with a similar ratio for a relevant comparison person.[22] The comparison process is as follows:[23]

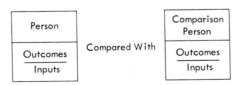

When person finds that his or her outcomes and inputs are not in balance with those of a comparison person, feelings of inequity result.

Input–Output Factors

Inputs include anything that the individual perceives as an investment in the job and is worthy of some return, that is, skill, seniority, education, age, effort, physical fitness, risk incurred, and the like. Outcomes are anything that is perceived as a return from the work situation. Positively valued outcomes include pay, rewards intrinsic to the job, satisfying supervision, seniority benefits, job status and status symbols, and various prerequisites. However, outcomes may have a negative value. Negatively valued outcomes include poor working conditions, monotony, job uncertainty, and the dissatisfiers or hygienic factors listed by Herzberg.

Inequity comparisons.

Although the comparison person is usually a different individual, it may be the individual himself or herself in a previous job. In this case, the individual is comparing his or her *present* and *past* outcomes and inputs to determine whether they are equitable. The terms person and comparison person also may refer to groups rather than to individuals.

Whenever a person compares the ratio of his or her outcomes to inputs with a comparison person, three things happen. If the ratios are equal, *equity* exists. However, if a person perceives his or her ratio of outcomes to inputs as being *less than* or *greater than* those of the comparison person, inequity exists.

Equity can be expressed as

$$\frac{O_p}{I_p} = \frac{O_{cp}}{I_{cp}}$$

The O and I refer to outputs and inputs, respectively. Subscript "p" refers to person, and comparison person is noted as "cp."

Inequity, as noted, is experienced in two ways, one of which is a "less than" condition.

$$\frac{O_p}{I_p} < \frac{O_{cp}}{I_{cp}}$$

When a person's output-input ratio is less than that of the comparison person, a general condition labeled "underpayment" exists. Conversely, a "greater than" situation is perceived to exist when there is "overpayment." This is expressed as

$$\frac{O_p}{I_p} > \frac{O_{cp}}{I_{cp}}$$

In this case, the person's output–input ratio is greater than that of the comparison person.

Motivation

Inequity results in dissatisfaction or an unpleasant emotional state within an individual. The consequences are twofold. First, the perception of inequity by the person creates internal tension. The tension is proportional to the amount of inequity present; the greater the inequity, the greater the tension. Second, the tension created in a person will motivate him or her to eliminate or reduce such tension. The strength of the motivation is proportional to the tension created; that is, the greater the tension experienced, the higher the motivation to reduce it. The person will seek to achieve equity or reduce inequity, the strength of his or her motivation to do so depending directly upon the amount of inequity experienced.

Reducing inequity

Evidence accumulated in laboratory and field studies indicates that inequity may be reduced in several ways.

1. *The person can alter his or her inputs:* The person can vary his or her inputs by increasing or decreasing them depending on whether the inequity is "overpayment" or "underpayment." Increasing inputs will reduce felt inequity if there is overpayment; for example, the person may increase his or her productivity or effort. If underpayment exists, the person may decrease his or her inputs by working less.
2. *The person can alter his or her outputs:* The person can increase his or her outcomes if the ratio of outputs to inputs is less than that of the comparison person. Conversely, decreasing outcomes will reduce inequity if the person's ratio is greater than that of the comparison person.
3. *The person can subjectively change his or her inputs and outputs:* The person may subjectively distort his or her inputs and outputs by reevaluating their utility, importance, and relevance. This is equivalent to changing the weights of inputs and outputs. For example, less significance might be attached to education in reducing inequity.
4. *The person may leave the field:* Quitting the job, obtaining a transfer, and absenteeism are common means that employees use in leaving the field.
5. *The person may act on the comparison person:* The person may subjectively distort the inputs or outputs of the comparison person. Additionally, the person may seek to get the comparison person to accept greater outputs, lower his or her inputs, or leave the field.
6. *The person may change the object of his or her comparison:* While difficult to accomplish, the person may change the individual with whom he or she has been comparing himself or herself.

If the person experiences inequity, any of these means can be used to redress the imbalance. However, an individual will tend to maximize favorable outcomes and minimize increasing inputs that require great effort and personal cost. Also one will resist changes that are central to one's self-concept and self-esteem. Leaving the field by quitting the job is not a likely choice unless the inequity is great and alternative means of reducing inequity are unavailable. Research has generally confirmed the various ways shown above that individuals may use to reduce inequities.[24]

Equity theory reinforces the observation that morale and performance problems arise when employees believe that they are not being rewarded equitably. Wage and salary programs are geared to provide individuals and occupational groups comparable pay for similar work. Furthermore, the absolute amount of pay may not be as important as relative pay, that is, what others are receiving under the same conditions. In equity terms, the employee is evaluating his or her ratio of outputs to inputs to relevant comparison persons.

MOTIVATION IN AN ORGANIZATIONAL CONTEXT

Motivation theories provide significant insights but are inadequate for explaining the entire process. Other factors must be examined if motivation and performance are to be more completely explained. The theories already discussed looked at the individual's needs, the job itself, or situational factors. These factors must be expanded for a more comprehensive understanding and utilization of the motivation process in an organization. Individual characteristics, job characteristics, and organizational climate characteristics will be examined further.[25]

Individual Characteristics

The content theories of motivation provide considerable insight into needs that stimulate goal-directed behavior. However, the individual must also have the capacities and skills required before motivation can occur. Many organizations screen and select applicants on the basis of capacities and skills. Subsequent training is designed to develop skills and capacities to an acceptable level. At this point motivation is a matter of developing a "will to do" what the individual "can do."

In addition to the "can do" factors, an employee's attitudes or beliefs play an important role in the motivation to perform. As noted in Chapter 2, employees have positive or negative feelings about all facets of their work life—job, supervisor, work groups, and so on. Dissatisfaction may reach a point where effort is affected, with the result reflected in performance quality and/or quantity.

Additionally, an individual's self-concept or self-perception may influence the motivation process. One's self-esteem, an accumulation of past experiences, affects the effort expended to attain a performance objective. Individuals with low self-esteem tend to underestimate the likelihood that they can perform well or be successful. As a result, performance is generally low, which confirms the low self-concept. Motivating persons with low self-esteem to perform well is difficult. The right kind of job, training, coaching, and leadership may help such an individual, but there is no guarantee of success.

Finally, one's interest affects the motivation process. Occupational guidance and counseling give careful attention to this factor. A person's work performance will tend to vary with the interest that he or she has in the task.

Characteristics of the Job

What an individual does at work also will influence the motivation process. Some jobs are routine, others are quite varied. Jobs also differ in the degree of autonomy and the amount of performance feedback provided the job incumbent. Also, jobs vary drastically in terms of the amount and kinds of intrinsic rewards available to employees. Jobs may be redesigned to build in motivators as a means for increasing performance and satisfaction.

Finally, role or job clarity is a factor affecting motivation. An employee must have a clear understanding of what the job requires if he or she is expected to perform adequately. Even if one is highly motivated and has the required abilities, not knowing exactly what should be done leads to wasted effort and poor performance.

Characteristics of the Work Environment

The work environment can be divided into two broad categories: (1) the immediate work environment, consisting of peers and supervisor, and (2) the organizational climate, including the reward system, conflict versus cooperation, flexibility and innovation, decision centralization, supportiveness, and so on. Although both categories are discussed in later chapters, a few comments will show their relevance to the motivation process.

The immediate work group can significantly affect an employee's effort. Output levels become norms of acceptable behavior, and group pressure is exercised to ensure compliance. The motivational influence of peers can outweigh that of managerial officials in some instances. However, supervisors can influence efforts and performance through their use of rewards to reinforce desired behavior.

Finally, the organizational climate has an influence upon motivation. Work groups and leadership are two determinants of climate. Technology, organizational structure, management philosophy and values, and even the external environment also are factors that contribute to an organization's climate. The climate is experienced by the organization's members and it influences their behavior.

Motivation theories by themselves do not explain the complete motivation process and the resulting job performance and effort. As we have seen, motivation may be influenced by many factors not incorporated in such theories. While a theory cannot include all factors that may be involved, systems thinking requires a more comprehensive viewpoint. An indication of some of the more relevant factors involved and their interaction is given in Table 3-2.

Table 3-2

Variables Affecting the Motivation Process

Environmental Stimuli	Individual	Behavior
Work environment characteristics	Interest	Job performance
Immediate work environment	Attitudes toward	Effort
Peers	Self	
Supervisor	Job	
Organization climate	Work situation	
Reward system	"Can do" factors	
Supportiveness, etc.	Capacities	
Job Characteristics	Abilities	
Task variety	Skills	
Performance feedback	Needs	
Autonomy	Security	
Intrinsic rewards	Social	
Role clarity	Achievement	

Source: Adapted from Richard M. Steers and Lyman W. Porter, *Motivation and Work Behavior* 2nd ed., (New York: McGraw-Hill, 1978), p. 21.

From the table one can surmise that many factors may be involved if an employee's behavior reflects poor job performance or low effort. Effective remedial measures for such behavior will require a thorough problem-solving approach. It is doubtful if a single theory of motivation will provide the complete answer. Rather, the theory must be used with the realization that other potential causal factors may be present. Many of the variables shown will be treated in later chapters.

ASSUMPTIONS ABOUT MOTIVATION

There is a crisis in motivation that is to some extent due to unconscious assumptions about motivation.[26] Executives were asked, "What is the dominant philosophy of motivation in American management?" Almost invariably they agreed that it was the carrot-and-stick philosophy, that is, reward and punishment. Additionally, when asked to form a mental picture of a carrot at one end and a stick at the other end and then describe the central image between these two items, the executives most frequently saw a jackass.

From this association, it was concluded that many organizational officials unconsciously assume that they are dealing with "jackasses" who must be manipulated and controlled. The characteristics of a "jackass" are stubbornness, stupidity, willfulness, and unwillingness to go where someone is driving him or her. Such an underlying assumption leads to self-fulfilling prophecy; if managers assume that employees are unmotivated, they will become unmotivated. Levinson labeled this motivation assumption "the jackass fallacy."

Douglas McGregor popularized two divergent sets of assumptions about people: Theory X and Theory Y.[27] These beliefs about the nature of man are as follows:

> Theory X: Without active intervention by management, people would be passive—even resistant—to organizational needs. They must therefore be persuaded, rewarded, punished, controlled—their activities must be directed. Additional beliefs include the following:
>
> 1. People generally are by nature indolent; they work as little as possible.
> 2. They lack ambition, dislike responsibility, prefer to be led.
> 3. They are inherently self-centered and indifferent to organizational needs.
> 4. They are by nature resistant to change.
> 5. They are gullible, not very bright, the ready dupe of the charlatan and the demagogue.
>
> Theory Y: People are not by nature passive or resistant to organizational needs. They have become so as a result of experience in organizations. Beliefs stemming from this premise include the following.
>
> 1. The motivation, the potential for development, the capacity for assuming responsibility, and the readiness to direct behavior toward organizational goals are all present in people. Management does not put them there.
> 2. People are capable of self-direction and self-control.

While it is possible to have other sets of assumptions about human behavior, McGregor maintained that Theory Y assumptions were most consistent with what is known about adult human behavior.

The significance of these assumptions is that the behavior exhibited toward others tends to reflect such assumptions. Theory X assumptions influence one to motivate others by fear and/or economic incentives. Manipulation and control play a large part in the motivation process. In contrast, Theory Y assumptions predispose one to make use of Herzberg's motivators and involve others by participative methods.

However, Y assumptions do not make participative methods or the creation of opportunities for self-actualization mandatory. As one investigator has noted, if one holds to Theory Y assumptions, he or she is more likely to examine all available alternatives and choose wisely from among them.[28] Such an analysis would take into account the technological, economic, work group, and organizational climate factors. This is contingency thinking that may or may not suggest the possibility of significant linking of personal and organizaional goals. For example, a manager directing a routine, stable, highly repetitive operation is faced with definite constraints in motivating his or her group even though that manager holds Theory Y assumptions about people. Opportunities for self-direction and self-control may be extremely limited.

GUIDELINES FOR MOTIVATING

Unlike the physicist or chemist, the student of organizational behavior has no uniform formula(s) to apply for achieving desired results.[29] This is especially true of motivation. Motives cannot be seen; they must be inferred from what the individual does or says. Such inferences are complicated because the employee may not be conscious of his or her needs or may not express them adequately. Also, a single act may be an expression of several needs. An employee, for example, may improve his or her performance to satisfy the needs for more pay, a promotion, or recognition. Likewise, a single motive may be satisfied by a variety of incentives or activities. One's needs for socialization may be met by seeking acceptance of the work group, joining a bowling team, or becoming involved in community projects.

Although there is no formula for motivating others, several guidelines may be profitably considered and followed:

1. *Know the basic human needs and motivation processes:* Human needs are the energizers of behavior. Insight into general and work-related needs and the interrelationship of variables is the first step toward understanding motivation.

2. *Examine your basic beliefs or assumptions about others:* One's basic beliefs provide a framework within which a motivation effort takes place. Whether these assumptions are of the Theory X or Theory Y variety, or some-

where in between, they will influence how others are induced to perform. One's personal view of others may limit or expand the motivating options perceived to be available.

3. *Put the motivation process into the "total" organizational context:* Motivation is more than human needs and personal attributes. It is affected by the job characteristics and the entire organizational situation or climate. Motivation is a result of many direct and indirect factors.

4. *Remember that individuals differ:* No two people are exactly alike; the principle of individual differences prevails. Consequently, what motivates one person may not do so for another because their need structures differ. Equally important, do not assume that others have the same needs as you do or will be motivated by the same incentives.

5. *Know your people as individuals:* Anyone in a supervisory capacity usually spends some time with those being directed. Such contact provides opportunities to learn their needs, aspirations, and frustrations. Openness, trust, and two-way communication will facilitate determining what makes others tick. Such insight, supplemented by observing to what and how they respond, gives cues for the motivating process.

6. *Watch for threats to present need satisfaction:* Most organizations change work flows, jobs, policies, procedures, and so on that may reduce needs being satisfied. Sensitivity to the potential impact of such changes can lead to the development of other alternatives that can minimize the negative impact on the motivating process.

7. *Promote changes conducive to satisfying human needs:* One may promote or initiate changes that have promise of satisfying individual and group needs. Such changes are contingent on those involved, as some may feel threatened rather than having been given an opportunity to improve the quality of their work life.

SUMMARY

Motivation has been examined as a process that involves energizing by motives, behavior or goal-directed activity, and an incentive or goal that reduces the energizing need. Six theories of motivation were presented. Each theory has its own view of motivation. Collectively, however, the theories provide considerable insight into the motivating process. The diversity of the theories is reflected in Table 3-3.

The motivation process is imbedded in a broad organizational setting. Problems of motivation, as reflected in performance, can only be understood by considering characteristics of the individual, the job, and the organizational climate. No one theory of motivation includes all the factors that influence the motivation process. Understanding, predicting, and influencing motivation, however, requires an examination and evaluation of all relevant variables.

Table 3-3

Summary of Motivational Theories

	Theory	Behavior Is due to
Content	Maslow: Need Hierarchy	Personal needs
	Alderfer: E.R.G.	Personal needs
	Herzberg: Motivation–Hygiene	Job content
	McClelland: Achievement	Personal motives and situation
Process	Vroom: Expectancy	Valence instrumentality, and expectancy
	Adams: Equity–Inequity	Perceived equity of situation

Equally significant for the motivation process are the assumptions made about other people. If others are seen as passive, lazy, resistant to change, and so on, then motivation methods are likely to take some form of manipulation and control. On the other hand, if people are seen as capable of self-direction and self-control, then a broad range of motivating methods becomes feasible. Theory X and Theory Y provide two divergent sets of beliefs about the nature of man.

Finally, one should understand not only the general motivation process but also his or her assumptions about others, the total organization context, the principle of individual differences, and the factors that motivate each person supervised. Such insights increase the possibility of successfully motivating others.

QUESTIONS FOR STUDY AND DISCUSSION

1. How does one's level of aspiration affect each phase of the motivation process? Give an example of this.

2. How do content theories and process theories of motivation differ?

3. Compare Maslow's need hierarchy and Herzberg's two-factor theory. Are there any similarities? What are the similarities in the theories of Maslow and Alderfer?

4. Think of the satisfying and dissatisfying experiences you have had in work. Make a list of the causes of your satisfaction and another for the causes of your dissatisfactions. Relate your list to Herzberg's motivators and hygienic factors, respectively. Does your experience support Herzberg's work? Where are they similar? Different? Why?

5. How can a manager apply the expectancy theory of motivation to obtain effort from his employees?

6. How does experiencing inequity affect motivation? Give an example of this.

7. What insight does an appraisal of the organization context add to the motivation process? See Table 3-2.

8. How do the assumptions one makes about people influence efforts to motivate them? What are some limiting factors one must deal with regardless of personal assumptions?

NOTES

[1]Steers, Richard M. and Lyman W. Porter, eds., *Motivation and Work Behavior* (New York: McGraw-Hill, 1973), pp. 6–9.

[2]Campbell, J. P., M. D. Dunnette, E. E. Lawler, III, and K. E. Weick, *Managerial Behavior, Performance, and Effectiveness* (New York: McGraw-Hill, 1970), p. 341.

[3]Maslow, A. H., "A Theory of Human Motivation," *Psychological Review* 50 (1943): 370–396.

[4]Lawler, Edward E., III, and J. Lloyd Suttle, "A Casual Correlation Test of Need Hierarchy Concept," *Organizational Behavior and Human Performance* (1972): 265–287.

[5]Mitchell, Vance F. and Pravin Moudgill, "Management of Maslow's Need Hierarchy," *Organizational Behavior and Human Performance* 16 (1976): 334–349.

[6]Alderfer, Clayton P., "An Empirical Test of a New Theory of Human Needs," *Organizational Behavior and Human Performance* 4 (1969): 142–175.

[7]Alderfer, Clayton P., *Existence, Relatedness, and Growth* (New York: Free Press, 1972), p. 124.

[8]Herzberg, F., G. Mausner, and B. Snyderman, *The Motivation to Work* (New York: Wiley, 1959).

[9]Herzberg, F., "One More Time: How Do You Motivate Employees?" *Harvard Business Review* (January–February 1968): 53–63.

[10]Herzberg, F., B. Mausner, R. Peterson, and D. F. Capwell, *Job Attitudes: Review of Research and Opinion* (Pittsburgh: Psychological Services of Pittsburg, 1957).

[11]Vroom, V. H., *Work and Motivation* (New York: John Wiley, 1964).

[12]House, Robert J. and Lawrence A. Wigdor, "Herzberg's Dual-Factor Theory of Job Satisfaction and Motivation: A Review of the Evidence and a Criticism," *Personnel Psychology* 20 (1967): 369–389; King, Nathan, "Clarification and Evaluation of the Two-Factor Theory of Job Satisfaction," *Psychological Bulletin* 74 (1970), 18–31; Backman V. M., "The Herzberg Controversy," *Personnel Psychology* (1971), 155–189.

[13]McClelland, David C., *The Achieving Society* (Princeton, N.J.: Van Nostrand, 1961).

[14]Litwin, G. H. and R. A. Stringer, Jr., *Motivation and Organizational Climate* (Boston: Division of Research, Graduate School of Business Administration, Harvard University, 1968), p. 12.

[15]McClelland, David D., "Business Drive and National Achievement," *Harvard Business Review* 40 (July–August 1962): 99–112.

[16]Wainer, H. A. and I. M. Rubin, "Motivation of Research and Development Entrepreneurs: Determinants of Company Success," Part I, *Journal of Applied Psychology* (June 1969): 178–184.

[17]McClelland, David C., "Toward a Theory of Motive Acquisition," *American Psychologist* 20 (1965): 321–333.

[18]Hampton, David R., "Selection and Motivation," *Human Resource Management,* Vol. 14 (Summer 1976): 23–29.

[19]Vroom, *op. cit.*

[20]Lawler, Edward E., III, "Expectancy Theory," in *Motivation and Work Behavior,* Richard M. Steers and Lyman W. Porter, eds. (New York: McGraw-Hill, 1975), pp. 190–200.

[21]Mitchell, Terance R., "Expectancy Models of Job Satisfaction, Occupational Preference and Effort: A Theoretical, Methodological, and Empirical Appraisal," *Psychological Bulletin* (1974): 1053–1075.

[22]Adams, Stacy J., "Inequity in Social Exchange" in L. Berkowitz, ed., *Advances in Experimental Social Psychology* (New York: Academic Press, 1975): 276–299.

[23]Campbell et al., *op. cit.,* p. 349.

[24]Goodman, Paul S. and Abraham Friedman, "An Examination of Adams' Theory of Inequity," *Administrative Science Quarterly* 16 (December 1971): 271–288. See also Starke, Frederick A. and Orlando Behling "A Test of Two Postulates Underlying Expectancy Theory" *Academy of Management Journal* 18 (December 1975): 703–714.

[25]Steers, Richard M. and Lyman W. Porter, *op. cit.,* pp. 21–24.

[26]Levinson, Harry, "Assinine Attitudes toward Motivation," *Harvard Business Review* (January–February 1973): 70–76.

[27]McGregor, Douglas, *The Human Side of Enterprise* (New York: McGraw-Hill, 1960).

[28]Schein, Edgar H., "In Defense of Theory Y," *Organizational Dynamics* 4 (Summer 1975): 17–30.

[29]Pinder, Craig C., "Concerning the Application of Human Motivation Theories in Organizational Settings," *Academy of Management Review* 2 (July 1977): 384–397.

cases cases cases

Case Study: The Drafting Room

PART I: BEFORE CHANGE

During the early 1970s, the drafting room was experiencing a severe increase in demand for distribution drawings. The drafting room prepared drawings for the company's Construction, Maintenance, and Engineering departments. These drawings involved ten different fields, such as mapping, electrical wiring, relay and distribution, and the like. When a drawing was requested by an outside department, the chief draftsman assigned the drawing to any one of the ten draftsmen, depending on who was free at the time. Each draftsman was therefore required to have a ready knowledge in all ten drafting fields. He was not a specialist, but a general draftsman who prepared one one type of drawing today and another type tomorrow.

All ten draftsmen worked in one large group under the chief draftsman. The chief draftsman, involved as he was in everyday operating problems, was unable to keep the drafting room "organized." He had no system of review and evaluation of worker performance. When a draftsman asked about his performance or future with the company, the chief draftsman could give no answer.

CASE QUESTIONS

1. Evaluate this situation. What needs of the draftsmen are being met? Frustrated?

2. How would you change this work situation? What are the reasons for your change?

PART II: AFTER CHANGE

Management decided to divide the drafting room into three groups, each headed by a group leader. The chief draftsman retired and was replaced by a promoted draftsman. The three group leader positions were also filled by promoted draftsmen. The drafting operation was reorganized as follows:

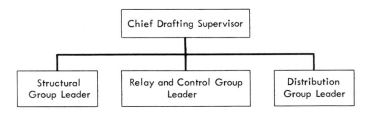

The group breakdown was welcomed by the draftsmen, although they were not consulted in advance about the change. Management made the change very gradually, in fact, it required almost one year. A few draftsmen retired, a few were promoted, a few were transferred, but many more were hired. Draftsmen were assigned to one of the three groups based on their suitability and interest. Now they worked on only a limited number of drawing types in a smaller group. A draftsmen's club was established and avidly supported by the draftsmen.

The chief draftsman let the group leaders run the groups as they saw fit, but encouraged them to come to him when they had problems. He never directly supervised the draftsmen, but always worked through their group leader. The group leaders were able to give more attention and recognition to the draftsmen than the chief draftsman had under the old arrangement. A Review and Evaluation Program was established. Each worker was evaluated and interviewed every six months by the chief draftsman, who was furnished performance reports by the group leader and the draftsman involved.

The chief draftsman's immediate superior reported that the draftsmen derived greater satisfaction from specific job assignments and responsibilities and that he was entirely pleased with their output. Although their job was narrowed, they performed the drawing from the beginning to completion. Consequently, their contribution opportunity was not lessened by specialization.

Several additional changes also were made that affected the draftsmen. First, the company reimbursed draftsmen for after-work education courses. Second, the company adopted the procedure of rotating jobs within groups to give each draftsman a broader background. Third, in each of the three groups, the draftsmen worked in groups of two. The group leader assigned the drawing to an older, experienced draftsman who worked with a younger, less experienced one. Fourth, the company initiated a policy of promotion from within.

CASE QUESTIONS

1. Use the Maslow and Herzberg theories of motivation to analyze what happened in the drafting room.

2. Relate the changes to the organizational context (Table 3-2). What factors were altered? What was the impact or result?

cases cases cases

Case Study: A Theory Y Manager?

Mr. Grey is a certified public accountant and the owner of a small firm called Accounting and Bookkeeping Services. He is an easygoing person and gets along very well with his employees. Two senior accountants play a major role in the firm. Mrs. Duston has been with the firm for eight years. Although she has no formal accounting training, Mrs. Duston does much of the bookkeeping and is in charge of most of the work done in the office but does not have the knowledge to cope with many of the problems encountered. Consequently, work is often held up until Mr. Grey is present, resulting in a serious waste of time. Two other major problems stem from Mrs. Duston's limitations. First, she assigns each person something to do according to what is most pressing. Because of this, different people work on the same set of books, causing a lack of consistency since employees do the same thing in different ways. Secondly, because Mrs. Duston alone assigns work, each time someone needs something to do, she has to stop what she is doing and get the employee started on a new assignment. Many hours are wasted because she frequently cannot terminate her work to find the part-time help something to do. On one occasion Mrs. Duston had a day off while Mr. Grey was also out of the office. Nearly the entire day was wasted by everyone because there were no work instructions.

New employees encounter a similar problem. They are given work without an adequate explanation of how to proceed and often resort to the trial-and-error methods until someone can explain the proper procedures.

Mrs. Duston works only because she wants to and not of necessity. As a result, she feels free to work or take a break when she wants; this attitude spreads to other employees. Frequently when Mr. Grey is out of the office, discussions on religion or politics take place. There seems to be an attitude of "I can work when I want and stop when I want."

Mr. Levitt, the other senior accountant, has worked off and on for several years with the company. He has no accounting degree and his accounting knowledge has been acquired from experience. Much of Mr. Levitt's work is done outside the office on audits with Mr. Grey although he does do some work in the office.

Mr. Eason is an elderly man, past retirement age, who does book-work in the office. He is a little slow, has difficulty understanding instructions, and makes numerous mistakes. He only works in the morning, about twenty hours a week. Mrs. Towns is Mr. Grey's secretary and receptionist. She does some bookkeeping, payroll taxes, and all of the typing. Mr. Ritter, a part-time employee and college student, works on books, financial statements, and payroll taxes.

The present organization evolved as a matter of necessity and was never planned or formalized. The following organization chart shows how the firm appears to be structured.

Accounting & Bookkeeping Services

Although Mr. Grey is out of the office much of the time, he feels the human relations of his small firm are very good; everyone fits into the group and seems happy. Furthermore, Mr. Grey considers himself to be a

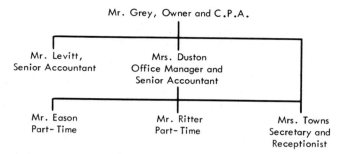

Mr. Grey, Owner and C.P.A.

Mr. Levitt,
Senior Accountant

Mrs. Duston
Office Manager and
Senior Accountant

Mr. Eason
Part-Time

Mr. Ritter
Part-Time

Mrs. Towns
Secretary and
Receptionist

"Theory Y" type manager he has read about; he is easygoing and doesn't push his employees. Mr. Grey is perturbed, however, because productivity and efficiency are lower than they should be.

QUESTIONS

1. Is Mr. Grey a "Theory Y" manager?
2. How does a "Theory Y" manager manage?

CHAPTER 4

Individual Effectiveness

LEARNING OBJECTIVES

When you have finished this chapter you should be able to:

- *Explain how an organization's personnel philosophy influences the way people are utilized.*
- *Understand how essential manpower activities affect individual effectiveness.*
- *Describe how job conflict and job ambiguity impact on individual performance.*
- *Outline and describe Herzberg's approach to job redesign.*

In this chapter we will be exploring the topic of individual effectiveness, that is, ways in which an employee may become more productive. Chapter 3 dealt with motivation, which is obviously concerned with increasing effectiveness and, viewed more broadly, integrating the needs and aspirations of individuals with the goals of the organization; now we turn to some techniques that have been employed to implement the blending of individual and organizational goals. First, however, we will briefly examine the organizational setting in which such effectiveness efforts are undertaken. That is, we will be looking at personnel philosophy, the manpower function, and job conflict and ambiguity.

PERSONNEL PHILOSOPHY

One of the most intangible but significant determinants of how individuals are utilized in an organization is the organization's personnel philosophy. Specifically, a personnel philosophy "represents the fundamental beliefs, ideals, principles and views held by management with respect to organizing and treating individuals at work...".[1] Whether explicit or implicit, such a philosophy will be found in every organization and will influence organizational behavior at all levels. For example, managements that make the assumption that their employees are responsible and capable of self-control will create different work environments than will those organizations emphasizing close supervision and control. The factors influencing the development of personnel philosophy are shown in Figure 4-1.[2]

The variables contributing to personnel philosophy have changed over time and differ to some extent for each organization. One potential determinant of personnel philosophy is of particular interest to us as we study organizational behavior—behavioral scientific disciplines. The philosophy of organizations varies widely to the extent that scientific findings influence or shape the management of human resources.

In the course of examining the emergence and development of personnel philosophies, six rationales are discernible. Two of these—*laissez-faire* and paternalism—are primarily of historical interest. The do-nothing, technique, humanistic, and idealized "total personality" philosophies are currently in use in business and industry today.

Attitudes toward Employees

The prevailing philosophy of an employer or chief executive will be largely determined by his or her concept of labor, and in turn his or her basic attitude will affect the consideration and treatment accorded employees. A number of distinct employer attitudes can be identified.[3] For example, a manager who accepts the "commodity concept of labor" considers the employees to be like any other physical resource necessary to produce a product. When the supply of labor is scarce, the price becomes high; when plentiful, the price is low. As an impersonal commodity, no consideration is given employees as individuals with psychological needs that may be gratified within the industrial structure. No responsibility is acknowledged for the psychological or economic welfare of workers.

Some managers have regarded employees as machines or mere appendages of machines, capable of a specific output. The employment

Figure 4-1
Factors Influencing the Development
of Personnel Philosophy

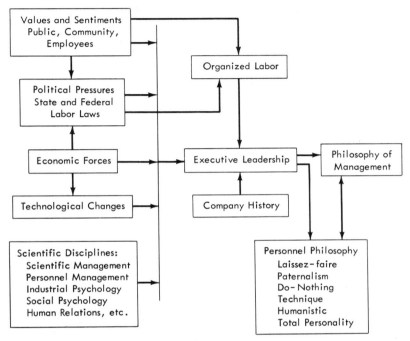

Source: Charles R. Milton, *Ethics and Expediency in Personnel Management* (Columbia: University of South Carolina Press, 1970), p. 15.

relationship is maintained only if the worker attains his or her assigned production quota. Assuming that employees are primarily economically motivated, wage incentive plans are utilized to ensure that full productive potentials are realized. Like the commodity viewpoint, the "machine concept" does not view the employees as endowed with human attributes or a multiplicity of human needs.

Conversely, the manager who adopts a paternalistic attitude toward employees recognizes that their welfare has a direct effect on their satisfaction on the job and on productivity. Accordingly, many employers decide to "do good" and provide adequate work conditions, rest rooms, cafeterias, and fringe benefits for their employees. In turn, they expect workers to be grateful, loyal, and productive. This approach, however, fails to recognize the need of employees for independence and self-respect.

An "individual differences" view of labor evolved from the applications of psychology. People are characterized by differences in their basic capacities, abilities, and personalities. Some employees perform certain tasks better than others and therefore cannot be indiscriminately placed on the job, transferred, or promoted. Employee satisfaction on the job and productivity are promoted if such differences are utilized wisely, that is, if the person is matched with a job requiring the abilities and attitudes that he or she possesses.

The manager with a "humanistic concept of labor" approaches the problem of work from the human as well as the productive point of view. Such a manager's approach is founded upon a concern for both the economic and psychological aspects of work. Management endeavors to enlist the worker's interest, goodwill, and cooperation by treating him or her as a human being with definite needs, desires, and aspirations that are attainable within the industrial organization.

A broader view is conveyed by the "citizenship concept" under which managers hold that employees are entitled to have a voice in determining some of the conditions affecting their welfare in the work environment. An employee's investment of his or her labor in industry is thought to convey rights similar to those of community citizenship, wherein each individual has inherent rights and is entitled to a voice and a vote in determining civil matters. The citizenship concept of labor has been reflected in personnel practices that provide for such things as shop committees, employee representation, union–management representation, and participation of employees in the decision-making processes of management.

A "partnership concept" of labor is based upon a belief in the mutuality of interests between management and employees. Although their interests may be divergent in the short run on some issues, in the long run the needs of both employers and employees tend to coincide so that both can attain their respective objectives. Mutual confidence and respect are implied in this attitude and have been manifested in stock ownership and profit-sharing plans used to secure the cooperation, productivity, and identification of employees with company objectives.

Management with a "social attitude" toward labor recognizes that work has a social function, that the worker has social as well as egoistic needs. The work environment is viewed as consisting of informal work groups having definite values and attitudes; and the employee, while exerting an influence upon the group, is also thought to be regulated and controlled by group sentiments. Economic incentives may be ineffective if they are not consistent with group values and norms; however, changes in harmony with group values are less threatening and less likely to produce resistance to innovation and production. It follows, therefore, that management or supervision is in part a social skill and that socially sound leadership requires the use of two-way communication, consultation, and participation at the work group level. The employment relationship is influenced by the different attitudes of management toward labor. Whether work is a productive and satisfying experience depends on the value placed upon the human factor.

MANPOWER FUNCTION

Whatever the personnel philosophy of an organization, certain manpower functions must be established and maintained if the organization is to remain viable. These functions are shown in Figure 4-2.[4] While the essential manpower activities are typically associated with staff personnel in the personnel department, it is well to note that operating or "line" personnel are deeply involved in the manpower function. As the figure shows, the amount of involvement of these two groups depends on the kind of manpower activity involved, but both are concerned with the maximum utilization of human resources. Concern with individual effectiveness begins with recruitment and selection—the employment function—and is designed to find the right person for the right job. Obviously, this is the first step in increasing individual effectiveness, which is a relevant objective for each manpower activity. The development activity is concerned with training, coaching, and performance appraisal. Maintenance activities are implemented through safety plans, medical plans, and employee relations in general.

The utilization of manpower is the function that concerns us in this chapter. Utilization is probably the most vital of the manpower subsystems because effective use of manpower as a resource takes place here. The right person may be selected, trained, compensated, and protected by various maintenance programs but can still be underutilized. Utilization is achieved by means of participation, delegation of authority, special assignment, job enrichment, and so on. The use of such techniques, however, is contingent upon the kind of leadership provided by the organization and its managers.

Although the manpower function provides the basic activities necessary to obtain and retain competent personnel, its impact on the individual must be examined in more detail. Figure 4-3 is a model of individual effectiveness, which is a primary concern of the manpower function.[5]

In the model of individual effectiveness, we see that an employee's characteristics interact with the demands of the job. Even though the employment process, via recruitment and selection, attempts to match the person with the job, the process may be incomplete. The individual may still have much more to contribute or give than the job demands. Job performance is also influenced by training and development activities. Additionally, performance may be influenced by the reward structure, that is, whether or not it is perceived as fair and equitable as compared with other employees' situations and whether or not good performance is appropri-

Figure 4-2
Essential Manpower Activities

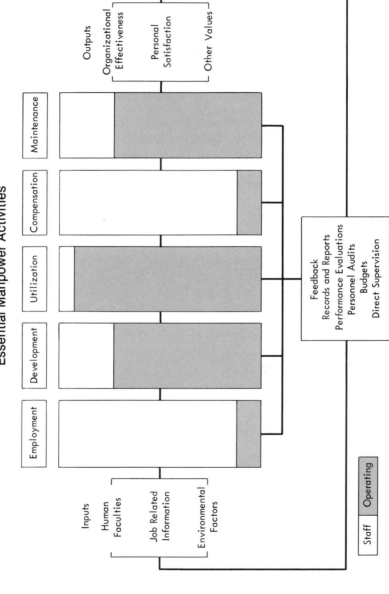

Source: Edgar G. Williams, "A Systems Approach to Manpower Management," *Business Horizons*, Winter 1964, p. 60. Copyright, 1964, by the Foundation for the School of Business at Indiana University. Reprinted by permission.

Figure 4-3

Model of Individual Effectiveness

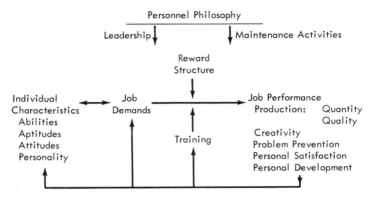

Source: Adapted from J. P. Campbell et al., *Managerial Behavior, Performance and Effectiveness* (New York: McGraw-Hill, 1970), p. 475.

ately rewarded. This, of course, is part of the manpower activity generally referred to as the compensation system. However, these determinants of performance are imbedded in a context known as the organizational climate. While the topic of climate will be treated in Chapter 15, the figure does indicate the leadership and maintenance activities (medical and safety programs) influencing to some extent the employee's performance or effectiveness. Frequently, the impact is quite direct and tangible; at other times the influence is intangible. Finally, the model depicts several possible measures of individual effectiveness; these, of course, depend on the job being considered. Performance effectiveness measures reflect the adequacy of the organization's reward structures and its training programs. Also the performance measures may indicate a need to increase or decrease job demands upon the employee to achieve a more desirable set of performance outputs. Also, the same performance measures may reflect a need for different abilities and aptitudes for individuals performing on the job and result in modified selection criteria.

One of the more crucial elements in the individual effectiveness model is the task demands placed upon the employee. Such demands may result in underutilization for some and contribute to or cause low efficiency. On the other hand, the demands or requirements of the job itself may not be clear to the employee. Consequently, we will turn to an examination of the job itself, the clarity of its demands, and the potential consequences if job requirements are not explicit.

When considering individual effectiveness, we must examine the job that an individual holds. We may assume that management designs the job and that the employee simply performs the function of that job. This is an over-simplification! Role theory gives us some significant insight into this complicated process. Ideally, a role is a standardized pattern of behavior that is expected of everyone in a particular position, regardless of personal wishes, and sanctions are employed to compel compliance with the role. However, the job is not usually that simple. There are several "significant others" that exercise some influence on the job or role that an individual fills. The formal organization or management through job design, subsequent job description, and sanctions provides significant inputs for role or job behavior. One's supervisor may hold expectations of the job incumbent and the role played that differ from expectations elsewhere in the management system. Also an employee's peers or work group may have their own expectations that can vary quite significantly from the expectations of the formal system or the immediate supervisor. Finally, the job incumbent's own expectations and self-concept influence how the job is perceived, how it should be done, and how the expectations of other role senders are interpreted. Figure 4-4 depicts the impact of various role senders on the job incumbent.

Figure 4-4

Impact of Role Senders on Job Incumbent

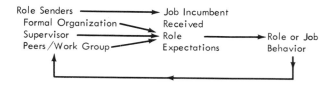

Role behavior is the job incumbent's response to the role or job situation and influences the attempts of role senders. The actual role behaviors may not fit the expectations of one or more role senders, and an effort will be made to influence the job behavior of the job incumbent. This type of feedback is noted by the line from job behavior to the role senders. Such feedback may result in additional attempts to communicate or influence the job incumbent. The role senders, as part of an existing social system, may give positive sanctions when the job incumbent properly enacts the role as prescribed or, conversely, they may provide negative sanctions to those failing to meet expectations.

Role Conflict

The fact that the expectations of role senders may vary or differ from one another sets the stage for role conflict. Incompatible expectations and/or conflicting roles are the general sources of such conflict, but these may appear in several forms.

Intrasender conflict

In this source of conflict, there is *one* role sender who presents separate required job behaviors to the jobholder that are incompatible with one another. For example, the supervisor may push for quantity and quality when the two are inconsistent with each other.

Intersender conflict

This source of conflict is initiated when the job behavior expected by one role sender is inconsistent with that of another sender. One example is the foreman who is caught between the conflicting expectations of his or her subordinates and higher management. Equally important is the employee caught between the expectations of his or her peers and work group and the requirements of the formal management system. Newly developed jobs often lack clarity as do jobs that have been altered significantly.

A job incumbent and his or her role partners or senders may disagree in the following ways:[6]

1. As to what expectations are included in a given job or role.
2. As to the range of permitted or prohibited behavior.
3. As to the situations in which the role applies.
4. As to whether the expected behavior is mandatory or simply preferred.
5. As to which should be honored first when one expectation conflicts with another.

Some organizations attempt to cope with the first four potential sources of conflict by training their employees or developing manuals of operation that attempt to make explicit what is expected of each position. The fifth potential source—not knowing which expectation to honor first—arises, for example, when one secretary is assigned to a number of persons. Should one person's work have a higher priority than another's? Each feels that his or her work is of utmost importance and should be finished as soon as possible. The secretary feels harassed, frustrated, and embarrased. A frequent solution is to assign priorities to the various kinds of projects. Further protection is offered to the secretary by requiring a differing number of days' lead time for each priority classification or by recognizing the working rule of "first in has working priority."

Interrole conflict

This kind of conflict arises when separate roles held by the same individual make conflicting demands. Such a possibility may happen to anyone as we all have multiple roles to fulfill. An individual may be an employee in an organization, a husband, a father, a church member, a lodge member, and so on. Each role is associated with different expectations from each set of role partners. Frequently, these differing roles may make conflicting demands on the individual. The organization expects the employee to work overtime on Saturday when necessary. However, the employee's role as a father dictates that he spend time at home with the children. Interrole conflict!

A similar situation exists when there are different facets to one's role. The foreman is expected to be helpful and supportive but also a disciplinarian; he or she is expected to train and coach but also to periodically evaluate performance. The military chaplin is expected to be a religious leader to enlisted personnel but also to be a military officer. There is conflict inherent in playing such divergent roles.

Job incumbent role conflict

Although job incumbents receive expectation messages from other role senders, the role-sending process is not completely one way. Job incumbents strive to get others to behave toward them in ways that are consistent with the picture that they have of themselves—their self-concepts. Expected behaviors that are inconsistent with employees' self-concepts will be resisted and perhaps induce role conflict in others or in the position itself. For example, the job incumbents' internal standards or values may conflict with defined role behavior.

An empirical study

Role theory indicates that, when the behaviors expected of individuals are inconsistent, they will experience stress, become dissatisfied, and perform less effectively. These associations can be conceptualized as follows:

$$\text{Inconsistent Expectations} \longrightarrow \text{Stress} \longrightarrow \text{Dissatisfaction} \longrightarrow \text{Impaired Performance}$$

Rizzo and his associates surveyed numerous studies of the relationship of conflict to member satisfaction and performance and concluded that role conflict was associated with decreased satisfaction, behavior detrimental to the organization, stress and anxiety.[7] The researchers also found that positive answers to the following test items were effective measures of role conflict.

> *I have to do things that should be done differently.*
> *I lack policies and guidelines to help me.*
> *I work under incompatible policies and guidelines.*
> *I receive an assignment without the manpower to complete it.*
> *I have to buck a rule or policy to carry out an assignment.*
> *I have to "feel my way" in performing my duties.*
> *I work with two or more groups who operate quite differently.*
> *I receive incompatible requests from two or more people.*
> *I do things that are apt to be accepted by one person and not accepted by others.*
> *I receive an assignment without adequate resources and materials to execute it.*
> *I work on unnecessary things.*
> *I have to work under vague directions or orders.*
> *I do not know if my work will be acceptable to my boss.*

Classical Organization Theory and Role Conflict

In classical organization theory, the principles of chain of command and unity of command were formulated to prevent conflict and ambiguity. The chain of command stipulates that there should be a clear and single flow of authority from the top to the bottom of the organization. Such a line of authority would result in more effective economic performance, goal achievement, and systematic controls.

Research evidence indicates that multiple lines of authority, such as those frequently found in professional organizations, are accompanied by role conflict and dissatisfaction among the members and the loss of organizational efficiency and effectiveness. However, these undesirable results appear to be necessary costs of providing professional control over the technical aspects of the organization's activities.

Closely associated with the chain of command is the unity-of-command principle, which states that, since responsibility is a personal matter and that the superior–subordinate relationship a very personal one, each subordinate should have only one superior. An organization structured on this basis should prevent incompatible orders and expectations from more than one boss and ensure consistent reporting, evaluation, and control. Job or role conflict would result from violating the unity-of-command principle. Several studies support the position that violating the principle of unity of command or single accountability frequently results in increased role conflict, dissatisfaction, lower performance, and poor use of time.[8]

Role Ambiguity

Classical organization theory states that every position in a formal organization should have a set of specified tasks and responsibilities. The principle of delegation requires the assignment of duties, the delegation of sufficient authority to accomplish such duties, and the holding of the subordinate responsible for accomplishing duties and utilizing authority appropriately. Unless employees know what they must accomplish, what authority they can exercise, and how they will be evaluated, performance will suffer. Such a condition is known as role ambiguity, namely the lack of necessary information available to adequately perform a given organizational position. Role ambiguity will increase the probability of an employee's being dissatisfied with his or her job, experiencing anxiety, and consequently performing less effectively.

Research supports the proposition that role ambiguity is associated with diminished individual and organizational efficiency. According to another study, role ambiguity is produced when[9]

1. organization size and complexity exceed the employee's comprehension
2. rapid organization growth is accompanied by frequent reorganizations
3. frequent technological change requires changes in the social structure
4. frequent personnel changes disturb interdependencies
5. environmental changes impose new demands on employees
6. management practices restrict the flow of information throughout the organization

The study indicated that 35 percent of a national sample of employees were disturbed by the lack of a clear idea of the scope and responsibilities of their job. Interviews with these employees indicated that high role ambiguity was associated with increased tension, anxiety, fear and hostility, decreased job satisfaction, loss of self-confidence, and often lower productivity. Field and laboratory studies by other researchers have demonstrated similar results.

In the study by Rizzo referred to previously, test items also were developed to measure role ambiguity.[10] These items, outlined as follows, provide some insight into the various facets of role ambiguity, but they are stated in terms of role clarity.

I feel certain about how much authority I have.
I have clear, planned goals and objectives for my job.
I am able to act the same regardless of the group I am with.
I know that I have divided my time properly.
I know what my responsibilities are.
I do not have to "feel my way" in performing my duties.

I feel certain how I will be evaluated for a raise or promotion.
I have just the right amount of work to do.
I know exactly what is expected of me.
I am clear on what has to be done.
I perform work that suits my values.

These items, as measures of role ambiguity, and the role conflict items noted previously were found to comprise two separate dimension using factor analysis. These two variables were then related to satisfaction, leadership, and organizational practices responses of managerial and technical personnel, first-level foremen, and clerical employees. Summarized very briefly, the investigation found the following:[11]

1. High role conflict and role ambiguity was associated with lowered degrees of need fulfillment derived from the work itself, the reward system, and the pleasantness of the social environment.
2. Role conflict and role ambiguity tended to be lower under conditions in which superiors were described as more frequently engaged in emphasizing production under conditions of uncertainty, providing structure and standards, facilitating teamwork, tolerating freedom, and exerting upward influence.
3. High role conflict and role ambiguity tended to be associated with goal conflict and inconsistency, delay in decisions, distortion and suppression of information, and violations of the chain of command. Conversely, *low* role conflict and role ambiguity were associated with an emphasis on personal development, formalization, adequacy of communication, planning, horizontal communication, top management receptiveness to ideas, coordination of work flow, adaptability to change, and adequacy of authority.

In essence the study demonstrated that leadership behaviors and organizational practices can be a cause of a role conflict and role ambiguity. Additionally, role conflict and role ambiguity are associated with diminished need satisfaction.

APPROACHES TO IMPROVING
INDIVIDUAL EFFICIENCY

When examining efforts to improve individual efficiency since the turn of the century, we can observe three approaches: scientific management, human relations, and human resources management.

The *scientific management approach* is most closely associated with Frederick W. Taylor. From firsthand experience and research, Taylor concluded that employers lacked specific knowledge of the various kinds of work performed. To remedy this, he felt that it was necessary to develop a science for each element of an employee's work. Jobs should be simple, repetitive, easily learned operations. Under such conditions, management could then establish what constituted a fair day's work and a fair day's pay. Supplementary managerial duties consisted of scientific selection and training that would develop each employee to a state of maximum efficiency. The basic premise was that employees were motivated primarily by economic interests and that incentive systems would induce better performance.

The *human relations approach* began with the famous Hawthorne experiments conducted in the late 1920s and early 1930s. In these investigations work was found to have a social function. Task groups were found to consist of informal groupings in which each employee had a special position. Having assimilated the general values and attitudes of the group, employee behavior was extensively regulated and controlled by group sentiments. Therefore, to understand employee behavior, it was necessary to consider the worker's social environment. Of special significance was the conclusion that economic incentives might not be effective if they were inconsistent with group norms and values. For example, employees frequently acted contrary to their own economic advantage by following production norms established by the work group, although they were capable of greater output. In essence, economic incentives were found to be less effective than were social incentives. Furthermore, technological changes instigated by management were resisted, although they were to the employees' economic advantage, because such modifications might threaten an individual's social position within the groups or the group's social standing within the organization.

To promote cooperative employee behavior, it was necessary to maintain effective two-way channels of communication throughout the organization. Management had to be informed of employees' thoughts and actions, and in turn, employees needed to be informed of managerial expectations and proposed courses of action. An integral part of planned communication was employee consultation; this would convey that workers were important members in the organization and that their views were welcomed and duly considered. Participation provided an opportunity to contribute to company development and minimize resistance to technological changes. For these findings to be effectively utilized, a new style of leadership by supervision and managerial personnel was needed.

The human relations approach, however, did not challenge the thrust of scientific management toward standardization or specialization. Technology, organization structure, and job design were accepted as given. The work context was humanized, but the nature of work itself was not considered. The human relations approach to efficiency was the subject of increasing questioning and doubt, and by 1960 a new perspective was clearly evident—human resources management.

The *human resources approach* is based on the premise that people want more than physical, economic, and social rewards; individuals also want recognition and fulfillment from their jobs. Standardized and specialized jobs had to give way to jobs that provided greater opportunities for accomplishment and achievement. Consequently, job enrichment, management by objectives, and self-controlled work teams evolved to utilize human resources more efficiently. Central to some of the newer approaches is participation in the formulation of performance goals and the exercise of responsible self-control for the achievement of such goals. The following material will examine some of these newer approaches to increasing employee efficiency.

JOB REDESIGN

The past decade has witnessed unprecedented concern about the alienation and underutilization of employees. To some extent, both problems are seen as associated with each other and frequently a common solution is proposed —job redesign. Since terminology in the area is rather imprecise, it will be necessary to indicate how we will use the terms. *Job enlargement* is used to describe efforts to increase the number of tasks and responsibilities that a worker is given so that the jobs expand or grow and perhaps become more interesting to the employees, but this does not necessarily result in increases in challenge, scope of decision making, or authority. Frederick Herzberg has labeled such efforts as horizontal job loading, which he sees as merely enlarging the meaninglessness of the job.[12] In rather picturesque terms he describes this approach and its effect as follows:

> Challenging the employee by increasing the amount of production expected of him. If he tightens 10,000 bolts a day, see if he can tighten 20,000 bolts a day. The arithmetic involved shows that multiplying zero by zero still equals zero.

> Adding another meaningless task to the existing one, usually some routine clerical activity. The arithmetic here is adding zero to zero.

> Rotating the assignments of a number of jobs that need to be enriched. This means washing dishes for a while, then washing silverware. The arithmetic is substituting one zero for another zero.

Job enrichment, on the other hand, refers to redesigning the jobs so as to enrich the work by adding greater challenge, responsibility, and so forth. This is called vertical job loading, which has as an objective the building of motivation into the job. The objective of such job enrichment is to create jobs that will be more motivating and satisfying and also result in increased performance and productivity.[13]

The Herzberg Model

The most widely known and utilized approach to job restructuring has been developed by Herzberg. As we noted in the previous chapter, he makes a clear distinction between hygienic factors and motivators. Herzberg's approach to job enrichment is an application of his theory of motivation and, more specifically, is directed at designing motivators into diluted, overspecialized jobs. The principles of job restructuring and the motivation involved are shown in Table 4-1. These principles serve as guides to redesigning jobs and indicate the motivators involved for each job change.[14]

Table 4-1

Principles of Vertical Job Loading

Principle	Motivators
Removing some controls while retaining accountability	Responsibility and personal achievement
Increasing the accountability of individuals for own work	Responsibility and recognition
Giving a person a complete natural unit of work (module, division, area, and so on)	Responsibility, achievement, and recognition
Granting additional authority to an employee in his or her activity; job freedom	Responsibility, achievement, and recognition
Making periodic reports directly available to the worker himself or herself rather than to the supervisor	Internal recognition
Introducing new and more difficult tasks not previously handled	Growth and learning
Assigning individuals specific or specialized tasks, enabling them to become experts	Responsibility, growth, and advancement

The steps that managers should take in using the principles of job enrichment are outlined briefly by Herzberg as follows.[15]

1. Select the jobs to be enriched on the basis of the following criteria:
   a. investment in industrial engineering or technological modifications do not make a change too costly
   b. attitudes are poor
   c. providing hygiene factors is becoming very expensive
   d. motivation will make a difference in performance

2. Brainstorm a list of changes that may enrich the job, without concern for their practicality or merit.
3. Screen the list to eliminate
   a. hygiene suggestions
   b. generalities that sound impressive but have no substance such as "give more responsibility"
   c. horizontal loading suggestions
4. Avoid direct participation by the employees whose jobs are being enriched since the job content itself will produce motivation, not attitudes about being involved or the challenge in changing the job.
5. In the initial introduction of job enrichment, set up a controlled experiment by selecting two equivalent groups—one an experimental group and the other a control group. The motivators are systematically introduced over a period of time for the experimental group while no changes are made for the control group. Pre- and post-job enrichment tests of performance and job attitudes are made to evaluate the effectiveness of the program.

In addition to these steps, several warnings were given. Anticipate a decline in the experimental group's performance and efficiency for several weeks as new tasks are learned and adjustments made. Additionally, expect the first-line supervisor to experience some anxiety and hostility concerning the changes being made. His or her unit may well have a poorer performance record as a result of the change. Also supervisors frequently experience misgivings about their own function or role that is altered as their subordinates assume more responsibility with their expanded jobs. Usually the supervisor discovers the basic managerial functions that he or she has neglected, that is, planning, organizing, and directing. When a supervisor devotes more time to these tasks, that person will become a better manager.

Model of a Restructured Job

From the foregoing principles of job enrichment, one may still have difficulty visualizing what well-designed jobs look like. If so, an interesting descriptive model of such a job is as follows.[16]

First of all, it is a complete piece of work; the person who is doing the job can tell where his work begins and where it ends, and in that way can determine what responsibilities are his and what are someone else's. In addition, he should be able to carry the task through to a natural finishing point in the process. These natural "modules" are found in almost all work situations. It is also important for him to have an identifiable receiver or "customer" of the work— that is, a person or group affected directly by the task performed.

Secondly, the job permits a high degree of decision making and control. The job holder may decide what procedures to use, what his priorities are, and, most important, what to do in situations involving correction or problem solving. There are, or course, justifiable limitations to the possibilities here; differences in workers' capability levels or in requirements for coordinated results might make it unwise to extend some types of decision making to certain jobs. If, however, the job holder must follow prescribed methods and refer any unusual situation to his supervisor or to some other person in authority, the assignment has been poorly designed for enrichment.

Finally, the person performing the work receives frequent and direct non-supervisory feedback on his performance. Feedback from the supervisor obviously is important; but if the job holder, in its absence, cannot tell how well he is doing, the job is poorly designed. Where possible, the feedback should come from the previously mentioned "customers." Moreover, it should be individual in the sense that it informs each person about what his particular contribution is to the performance of the group of the department.

What principles of job enrichment do you see reflected in this job description? A natural unit of work has been provided, and additional authority has been granted to the job incumbent. Additionally, some controls have been removed, and the individual has been made accountable for his or her own work. Finally, performance reports are given directly to the employee.

A Restructuring Study

The Bankers Trust Company, a New York commercial bank, made the decision in late 1969 to undertake job enrichment in a division handling stock transfer operations.[17] The model for this application of job enrichment was essentially the approach that uses the supervisory and lower management team as the primary resource for job analysis and ideas for changes in job design. Change items were introduced selectively according to ability; that is, the bank did not implement "broadside" modifications involving all employees at once. A deviation in the basic implementation model, however, created added interest in this case history. During the search for work modules, it was initially felt that fully individual modules were not practical in all cases. *Small-group modules* were decided upon in an effort to gain motivational advantages similar to those found in individual modules, even though some dilution of impact was expected. This is an example of the new and more flexible model for implementation that is gaining favor.

The job

Bankers Trust acts as the stock transfer agent for a large number of corporations. The production typist must type and record stock transfer data into many "blocks" on large forms. There are approximately one hundred typists on each of two shifts. Because errors create serious problems such as improper registration, lost certificates, and misdirected dividend checks that lead, among other things, to customer irritation, there is one checker for each typist, with few exceptions. The checker verifies the accuracy of every form completed by the typist. Errors are noted and returned to a special group for correction. The forms are then certified a second time by another checker. Finally, the information is put on magnetic tape and fed into a computer for official recording of the transaction.

Management saw this area of the operation as a serious problem. Production was low, quality was poor, absenteeism and turnover were high, and employee attitudes were considered poor. The jobs were viewed as routine, repetitive, and completely devoid of intrinsic interest. The production typist job was to be the focal point of change.

Postworkshop implementation

Following a workshop designed to give management an understanding of the principles of job enrichment, each supervisory team met weekly to plan the introduction of various job changes, working from a list of fifty-two possible changes for the production typist job developed during the workshop. Additional items were added, and some items were dropped from the original list.

Within two weeks, the first motivator was introduced to the job. Certain typists were permitted to change their own computer input tapes. This had always been the responsibility of the group leader. The variety of feeling about this change was meaningful. Whereas higher management was fearful of the risk of losing information and reluctant to transfer this responsibility to the typists, the section supervisors considered tape-changing inconsequential. They wanted to press on to implementing more "important" items. The typists reacted immediately to their new responsibility with such remarks as "Well, it's about time," and "It's good to be trusted." Within six months a dozen motivators had been introduced on the job in varying degrees.

However, section supervisors realized early in the effort that no one felt responsible for his or her own work. This was seen as a major problem. The following changes came about as they addressed this important problem.

Customer identification

Prior to implementation, the employee was assigned work in a random manner by the supervisor. There was little or no concern for establishing work modules to give each individual a "customer territory." The work was rearranged so that several typists were given continuing responsibility for a group of customers. They would draw new certificates from the vault, prepare them, and enter the shareowner's name and address. They typed the transfer information onto the sheets. Finally, they checked their own work and corrected their own errors. These typists were no longer dependent on the supervisor for work assignment and control. While working at servicing the customer group assigned to his or her team, each typist was able to project the work load for the balance of the day. Tasks related to final typing were drawn into the typist's job. These tasks eventually became an integral part of the production typist's job design, which had become a diversified module. Figure 4-5 is a schematic of the old work flow and the new module or job design.

Figure 4-5

Prejob-Enrichment Work Flow and New Modular Design

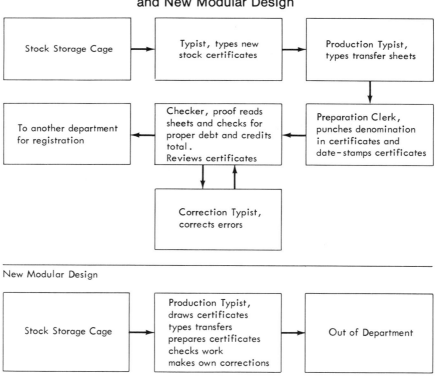

Source: William W. Dettelback and Philip Kraft, "Organization Change Through Job Enrichment." Reproduced by special permission from the August, 1971 TRAINING AND DEVELOPMENT JOURNAL. Copyright 1971 by the American Society for Training and Development, Inc.

Group responsibility

While certain employees could take total responsibility for a group of customers, other typists were less accurate but nevertheless ready for additional responsibility. These employees were assigned to specific teams of varied size. Each team was responsible for a group of customers. Typists and checkers scheduled their own work, corrected their own errors, kept their own production counts, and maintained individual quality records. Errors picked up by teammates were fed directly back to the typist who made the mistake for correction.

Accountability

The degree of checking was gradually reduced for those typists who demonstrated accuracy. There were fewer typing errors in spite of the absence of checking for this group. Typists who were accountable for their own work showed far greater concern for quality.

Growth and learning

Before job enrichment only certain experienced typists were allowed to do "specials." Shortly, however, all but three employees were trained and showed proficiency on these "specials." The training, in fact, was done by the few typists who were initially familiar with the procedures. The newly trained typists found their work more interesting, and the experienced typists found satisfaction in their roles as trainers.

Results

The primary objective for management was to improve productivity. Supervisors were reluctant to implement any items that might be detrimental to their production records. To gain a success, then, the job-enrichment process had to produce immediate productivity gains in an adverse environment. During the early implementation phase, individual typist output showed some decrease for those who had no checker. Responding to the increased responsibility, the typist was more careful and his or her work rate slowed down. The net result, however, was that typed transactions were turned out at a much faster rate. So much time was saved by clearing delays and eliminating or combining functions in the new module design (see Figure 4-5) that output direct from the typist sections increased dramatically. Table 4-2 gives the before-and-after comparison. The division is well on the way to eliminating checkers for half the typists, which will allow a savings of $300,000 annually in checker salaries.

Table 4-2

Before-and-After Job-Enrichment Production Rates

	Completed Transactions per Hour by Section		
Section	1	2	3
Prior job module	10	12	14
Current job module	22	23	30
Percentage improvement	110%	92%	114%

Source: William W. Dettelback and Philip Kraft, "Organization Change Through Job Enrichment." Reproduced by special permission from the August, 1971 TRAINING AND DEVELOPMENT JOURNAL. Copyright 1971 by the American Society for Training and Development, Inc.

Quality

Quality had never been measured or analyzed consistently. Serious errors, detected by the shareowners themselves, were brought to the attention of supervisors but rarely discussed with the employee responsible. Indeed, the supervisor had no way of knowing who was responsible. In most cases more than one person was involved in the error because the work was so fragmented. Individual accountability was impossible.

Acting upon a suggestion from the first-line supervisors, a computer program was designed to detect the most common errors prior to issuance and to cite the typist responsible. Each day the errors were fed back directly to the typist responsible. Many of the clerks recorded their own mistakes and maintained error charts. Most impressive was the fact that error rates showed no increase among those typists whose checkers were removed.

Attitude

A most rewarding result during the first six months was the improved attitude of the employees toward their work experiences. A job reaction survey of eight questions was developed and administered to all employees prior to the project. The survey was designed to obtain a quantitative measure of the various motivating factors in a given job as experienced and reported by the employees. At the end of six months, the survey was again administered to a random 20 percent of the work group. Individual scores were compared by pairing before job-enrichment scores for the same individual with scores after they had been in the job redesign group for six months. There was a significant improvement in all eight question categories as shown in Figure 4-6.

Figure 4-6

Employee Reactions to Their Job Before and
After the Job Enrichment

Reactions to Your Job

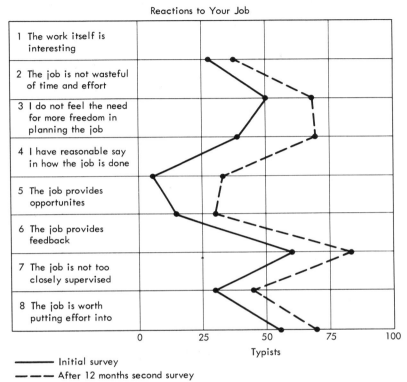

——— Initial survey

— — — After 12 months second survey

Source: William W. Dettelback and Philip Kraft, "Organization Change Through Job Enrichment." Reproduced by special permission from the August, 1971 TRAINING AND DEVEL-OPMENT JOURNAL. Copyright 1971 by the American Society for Training and Development, Inc.

Interviews

In addition, a large number of interviews were conducted and taped prior to the workshop. These interviews were designed, like the survey, to determine reactions to the work itself. Some of the employees were interviewed again after six months. This kind of interviewing, though not an accurate tool for measuring the program, can give the broad outline of problems and give signs of change. The anecdotal information can also be of great help during discussions of program progress with higher management. The change in tone of these before-and-after interviews is striking.

Prior to job enrichment interviews were filled with comments such as the following:

"I don't see anything good in the job—not anything. What could you learn from typing names and addresses?"

"The same sheeting every day. You don't know when you make errors."

"The work is just routine. You have no say so in the programming of the work."

"I have five bosses to account to. It is ridiculous. I like to be treated like an adult."

After six months comments such as these were more frequent:

"I have had more duties added to me which I do appreciate. More work, but I enjoy it."

"My work is more important."

"I feel I am responsible for something. I know if anything happens it's going to come back to me and I'm going to feel bad about it."

"My absence and lateness was terrible . . . but now I say, 'If I don't come in, who is going to do my work?' I can't stay out."

Supervision

In addition to the improvements found in productivity and employee attitudes, job enrichment also generated a serious review of the first-line supervisor's function. This had been contemplated initially, but it eventually became imperative. Many of the motivators introduced to the typists' job had formerly been the responsibility of the supervisor. As these duties were given to responsible subordinates, vacuums were created in the supervisor's job. Many of them had difficulty adjusting to the new role. Without the volume of work to check and nonsupervisory production tasks to perform, many supervisors were uncertain about how to use their newly acquired blocks of time. This was identified as a crucial transition for supervisors. They were assisted individually to accommodate special needs through counseling and some remedial skill training in developmental methods. They began to use their time to coach, develop, and instruct; they assumed a new role centered on managing human resources. As the employees grew in their knowledge of and commitment to the work, the supervisory group concurrently developed the ability to manage talent through the process of matching talent to jobs and measuring progress. Their attitude toward the clerks showed increased concern for individual needs as they became better equipped to measure and reward quality work.

Supervisors found through this job enrichment effort their proper developmental role and have made great progress toward fulfilling it. They have also become better planners, better organizers, and better managers of time, all of which results in better work unit performance.

SUMMARY

In this chapter we examined individual effectiveness. Measures to increase employee productivity are influenced by numerous factors other than those emphasizing the task–person linkages. One of the most significant determinants is an organization's personnel philosophy, which conveys management's views on organizing and treating its employees at work. Whether people are viewed simply as a factor of production, and nothing more, or are seen as entitled to rights and dignity, impacts on individual efficiency and also the quality of work life.

Within the framework of a personnel philosophy, an organization, regardless of its size, must implement a manpower function consisting of employment, development, utilization, compensation, and maintenance activities. Employee effectiveness is shaped by each of these functions—from recruitment to retirement.

Individual effectiveness is also influenced by the clarity of the job, which may present some unanticipated difficulties. Management does not simply design the job and the employee perform as instructed. The organization—supervisor, peers, and job incumbent—may all hold different views of what the duties are and how such duties should be performed. Such divergent expectations can produce varying amounts of job conflict and may have a detrimental effect on employee efficiency. Similar results are generated when insufficient job information is provided to an employee, that is, role ambiguity.

Finally, we explored job redesign as a possible solution to the underutilization of employees and as a means of enhancing employee efficiency, and we considered Frederick Herzberg's approach of building motivators into redesigned jobs. A distinction was made between horizontal job loading—enlarging the meaninglessness of the job—and vertical job loading—building motivation into the job.

QUESTIONS FOR STUDY AND DISCUSSION

1. What are the determinants of personnel philosophy? Are some determinants more important than others? Why is an organization's personnel philosophy important?

2. Why is the utilization of manpower so important? How is this function related to job enrichment?

3. How does role theory help to explain role conflict?

4. What are the sources of role conflict? How can an organization deal with the sources of role conflict?

5. What is role ambiguity? How can an organization minimize role ambiguity?

6. How do job enlargement and job enrichment differ?

7. What "motivators" does Herzberg's model of job enrichment seek to build into redesigned jobs?

8. Why do supervisors usually fear job enrichment? Are such fears justified? Why?

NOTES

[1]Johnson, Lewis K., "Personnel Philosophy," *Personnel Journal* 25 (June 1946): 42.

[2]Milton, Charles R., *Ethics and Expediency in Personnel Management* (Columbia: University of South Carolina Press, 1970), p. 15.

[3]*Ibid.,* pp. 9–13.

[4]Edgar G. Williams, "A Systems Approach to Manpower Management," *Business Horizons,* Winter 1964, pp. 59-60.

[5]Campbell, J., M. Dunnette, E. Lawler, and K. Weick, *Managerial Behavior, Performance and Effectiveness* (New York: McGraw-Hill, 1970), p. 475.

[6]Secord, Paul F. and Carl W. Backman, *Social Psychology* (New York: McGraw-Hill, 1964), p. 472.

[7]Rizzo, John R., Robert J. House, and Sidney I. Lirtzman, "Role Conflict and Ambiguity in Complex Organizations," *Administrative Science Quarterly* 15 (March 1970): 150–163.

[8]*Ibid.,* p. 151.

[9]Kahn, Robert L., Donald M. Wolfe, Robert P. Quinn, J. Diedrick Snoek, and Robert A. Rosenthal, *Organization Stress* (New York: Wiley, 1964).

[10]Rizzo et al., *op cit.*

[11]Rizzo et al., *op cit.* See also Valenzi, Enzo and Gary Dessler, "Relationship of Leader Behavior, Subordinate Role Ambiguity and Subordinate Job Satisfaction," *Academy of Management Journal* 21 (December 1978), 671–678; Morris, James H., Richard M. Steers, and James L. Koch, "Influence of Organizational Structure on Role Conflict and Ambiguity for Three Occupational Groupings," *Academy of Management Journal* 22 (March, 1979), 58-76.

[12]Herzberg, Frederic, "One More Time: How Do You Motivate Employees?" *Harvard Business Review* (January–February 1968): 53–62.

[13]Chung, Kae and Monica F. Ross, "Differences in Motivational Properties Between Job Enlargement and Job Enrichment," *Academy of Management Review* 2 (January 1977), 113–122.

[14]Herzberg, *op. cit.,* p. 59.

[15]*Ibid.*

[16]Whitsett, David A., "Where Are Your Unenriched Jobs?" *Harvard Business Review* (January–February 1975): 74–80.

[17]Dettelback, William W. and Philip Kraft, "Organization Change through Job Enrichment," *Training and Development Journal* (August 1971): 2-6.

cases cases cases

Case Study: A Job Change

The Inspection and Rating Bureau is a division of the Underwriters Association that acts as a service agency to all member insurance companies. The services performed for members involve fire-rating inspection of any form of building except private dwellings. A request is made by an insurance company for a particular building to be rated due to its newness, a new occupant, or a change in the environment surrounding the building (more fire hydrants, for example). Upon receipt of the request, an agent is assigned to the job and subsequently makes the necessary observations. When this has been done, the agent returns to the home office and fills out the required data sheets and actually computes the rate. This rate is turned over to the requesting insurance company who then adjusts its customers' premiums accordingly.

PART I: BEFORE THE CHANGE

For years, each agent has had a specific territory in the state. In this way, the agent had a chance to become very familiar with all the roads, buildings, and businesspeople with whom he or she would come in daily contact. The insurance companies therefore know which agents were concerned when a rating was necessary. Due to this fact, much formality was bypassed. If an insurance company wished to have a building in Norfolk rated, it simply asked the Norfolk agent to do the job next time he or she went on a rating trip. All this was done on a very informal and personal basis.

CASE QUESTIONS

1. Apply Herzberg's principles of vertical job loading to the agent's job. Which principles are relevant? What motivators are likely to be involved?
2. Would you suggest any changes in the agent's job or in the existing organization of work? If you suggest any changes, what results do you expect to achieve?

PART II: CHANGE RESULTS

An efficiency study group was employed to set up an efficiency program. The efficiency experts sat in the office and took notes on work patterns and time requirements for different jobs. Eventually, they established an efficiency program based on a point system in which each unit of output of work was associated with a certain number of points. A total of 300 points was considered to be a very good, productive day. The manager, however, found this number to be slightly high and lowered it to 275 points per day. The point sheet that each agent had to fill out as the day progressed became known as "the idiot sheet."

In addition to the point system, the position of job allocator was created to allocate the requests of insurance companies to the different agents. The agents no longer had a specific territory of their own as assignments were made on the basis of whose "turn" it was to make an investigation.

CASE QUESTIONS

1. Evaluate the point system as an incentive to work. Merits? Limitations?

2. Outline the advantages and disadvantages of this operation *before* and *after* the change. What conclusions do you draw from this comparison?

3. What will be the response of the agents to the changes made? Why?

cases cases cases

Case Study: A Change in Operations

The Proof and Transit Department is a subdivision of bank XYZ's Operations Department that performs two major functions. The proof function is to verify the dollar amount of checks that go through the department while in transit to the Federal Reserve banks. The transit function involves the handling of checks that are to be sent to the various Federal Reserve banks. Checks are sent to the department from the bank's branches, from banks that are not allowed to deal directly with the Federal Reserve because they are not members of the Federal Deposit Insurance Corporation and from banks that purchase these services because they are too small to have proof and transit facilities of their own.

The focal point of this episode is fifteen proof operators and their department manager, shown in the following organizational chart.

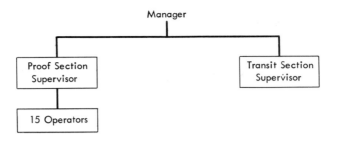

PART I: MANAGER A

The manager, Mr. Able, was a college graduate who was withdrawn from the bank's training program before finishing so that he could assume the position of manager of the Proof and Transit Department. To facilitate handling some of the department's problems, he held weekly meetings with the operators. The meetings were long and generally considered boring and punitive. They were usually not too informative or productive.

Mr. Able allowed the operators great independence. That is, the operators were to check their machines when they finished their work. This was to make sure that no checks were left in the machines, thus reducing the number of errors. But, because there was no certification procedure to verify that the operators really had checked the machines, the machines were often not examined. Checks left in the machines were the predominate sources of errors. If an operator's machine got out of balance, it was up to that individual to trace the error. The operator had to do this alone, and it was often time consuming, causing a bottleneck in the flow of operations.

Mr. Able did not set a specific daily starting time for reporting to work. Because of fluctuations in the volume of work to be done each day, he felt that he could estimate how much work had to be done the subsequent day. Consequently, he would always tell the operators the previous day what time they were to come in the following morning. The starting time would vary from 8:00 A.M. to 9:30 A.M. However, because he was not always able to accurately forecast the amount of work to be done, the operators frequently had to stay quite late. This was a source of much tension and dissatisfaction. However, the operators were allowed to leave individually as soon as they finished their work.

Mr. Able was replaced after a year plagued by numerous difficulties.

QUESTIONS

1. Why did employees fail to check their machines or work when it is quite easy to do so? Does this prove Theory X assumptions about human nature?

117

2. Each operator had to trace his or her own error. Is this a reasonable practice if it caused bottlenecks in the flow of operation? How can each operator be held responsible for his or her errors but not at the expense of work stoppage or depriving that person of learning from his or her mistakes?

3. The operators have responsibility and autonomy but do not seem to be responding very well. Why?

PART II: MANAGER B

Mr. Baker, the new manager, was not a college graduate, but he had many years of experience in the operations aspect of banking. He kept up with newer managerial techniques and practices by doing research on his own when he was faced with a problem. Within a week things began to change in the department.

The first change was in the varied time reporting for work; he required everyone to be at work at 8:00 A.M. every day. This change generally pleased the operators because it allowed them to get off work earlier and to formalize a regular routine. Mr. Baker required the operators to wait until everyone was finished before they were allowed to leave work. While they were waiting, they were required to help the slower operators wherever they could. It was also to be a group effort if a proof machine got out of balance. This helped to eliminate many previous bottlenecks to output. When the faster operators finished and no other operator needed assistance, they were allowed to talk among themselves. This interaction resulted in better working relations. The practice of requiring all the operators to leave at the same time caused the faster operators to apply pressure on the slower ones to work more rapidly. The operators now had more *espirit de corps* because they had more opportunity to identify one with another.

Mr. Baker instituted the practice of calling small groups of operators into his office to find out what problems they were having and how they thought improvements could be made in the department. He also held regular meetings with his two supervisors to tackle and help with problems they were having. As a result of the manager–supervisory sessions, there developed a consistency and mutuality of purposes and objectives.

A procedure was installed to verify the fact that each operator had examined his or her machine for missing checks when that operator had finished for the day. This drastically reduced the number of errors that each operator made. Each operator was evaluated periodically to make sure that she was not making an excessive number of errors. Whenever an operator made an error it was entered into his or her file. The procedure was to notify the specific operator every time that the operator had caused an error. The error was stated in writing telling what had happened and why.

The supervisor would add any comments she might have and then give the notice to the operator. The operator would give any explanation he or she might have, sign the notice, and return it to the supervisor to be placed in his or her file. This turned out to be a very effective method of preventing errors. When an operator received a notice of error, all the co-workers knew about it. The typical operator was usually embarrassed to receive an error notice and, therefore, tried to avoid further errors. The operators knew that if they made too many mistakes they would be called into the manager's office to discuss the problem and what might be done about it.

A record system was developed using this information to evaluate each operator's performance. Additionally, another file was maintained that indicated how many items each operator processed per day.

Another change made by Mr. Baker was to allow the operators who had to work on Saturday to take a day off during the week. Since only one third of the operators were needed each of three Saturdays a month, it was necessary for each one to work only one Saturday per month. Everyone appreciated not having to work a six-day week once a month as was the previous practice.

There was also a change in the weekly meetings. They were only held when there was a new policy change or when some other important announcement had to be made. He discovered that the operators were hostile toward meetings that did not cover anything of interest to or had no effect on them.

QUESTIONS

1. Are any of Herzberg's principles of job redesign reflected in the changes made by Mr. Baker?

2. Have any hygienic factors been altered by the change? What are the results?

3. What conclusions can you draw about hygienic factors based on this case?

CHAPTER 5

Individual Effectiveness (Continued)

LEARNING OBJECTIVES

When you have finished this chapter, you should be able to:

- *Explain the Job Diagnostic Survey Model of job redesign.*
- *Outline the Problem-Solving-Goal-Setting approach to job redesign.*
- *Understand the socio-technical approach to structuring work.*
- *Cite the critical arguments that have been leveled against job redesign and enrichment.*

In the previous chapter, we examined aspects of individual efficiency and the Herzberg model of job redesign. In this chapter, we consider additional methods of job design. Unsatisfactory experiences with job enrichment in numerous work settings prompted a closer look at what was being done. The Job Diagnostic Survey approach to job redesign discussed in this chapter represents an effort to cope with the deficiencies encountered. Still another approach to job enrichment is the use of problem-solving and goal-setting, which is designed to involve employees in the planning and control process, not just performing the job. The final job design approach presented is a sociotechnical one that requires a blending of the production and social systems to structure an autonomous work group responsible for the total task. The chapter concludes with a critical examination of the assumptions underlying job enrichment and some of the variables that may be overlooked in job design.

THE JOB DIAGNOSTIC SURVEY MODEL

Job enrichment, which began with the work of Herzberg and his associates, has not always been successful in increasing motivation, satisfaction, and production. This failure has led to an examination of job enrichment, its theoretical base, mode of application, and the occupational classifications affected by redesigned jobs. Hackman and Oldham have developed a new strategy for the redesign of work that builds upon and complements the previous work by Herzberg and others,[1] providing for the first time a set of tools for diagnosing jobs and procedures for translating the diagnostic results into specific action steps for change. This approach suggests that there are three critical psychological states whose presence is necessary to get people motivated by work:

1. Experienced meaningfulness: The individual must perceive his or her work as worthwhile or important by the values that he or she accepts.
2. Experienced responsibility: The individual must believe that he or she personally is accountable for the outcomes or results of his or her efforts.
3. Knowledge of results: The individual must be able to determine, on some fairly regular basis, whether or not the results of his or her work are satisfactory.

When these three conditions are present, a person is generally presumed to be motivated and is expected to experience satisfaction on the job; additionally, high-quality work performance, low absenteeism, and low turnover also should result. If one of the three psychological states is missing, motivation drops markedly. Obviously, desirable job results do not generally happen by chance; five specific job characteristics or dimensions elicit the psychological states cited here.

Job Dimensions or Characteristics

Three of the five core dimensions contribute to a job's *meaningfulness:*

1. Skill variety: the degree to which a job requires the worker to perform activities that challenge his or her skills and abilities. When several skills

are involved, the job has the potential of appealing to the whole person and also of avoiding the monotony of performing the same task repeatedly.

2. Task identity: the degree to which the job requires completion of a "whole" and identifiable piece of work, that is, doing a job from beginning to end with a visible outcome. For example, it is clearly more meaningful if an employee builds a complete toaster rather than attaches one electrical cord after another.

3. Task significance: the degree to which the job has a substantial and perceivable impact on the lives of other people, whether in the immediate organization or the world at large.

Each of these job dimensions is an important contributor to meaningfulness. If a job is low in any one of the three dimensions, there will be a drop in overall experienced meaningfulness. Even when two dimensions are low, the employee may find the job meaningful if the third is high enough since it is not necessary that all three dimensions be high.

4. Autonomy: the degree to which the job gives the worker freedom, independence, and discretion in scheduling work and its implementation. By experiencing increased responsibility on the job, one becomes personally responsible for his or her successes and failures.

5. Feedback: the knowledge of results. This information indicates the effectiveness of work effort and is most valuable when it comes from the work itself. One learns from the feedback process.

Figure 5-1 shows how the five core dimensions combine to affect the critical psychological states that are necessary in determining whether or not an employee will be internally motivated to work effectively. Whether or not desirable personal or work outcomes result depends upon the extent to which critical psychological states are produced by the job itself.

Using a questionnaire based on the preceding five job dimensions, it is possible to compute a "motivating potential score" (MPS) for any job. The MPS is determined as follows:

$$\text{MPS} = \frac{\textit{Skill variety} + \textit{task identity} + \textit{task significance}}{3} \times \text{autonomy} \times \text{feedback}$$

The motivating potential score provides a single summary index of the degree to which the objective characteristics of the job will prompt high internal work motivation. A job high in motivating potential must be high in at least one of the three dimensions that lead to experienced meaningfulness and high in both autonomy and feedback. The MPS is useful in diagnosing jobs and in assessing the effectiveness of job-enrichment activities.

Figure 5-1

Relationships among Core Job Dimensions, Critical Psychological States, and On-the-Job Outcomes

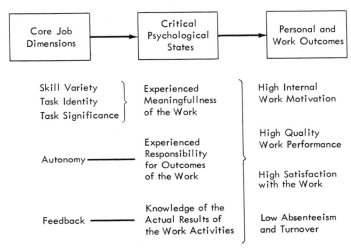

Source: J. Richard Hackman and Greg R. Oldham, "Motivation Through the Design of Work: Test of a Theory," *Organizational Behavior and Human Performance* 16 (August 1976): 256.

The questionnaire that provides the data for a motivation potential score also measures the satisfaction and work performance of employees on the job. Additionally, measures are taken of how people feel about other aspects of their work setting such as pay, supervision, and relationships with co-workers. Finally, the instruments gauge the extent of employees' growth needs. Some people have strong needs for personal accomplishment, learning, self-development, stimulation and challenge; some, however, do not. The growth-need measure makes it possible to identify which persons should be initially utilized in the job redesign and which employees may need help in adapting to the enriched job.

Using these diagnostic tools and data, the following sequence of questions is relevant for a job diagnosis.

1. Are motivation and satisfaction central to the problem? If not, look to other aspects of the work situation such as a poorly designed production system, inadequate training, and so on to identify the real problem rather than mistakenly apply job enrichment.

2. Is the job low in motivating potential? The motivating potential score of the target job as compared with other jobs will answer this question. If, on the other hand, this score is high, other motivational difficulties such as the pay system or supervision may be the problem.

3. What specific aspects of the job are causing difficulty? Each of the five job core dimensions scores is examined to pinpoint the specific strengths and weaknesses of the job as it is currently structured.
4. How "ready" are the employees for change? Once the need for job improvement has been demonstrated and the troublesome aspects of the job identified, specific steps must be taken to enrich the job. An important factor in such planning is the level of growth needs of the employees, since those high on such needs usually respond more readily to job enrichment than do employees with little need for growth. The high-growth-need employees should be among the first to have their jobs changed.

Changing the Job

After completing the diagnosis of a job, the core dimensions most in need of remedial attention can be identified. Specific action steps are relevant for improving each core job dimension and the subsequent quality of the working experience for the individual and his or her work productivity. The remedial actions for enriching the job are combining tasks, forming natural work units, establishing client relationships, loading jobs vertically, and opening feedback channels. Each remedial action and the job dimensions affected is examined in the following paragraphs.

Combining tasks

The principle of combining tasks suggests that, whenever possible, existing and fractionalized tasks should be combined to form new and larger modules of work.,For example, the assembly of a laboratory hot plate may be changed from a series of specific activities performed by different individuals to one in which each hot plate is assembled from start to finish by one operator. However, some tasks, if combined into a meaningful module of work, are more than an individual could do alone. In such cases it may be possible to assign the larger task to a small team of workers who are given greater autonomy for its completion.

Combining tasks expands the task identity of the job. The hot-plate assembler, for example, can see and identify with a finished product rather than with some minute facet of its assembly. Moreover, the more tasks combined into a single worker's job, the greater the variety of skills that must be utilized in performing the job. So combining tasks can affect both task and skill variety.

Forming natural work units

The principle underlying natural units of work is that of providing the worker with a sense of continuing responsibility for an identifiable body of work, namely, ownership. Two steps are involved in creating natural work units. The first is to identify the basic work items. In a typing pool, for example, the items might be "pages to be typed." The second step is to group the items in natural categories. In the typical typing pool, jobs are randomly assigned, and consequently there is no basis for identifying with the work, the person, or department for whom the work is performed or for placing any personal value upon it. On the other hand, if work is assigned naturally by departments, the typist has a greater chance of performing a job to completion (task identity) and developing an appreciation of how the work affects those serviced (task significance). The ownership fostered by natural units of work can make the difference between feeling that work is meaningful and rewarding and the feeling that it is irrelevant and boring.

Establishing client relationships

One consequence of job specialization is that the typical employee has no awareness of or contact with the ultimate user of his or her product or service. Creating client relationships is a three-step process. First, the client must be identified, and, second, the most direct contact must be established between the worker and the client. Third, criteria must be formulated to permit the client to judge the product or service quality and, if possible, relay his or her evaluations directly to the worker. By establishing such communications, improvements may be realized simultaneously on three job core dimensions. Feedback increases because the worker has additional opportunities to receive direct praise or criticism for his or her work output. Skill variety often increases because of the need to develop and exercise interpersonal skills in maintaining the client relationship. And, finally, autonomy can increase because the individual worker often is given personal responsibility for deciding how to manage his or her relationships with those who receive his or her work.

Vertical loading

The principle underlying vertical loading is that responsibilities and controls formerly reserved for higher levels of management are added to the job. Efficiency through specialization—the scientific management approach—has tended to separate the planning and controlling from the doing or performing of the job. The result has been an unexpected but significant cost in motivation and work quality. In vertical loading, the intent is to partially restore the planning and controlling parts of the job. There are many ways to accomplish this:

1. More responsibility: Return to the jobholder greater discretion in setting schedules, deciding on work methods, checking on quality, and advising or helping to train less experienced workers.

2. Additional authority: The objective should be to advance workers from a position of no authority or highly restricted authority to positions of reviewed authority and eventually nearly total authority for his or her own work.

3. Time management: The jobholder should have the greatest possible freedom to decide when to start and stop work, when to break, and how to assign priorities.

4. Troubleshooting and crisis decisions: Workers should be encouraged to seek problem solutions on their own rather than call immediately for the supervisor.

5. Financial controls: Some degree of knowledge and control over budgets and other financial aspects of a job can often be highly motivating. However, access to this information frequently tends to be restricted. Workers can benefit from knowing something about the costs of their jobs, the potential effect upon profit, and various financial and budgetary alternatives.

When a job is vertically loaded, it will inevitably increase in autonomy. And, as shown in Figure 5-1, this increase in objective personal control over the work can also lead to an increased feeling of personal responsibility for the work and, ultimately, to higher internal work motivation.

Opening feedback channels

The principle of feedback suggests that it is generally better for a worker to learn about his or her performance directly as the job is being performed rather than to hear from management on an occasional basis. Job-provided feedback is usually more immediate and private than supervisor-supplied feedback. Moreover, it avoids many of the potentially disruptive interpersonal problems that can develop if the worker's boss handles the feedback matter poorly. In virtually all jobs there are ways to open feedback channels to individuals or teams to help them learn whether their performance is improving, deteriorating, or remaining at a constant level.

The means for opening channels for job-provided feedback will vary from job to job and organization to organization. In many cases the change simply involves removing existing blocks that isolate the worker from naturally occurring data about performance rather than creating entirely new feedback mechanisms. Some examples are the following.

1. Establishing direct client relationships often removes blocks between the worker and external sources of data about his or her work.

2. Quality-control efforts in many organizations often eliminate a natural source of feedback. The quality check on a product or service is done by persons other than those responsible for the work. Feedback to the workers, if there is any, is belated and diluted. It often fosters a tendency

to think of quality as "someone else's concern." By placing quality control close to the worker (perhaps even in his or her own hands), the quantity and quality of data about performance available to that worker can increase dramatically.

3. Tradition and established procedure in many organizations dictate that records about performance be kept by a supervisor and transmitted up (not down) in the organizational hierarchy. Sometimes supervisors even check the work and correct any errors themselves. The worker who made the error never knows that it occurred and, therefore, is denied the very information that could enhance both his or her internal work motivation and the technical adequacy of his or her performance. In many cases it is possible to provide standard summaries of performance records directly to the worker (as well as to his or her superior), thereby giving that worker personally and regularly the data needed to improve his or her performance.

4. Computers and other automated operations sometimes can be used to provide the individual with data now blocked from him or her. Many clerical operations, for example, are now performed on computer consoles. These consoles often can be programmed to provide the clerk with immediate feedback in the form of a display or a printout indicating that an error has been made. Some systems even have been programmed to provide the operator with a positive feedback message when a period of error-free performance had been sustained.

Many organizations simply have not recognized the importance of feedback as a motivator. Data on quality and other aspects of performance are viewed as being of interest only to management. Worse still, the standards for acceptable performance often are kept from workers as well. As a result, workers who would be interested in following the daily or weekly ups and downs of their performance, and in trying accordingly to improve, are deprived of the very guidelines they need to do so.

Is the job-enrichment theory outlined here correct? The Job Diagnostic Survey has been taken by more than 1,000 employees working on about 100 diverse jobs in more than a dozen organizations over a two-year period.[2] These data were analyzed to test the basic motivational theory and the impact of the core job dimensions on worker motivation, satisfaction, and behavior on the job. Some of the findings are summarized as follows.

1. People who work on jobs high on core dimensions are more motivated and satisfied than are people who work on jobs that score low on the dimensions. Employees with high motivational potential scores also were higher on experienced meaningfulness, experienced responsibility, knowledge of results, and "growth" satisfaction.

2. Absenteeism was lower and job performance higher for employees with jobs high in motivational potential.

3. Responses to jobs high in motivating potential are more positive for people who have strong growth needs than for people with weak needs for growth.

A Test of the Theory by Application

The ultimate test of this approach to job enrichment is whether the change strategy really leads to measurable and significant improvements in productivity and job satisfaction when applied in an actual organizational setting. The following is a summary of a job-enrichment project conducted at the Travelers Insurance Companies that illustrates how the change procedures work in practice.[3]

The Travelers project was designed with two purposes in mind. One was to achieve improvements in morale, productivity, and other indicators of employee well-being. The other was to test the general effectiveness of the strategy for job enrichment.

The work group chosen was a keypunching operation. The group's function was to transfer information from printed or written documents onto punched cards for computer input. The work group consisted of ninety-eight keypunch operators and verifiers (both in the same job classification) plus seven assignment clerks. All reported to a supervisor who, in turn, reported to the assistant manager and manager of the data input division. The size of individual punching orders varied considerably, from a few cards to as many as 2,500. Some work came to the work group with a specified delivery date, while other orders were to be given routine service on a predetermined schedule.

Assignment clerks received the jobs from the user departments. After reviewing the work for obvious errors, omissions, and legibility problems, the assignment clerk assigned batches expected to take about one hour. If the clerk found that the work was not suitable for punching, it went to the supervisor, who either returned the work to the user department or cleared up the problems by phone. When work went to operators for punching, it was with the instruction, "Punch only what you see. Don't correct errors, no matter how obvious they look."

Because of the high cost of computer time, keypunched work was 100 percent verified—a task that consumed nearly as many labor-hours as the punching itself. Then the cards went to the supervisor, who screened the jobs for due dates before sending them to the computer. Errors detected in verification were assigned to various operators at random for correction. The computer output from the cards was sent to the originating department, accompanied by a printout of errors. Eventually, the printout went back to the supervisor for final correction.

A number of phenomena indicated that the problems being experienced in the work group might be the result of poor motivation. As the only person performing supervisory functions of any kind, the supervisor spent most of his time responding to crisis situations, which recurred continually. He also had to deal almost daily with employees' salary grievances or other complaints. Employees frequently showed apathy or outright hostility toward their jobs. Rates of work output, by accepted work measurement standards, were inadequate. Error rates were high. Due dates and schedules were frequently missed. Absenteeism was higher than average, especially before and after weekends and holidays. The single, rather unusual, exception was turnover. It was lower than the companywide average for similar jobs. The company attributed this fact to a poor job market in the base period just before the project began and to an older, relatively more settled work force, made up entirely of women.

The diagnosis

Using some of the tools and techniques we have outlined, it was concluded that the keypunch operator's job exhibited the following serious weaknesses in terms of the core dimensions.

Skill variety: None. Only a single skill was involved—the ability to punch adequately the data on the batch of documents.

Task identity: Virtually nonexistent. Batches were assembled to provide an even work load but not whole identifiable jobs.

Task significance: Not apparent. The keypunching operation was a necessary step in providing service to the company's customers. The individual operator was isolated by an assignment clerk and a supervisor from any knowledge of what the operation meant to the using department or its meaning to the ultimate customer.

Autonomy: None. The operators had no freedom to arrange their daily tasks to meet schedules, to resolve problems with the using department, or even to correct, in punching, information that was obviously wrong.

Feedback: None. Once a batch was out of the operator's hands, she had no assured chance of seeing evidence of its quality.

Design of the experimental trial

Since the diagnosis indicated that the motivating potential of the job was extremely low, it was decided to attempt to improve the motivation and productivity of the work group through job enrichment. Moreover, it was possible to design an experimental test of the effects of the changes to be introduced. The results of changes made in the target work group were to be compared with trends in a control work group of similar size and demographic makeup. Since the control group was located more than a mile away, there appeared to be little risk of communication between members of the two groups.

A base period was defined before the start of the experimental trial period, and appropriate data were gathered on the productivity, absenteeism, and work attitudes of members of both groups. Data were also available on turnover, but, since turnover was already below average in the target group, prospective changes in this measure were deemed insignificant.

An educational session was conducted with supervisors, at which time they were given the theory and implementing concepts and actually helped to design the job changes themselves. Out of this session came an active plan consisting of about twenty-five change items that would significantly affect the design of the target jobs.

The implementing concepts and the changes. Because the job as it existed was uniformly low on the core job dimensions, all five implementing concepts were used in enriching it.

Natural units of work. The assignment of work in random batches was replaced by assigning to each operator continuing responsibility for certain accounts—either particular departments or particular recurring jobs. Any work for those accounts would now always go to the same operator.

Task combination. Some planning and controlling functions were combined with the central task of keypunching. However, these additions are more suitably discussed under the remaining three implementing concepts.

Client relationships. Each operator was given several channels of direct contact with clients. The operators, not their assignment clerks, then inspected their documents for correctness and legibility. When problems arose, the operator, not the supervisor, took them up with the client.

Feedback. In addition to feedback from client contact, the operators were provided with a number of additional sources of data about their performance. The computer department returned incorrect cards to the operators who punched them, and operators corrected their own errors. Each operator kept her own file of copies of her errors that could be reviewed to determine trends in error frequency and types of errors. Each operator received weekly a computer printout of her errors and productivity, sent directly, not handed out by the supervisor.

Vertical loading. Besides consulting directly with clients about work questions, operators now had the authority to correct obvious coding errors on their own. Operators set their own schedules and planned their daily work, as long as they met schedules. Some competent operators were given the options of not verifying their work and making their own program changes.

Results of the trial. The results were dramatic. The number of operators declined from ninety-eight to sixty. This occurred partly through attrition and partly through transfer to other departments. Some of the operators were promoted to higher-paying jobs in departments whose cards they had been handling—something that had never occurred before. The following outlines some details of the results.

Quantity of work. The control group, with no job changes made, showed an increase in productivity of 8.1 percent during the trial period. The experimental group showed an increase of 39.6 percent.

Error rates. To assess work quality, error rates were recorded for about forty operators in the experimental group. All were experienced and all had been in their jobs before the job-enrichment program began. For two months before the study, these operators had a collective error rate of 1.53 percent. For two months toward the end of the study, the collective error rate was 0.99 percent. By the end of the study the number of operators with poor performance had dropped from 11.1 percent to 5.5 percent.

Absenteeism. The experimental group registered a 24.1 percent decline in absences. The control group, by contrast, showed a 29.0 percent increase.

Attitudes toward the job. An attitude survey given at the start of the project showed that the two groups scored about average, and nearly identically, in nine different areas of work satisfaction. At the end of the project the survey was repeated. The control group showed an insignificant 0.5 percent improvement, whereas the experimental group's overall satisfaction score rose 16.5 percent.

Selective elimination of controls. Demonstrated improvements in operator proficiency permitted them to work with fewer controls. Travelers estimates that the reduction of controls had the same effect as adding seven operators—a savings even beyond the effects of improved productivity and lowered absenteeism.

Role of the supervisor. One of the most significant findings in the Travelers experiment was the effect of the changes on the supervisor's job and, thus, on the rest of the organization. The operators took on many responsibilities that had been reserved for the unit leaders and sometimes for the supervisor. The unit leaders, in turn, assumed some of the day-to-day supervisory functions that had plagued the supervisor. Instead of spending his days supervising the behavior of subordinates and dealing with crises, he was able to devote time to developing feedback systems, setting up work modules, and spearheading the enrichment effort—in other words, managing. It should be noted, however, that helping supervisors change their own work activities when their subordinates' jobs have been enriched is itself a challenging task. And, if appropriate attention and help are not given to supervisors in such cases, they rapidly can become dissatisfied, and a job-enrichment "backlash" can result.

Summary

By applying work measurement standards to the changes produced by job enrichment—attitude and quality, absenteeism, and selective administration of controls—Travelers was able to estimate the total dollar impact of the project. Actual savings in salaries and machine rental charges during the first year totaled $64,305. Potential savings by further application of the changes were put at $91,937 annually. Thus, by almost any measure used—from the work attitudes of individual employees to dollar savings for the company as a whole—the Travelers test of the job-enrichment strategy proved a success.

PROBLEM SOLVING AND GOAL SETTING

Developed at Texas Instruments, the problem-solving–goal-setting approach is based upon building motivators into work by the application of Herzberg's motivator–hygiene theory.[4] The problem-solving–goal-setting application is different, however, in that the change is made by the work group rather than by supervisors or higher-level managers. Additionally, the approach seeks to add management responsibilities to the employees' jobs rather than to focus primarily upon the nature of the work performed.

The Basic Approach

The problem-solving–goal-setting theory notes that there are three broad approaches to work—planning, doing, and controlling. Planning and controlling, which involve problem solving, goal setting, using resources, and checking performance against goals, are traditional managerial functions; the doing of the work, or implementation of the planning, is the role usually assigned to employees. However, the motivators are more likely to be an inherent part of planning and control, not the work itself. Consequently, to be meaningful, the employees' work should be expanded to include planning and control. Planning makes work meaningful because it ties the performing or the doing of the work to setting goals. Likewise, controlling makes work more meaningful because it provides the feedback needed for improvement, growth, and satisfaction. The most meaningful and motivating work involves all three activities—planning, doing, and controlling. Every employee becomes a manager when jobs are redesigned following this approach.

The Problem-Solving–Goal-Setting Process

Although the employees are to be involved in planning, doing, and controlling, the supervisor is central to the process. The supervisor must be familiar with motivation theory and the meaningful ingredients of work.

This serves as a basis for determining the difference between existing work group conditions and the meaningful work model. In addition, the supervisor evaluates the work group to determine if its members are prepared to plan, do, and control. To achieve this purpose, the supervisor seeks answers to such questions as the following.

Plan: Can the group—

Name customers and state delivery dates for products and services?
State the product quality and quantity commitments?
Organize their work layouts and influence assignments?
Set goals and standards based on customer needs and fix priorities?
State the sources of their materials and problems in obtaining them?
List direct and overhead costs, selling price, and other profit and loss information?

Do: Does the job—

Utilize people's talents and require their attention?
Enable people to see the relationship of their work to other operations?
Provide access to all the information they need to do their work?
Have a satisfactory work cycle—neither too long nor too short?
Give people feedback on how well they are doing?
Enable them to see how they contribute to the usefulness of the product?

Control: Can the group—

State customer quality requirements and reasons for these standards?
Keep their own records of quality and quantity?
Check quality and quantity of work and revise procedures?
Evaluate and modify work layout on their own initiative?
Identify and correct unsafe work conditions?
Obtain information from people outside the group as a means of evaluating performance?

Planning and control responsibilities are added to the employees' jobs by having them participate in customer problems and the group's problems in serving customer needs. Problem-solving–goal-setting conferences provide the setting for this. The following steps outline the flow of events in such a setting.

1. Supervisor presents the customer problem and background information to his or her work group.
2. Supervisor details the costs, profits, and schedules relating to the problem.
3. Group helps to define the problem and suggests possible solutions. No evaluation of ideas is made at this point.
4. Supervisor records and displays suggestions. Supervisor does not contribute ideas or evaluate the group's ideas.
5. Ideas are classified, grouped, and evaluated, and applications are planned for the most promising ideas by the group.

6. Group sets a new performance goal in the problem area and returns to work.
7. Group members receive a summary of problems, suggestions, and goals made in the conference.
8. Ideas are implemented in the work area; technical assistance is provided if needed.
9. Problem-solving group is reconvened to review results and present suggestions.

The group may be expanded to broaden its scope of technical competence if necessary after the last step. For example, engineering or staff assistance may be requested. With the enlarged group, the group again lists and evaluates suggestions; then new goals are set. Working as an expanded group takes place only as deemed necessary.

An Application

Successful applications of the problem-solving–goal-setting job enrichment technique have been reported at Texas Instruments.[5] One notable example occurred with a group of women employees who assembled a complex instrument according to methods prescribed by the engineering department. The standard time for assembly had been calculated at 100 hours, but it had actually taken the group 138 hours. The employees were paid on an hourly basis and the company was losing money on the contract.

A problem-solving–goal-setting conference was held by the supervisor. After deciding on new assembly methods, the group set a goal of assembling the instrument in eighty-six hours, or fifty-two hours less than previously and fourteen hours less than the standard one hundred hours. The new assembly time was actually lowered to seventy-five hours, and after another group conference a new goal of sixty-five hours was set. Again the goal was surpassed, and actual assembly required only fifty-seven hours. After another session, an assembly time of thirty-two hours was achieved on a consistent basis. Not only was productivity increased and cost reduced but the group experienced more satisfaction as measured by an attitude survey.

SOCIOTECHNICAL APPROACH

The concept of a production system as a sociotechnical system was introduced by Trist and Bamforth.[6] Any production system requires both a technology—machines, plant layout, raw materials—and a work relationship structure that relates the human operators both to the technology and to each other. The technology makes demands and places limits on the type of work structure possible, whereas the work structure itself has social and psychological properties that generate their own unique requirements with regard to the task to be done.

When the sociotechnical concept is applied or utilized as a basis for job redesign, it involves structuring work around self-regulating work teams that perform relatively whole tasks. This requires a good deal of planning and spelling out of what the organization should delegate to the autonomous work group and what decisions management should retain. Workgroups are organized around relatively whole tasks and set their own standards within the broad limits determined by higher management. Typical changes in the work situation include increases in autonomy, task variety, information feedback, technical or machine support, and the use of small items.

The British Coal Industries

The authors of the sociotechnical approach applied it in a series of studies investigating changes in the British coal mining industry.[7] Changes in the industry were due to economic and technical pressures. Mechanized systems of coal extraction had reduced costs but alternative energy sources had still become more competitive.

In the original production system, a small group of men worked autonomously, shared all the required tasks among them, and experienced the entire cycle of operations. The new "longwall" method which utilized modern technology, permitted work on a single long face of coal. Work was segmented into three cycles whereby each shift had different tasks to perform. The work team became a unit of forty men distributed over three specialized work shifts. Each worker was assigned to one job category.

The small-group system was in effect replaced by a production line system. The technological change, however, had the potential for enormous economic advantages, but the change in the social system of the mine was detrimental to the workers and their output. Incomplete work and bad preparation on one shift disrupted the work of the next shift, created more danger, and resulted in harder work but less pay. The system created tension and anxiety in the workers; absenteeism increased and men simply left the mines. A subsequent study combined some of the social system characteristics of the traditional system with the improved mechanized equipment to produce the "composite longwall." The composite method proved to be superior in every respect when compared with a conventional longwall mining operation.

Recent Sociotechnical Studies

Several additional efforts in the sociotechnical mode of job redesign are noted here to illustrate some of the approaches taken and the results obtained.[8] Most of the serious efforts have taken place outside of the United States.

At Phillips N.V. in the Netherlands, for example, groups of seven or eight employees were given total responsibility for assembling black-and-white TV sets and color selectors for color TV sets, a task equivalent in complexity to assembling a black-and-white set from scratch. Group responsibilities for assembling the black-and-white sets also involved dealing with staff groups such as procurement, quality, and stores, with no supervisor or foreman to act as intermediary or expediter. Results have been mixed. It required about six months for the groups to become accustomed to the increased pressures and responsibilities. Training costs, as one would expect, increased. Most significantly, however, the small, autonomous groups required new and smaller machines to perform their previous assembly line tasks. On the other hand, production costs in labor-hours dropped 10 percent, waiting times decreased, and quality levels increased by small, but still meaningful, amounts.

Saab-Scania initiated limited experiments that involved several sections of their production effort. In the truck chassis assembly operation, production groups of five to twelve workers decide among themselves how they will do their jobs, within the quality and production standards defined by higher management. Members of the work team can rotate job assignments, that is, do a smaller or larger part of the overall task. The jobs of all production members have been enlarged by making the team responsible for simple services and maintenance activities, housekeeping, and quality control in their work area. Employee reception of the production group work arrangement has been mixed but largely positive. Nothing was done to measure the results quantitatively.

In one of its truck assembly plants, Volvo also has developed production teams of five to twelve persons with a common work assignment. Each group elects its own chargehand, schedules its own output within the standard set by higher management, distributes work among its members, and is responsible for its own quality control. In these teams, group piecework replaces individual piecework, and everyone earns the same amount. Even though these jobs were considered inherently more complex and interesting prior to redesign, the change to teams has resulted in less labor turnover, less absenteeism, an improvement in quality, and fewer final adjustments.

The General Foods Corporation structured an entire plant in Topeka to provide a high-quality work life, enlist human involvement, and improve productivity.[9] To achieve these objectives, the total work force of approximately seventy employees was organized into six self-managed work teams who were given responsibility for large segments of the production process. The teams varied in size from seven to fourteen members, and each has an appointed, or formal, group leader. Assignments of individuals to sets of tasks are subject to team consensus. Although an operator has primary responsibility for a set of tasks, some tasks can be shared by several operators. Moreover, tasks can be redefined by the team in light of individual capabilities and interests. In contrast to traditional work design, the teams coordinate and handle production problems, screen and select new team members, repair all but the most complicated of the machines that they operate, inspect their own work, and counsel team members who fail to meet group production and attendance standards. The results have been impressive. Seventy workers operate the plant rather than the one hundred and ten previously estimated to be necessary, quality rejects are 92 percent below the industry average, absenteeism is 9 percent below the industry norm, turnover is below average for the company, and there has been an annual savings of $600,000 from reductions in variable manufacturing costs.

From these examples, we can see that the sociotechnical approach is similar to job redesign, wherein simple elements of a job previously distributed among individual workers are recombined into a larger whole. However, in the sociotechnical approach, the reconstructed jobs are assigned to a group rather than to individuals. The objective is to establish a cohesive social unit of workers that is integrated with meaningful technological arrangements. The work group also has sufficient autonomy and responsibility as a group for the total task.[10]

SOME CRITICAL COMMENTS

As we have seen, the Job Diagnostic Survey was designed to meet some of the limitations of job redesign. However, further note must be taken of these limitations and the questions that have been raised about job design.[11]

Congruency Test

The focus upon tasks to achieve an optimal structure of job duties may cause one to overlook other significant but interdependent factors. A fit must exist among the task, people, social structure, and the formal system.[12] A short description of what each includes follows.

1. Task—what the employees do to perform effectively.
2. People—capabilities, background, and expectations.
3. Social structure—informal statuses and relationships.
4. Formal system—setting objectives, measuring performance, and the reward system.

These factors comprise the elements of a system, and, as such, their interdependence must be considered.

As noted, job design has often failed to "pay off" because the capacities, background, needs, and expectations of the employees were ignored. Equally important is the social system that is affected by job redesign and the flow of work. Jobs may be made independent of one another or relatively separated from one another. Both factors may alter informal statuses and relations and deprive the workers of social and other satisfactions derived from the existing social system. Improvements in performance may be short-lived if the social or informal interactions are threatened. The social system may turn against management and the redesigned jobs. All these considerations point to the danger inherent in redesigning without evaluating its impact or its implications for the social structure of the work group. Chapter 8 will take a close look at the work group and its implications for performance and employee satisfactions.

Finally, once jobs have been redesigned, they must be subject to some degree of formal management control. This is evident in measurements, evaluation, and rewards, which are tied together. Performance measurements are used in the evaluation of employees, and evaluation becomes the basis for administering rewards. Redesigned job performance must be measured, evaluated, and rewarded if employee expectations of fair treatment and justice are to be met.

Job redesign affects the task, people, social structure, and the formal system.[13] Failure to consider all these factors invites an inadequate change effort. The sociotechnical method of job redesign directs more attention to the interrelationship of these factors than do other approaches.

Community Variables

Several industrial field studies have indicated the importance of community variables as determiners of workers' performance and satisfaction. Others indicated that the effects of job reengineering on job satisfaction and/or motivaton may be applicable only to certain segments of the working population. From these studies and from the sociological studies of alienation, Blood and Hulin formulated and tested a construct for predicting workers' responses to job redesign.[14] This construct stipulates there is a continuum of alienation running from "integration with middle class norms" to "alienation from middle-class norms." The characteristics of workers at these two extremes are shown on the next page.

Drawing upon other studies, the investigators sought to determine what environmental factors led to alienation from middle-class norms. It was concluded that "alienation from middle-class norms" results from lack

Integrated with Middle-Class Norms	Alienated from Middle-Class Norms
Personal job involvement	Job is means for obtaining extra-occupational goals
Occupational aspirations	Concern is for money
Upward mobility	Concern is minimal for personal involvement, increased responsibilty, high status, and more autonomy

of socialization to these norms. Alienation is fostered by industrialized, socially diversified, metropolitan conditions. Workers in large cities with heterogeneous social cultures are less likely to develop or adopt middle-class values of hard work, attainment of responsible positions, and the like. Alienated workers are not normless but simply have norms that differ from those of the middle class. Their segment of society in urban centers is large enough to sustain their own culture and socialize their members into that culture. Workers separated from middle-class identification by low educational attainment or low occupational status and by living in ghettos, slums, and highly industrialized communities are likely to develop and sustain a different norm system. On the other hand, workers from small, rural locations readily internalize middle-class values that are perpetuated by their families and communities.

The investigators based their analysis on 1,390 blue-collar and 511 white-collar workers employed in 21 plants located throughout the eastern half of the country. The plants were classified according to community characteristics such as extent of slums, urbanization, population density, standard of living, and so on. These dimensions were considered to indicate the degree to which workers in the communities would feel alienated from middle-class work norms and would be reflected in preparation for retirement, work satisfactions, pay satisfactions, and the like. Two predictions were confirmed beyond the chance level.

1. Blue-collar workers having a low standard of living, from small communities, slums, and so on responded in a manner consistent with middle-class behavior. White-collar workers respond in the same manner.
2. Workers from large, industrialized communities and large slum areas did not respond as expected or responded in a manner opposite to middle-class behaviors.

Using an urban–rural division to classify worker alienation from middle-class work norms gave the following overview.[15]

Type of Worker	Urban Location	Rural Location
Blue collar	Alienated	Nonalienated
White collar	Nonalienated	Nonalienated

The investigators concluded the nonalienated subgroups would respond positively to redesigned jobs, whereas the alienated blue-collar workers from an urban location would not likely do so. Alienated workers may be happiest when given a job that demands little personal involvement either in terms of task skills or identification with the goals of management. Consequently, there are dangers in assuming that the basic human needs of all people include self-actualization, autonomy, responsibility, a demanding job, and so on.[16] The investigators conceded that alienation from middle-class norms is not the only explanation of their findings. An explanation based on differing "needs" being generated by urban and rural environments is equally plausible.

A Questionable Assumption

A basic assumption of job enrichment is that, as jobs become increasingly specialized and fragmented, the unchanging nature of the job from minute to minute produces monotony.[17] Concomitantly, monotony is associated with feelings of boredom and job dissatisfaction, which in turn leads to undesirable behavior. This reasoning has been diagrammed as follows:

The line of reasoning, however, ignores individual differences. Does repetitiveness always lead to monotony? Are all workers on the same job susceptible to monotony? One investigator indicates that some workers do not report feelings of monotony when working on a job with an extremely short work cycle. Another researcher has noted that repetitive work can be positively motivating and tends to pull the worker along. Consequently, it would seem that the assumption that repetitiveness leads to monotony ignores the potential effect of individual differences. The same applies to the implication that monotony leads to boredom and job dissatisfaction. People may not respond in this manner! The possibility exists that some workers prefer the safety of little job variety and no decision making. Finally, since employees may have differential emotional responses to monotony, that is, the presence or absence of boredom and job dissatisfaction, it does not follow that absenteeism or turnover will be higher or that output will be restricted. However, if job enrichment had no other result than decreased boredom and increased job satisfaction, it could be an appropriate change.

Another study dealt with individual differences that were labeled "higher-order need strength" to gauge an individual's receptivity to job enrichment.[18] This variable is measured by a questionnaire requesting expressions of belief or disbelief in a number of statements related to Maslow's self-actualization needs. Some people are high in "growth need strength" and typically report greater satisfaction if their jobs have a great deal of variety and autonomy. Workers whose growth needs are not so strong may balk at being "pushed" or "stretched" too far by enriched jobs. From such measures of higher-order needs, it is possible to predict who is likely to become internally motivated on a job and who will be less willing or able to do so.

The varied worker reactions to repetitive jobs may be due to intrinsic job and personal characteristics not appreciated by job-enrichment advocates. Many employees may perceive work as a form of punishment that is uninteresting, demeaning, oppressive, and inconsistent with personal goals. However, work is an activity that they take in stride or an unpleasantness that they are willing to endure to get the money needed to buy goods and services that are related to personal goals. Apart from the needs satisfied through job income, work, however dull and menial, satisfies a wide variety of motives:[19]

> Work reduces role ambiguity. It establishes the worker's identity and, though the self-image may not be an attractive one, for most it is better than an undefined role.

> Work offers socializing opportunities. Close and sustained association with others having similar job goals, socioeconomic backgrounds, and interests are natural conditions for social compatibility.

> Work increases solidarity. The performance of similar tasks, however routine, is a shared ritual which provides a basis for equality and role acceptance.

> Work bolsters security feelings. Apart from the security related to economics, for many persons, feelings of security require continuous affirmation from authority figures. Authority-oriented people, particularly when deprived of meaningful work roles, have unusually high requirements for feedback from the supervisor to satisfy their security and achievement needs.

Work is a substitute for unrealized potential. "Keeping busy" channels energy or thwarted intellectual capability and helps obscure the reality of unfulfilled potential. Though it is an escape mechanism, at least it is less punishing than alcoholism or other means of escape, and it helps to buy freedom and opportunity off the job which gives better expression to talent. Furthermore, fatigue from an "honest day's work" evokes social approval.

Work is an escape from the home environment. Particularly for women whose homemaking roles are unfulfilled or completed, a job provides an opportunity for getting away from home. Other reasons for wanting to get away from home include domestic conflict, neighborhood friction, unattractive home facilities, and loneliness.

Work reduces feelings of guilt and anxiety. In an achieving society where dignity and pride are earned through the traits of ambition, initiative, industriousness, and perseverance, idleness violates deep-seated values, and work for work's sake is virtuous. By Protestant ethic standards, idleness is the equivalent of stealing, and a strong conscience is a key motive for staying on the job.

These observations illustrate unanticipated potential reactions and adjustments by some workers that are not fully appreciated. Additionally, such reactions may explain the unpredictable reactions to job design and especially the failure of some efforts to appreciably change job satisfaction, productivity, turnover, and absenteeism to the extent anticipated by managers and job researchers. Despite some failures, a summary of reports on job redesign projects indicate the following results.[20]

1. Turnover and absenteeism have generally decreased.
2. Quality of output has improved.
3. Satisfaction has increased.
4. Some, but not universal, improvements in productivity and output rates have been achieved.

Much of the job enrichment work has been done on white-collar jobs. Some critics argue that its application is appropriate primarily for white-collar and professional employees because it is extremely difficult to change blue-collar jobs without large economic costs. There is no doubt that real and encompassing constraints are imposed by the technology with which work is done and that change requires considerable investment in new equipment or facilities.[21] However, the belief that technology makes any change impossible for large classes of jobs is ill founded. The sociotechnical experiences cited in this chapter (and others at Maytag, Morotola, and Non Linear Systems) refute this belief. In the factory, as well as in the office, significant job enrichment has been effected and major performance improvements have been achieved.

SUMMARY

Several approaches to job design have been presented and evaluated. The Job Diagnostic Survey provides not only a different theoretical foundation for job design but also a questionnaire to analyze the characteristics of the total job setting in a systematic manner. The employees to be involved and subsequent job changes are determined by a careful diagnostic procedure that overcomes many of the weaknesses of previous job redesign applications.

The problem-solving–goal-setting approach to job redesign provides a manager with still another option. Expanding the employee's role from merely performing the job to include planning and controlling functions is used to enrich the job. Changes are originated and implemented by the employees who function as a group. While the job may be changed, this is not the central focus or concern of this method. Every employer becomes a manager with planning, performing, and controlling responsibilities.

The sociotechnical approach to job enrichment emphasizes the work group's social structure and technological aspects of work. This requires structuring work around self-regulating work teams that perform relatively whole tasks. Contrary to other job redesign methods, the reengineered jobs are assigned to a group rather than to individuals.

Finally, a critical look was taken of job enrichment. Monotony and boredom is not experienced by everyone with repetitive, short-time-cycle jobs. Dull and menial work may satisfy various needs to an extent not really appreciated by managers. Finally, the theme of individual differences was interjected into job enrichment. Not everyone desires challenge, achievement, or a greater decision-making role!

QUESTIONS FOR STUDY AND DISCUSSION

1. According to Hackman and Oldham what are the three critical psychological states necessary for motivation? What job characteristics are associated with or produce each psychological state?

2. Compare the Herzberg approach to job enrichment given in the previous chapter with that of Hackman and Oldham's Job Diagnostic Survey. Similarities? Differences?

3. What does "every employee a manager" mean? How is this achieved?

4. What is the role of the work group in problem solving and goal setting? The supervisor?

5. What does the sociotechnical approach to job design mean? How is it implemented?

6. Relate the "congruency test" to the various job redesign approaches. Do some seem to meet this test better than others? Which one(s)?

7. What is the basic assumption of job enrichment? What are its weaknesses?

8. As a manager, would you undertake a program of job enrichment? What results would you expect?

NOTES

[1]Hackman, Richard J., Greg Oldham, Robert Janson, and Kenneth Purdy, "A New Strategy for Job Enrichment," *California Management Review,* 17 (Summer, 1975), 55–71. Also See Dunham, Randall B., Ramon J. Aldag, and Arthur P. Brief, "Dimensionality of Task Design as Measured by the Job Diagnostic Survey," *Academy of Management Journal,* 20, (June 1977), 209–223.

[2]*Ibid.,* p. 66.

[3]*Ibid.,* pp. 67–69.

[4]Myers, Scott M., *Every Employee a Manager* (New York: McGraw-Hill, 1970), pp. 70–80.

[5]Foulkes, Fred K., *Creating More Meaningful Work* (New York: American Management Association, 1969), pp. 56–96.

[6]Trist, E. L., and K. W. Bamforth, "Some Social and Psychological Consequences of the Longwall Method of Coal-Getting," *Human Relations* 4 (1951), 3–38.

[7]Trist, E. L., G. Higgins, H. E. Pollock, and H. A. Murray, *Organizational Choice,* (London: Tavistock, 1963).

[8]Editor, "Job Redesign on the Assembly Line: Farewell to Blue-Collar Blues?" *Organizational Dynamics* 2, (1973), 51–67.

[9]Walton, Richard E., "How to Counter Alienation in the Plant," *Harvard Business Review,* 50, (Nov.-Dec. 1972), 70–81.

[10]Cummings, Thomas G., "Self-Regulating Work Groups: A Socio-Technical Synthesis," *Academy of Management Review* 3, (July 1978), 625–634.

[11]Pierce, Jon L. and Randall B. Dunham, "Task Design: A Literature Review," *Academy of Management Review,* 1, (October 1976), 83–97.

[12]Dalton, Gene W. and Paul R. Lawrence, *Motivation and Control in Organizations* (Homewood, Ill.: Irwin, 1971), pp. 20–35.

[13]Pierce, Jon L., Randall B. Dunham, and Richard S. Blackburn, "Social System Structure, Job Design, and Growth Need Strength: A Test of a Congruency Model," *Academy of Management Journal* 22, (June 1979), 223–240.

[14]Blood, Milton R., and Charles L. Hulin, "Alienation, Environmental Characteristics, and Worker Responses," *Journal of Applied Psychology* 51, (June, 1967), 284–290.

[15]Hulin, Charles L., and Milton R. Blood, "Job Enlargement, Individual Differences, and Worker Responses," *Psychological Bulletin* 69, (1968), 41–55.

[16]Steers, Richard M., and Richard T. Mowday, "The Motivational Properties of Task," *Academy of Management Review* 2, (October 1977), 645–658.

[17]Hulin, Charles L., "Individual Differences and Job Enrichment—The Case Against General Treatments," in Richard M. Steers and Lyman W. Porter, eds., *Motivation and Work Behavior* (New York: McGraw-Hill, 1975), pp. 425–436.

[18]Hackman, J. R. and E. E. Lawler, "Employee Reactions to Job Characteristics," *Journal of Applied Psychology* 55, (June 1971), 259–286.

[19]Myers, *op. cit.,* pp. 67–69.

[20]Steers, Richard M. and Lyman W. Porter, *Motivation and Work Behavior,* 2nd ed., (New York: McGraw-Hill, 1979), 392.

[21]Sirota, David and Alan D. Wofson, "Job Enrichment: What are the Obstacles?" *Personnel* 49, (May-June 1972), 8–17.

cases cases cases

Case Study: Problems in a Profession

The managing partner summed up his major problem:

"Personnel turnover has been our biggest problem. Every time we have built our staff to meet our requirements, something happens. We lose key people, obtain a client with a pressing deadline for an SEC filing, or have to loan our people out to other offices because they're short. It puts an additional burden on the rest of the staff, causing increased overtime and out-of-town travel, which are the major causes of our turnover. It's a vicious cycle. But that's part of the business. It's been that way all during my career, and it will probably never change. We plan for the turnover, but when it comes it's always a shock. I don't understand it though. Right now there's more opportunity for a person who's willing to put forth the time and effort than in any other profession. You'd think people would realize this. Almost every one of them would have made more money with us than where they've gone. They have severely limited themselves by leaving the firm.

"Where the turnover really hurts is in the staff level—people with one to three years of experience. A high turnover in this level disrupts the normal replacement of seniors and managers. We've experienced a higher turnover than expected in this level. It seems that we are hiring a different type of individual today. They are impatient. They want everything right now. They don't seem to believe in working for their promotions and earning additional responsibilities. They don't realize that it takes time to gain experience in this business so that they know what they're doing."

The accounting firm provides the following types of service to its clients.

Description	% of Total
Audits, opinions on examinations of financial statements	60%
Tax services	25
Management advisory services, consultant services	15

The professional staff is segregated into four levels; staff, senior, manager, and partner. The "average" progression is about three years to promotion to senior, six years to manager, and ten to fifteen years to partner.

Heavy amounts of overtime and out-of-town travel are the rule. The jobs are generally understaffed at the senior and manager levels. Audits are often being made by staff with no more than a year's experience.

When the junior accountants are required to travel, a regular occurrence during the tax season, they are expected to leave as early as 4:00 A.M. to ensure an eight-hour work day on location. This travel time is not considered part of the employee's working time, so no remuneration is received for these hours. The same is true of the return trips, which result in the employees' arriving home as late as 9:00 P.M., three and one-half hours after ceasing to be paid. They are often notified at the last minute of proposed travel obligations and are sometimes forced to return home to pack for a trip that had been planned days earlier by superiors.

The following information was obtained from two persons leaving the firm. An audit manager summed up his reasons for leaving:

"I've been working like a slave for the last six years. There's no prospect of its letting up in the future. They won't hire the people we need to do the work. And I sure am sick of doing the same work year after year. It doesn't look like there's anybody to take my place so I can move on to something different.

"The boss won't let go of the damn jobs, either. He's always into my jobs, nosing into things that I should take care of and then bitching about the time charges. The previous manager made me work like a dog, but at least he let me run my own jobs and make my own mistakes."

In a conversation with a staff accountant prior to his leaving,

"I know the first couple of years you get only grunt work—a lot of the routine work that someone has to do. I don't mind doing it. What I mind is doing it long after I can learn from it because there's no one else to do it. Nobody's coming up to take my place. I've had one year's experience two times. I'm not staying around for a third time."

Before leaving, another audit manager stated,

"It's a real dilemma. All firms want intelligent, well-educated people.

The ones that can afford it hire the cream of the crop from the best schools and tell them they will be challenged, that they will need to be creative and imaginative in their work. Then what happens? The firms hand them a canned program and tell them to hit the audit trail. If they deviate from the program, it takes more time and effort for them to justify the deviation than it does to follow the program. This may be an oversimplification, but more often than not there is a premium on routine, mechanical, repetitious activity.

"The work as an end in itself is unrewarding and uninteresting. Who really cares about a 'good' audit? It's an intangible and almost unmeasurable; it's a negative type of effort—you only hear about your mistakes. The work has to be viewed as a means to another end and that requires a motivator."

QUESTIONS

1. Evaluate the managing partner's comments at the beginning of the case. How does his perception of the situation differ from the perceptions of those leaving the firm?

2. Referring to the Job Diagnostic Survey's three critical psychological states necessary for motivation, which one(s) appear missing according to the comments of those leaving the firm.

3. Relate the statements of terminating personnel to the five job dimensions or characteristics in the job-enrichment model. What inferences do you draw from this comparison?

4. What recommendations would you make to the managing partner of the firm?

cases cases cases

Case Study: A Redesigned Job

Mr. Metz, cost accounting supervisor, has reporting to him two cost clerks: Mrs. Lawson and Mrs. Rabinerwitz.

Mrs. Lawson is fifty-four years of age and has been employed in the cost accounting department for five years. After five years of employment, she still maintains the same job grade. Her grade position is held by all newly employed clerks. Her hourly wage is $3.30 per hour, and she was once denied a yearly pay increase.

At the time that Mr. Metz asumed his new responsibilities as Mrs. Lawson's supervisor, her job assignment included:

1. posting invoices to a purchased inventory control sheet
2. transferring certain numerical values from computer reports to the weekly Manufacturing Performance Analysis Work Sheet and the Period Variable Manufacturing Expense Analysis
3. totaling and posting production records on computer cards and, after the computer runs, sorting and mailing these reports to the mill managers

Because Mrs. Lawson did not have a full job assignment, she was often asked to perform other work that was very tedious and repetitious. Included in this work were:

1. the extending of physical inventories
2. adding and multiplying long columns of numbers
3. various other tasks

All her weekly and period work was such that she would perform the calculations using prenumbered forms, after which Mr. Metz or Mrs. Rabinerwitz would use these calculations for the closing entries. Because Mrs. Lawson was never allowed to make these entries, she was never able to understand how her work fitted into the overall accounting picture. By not allowing her to follow through and make these entries, she was never able to trace her contribution to the financial statements. Therefore, she could not understand how the computer application took these numbers and printed them into income statements, variance analyses, and balance sheets that were used by management.

For eight months, Mr. Metz allowed the job duties to remain as they had at the time of his arrival. During this time, Mr. Metz noticed that Mrs. Lawson was constantly engaged in lengthy outside conversations with many of the other clerks in the office. He also noticed that she began to extend the length of her coffee breaks and lunch hours and was constantly disrupting some of the other cost personnel with her outside conversations. During the same span of time, Mr. Metz observed Mrs. Lawson on numerous occasions daydreaming during working hours. Even though able to complete her work assignment, she was not performing at the level of her capability. Mr. Metz wrote a new job description for Mrs. Lawson.

1. Preparation of all product information and product reference specifications for computer input.
2. Development and completion of all cost sheets for the five mills.

3. Preparation of all cost ledger closing entries.
4. Audit of all financial statements after period closing.
5. Preparation of the weekly Manufacturing Performance Analysis Work Sheet and Period Variable Manufacturing Expense Analysis.

Mr. Metz began to have informal training sessions with Mrs. Lawson. They discussed each phase of the cost sheets and some of the journal entries that she would be preparing during closing week. Also, during the informal training period, Mr. Metz took each computer report and explained in detail how these reports would be used in her closing work. After approximately four weeks of training, Mrs. Lawson began to work on the cost sheets with very little assistance from Mr. Metz. After auditing a number of the sheets, Mr. Metz found that Mrs. Lawson no longer needed his help in performing this part of her job. While she was gaining experience and a working knowledge of each cost sheet, Mr. Metz began to brief Mrs. Lawson on the procedure that would be used in her period closing work. During the first closing week after this briefing, Mrs. Lawson began to perform the second function in her job description, closing the books of the five mills.

Mrs. Lawson was also seeing the final results of her weekly and period work and was gaining a better understanding of how this information was being used by the management as a tool in evaluating the performance of each of the mills. Although Mrs. Lawson had not completely mastered all phases of her new job assignment, she began to show a concern for the mastering of each phase. She had accepted the new responsibility as a challenge, and, with each day, Mr. Metz noticed that the outside conversations and disturbances that Mrs. Lawson had been creating had stopped.

During the following week, Mr. Metz continually observed the quantity and quality of work that she was performing. He could see a marked improvement in her work and also noticed that coffee and lunch break rules were being followed too. Mrs. Lawson was consulted with on various projects, such as budget work, and began to make a number of contributions on means of improving product cost sheets and cost work sheets that were needed in her period closing work. Also during this time. Mr. Metz asked her to prepare her weekly plans and submit them to him every Monday morning.

QUESTIONS

1. Make an analysis of Mrs. Lawson's job *before* and *after* the job redesign.
2. Analyze Mrs. Lawson's personal behaviors and work performance *before* and *after* the job redesign.
3. What risk was Mr. Metz taking in changing Mrs. Lawson's job?

CHAPTER 6

Job Satisfaction

LEARNING OBJECTIVES

When you have finished this chapter, you should be able to:

- *Make a distinction between job satisfaction and morale.*
- *Explain two models that point to alienated workers.*
- *Evaluate the two positions taken on the connection between job satisfaction and job performance.*
- *Give seven classes of variables associated with job satisfaction and some of the related research findings.*
- *Give four approaches to promote productivity and job satisfaction and their relative effectiveness.*
- *Present the pros and cons of quality of work life indicators.*

In the last chapter we examined several of the factors contributing to individual efficiency as well as approaches that have been used to improve efficiency. In this chapter our primary concern is employee satisfaction.

First, we will examine the role of work in life. Second, we will look at the extent of dissatisfaction and alienation among American workers. Is work central and preeminent to our existence or have other values assumed equal or more importance? Next, we will consider the many factors affecting job satisfaction, concluding with a look at potential integrative mechanisms for a more satisfying organization–people linkage.

SATISFACTION AND MORALE: DEFINITIONS

Our attention must first be directed to the meaning of the terms job satisfaction and morale. Both terms are related but distinguishable from one another. In general, job satisfaction relates to workers' opinions concerning their jobs and their employers; more specifically, job satisfaction may be defined as a pleasurable or positive emotional state resulting from the appraisal of one's job experiences. However, one's affective reaction to his or her job will depend upon the extent to which the job fulfills physical and psychological needs so crucial to survival and well-being. The discrepancy between what one's work offers and what one expects becomes the basis for satisfaction or dissatisfaction.

As we noted previously, job satisfaction and morale are different but interrelated concepts. Morale is[1]

1. an attitude of satisfaction with
2. a desire to continue in and
3. a willingness to strive for the goals of a particular group or organization.

From this definition we see that morale is a group phenomenon, whereas satisfaction refers to the appraisal made by a single individual of his or her job situation. Morale is a reflection of the summed motivation of group members to work together toward a common goal. Also morale is more future oriented, whereas satisfaction is more present and past oriented.

The characteristics of high and low morale have been well outlined as follows.[2] High morale is indicated when

1. the group is held together through internal cohesiveness rather than through external pressures, that is, when there is a strong need to maintain the identity and integrity of the group.
2. there are few disruptive frictions and the group is able to cope with these.
3. the group is adaptable to change that facilitates its development and growth while achieving effectiveness.
4. positive attraction and goodwill exist between group members.
5. the group agrees as to its goals and values.

6. a consensus concerning objectives and style of leadership permits the interactions appropriate to attaining their goal.
7. the group has a strong desire to maintain or continue its existence.

Low morale is indicated when

1. the group disintegrates under pressure and breaks into hostile subgroups.
2. internal strife arises from distrust and criticism.
3. the group cannot resolve its problems when faced with anxiety-generating situations.
4. the absence of friendly emotionalities among members makes it difficult for the group to innovate and create new solutions necessary for survival.
5. there is a lack of consensus on group objectives and values, that is, when individual members have aims that differ from group objectives and negative attitudes toward group purposes.
6. members lack a sense of identification with their group.

Despite the distinctions, one may view morale as being partially caused by job satisfaction; that is, job satisfaction is a component of morale. Some researchers make a distinction between morale and job satisfaction but view the components of each concept as the same in many respects. However, a distinction is made that reserves the term satisfaction for individuals and morale for groups. The text uses these terms in this manner.

THE ROLE OF WORK IN LIFE

How important is work in human life? We all know people whose life is centered around their work (job centered) and others who are community and home centered. Stated differently, work is expressive, a valued end in itself for some persons. For others, the orientation to work is instrumental, that is, the means to earn more money, obtain greater job security, and enjoy more leisure. An instrumental orientation does not mean that one is totally unconcerned as to whether or not his or her job provides intrinsic interest or challenge. Rather, such workers prefer jobs that are highly paid to those that are interesting.[3]

However, an instrumental orientation does not mean that the worker prefers not to work at all. Evidence of the role of work is provided in research that asked a sample of white male workers, "If by chance you inherited enough money to live comfortably without working, do you think you would work anyway?"[4] The vast majority of all workers answered affirmatively; the percentages, however, were somewhat higher for middle-class (86 percent) than for working-class workers (76 percent). Why would they work? The main reason that the middle class (an expressive orientation) would continue to work was related to "interest and accomplishment"; for blue-collar workers (many instrumentally oriented), the main reason for continuing to work was "to keep occupied." The blue-collar workers would rather work than not work, even though working involves just filling time. Working provides organization and structure to their lives!

Although many workers would prefer to work rather than to forego work, there is no doubt that the work ethic is undergoing some change. In Chapter 2, we noted that both college and noncollege persons under twenty-five years of age felt that there must be something more to life than making a living or struggling to make ends meet. The college group and increasingly the older generation do not feel the need to submerge their "real selves" in their work. Self-fulfillment with the material accompaniments are of utmost importance, but subordinate to the main goals of finding just the right life-style for expressing their psychological potential. Even the noncollege youth, including those working in blue-collar jobs, are seeking the kind of success that emphasizes self-fulfillment and quality of life as well as money and security.[5]

Managers can no longer assume that employees hold the same work values as they do, will respond to the same incentives, or accept the traditional quality of work life. For example, one chief executive who has always expected his lieutenants to put in the same seventy-hour work week as he does has been getting a growing number of complaints from departing employees.[6] Even those industries with a "workaholic" reputation—electronics and project-oriented firms—find that professionals and middle-level managers are growing less tolerant of any atmosphere that smacks of workaholism and of executives who assign back-breaking projects without breathers in between. Executive recruiters, who are in an ideal position to spot changing attitudes in companies and employers, say that such situations are becoming more frequent. It is very rare to find younger managers who are wedded to their jobs.

SATISFACTION–DISSATISFACTION: HOW MUCH ALIENATION?

Most Americans spend nearly 25 percent of their total weekly hours working. Predictably, the quality of work life has become of interest to society in general and managers in particular. Terms such as "blue-collar blues," "dehumanization of work," and "worker alienation" have become part of our current vocabulary. However, the question remains whether or not such widely publicized descriptive terms are characteristic of the American work force. How dissatisfied is the average worker with his or her lot?

Two Models of Despair

The potential conflict between the nature of men and women and the technological demands of organization has been debated by many writers. Two excellent models of the variables involved and possible consequences will be presented. Neither model, however, gives empirical results that would indicate the degree of alienation.

Personality versus the Organization Model

The interaction between personality characteristics and the properties of formal organization have been presented by Chris Argyris.[7] In our culture the self tends to develop on specific, observable dimensions as one moves from being an infant to an adult. These growth trends are shown in Table 6-1. One does not necessarily obtain maximal expression of each development trend; rather, by adjusting and adapting, it is hoped that one finds optimal expression.

Table 6-1

Growth Trends of Personality Dimensions

Infant	Adult
Passive	Increasing activity
Dependence	Independence
Behaving in few ways	Behaving in different ways
Few, shallow interests	Deepening of interests
Present determines behavior	Past and future affects on behavior
Subordinate position	Equal and superordinate
Lack of self-awareness	Awareness and control of self

In addition to the model of personality growth Argyris focuses on the properties of formal organizations. Organizations are guided by the following principles.

1. People will behave rationally, that is, as the organization requires.
2. Efficiency is promoted by task specialization.
3. Organizational efficiency is increased by a hierarchy of authority (unity of command).
4. Unity of effort is enhanced by specialization and direction by a single leader.

The net results of these principles are that employees will tend to work in an environment in which (1) they have no control over their workaday world; (2) they are expected to be passive, dependent, subordinate; (3) they are expected to have a short-time perspective; (4) they are induced to perfect and value the frequent use of a few shallow abilities; and (5) they are expected to produce under conditions leading to psychological failure.

All these conditions are inconsistent with those of healthy, mature adults. Such incongruency increases as employees are of increasing maturity, as the formal organization is made more clear-cut for maximum effectiveness, as one goes down the chain of command, and as jobs become more assembly line in nature. What are the results of all this? The employee adapts by:

1. leaving the organization,
2. climbing the organizational ladder,
3. manifesting defense reactions such as daydreaming and aggression,
4. becoming apathetic about organizational goals,
5. reducing the number and potency of needs expected to be fulfilled at work,
6. creating informal groups to sanction defensive reactions and develop group norms to perpetuate such reactions, and
7. emphasizing material factors while minimizing the human or nonmaterial.

Needless to say, these organizational characteristics and resulting behaviors are found to some degree in any organization. Later we will examine methods used to integrate the needs of healthy humans and the objectives of organizations.

An Environmental–Organization Model

A wide-ranging account of the potential sources of dissatisfaction and alienation has been proposed by Richard E. Walton.[8] Like Chris Argyris he also notes the contribution of traditional organizational methods, but he examines broad changes in society as influencing employee alienation from work and organization. Figure 6-1 presents this diagnosis. Social forces—rising levels of wealth and security; declining achievement motivation; rising educational levels; declining emphasis on socialized obedience in schools, families, and churches; and a shifting emphasis from individualism to social commitment—have changed the expectations of employees. Such expectations and forces have been translated into perspectives of personal growth, and the like, as shown in Figure 6-1. The gap between these, as well as other expectations, and what organizations provide generates the potential for alienation.

Some Empirical Evidence of Alienation

Job satisfaction has never been measured systematically and continually as wages, hours, and unemployment. Nevertheless, some idea about national trends in overall job satisfaction have been obtained by comparing

Figure 6-1

Diagnosis of Alienation

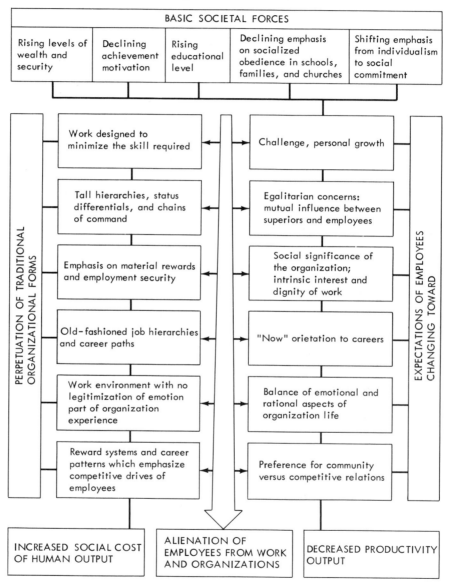

BASIC SOCIETAL FORCES

| Rising levels of wealth and security | Declining achievement motivation | Rising educational level | Declining emphasis on socialized obedience in schools, families, and churches | Shifting emphasis from individualism to social commitment |

PERPETUATION OF TRADITIONAL ORGANIZATIONAL FORMS

EXPECTATIONS OF EMPLOYEES CHANGING TOWARD

Work designed to minimize the skill required	Challenge, personal growth
Tall hierarchies, status differentials, and chains of command	Egalitarian concerns: mutual influence between superiors and employees
Emphasis on material rewards and employment security	Social significance of the organization; intrinsic interest and dignity of work
Old-fashioned job hierarchies and career paths	"Now" orietation to careers
Work environment with no legitimization of emotion part of organization experience	Balance of emotional and rational aspects of organization life
Reward systems and career patterns which emphasize competitive drives of employees	Preference for community versus competitive relations

INCREASED SOCIAL COST OF HUMAN OUTPUT

ALIENATION OF EMPLOYEES FROM WORK AND ORGANIZATIONS

DECREASED PRODUCTIVITY OUTPUT

Source: Dorothy H. Harlow and Jean J. Hanke, *Behavior in Organizations* (Boston: Little, Brown, 1975), p. 508. Reprinted by permission of the Harvard Business Review. Figure adapted from "How to counter alienation in the plant" by Richard E. Walton (November-December 1972.) Copyright ©1972 by the President and Fellows of Harvard College; all rights reserved.

the results of seven national surveys conducted since 1958.[9] The National Opinion Research Center and the Survey Research Centers at the University of Michigan and the University of California all asked the same single question, "All in all, how satisfied are you with your job?" The percentages of workers reporting that they were satisfied with their jobs are shown in Figure 6-2. Spanning a fifteen-year period from 1958 to 1973, the surveys show that job satisfaction for the working population as a whole in-

Figure 6-2

Percentage of "Satisfied" Workers, 1958–1973, Based on Seven National Surveys

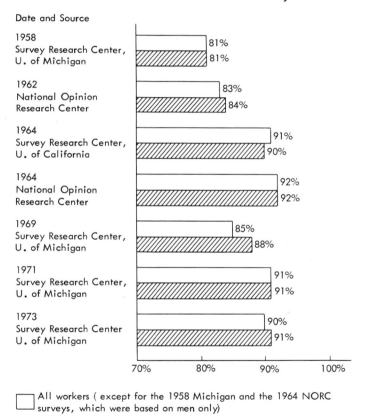

Date and Source

1958
Survey Research Center, U. of Michigan
81%
81%

1962
National Opinion Research Center
83%
84%

1964
Survey Research Center, U. of California
91%
90%

1964
National Opinion Research Center
92%
92%

1969
Survey Research Center, U. of Michigan
85%
88%

1971
Survey Research Center, U. of Michigan
91%
91%

1973
Survey Research Center U. of Michigan
90%
91%

70%   80%   90%   100%

All workers (except for the 1958 Michigan and the 1964 NORC surveys, which were based on men only)

Men only, ages 21 through 65 (except for the 1958 survey, which was based on men 21 or older and which was not available for reanalysis)

Source: Robert P. Quinn, Graham L. Staines, and Margaret R. McCullough, *Job Satisfaction: Is There a Trend?* Manpower Research Monograph No. 30 (Washington, D.C.: Department of Labor, 1974), p. 4.

creased between 1962 and 1964 and remained high until 1973, the last survey year. Comparable results were obtained from eight Gallup polls asking a similar question of men only who were between twenty-one and sixty-five years of age.

From Figure 6-2, it seems clear that there was no substantial change in overall levels of job satisfaction between 1958 and 1973. Since the overall index of satisfaction may mask a number of trends that offset one another, segments of the work force were also analyzed, that is, by race, education, age, and sex. The results disclosed no significant change in the overall satisfaction of blacks, women, and younger workers.

The third, and latest, survey by the University of Michigan Survey Research Center, however, interjects a note of concern. In 1977 a household survey was conducted of 1,515 workers representative of all major demographic and occupational groups. Survey results disclosed an appreciable drop in job satisfaction between 1973 and 1977. This is shown in Figure 6-3.[10]

The decline is significant because it is the first confirmed decline in the national level of job satisfaction and portends trouble if it continues. Although work is highly valued, many workers have a growing disdain for their jobs. This may lead to alienation unless jobs are made more challenging and job-related matters are adjusted to meet expectations.

Figure 6-3

Decline in Overall Job Satisfaction

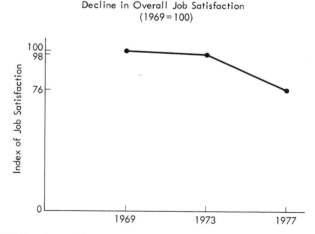

Source: IRS Newsletter, "Study Shows Job Satisfaction Has Decreased," (Ann Arbor: Institute For Social Research, University of Michigan), Spring 1979, p. 10.

MEASURING JOB SATISFACTION

Why do we want to measure job satisfaction? Several purposes are[11]

1. to understand the sources of satisfaction and dissatisfaction,
2. to understand the satisfaction–performance relationship,
3. to learn what areas of the workplace workers are satisfied with or dissatisfied with, and
4. to learn the relationship of satisfaction to training, absenteeism, turnover, and so on.

Moreover, it is generally agreed that most managers of human resources are primarily concerned with reasons 1 and 3 because of their concern with devising remedial measures. However, depending on an organization's philosophy of management, satisfaction may even be perceived as a legitimate goal.

Dimensions of Job Satisfaction

A job is not an entity, but a complex interrelationship of tasks, responsibilities, interactions, incentives, and rewards. Consequently, a thorough understanding of job attitudes requires that the job be analyzed in terms of its elements. The following dimensions of job satisfaction occur in most studies and research investigations.[12]

Work:	Including intrinsic interest, variety, opportunity for learning, difficulty, amount of work, chances for success, control over pace and methods
Pay:	Amount of pay, fairness or equity, method of payment
Promotions:	Opportunity for promotion, fairness, basis for promotion
Recognition:	Praise for accomplishment, credit for work done, criticism
Benefits:	Pension, medical, annual leave, paid vacations
Working conditions:	Hours, rest breaks, equipment, temperature, ventilation, humidity, location, physical layout
Supervision:	Supervisory style and influence, technical supervision, human relations, administrative skill
Co-workers:	Competence, helpfulness, friendliness
Company and management:	Concern for employee, pay, policies

While many factors affect job satisfaction, two kinds of perceptions—what *should be* and what *actually is*—are instrumental in determining satisfaction or dissatisfaction. The perception of conditions that should exist are the results of one's needs and values, prior job experiences, current social comparisons with others, and reference group influences that shape standards or criteria. The perception of actual job conditions such as compensation, supervision, and work itself provides a basis for comparison with what there should be. Figure 6-4 demonstrates the "mental calculus" involved in deciding the degree or extent of job satisfaction.[13]

Figure 6-4

A Hypothetical Model of Job Satisfaction Determinants

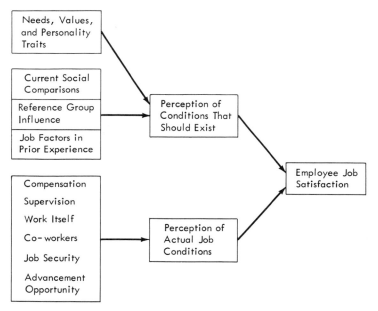

Source: Kenneth Wexley and Gary Yukl, *Organizational Behavior and Personnel Psychology* (Homewood, Ill.: Richard D. Irwin, 1977), p. 109. ©1977 by Richard D. Irwin, Inc.

Two Approaches

The potential connection between employee satisfaction and job performance has occupied the attention of researchers and managers for the past fifty years. In this span of time several conceptualizations of this relationship have emerged; we must examine these positions.[14]

Satisfaction ⟶ performance

The Hawthorne studies and the human relations movement that followed held that satisfaction leads to performance. When workers are satisfied with their job, production is greater and profits are higher. The moral? Keep your workers happy! Keep morale high! Interpretations of the work of Herzberg and his associates provide an example of this view. As you will recall from Chapter 3, job variables were separated into two groups: dissatisfiers (hygienic) and satisfiers (motivators). Included in the dissatisfiers were supervision, physical working conditions, wages, and company policies. Among the satisfiers were factors closely associated with work itself: achievement, recognition, and the like. From this it was concluded that satisfiers were causally related to performance. Build satisfiers into the job and increased productivity will follow. As noted in Chapter 5, improved productivity does not always occur.

Performance ⟶ satisfaction

The human relations movement had postulated that high levels of satisfaction result in high levels of performance, but an opposite view emerged later. The performance–satisfaction view of Porter and Lawler stresses the importance of variations in effort and performance as causes of variations in job satisfaction.[15] Figure 6-5 shows that performance causes

Figure 6-5

Performance ⟶ Satisfaction

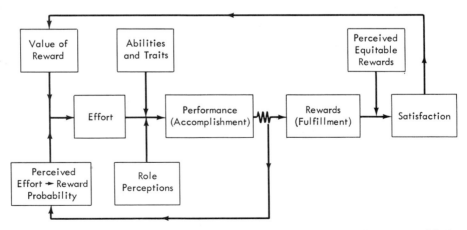

Source: Donald P. Schwab and Larry L. Cummings, "Theories of Performance and Satisfaction: A Review," *Industrial Relations* 9 (October 1970): 418.

satisfaction. This relationship is influenced, however, by both intrinsic rewards and the perceived equity of those rewards. In other words, satisfaction does not occur unless performance is properly rewarded and the employee sees the rewards as fair. For satisfaction to exert an influence on performance, it must affect the value of the rewards to the individual, which in turn interacts with the perceived effort–reward linkage to determine the levels of actual work effort. Finally, effort is influenced by the abilities and traits of the worker and also the role perceptions of clarity or ambiguity.

The Porter-Lawler model has definite administrative implications. It ties high performance to abilities and traits via the selection and training processes. Additionally, it suggests the importance for performance appraisal and wage administration in increasing the effort-reward and performance-reward probabilities. Also, a well-designed wage structure would likely influence the perceived equity of rewards.

A MODEL OF JOB SATISFACTION VARIABLES

From numerous studies Seashore and Taber have structured an overall model of the *clusters of variables* associated with job satisfaction.[16] Figure 6-6 presents a modified version of this model. At the top and to the left are rectangles representing classes of variables thought to be primarily causal in relation to job satisfaction. Environmental variables at the top are distinguished from person variables at the left. On the right are three classes of consequences associated with job satisfaction.

The environmental characteristics range from the macro political-economic environment to specific characteristics of the individual job. While little study has been made of the role of economic, political, and cultural factors, job characteristics and the immediate job environment have been examined intensively. Furthermore, the causes of job satisfaction lie substantially, although far from exclusively, in the immediate realities of jobs and job environments, and they lie even more strongly in the perceptions of these realities.

As noted in Figure 6-6, job satisfaction is affected by the personal characteristics of individual workers that range from demographic to personality characteristics. The situationally determined personality characteristics such as motivations, preferences, and expectations are not direct causes of job satisfaction; rather, they moderate or influence the individual's response to his or her job and work environment. Personality variables are likely to determine what job facets are potentially satisfying or dissatisfying; they do not directly determine the level of satisfaction.

Figure 6-6

Classes of Variables Correlated
with Job Satisfaction

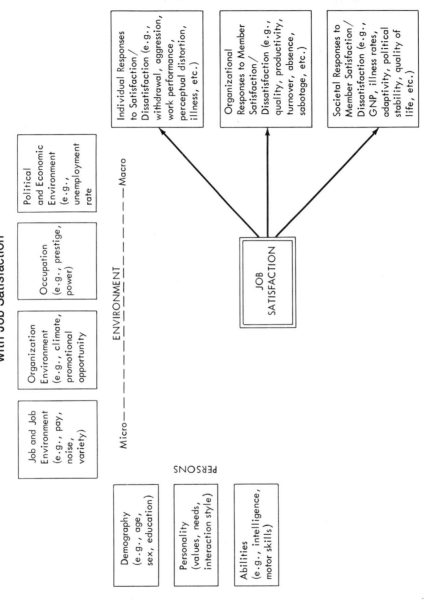

This figure drawn from "Job Satisfaction Indicators and Their Correlates" by Stanley E. Seashore and Thomas D. Taber is reprinted from *American Behavioral Scientist* Vol. 18, No. 3 (January/February 1975) pp. 333–368 by permission of the Publisher, Sage Publications, Inc.

Finally, the potential results of job satisfaction are shown on the right side of the figure. These responses are grouped into individual, organizational, and societal implications. Brief comments will be made on each category of variables associated with job satisfaction.

Environmental Factors and Job Satisfaction

Political and economic environment

No two people have the same orientation to work because of unique backgrounds and experiences. Such differences, as we noted in Chapter 2, are relevant to the shaping of values and attitudes. While very little systematic inquiry has been made into the role of cultural, economic, and political factors as related to job satisfaction, some evidence suggests that this class of variables is relevant. For example, it was found that characteristics of the communities in which workers reside must be considered to understand job satisfaction,[17] based on data obtained from 1,300 blue-collar workers employed in 21 plants in the eastern United States. The urban or rural location of the plant was used as an index of expected alienation from middle-class values such as accomplishment and upward mobility. The investigators found that none of the workers in rural locations were alienated from middle-class values, whereas those in urban locations were. One explanation advanced is that the workers in small towns are more likely influenced by middle-class, Protestant norms and values. Children are taught these values in school and attempt to reach goals defined in terms of these values by means of behavior consistent with these values. Children raised in urban areas are less likely to be Anglo-Saxon or Protestant and less responsive or sympathetic to such a value system. Criticism from peer groups and negative reinforcement tends to extinguish behavior and beliefs consistent with middle-class ideals.

Occupational characteristics

That job satisfaction is related to occupational levels and their general characteristics has been well documented. Among occupational categories, professional–technical workers and managers, officials, and proprietors have the highest level of job satisfaction and are more satisfied than others with the financial rewards and challenges offered by their jobs. Clerical workers, craftspersons, service workers, and farmers occupy the middle category. Operatives and laborers tend to have the lowest job satisfaction.[18] These results are shown in Table 6-2.

The mean values in the table are based on a twenty-eight-question measure of overall job satisfaction. A higher score indicates greater job

Table 6-2

Mean Job Satisfaction by
Major Occupational Groups

Occupational Group	Mean Job Satisfaction
Professional and technical ($N = 322$)	25
Managers, officials, proprietors ($N = 319$)	19
Sales ($N = 112$)	11
Craftsmen and foremen ($N = 270$)	8
Service workers, except private household	-11
Clerical ($N = 364$)	-14
Operatives ($N = 379$)	-35
Nonfarm laborers ($N = 72$)	-42

Source: Robert P. Quinn, Graham L. Staines, and Margaret R. McCullough, *Job Satisfaction: Is There a Trend?* Manpower Research Monograph No. 30 (Department of Labor, Washington, D.C.: 1974), p. 10.

satisfaction. Results similar to those shown have also been found in a survey of job satisfaction studies conducted up to 1960[19]. In that work, occupational differences in job satisfaction were explained as being partially due to occupational prestige and control of work, that is, time, movement, and pace.

Organizational environment

Structural variables such as size, shape, complexity, centralization, and formalization have been found in several studies to be antecedents to job satisfaction. Also decision-making styles, conflict management styles, team collaboration, and role conflict have been found related to job satisfaction. These variables will be explored further in subsequent chapters.

Porter and Lawler have made an excellent survey of studies designed to examine the relationship of facets of the organization structure and job attitudes and behavior.[20] Some of the findings are summarized as follows.

1. Job satisfaction or morale increases steadily with increasing levels of management; middle managers are more satisfied than those below them in the organization but less satisfied than those above. In addition several investigators have made extensive studies using a questionnaire designed to tap satisfaction of different types of needs relevant to a Maslow hierarchical classification of needs. Satisfaction increased with each higher level of management for esteem,

autonomy, and self-actualization needs, whereas, for security and social needs, satisfaction was approximately equal across all levels of management. Patterns of satisfaction are roughly similar *across* each organization level for managerial personnel.

2. The research literature on subunit size (number of employees in primary or work unit) shows that, for blue-collar workers, small-size subunits are characterized by higher job satisfaction, lower absence rates, lower turnover rates, and fewer labor disputes. No consistent relation was obtained for accident rates or productivity. Although small-sized units may not improve job performance directly, the accompanying low turnover and low absenteeism points to their value. The hypothesized effects of subunit size is as follows:

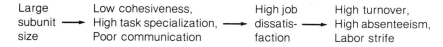

Large subunit size → Low cohesiveness, High task specialization, Poor communication → High job dissatisfaction → High turnover, High absenteeism, Labor strife

As subunits increase in size, it is probably increasingly difficult to maintain high cohesiveness and good communication. Further, task specialization may be more prevalent. Collectively, these factors have the potential for leading to high job dissatisfaction. (Subsequent chapters will deal with the dynamics of small groups.)

3. Tall and flat organizational structures are distinguished on the basis of the number of levels in the organization. A flat organization is one having few levels relative to the total size of the organization, whereas a tall one has many levels. Stated differently, for a flat structure the average number of employees supervised by each manager is high; for the tall structure the average is low. One cannot conclude that a flat organizational structure will definitely produce greater job satisfaction and improved production. Organization size seems to affect the relative advantages of these two forms of structures. In relatively small organizations, a flat structure appears to be advantageous in terms of producing job satisfaction. However, for relatively large organizations, one study found that the tall structure produced greater job satisfaction and, in another study, greater productivity. Consequently, it appears that the advantages of a flat structure not only decrease with increasing organization size but that, in relatively large organizations, a flat structure may be a liability. The arguments for a flat structure have centered around the greater freedom and autonomy for decision making that are associated with greater job satisfaction. A tall structure, on the other hand, increases supervisory controls and facilitates coordination. Each form of structure permits effective coping when the organization is small or large, respectively.

4. There is no clear support for the proposition that decentralization of decision making is associated with improved job attitudes or performance. Due to the lack of experimental controls in all but a few studies, the benefits of decentralization must be considered as an article of faith rather than as proven.

Technology

Very little work has been conducted that examines the relationship of technology to job satisfaction. However, an analysis of the skills required of workers in different technological settings gives us some meaningful insights.[21] Table 6-3 shows this.

Table 6-3

Type of Worker and Skills Required

Type of Worker	Skills Required			
Craftsman	Manual	Motor	Conceptual	Perceptual
Machine tender and assembly-line worker	Manual	Motor		
Automation worker			Conceptual	Perceptual

Source: Leonard R. Sayles and George Strauss, *Human Behavior in Organizations* (Englewood Cliffs, N.J.: Prentice-Hall, 1966), p. 60. Adapted from *Industrial Organization: Theory and Practice* by Joan Woodward (London: Oxford University Press), pp. 63–64.

Of special interest is the automation worker found in a continuous-process technological setting. Plants in the chemical and petroleum, electrical power generation, and steel manufacturing industries utilize automation to provide a continuous product flow from the raw material stage to finished output. The typical employee under such conditions spends much of his or her time monitoring gauges and control instruments, with major work activities coming primarily during breakdowns, start-ups, and changeover periods. As noted, the skills required are conceptual and perceptual.

Such automated jobs provide interest and variety. Involvement in a tangible, complete activity produces job interest and satisfaction that grows out of meaningful activity. Employees develop a sense of commitment to the total process and feel responsible for keeping the expensive technology operating. In this instance, the technology itself is the source of job characteristics that are the objectives of deliberate design in many job-enrichment programs. The resulting experiences of accomplishment, autonomy, and identification are also some of the results attained. However not all job satisfaction problems are solved with continuous-process automation since there is monotony associated with the long periods of watching and waiting. But such dissatisfactions are more than balanced by the satisfaction experienced.

Given this information noted, one would expect more satisfaction and less alienation in those industries consisting of automation workers and craftsmen. There is little evidence on this with the exception of an analysis made by Blauner.[22] Basic to his work is the theme that, since there are structural differences within modern industry, it can be assumed that certain conditions are more alienating than others. Blauner compared four industries using different forms of technology: a printing firm (nonstandardized work processes), a textile plant (with spinning and weaving as its chief processes), an automotive firm, and an oil refinery (continuous-process technology). These industries were categorized according to level of technology, division of labor, degree of bureaucratization, and economic standing. Which industry would have the greatest amount of dissatisfaction? The least dissatisfaction? Refer to the type of worker and the skills to help in your evaluation! The degree of dissatisfaction and the lack of morale varied from industry to industry. The automotive industry had the higher level of alienation followed by the textile plant. The most satisfied groups of workers were in the oil refinery followed by the printing industry. Both the printing and especially refinery industries had high levels of technology, permitting more freedom and control over the work processes.

Job and Job Environment

In a survey of job satisfaction research, Locke concluded that work attributes related to work interest and satisfaction included the opportunity to use one's valued skills and abilities, the opportunity for new learning, creativity, variety, difficulty, amount of work, responsibility, nonarbitrary pressure for performance, control over work methods and work pace and complexity.[23]

Each of these factors shares a common element—mental challenge. If the challenge of the work is sufficiently great and accepted by the employee, interest and involvement should result. The exercise of judgment and choice make one the main causal agent in performance. However, too much challenge can also result in dissatisfaction. An inability to cope with challenge may produce a sense of failure and frustration. While there must be opportunities for job challenges, these must be successfully overcome for the employee to experience satisfaction. The worker does not have to experience final success for this to occur just so long as he or she experiences improvement or progress. As a final caveat, however, there is clear evidence that not all employees value, desire, or seek mentally challenging work; individual differences prevail.

In summarizing his extensive analysis of job satisfaction, Locke made the following observation.[24]

Job satisfaction results from the attainment of values which are compatible with one's needs. Among the most important values or conditions conducive to job satisfaction are: (1) mentally challenging work with which the individual can cope successfully; (2) personal interest in the work itself; (3) work which is not too physically tiring; (4) rewards for performance which are just, informative, and in line with the individual's personal aspiration; (5) working conditions which are compatible with the individual's physical needs and which facilitate the accomplishment of his work goals; (6) high self-esteem on the part of the employee; (7) agents in the place who help the employee to attain job values such as interesting work, pay, and promotions, whose basic values are similar to his own, and who minimize role conflict and ambiguity.

While the nature of the work itself is important, so is the compensation associated with the work. The impact of pay on motivation and job satisfaction has been the subject of considerable controversy during the twentieth century. Scientific management advocates at the turn of the century held that pay was most important to employees and incentive wage plans were designed to motivate performance. The "economic man" was paramount! After the Hawthorne investigations in the late 1920s, the importance of pay was downgraded. The "social man" was paramount! Research studies pointed to the key role played by the work group or the informal system, even to the extent of employees' sacrificing monetary rewards for group acceptance, which was partially based on the restriction of output. This viewpoint was touted by the Human Relations School of Thought.

As you may recall from Chapter 3, Herzberg maintains that money is a hygienic factor and a dissatisfier, not a satisfier or positive motivator. The value of money is to avoid economic deprivation and also the feelings of being treated unfairly. Today, money has a more central place in the thinking of students of organization behavior. Pay dissatisfaction is perceived as inequity by making social comparisons; that is, one's pay is compared with that of one's co-workers performing the same duties under similar conditions. An individual who has more work-related traits (seniority, experience, etc.) or who works harder or who holds a more demanding job thinks that he or she should receive more pay. If not, inequity is perceived and the employee is dissatisfied with his or her pay. In addition to the equity-inequity viewpoint, pay is considered important because of its perceived association with other things that are desired. If money is perceived as a significant means for attaining security, status, or prestige needs that have a positive valence, then pay will be important to the individual.

In addition to the equity and instrumental implications of money, pay satisfaction will be affected by one's needs. One will be more satisfied if his or her pay is sufficient to meet personal and family needs than if pay is less than required to maintain an adequate standard of living. As an employee's income increases, his or her standard of living rises and it becomes important to hold this level. Even if one does not aspire to a higher standard of living, inflation decreases one's satisfaction with any given level of pay. The importance of compensation will vary from one work situation to another, with changes in the economy and with the particular individual and his or her need for income.

Personal Factors in Job Satisfaction

In addition to environmental factors, Figure 6-6 shows that satisfaction is also affected by personal characteristics—demographic factors, abilities, and personality variables. The role of person variables in the causation of job satisfaction or dissatisfaction is to moderate the association between the work environment and the satisfaction response of the employee.

Demographics

Much job satisfaction literature is confined to personal characteristics found in historical and biographical information such as sex, age, education, and the like. Many of the demographic factors associated with job satisfaction are well known and researched. One of these studies is summarized as follows.[25]

1. Younger workers are less satisfied with their jobs than are older workers. The biggest gap among age groups involves those aged sixteen through twenty-nine, who are appreciably less satisfied than are older people.
2. Women workers by and large are about as contented with their jobs as are men. Considering the large wage gap between men and women and the overrepresentation of women in lower-status occupations, it is surprising that differences have not been observed.
3. Among workers without a college degree, there is little relationship between educational level and job satisfaction. Those with college degrees, however, have high levels of satisfaction. Low levels of satisfaction are registered by workers with some college education but no degree.

Abilities

There are few reports on individual abilities as the cause of job satisfaction. However, studies of employee selection show that abilities known to be valid predictors of subsequent job performance also predict behaviors presumed to reflect job dissatisfaction such as early voluntary quitting. Also, discrepancy between the abilities possessed and those required by the job is highly associated with the degree of job satisfaction.[26]

Personality characteristics

Few studies have sought to relate personality and job satisfaction. However, we do know that the relationship between job characteristics and job satisfaction is influenced by higher-order need strength, the need for achievement, and one's preference for intrinsic as compared with extrinsic rewards.[27]

Consequences of Job Satisfaction

As Figure 6-6 indicates the consequences of job satisfaction may be assessed at the individual level, the organizational level, and the societal level. While these categories may seem to overlap, they do provide a framework for analysis. The experience of varying degrees of satisfaction or dissatisfaction prompts some sort of accommodative or adaptive behavior and in this sense is a partial "cause" of that behavior. If the work experience is dissatisfying, the individual may respond by avoiding or decreasing contact with the source of dissatisfaction. Conversely, if satisfaction is produced by work, the individual will continue to repeat or perpetuate the behavior found satisfying. Individual accommodative processes become significant if they are prevalent and affect the integrity of the organization and/or society.

Individual responses

Growing interest in psychosomatic illness has focused attention on psychological factors that may contribute to heart disease, migraine, ulcers, and so on. Numerous studies have reported associations between coronary disease and job complaints such as boredom, feeling ill at ease, interpersonal conflict, fatigue, shortness of breath, and headaches. On the other hand, there is evidence of coronary-prone behavior patterns characterized by extreme competitiveness, impatience, perfectionism, and inability to relax. These studies suggest a causal relationship between psychological states and bodily functioning; social stress is frequently touted as the linking concept. Social stresses such as the following have been considered at one time or another and related to health.[28]

1. Not knowing what is expected on the job.
2. Experiencing conflicting demands from people with whom one works.
3. Having too much work to do in the time available.
4. Having work that requires more skills than one has.
5. Having poor relations with one's supervisor, subordinates, or co-workers.

6. Being unable to participate in decisions that affect one's work.
7. Being required to deal frequently with people who are in other departments or who work for other employers.
8. Being responsible for other people at work.

There is an increasing body of evidence that work may not only affect physical health but also mental health. The experience of dissatisfaction implies conflict because the employee is performing tasks that he or she would prefer to avoid, partially or completely. A relationship between satisfaction and mental health is a real possibility. A study of the relationship of job satisfaction to mental health was made in the automotive industry. An index of mental health consisting of six components was developed; these are anxiety and tension, self-esteem, hostility, sociability, life satisfaction, and personal morale. Within each skill level and among both younger and older workers, those who expressed below-average job satisfaction were judged to have poorer mental health. Thus, 86 percent of the young, semiskilled workers who were below average in job satisfaction had relatively ''poor'' mental health, as compared with 48 percent of those above average in job satisfaction.[29]

Such findings do not necessarily mean that job satisfaction causes poor mental health; however, they may share a number of common work-related sources such as working conditions, the work itself, shift work, supervision, wages, and promotions. An alternative explanation is that the poor fit between the job requirements and the employee's physical and mental capacities is one cause of both dissatisfaction and mental health problems. The problem is complicated, however, because certain traits of employees may predispose them to select jobs that prevent them from growing.

Organizational consequences

Although the studies relating job satisfaction to mental and physical health are few, numerous investigations have examined turnover, absenteeism, and productivity. The following material will attempt to convey some of these conclusions and will be based primarily upon the review of the literature by Porter and Steers.[30] The conclusions point to the importance of job satisfaction as a central factor in withdrawal from the job such as turnover and absenteeism.

1. Job satisfaction is a predictor of turnover. Employees leaving their organization were more dissatisfied and their expectations were not met on the job. Several studies have indicated that, when job applicants are provided with a realistic picture of the job environment—including its difficulties—prior to employment, they apparently adjusted their job expectations to more realistic levels, which reduced turnover.

2. Pay and promotional considerations often represent significant factors in the decision to quit one's job. Studies fairly consistently indicated the importance perceived inequity and unfilled expectations as significant to such decisions.

3. Supervisory style is a major factor in turnover. Supervisors who are "considerate", that is, friendly, praise good performance, listen to workers' opinions, and so on, are liked by employees.

4. The size of the work unit is related to both turnover and absenteeism among blue-collar workers. Smaller work groups have a better record.

5. The lack of satisfaction with co-workers has been found highly related to turnover but not universally so. Some workers have a low need for affiliation; also some organizational settings provide for more peer group interaction, which affects one's level of expectations.

6. Turnover is positively related to dissatisfaction with job content among both blue- and white-collar workers. Job requirements represent either a means for personal fulfillment and satisfaction or a source of frustration and internal conflict.

7. Task repetitiveness and perceived lack of sufficient job autonomy or responsibility are consistently related to turnover and absenteeism.

8. Age is strongly and negatively related to turnover and positively, although weakly, related to absenteeism.

Societal implications

Both individual and organizational responses to job satisfaction may have tangible or intangible implications for society. Workers whose jobs undermine their physical or mental health place an additional demand on overburdened systems of health care services.[31] Job termination frequently results in demands for unemployment compensation and drains local resources. Also, where workers express dissatisfaction in the form of decreased productivity or absenteeism, upward pressure is placed on prices, which adds to inflation. In addition to such monetary considerations, some authorities maintain that job dissatisfaction affects the employee's other life roles. The dissatisfied worker becomes the dissatisfied citizen prone to endorse radical causes or perhaps become completely apathetic to governmental processes. Family roles may be affected, or a general disenchantment with life may be experienced. While all these consequences are possible, there is little concrete empirical evidence to indicate the extent to which such consequences actually occur.

MONITORING THE ORGANIZATION

Monitoring the organization means to systematically gather information about how all employees feel about many facets of their "work world." Each employee is asked for his or her opinion or reaction to a series of questions about his or her job, supervision, pay, communications, training, work problems, and so on. Normally, this kind of information is not available to management and is assessed on the basis of inference or some kind of presumed insight. Many managers still hold the view of the worker as basically the "economic man." For example, both management and union leaders tend to overestimate the importance of pay and fringe benefits in assessing employee attitudes, and they underestimate the importance of job challenge, opportunities for advancement, job security, and the like for employees. The questionnaire approach, however, provides specific information of value in making management decisions and in appraising current practices and procedures on the basis of the degree of employee understanding, acceptance, and satisfaction with them.

Additionally, the monitoring process may be used as a management development tool. Each person with supervisory responsibility obtains findings that will permit the individual to analyze his or her effectiveness in directing the people that report to him or her. On the basis of such analysis, the supervisor can determine specifically how to take advantage of his or her strengths and how to make his or her group more effective by taking action in areas that need improvement. For one supervisor the need emerging from such analysis may be to improve communications, for another to develop improved employee job satisfaction.

There are three major steps to the process of monitoring the organization.

1. The collection and tabulation of information: This involves the completion of questionnaires from the top of the organization on down, questions being designed to measure the dimensions of job satisfaction previously outlined, that is, work, pay, promotion, recognition, benefits, working conditions, supervision, co-workers, and management.

2. Feedback of the results: Survey results can be broken down to convey reactions from any part of the organization. Each person having managerial responsibilities can determine how his or her group has responded. Such data can be aggregated to obtain the picture for departments, divisions, and the total organization; differences among organizational units or salaried and hourly paid workers as well as other meaningful comparisons can be presented.

Basically, the purpose of such analyses is to bring into focus the way in which employees perceive the many facets of their work life and the way in which management activities are being received. This enables any management group or individual manager to decide what kind of an organization he or she has at present so that he or she may proceed more effectively to attain the desired organization.

3. Organizational improvement: Improvement occurs as a result of applying survey findings. The process begins with each supervisor's receiving and presenting the results to his or her own group. Subsequently, the

supervisor determines what remedial actions or programs are necessary to improve the group. The supervisor discusses the overall results with his or her superintendent who then, with others of the same rank, meets with the department manager to examine their units' results; a total plan is devised to improve the organization in discussions between the plant manager and department managers. Consequently, there is a series of interlocking discussions between each managerial official and the people reporting to him or her running from the top to the bottom of the organization. Each level of management discusses, analyzes, interprets, and applies survey findings pertinent to its own situation. Each level initiates the necessary action within the scope of its authority or recommends action to the next higher level in the organization. The flow of such communications is shown in Figure 6-7.

Figure 6-7

Flow of Information in Monitoring an Organization

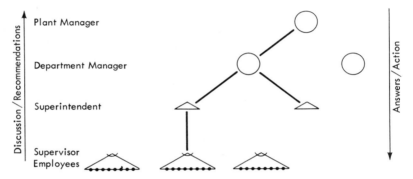

Two points must be noted. First, since there is no standardized terminology for levels in an organization or titles for persons holding managerial positions, the process described should be considered as a very generalized model. Second, the program for monitoring an organization is frequently called survey data feedback, one of the primary forms or techniques of organization development that will be examined in Chapter 13.

Organizations are not confined to surveys or polls for monitoring their operations, although, being organization-wide, this approach is the most effective and efficient. Interviews may be used to check on an organization. Interviews may be structured so that each interviewer follows the same pattern of questions, or they may be nondirective, to promote a free, less structured interchange. However, interviews are expensive and time consuming. Furthermore, the employee may not feel free to disclose his or her true feelings and reactions even though good rapport has been established by the interviewer.

Whenever an employee terminates his or her employment, some kind of exit contract is made with the departing employee. At this point an exit interview or questionnaire may be utilized to assess the organization's internal environment.[32] While the departing employee may be reluctant to express his or her real feelings, especially if he needs a recommendation, important information may be obtained. Additionally, the routine personnel reports on absenteeism, turnover, and grievances as well as productivity reports from the line may show symptoms of dissatisfaction. Such data may be followed up by interviewing employees or by examining exit data to disclose potential causes. Whatever the nature of an organization, profit or nonprofit, it has or may devise means for monitoring the level of satisfaction of its employees.

INTEGRATIVE MECHANISMS

In this chapter we have focused on job satisfaction; in the previous chapter we examined individual productivity. Both job satisfaction and performance are significant outcomes for any management. Such outcomes cannot be left to chance but require the appropriate blending of organization factors—goals, tasks, and technologies—with human factors—capacities, attitudes, and needs. At this point we must review the integrative mechanisms for effectively joining the organizational and people variables that have been considered up to this point. Figure 6-8 puts all these clearly before us.[33]

The integrative mechanisms have been examined previously with the exception of one—flextime. Basically, flextime is a system of flexible working hours that are often arranged to suit a worker's convenience; at both the beginning and end of the workday, employees arrive and leave at times of their own choosing. Many plants have a core time, which is a period when everybody in the plant and office is expected to be on the job—say, from 10:00 A.M. to 3:00 P.M. For workers, it provides a measure of control over their activities that can be rearranged into more meaningful patterns. Alterations relevant to transportation, leisure time use, personal business use, care for children, and so on, are possible for employees. For employers, there is the possibility of increased productivity, less tardiness, lower turnover, and better morale. The results are positive in terms of improved morale and higher productivity in most instances. Similar results and advantages have been found when organizations have adopted the compact workweek, that is, moving from the five-day, forty-hour week to a four-day week.[34]

Figure 6-8

Integrative Mechanisms

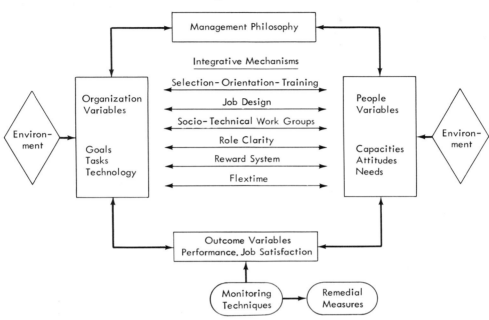

Source: Adapted from George Strauss et al., eds., *Organization Behavior: Research and Issues* (Madison: Industrial Relations Research Association, University of Wisconsin, 1974), p. 14.

Action Levers for Satisfaction and Productivity

In a comprehensive review of the empirical literature on job satisfaction, industrial organization, and productivity,[35] of 550 studies published between 1959 and 1974, only 57 dealt with organizational experiments in which actual changes were carried out under relatively controlled conditions. Using these field experiments, the investigators sought to evaluate strategies for improving productivity and the quality of work life. Those aspects of the organization that could be changed with assurances of success were designated as "action levers." Nine action levers were revealed that had a positive effect on productivity, job satisfaction, or both. The action levers and an example of each are as follows.

Pay and reward systems—introducing group bonus.

Autonomy and discretion—allowing workers to determine their own work methods.

Support services—providing service from technical support groups on demand.
Training—training all operators to perform every task in the department.
Organization structure—reducing the number of hierarchical levels.
Technical and physical—rearranging the layout of machinery.
Task variety—including preparatory and finishing tasks in machining jobs.
Information and feedback—providing direct feedback from user departments.
Interpersonal and group process—increasing the amount and kind of inter-action among group members.

Manipulation of these action levers resulted in positive outcomes on five criterion variables. The criterion variables and an example of each are as follows.

- *Costs—reducing direct labor cost per unit.*
- *Productivity—increasing units of output.*
- *Quality—lowering average rate of rejects.*
- *Withdrawal behavior—decreasing turnover and absenteeism.*
- *Attitudes—increasing job satisfaction.*

An examination of the experiments disclosed that action levers could be grouped to comprise four change orientations:

1. Sociotechnical and autonomous work groups: Structuring work around self-regulating work groups that perform relatively whole tasks.
2. Job restructuring: Expanding individual jobs horizontally and vertically.
3. Participative management: Increasing the amount of participation by workers in decisions that directly affect their work lives.
4. Structural change: Modifying the organizational structure by changing the number of hierarchical levels, scope of control, or information and feedback structures and processes.

Table 6-4 summarizes the manipulated action levers and the results obtained for each change approach category.[36] In the table, the action levers are referred to as an independent or manipulated variable and the results produced as dependent variables.

The findings revealed that each of the four change orientations led to increases in productivity and attitudes of self-fulfillment. Since most of the experiments changed more than one action lever, it was impossible to determine the specific effect of each manipulation of an action level. Some of the findings are as follows.

1. Participative management and job restructuring had the highest per-centage of totally positive attitudinal results, whereas structural change studies showed the lowest percentage of such results.

Table 6-4

A Summary of the Variables Manipulated and the Results Obtained in Field Experimental Studies

	Manipulated (Independent) Variables									Results (Dependent) Variables				
	Pay/ reward systems	Autonomy/ discretion	Support	Training	Organization structure	Technical/ physical	Task variety	Information/ feedback	Interpersonal/ group process	Costs	Productivity	Quality	Withdrawal	Attitudes
Sociotechnical and autonomous groups (N = 16)	56% (16)[1]	88% (16)	31% (16)	44% (16)	19% (16)	63% (16)	63% (16)	63% (16)	75% (16)	88%[2] (8)[1]	93% (15)	86% (7)	73% (7)	70% (10)
Job restructuring (N = 27)	14% (27)	92% (27)	22% (27)	33% (27)	14% (27)	22% (27)	79% (27)	45% (27)	4% (27)	90% (10)	75% (20)	100% (17)	86% (7)	76% (21)
Participaïve management (N = 7)		100% (7)		14% (7)	14% (7)					100% (1)	57% (7)	100% (1)	80% (5)	80% (5)
Organizational change (N = 7)	29% (7)	43% (7)	43% (7)	43% (7)	100% (7)	29% (7)	14% (7)	71% (7)	43% (7)	50% (2)	100% (4)	100% (2)	67% (3)	50% (6)

[1]Numbers in parentheses indicate the base number of studies on which the percentage is based—that is, the denominator.
[2]The percentages represent those studies that reported no negative, mixed, or zero-change findings for the dependent variable in that column—that is, studies that produced totally positive results.

Source: T. G. Cummings, E. S. Malloy, R. H. Glen, "Intervention Strategies for Improving Productivity and the Quality of Work Life," *Organizational Dynamics*, Summer, 1975 (New York: AMACOM, a division of American Management Associations, 1975), p. 57.

179

2. The participative management studies, with the exception of one, changed only autonomy and discretion yet produced the highest percentage of positive attitudinal results.

3. Participative management studies showed the lowest percentage of positive productivity increases when compared with the other three change approaches.

4. Information and feedback appeared to be the action lever with the single greatest impact on productivity but did not account for all the results because other action levers were manipulated at the same time. Rather, information and feedback, technical and physical, task variety, and interpersonal and group process jointly accounted for positive productivity results.

Although the studies on which this information is based are not ideal from the standpoint of research methodology, the authors concluded that they showed no systematic pattern of weaknesses. When problems of morale and productivity arise, the methods described, coupled with careful change strategies, can be applied with a high probability of success.

Quality-of-Work-Life Indicators

Many employees are conscious of serious deficiencies in the quality of their work lives. At the same time, the term "quality of work life" has come to mean much more than the needs satisfied by the forty-hour workweek, job guarantees, equal employment opportunity, or job-enrichment schemes. Walton believes that the term includes broader needs and aspirations that can be encompassed in eight categories.[37]

1. *Adequate and fair compensation*—Does pay received meet socially determined standards of sufficiency or the recipient's subjective standard? Does pay received for certain work bear an appropriate relationship to pay received for other work?

2. *Safe and healthy environment*—That employees should not be exposed to physical conditions or work arrangements that are unduly hazardous or unhealthy is widely accepted. In the future, when health will be less the issue than comfort, more stringent standards than today's will possibly be imposed. These may include minimizing odors, noise, or visual annoyances.

3. *Development of human capacities*—To varying degrees work has become fractionated, deskilled, and tightly controlled; planning the work is often separated from implementing it. So jobs differ in how much they enable the worker to use and develop his skills and knowledge, which affects his involvement, self-esteem, and the challenge obtained from the work itself.

4. *Growth and security*—Attention needs to be given to (a) the extent to which the worker's assignments contribute to maintaining and expanding his

capabilities, rather than leading to his obsolescence; (b) the degree to which expanded or newly acquired knowledge and skills can be utilized in future work assignments; and (c) the availability of opportunities to advance in organizational or career terms which peers, family members, or associates recognize.

5. *Social integration*—Whether the employee achieves personal identity and self-esteem is influenced by such attributes in the climate of his workplace as these: freedom from prejudice, a sense of community, interpersonal openness, the absence of stratification in the organization, and the existence of upward mobility.

6. *Constitutionalism*—What rights does the worker have and how can he (or she) protect these rights? Wide variations exist in the extent to which the organizational culture respects personal privacy, tolerates dissent, adheres to high standards of equity in distributing rewards, and provides for due process in all work-related matters.

7. *The total life space*—A person's work should have a balanced role in his life. This role encompasses schedules, career demands, and travel requirements that take a limited portion of the person's leisure and family time, as well as advancement and promotion that do not require repeated geographical moves.

8. *Social relevance*—Organizations acting in a socially irresponsible manner cause increasing numbers of their employees to deprecate the value of their work and careers. For example, does the worker perceive the organization to be socially responsible in its products, waste disposal, marketing techniques, employment practices, and participation in political campaigns?

Needless to say, the various facets of quality of work life will present even the best-managed organization with some degree of challenge. Furthermore, the question still remains, "Will gains in quality of work life result in gains in the organization's ability to perform its task?" While offering no empirical evidence, some believe that, if an organization fails to meet minimum employee expectations on each of the eight points, dissatisfaction will hamper effectiveness. On the other hand, satisfaction of an expectation may trigger the desire for more, and minimal standards of quality work life may move upward. However,[38]

Regardless of how we approach the issue of the quality of work life, we must acknowledge the diversity of human preferences—diversity relating to culture, social class, family rearing, education, and personality. Different definitions of a high-quality work life accompany differences in subcultures and lifestyles.

Can organizations tailor their work arrangements and assignments to fit such varied individual preferences? Will it pay in either human satisfaction or productivity?[39] Not everyone agrees that such changes can be made or that such favorable consequences will follow.

SUMMARY

Chapters 4 and 5 examined the concept of individual effectiveness and the ways in which management could influence output and productivity. The present chapter has considered a complementary topic—that of job satisfaction. Job satisfaction was defined as a pleasurable or positive emotional state resulting from the appraisal of one's job experiences. However, job satisfaction must be considered in context of the role of work in life. Individual differences prevail. For some, life is centered around their work; for others, work is primarily a means for attaining money, security, leisure, and so on. Although not conclusive, there appears to be some evidence that attitudes toward work are shifting to demand more personal self-fulfillment and an improved "quality of life." However, despite the eye-catching titles "worker alienation" and "rampant employee dissatisfaction," there does not appear any widespread unrest or dissatisfaction on the part of most American workers.

Employee satisfaction was considered to be the result of two perceptions—what should be found on the job and what actually existed in the various characteristics of the job itself and various job conditions. Such a viewpoint, however, leaves unanswered the question of whether job satisfaction leads to better performance, or vice versa. Conceptually, the "performance leads to satisfaction" linkage seems more plausible, but there is no conclusive evidence on this.

Next, we noted that job satisfaction is a many-faceted thing. We observed that categories of environmental and personal variables are associated with job satisfaction. Many of the variables have not been studied extensively or sufficiently well in terms of good research methodology. Additionally, some of the consequences of job satisfaction on the individual, organization, and society were noted. Since job satisfaction has such potentially significant implications, consideration was given to monitoring the organization. Systematically gathered information on how employees feel about the many work dimensions of their jobs provides the background needed for the formulation of remedial measures.

Finally, we examined the integrative mechanisms considered in both Chapters 5 and 6. Performance and job satisfaction are the two primary results of work activity. Both, however, depend upon an appropriate blending of organizational and people variables. The optimal mix of these two factors can be facilitated by selection, orientation, training; job design; sociotechnical work groups; role clarity; reward systems; and flextime. Other integrative mechanisms will be considered in the remainder of the book.

QUESTIONS FOR STUDY AND DISCUSSION

1. What is the difference between job satisfaction and morale?
2. What is the role of work in life?
3. How do the Argyris and Walton models of dissatisfaction differ?
4. Evaluate the two viewpoints on the connection between job satisfaction and performance.
5. What are the four classes of environmental variables that have been related to job satisfaction? Can you give several examples of each?
6. What are the consequences of job satisfaction?
7. Give four approaches to increasing productivity and job satisfaction. Which one seems to be most effective?
8. What are the arguments for and against improving the quality of work life?

NOTES

[1]Viteles, Morris S., *Motivation and Morale in Industry* (New York: Norton, 1953), p. 12.

[2]Krech, D. and R. S. Crutchfield, *Theory and Problems of Social Psychology* (New York: McGraw-Hill, 1948).

[3]Strauss, George, *Organizational Behavior: Research and Issues* (Madison: Industrial Relations Research Association, University of Wisconsin, 1974), p. 28.

[4]Morse, N. C. and R. S. Weiss, "The Function and Meaning of Work and the Job," in S. Nosow and W. H. Form, eds., *Man, Work, and Society* (New York: Basic Books, 1962), pp. 29–35.

[5]Yankelovich, Daniel, *The New Morality: A Profile of American Youth in the 70's* (New York: McGraw-Hill, 1974), pp. 5–6, 20–22, 28–29.

[6]*Business Week,* "The Growing Disaffection with 'Workaholism,'" February 27, 1978, pp. 97–98.

[7]Argyris, Chris, "The Individual and Organization: Some Problems of Mutual Adjustment," *Administrative Science Quarterly* (June 1957): 1–24.

[8]Harlow, Dorothy N. and Jean J. Hanke, *Behavior in Organizations* (Boston: Little, Brown, 1975), p. 508. Adapted from Richard E. Walton, "How to Counter Alienation in the Plant," *Harvard Business Review* (November-December 1972): 70–81.

[9]Quinn, Robert P., Graham L. Staines, and Margaret R. McCullough, *Job Satisfaction: Is There a Trend?* Manpower Research Monograph No. 30 (Washington, D.C.: Department of Labor, 1974).

[10]"Job Satisfaction Has Decreased," *IRS Newsletter* (Ann Arbor: Institute For Social Research, University of Michigan, Spring 1979), pp. 10–11.

[11]Carrell, Michael, "How to Measure Job Satisfaction," *Training* (November 1976): 25–27.

[12]Locke, Edwin A., "The Nature and Causes of Job Satisfaction," in Marvin D. Dunnette, ed., *Handbook of Industrial and Organizational Psychology* (Chicago: Rand McNally, 1976), p. 1302.

[13]Wexley, Kenneth N. and Gary A. Yukl, *Organizational Behavior and Personnel Psychology* (Homewood, Ill.: Irwin, 1977), p. 109.

[14]Schwab, Donald P. and Larry L. Cummings, "Theories of Performance and Satisfaction: A Review," *Industrial Relations* 9 (October 1970): 408–430.

[15]*Ibid.*, p. 418.

[16]Seashore, Stanley E. and Thomas D. Taber, "Job Satisfaction Indicators and Their Correlates," *The American Behavioral Scientist* 18 (January–February 1975): 333–368.

[17]Hulin, Charles and Milton R. Blood, "Job Enlargement, Individual Differences, and Workers' Responses," *Psychological Bulletin* 69 (1968): 41–55.

[18]Quinn, Staines, and McCullough, *op. cit.*, pp. 9–10.

[19]Blauner, Robert, "Extent of Satisfaction: A Review of General Research," in Timothy W. Costello and Sheldon S. Zalkind, eds., *Psychology In Administration* (Englewood Cliffs, N.J.: Prentice-Hall, 1963), pp. 80–95.

[20]Porter, Lyman W. and Edward E. Lawler, III, "Properties of Organization Structure in Relation to Job Attitudes and Job Behavior," in W. E. Scott and L. L. Cummings, eds., *Readings In Organizational Behavior and Human Performance*, rev. ed. (Homewood, Ill.: Irwin, 1973), pp. 303–327.

[21] Sayles, Leonard R. and George Strauss, *Human Behavior in Organizations*. (Englewood Cliffs, N.J.: Prentice-Hall, Inc., 1966), pp. 59–67.

[22]Blauner, R., *Alienation and Freedom* (Chicago: University of Chicago Press, 1964).

[23]Locke, *op. cit.*, pp. 1319–1328.

[24]*Ibid.*, p. 1328.

[25]Quinn, Staines, and McCullough, *op. cit.*, pp. 1–3.

[26]Seashore and Taber, *op. cit.*, pp. 354–355.

[27]*Ibid.*, p. 355.

[28]Quinn, Staines, and McCullough, *op. cit.*, p. 19. See Also McClean, Alan A. *Work Stress* (Reading, Mass.: Addison-Wesley, 1979), 37–87; Washaw, Leon J., *Managing Stress* (Reading, Mass.: Addison-Wesley, 1979), 3–26.

[29]*Ibid.*, p. 20.

[30]Porter, Lyman W. and Richard M. Steers, "Organizational, Work, and Personal Factors in Employee Turnover and Absenteeism," in their book *Motivation and Work Behavior* (New York: McGraw-Hill, 1975), pp. 276–292.

[31]Quinn, Staines, and McCullough, *op. cit.*, pp. 27–28.

[32]Bass, Bernard M., *Organizational Psychology* (Boston: Allyn & Bacon, 1965), p. 47.

[33]Strauss, *op. cit.*, pp. 13–15.

[34]*U.S. News & World Report*, "The Swelling Ranks of Workers Who Set Their Own Hours," August 1, 1977, pp. 62–63.

[35]Cummings, T. G., Edmond S. Molloy, and Roy H. Glen, "Intervention Strategies for Improving Productivity and the Quality of Work Life," *Organizational Dynamics* 4 (Summer 1975): 52–68.

[36]*Ibid.*, p. 57.

[37]Walton, Richard E., "Improving the Quality of Work Life," *Harvard Business Review* (May–June 1974): 12–16.

[38]*Ibid.*, p. 16.

[39]Wiggins, Ronald L. and Richard D. Steade, "Job Satisfaction as a Social Concern," *Academy of Management Review* 1 (October, 1976), 48–55.

cases cases cases

Case Study: The Tops?

The Acme Advertising Agency is a successful advertising and public relations firm. Over the years, the firm has developed a respectable clientele, including a number of banks, retail establishments, real estate companies, and nonprofit organizations. The working area is plush and ultra modern with red carpet and brightly covered panels. Most employees have individual offices with modern tables, cabinets, and cushioned chairs. Panels are used to separate the reception area, the conference area, and the art area. The photographer's darkroom is in the basement of the office building.

The employees are divided into three groups: (1) publications, (2) broadcasting—audio and video tapes for radio and television, and (3) copy —newspaper and magazine advertisements. Two secretaries do the work for all employees, although one secretary is mainly responsible for the president's work.

The work load depends on client demand, but there is usually more than enough work to be done. If employees do catch up, they are expected to develop new ideas. The company is known for its expertise in publications and always seems to have three deadlines to meet at once.

Following are excerpts of interviews with some of the employees.

Vernon Vaughn, President

Interviewer: How do you feel about your new job as president?

Vernon: Well, basically, I'll be doing the same job I've been doing over the past year since the previous president has been sick. I don't really see myself as lording it over people and don't feel like I really have that much charge. I see the position of boss almost as a necessary evil; there has to be someone who has the final say. But the fact that the staff is a group of professionals means that leadership comes not only from the president but from the others as well.

Interviewer: Do you see any problems in the company?

Vernon: You don't realize it until you are in charge because we all are so happy here, but there are a great many problems. We have to balance between doing jobs too quickly and turning out high-quality material. Also, there are individual problems, as you well know. Sally feels as if she needs more help, but I've pointed out to her that she can use any of the copy written by others. In the past, sometimes Sally has taken the role of a martyr. I don't know that I'm all that interested in administrating, but I do believe that people need a positive guide and also need to know what is expected of them.

185

Interviewer: Are there any problems with the work produced?

Vernon: Of course, there is a lot of pressure from clients. I'm going to stress that everybody get each decision in writing. When a client proofreads copy, we are going to have him sign a paper saying that he has approved. I also think that we need to be more accountable for hours spent. We need to be able to specify how many hours we spent on this and how many on that.

Sally Frick, Broadcasting

Interviewer: What do you like about your job?

Sally: I love selling ideas, and I get personal satisfaction from working with a number of clients. Also, the relationship between the staff here is extraordinary. My roommate works in a hospital and the atmosphere there is like a snakepit, ripe with gossip. As far as I know, gossip is nonexistent in this office.

The morale here is higher than at any of the other places I have worked, and I have often wondered why. I guess we have pride in our professionalism, and we all know that we are good so we don't have to go on ego trips to prove it.

Interviewer: Do you have any problems in your work?

Sally: Yes, I do have several gripes. One is that Vernon (the president) always yells about how important radio and TV advertising is, but he won't hire any help for me. I envy publications for all the people they have, but it doesn't make me paranoid because they need them too.

The previous president always considered everything as a major production and didn't give some things priority over others. Vernon, I think, will be better about this as he seems to know that some things can be dealt with in a 15-second spot while other things require a videotape.

And I guess another gripe is that sometimes I'm in on the tail end of a project. Just last week they wanted me to tape a convention on real estate salesmen. They had been working on this convention since January but didn't tell me about it until two weeks ago.

Pam Prentis, Copywriting

Interviewer: How do you like your job, Pam?

Pam: I like it very much. Writing is what I've wanted to do since the second grade. I can't think of anything I'd enjoy more.

Interviewer: How do you feel about working under Vernon?

Pam: Oh, very good. He is a fine administrator and trust is the key factor. I have confidence in his ethics.

Tom Koonze, Publications Assistant

Interviewer: How do you like your job?

Tom: It's great. We have a beautiful setup. It scares me sometimes that I started out in such a great office because I can't go anywhere but downhill if I leave here.

Interviewer: What do you like about it?

Tom: Vernon acknowledges our expertise. He gives us his ideas, but knows when to shut up and let us in the publications department take over. I think this whole office has an unusual concentration of intelligent, creative, and nice people. I'm so happy to be here rather than out in the world of banks and insurance. In a way it's an escape from the real world.

Interviewer: How do you feel about the leadership?

Tom: It's very appropriate. When clients complain to Vernon, he will stand up for us when we are right. If we have made a mistake, he will quietly tell us rather than in front of twenty people. I feel that if I did a bad job I'd be letting Vernon down. It would be like embarrassing my friends.

Mary Schmidt, Artist

Interviewer: Do you like your job?

Mary: I don't know. I'm always afraid that Sue (publications specialist) is going to come in and hit me with a bombshell that I'll have to hurry to finish in the next couple of days. Sue is so hard to read, and I feel that I don't have any control over what happens.

Interviewer: Are there any other problems?

Mary: Sometimes Tom (publications assistant) will give me some work and tell me to do it when I get around to it. I think this means in a couple of days. Then he'll come in one morning and say, "I stayed at the office until four this morning doing that brochure you hadn't done." He likes to play the role of a martyr and likes you to think that his job is so demanding he always has to work overtime. The reason he has to work overtime is because he always comes in late and goofs off in the mornings.

Interviewer: Do you think you'll stay here?

Mary: I don't know, maybe I'm just basically lazy, but I don't like having to always meet deadlines and not knowing what's going to happen next. I'm going to start looking for another job.

Fay Thompson, Secretary

Interviewer: How do you feel about your job?

Fay: Well, the work is interesting, and I get to meet a lot of different people. And I don't feel like I'm under anybody except Mr. Vaughn.

Interviewer: How do you feel about Vernon?

Fay: He's a hard worker. He wouldn't expect anything of anybody that he wouldn't do himself. If I feel pushed, I know he does too. He's not a dictator and has been understanding when I have to get off work because of my children.

Interviewer: Do you foresee any problems?

Fay: I don't know. In the past one thing that was bad was that everything decided about planning the future and all was so secretive. They all talked about it behind closed doors. Then we weren't even told about the former president's retiring in a meeting. Vernon just passed a copy of a memo around. I feel like, if they don't think we can be trusted, then they should hire someone who can be trusted rather than always hiding things.

QUESTIONS

1. Why are these employees satisfied?

2. What would you suggest that might help Mary Schmidt (artist)?

3. Do you see any actual or potential problems? What solutions would you propose?

cases cases cases

Case Study: The Pits?

PART I A NEW JOB

John reported to work as manager of Accounting Operations with extreme optimism. After a tour of the plant and a thumbnail sketch of its history, the personnel manager conducted John to the general office building and into the finance area, turning him over to Tom, the controller and chief financial officer. Tom's orientation was very brief, consisting mostly of an exchange of trivialities and walking John to an enclosed area that was to be his office. Tom sat down in the spare chair and said he was sory about not being able to have lunch with him but that he had a previous engagement and that he would make it soon. He turned the keys on the finance records over to John, told him that Finance was his baby now, to look things over, become familiar with the overall operation, and then get back to him. "I will introduce you to your people later."

The remainder of the week was spent pouring over records and financial data to determine the needs and requirements in a thoroughly unfamiliar corporation. During these days there were several brief conversations with Tom in which he made comments on the requirements of the manager of Accounting Operations, the financial and data requirements of the company, and the personnel—most of which consisted of pointing to an individual and calling his or her name and stating "you have to stay right behind her to get any work out of her" and so on.

Each day John expected Tom to introduce him to the employees. This and "lunch soon" to become better acquainted failed to materialize. After the lack of an introduction to the personnel by Tom and the polite, rather patronizing, "hellos" from the others as he walked through the area, John decided there was definitely something amiss and pondered the best method of getting to the root of the matter. Distrust and resentment of him seemed fairly obvious, so he decided to interview each employee in his department, find the source of strife, and seek a solution. Since Mary, the secretary, seemed the least hostile, he called her in first for a talk.

Each employee was interviewed and related a similar story—briefly "I am," "I have worked here," and "my job is"; no one would divulge the reason for the friction that appeared very evident or the reason for the resentment of the supervisors. Having failed with the interviews, John went to Tom to discuss the situation.

Tom stated that he was aware of the situation but that it was of no significance and was nothing to worry about. He further stated that most of the personnel were fairly capable, that all they needed was strict supervision and someone to lay out the work in detail; the only thing required was production. "These people are, according to my own survey, better paid than any in the area; all they need is someone to push them."

QUESTIONS

1. What personnel philosophy is reflected in the case at this point?
2. What assumptions about people seem to prevail?

PART II EMPLOYEE PROBLEMS

With the passage of time, John began to notice that not all the resentment was against him and the other management personnel but that Finance personnel tended to divide into two groups for breaks and for lunch. From time to time each group would complain about an unequal distribution of work.

Through observation and studies of the various jobs, John determined that some carried much greater work loads than others. A redistribution of all tasks was made; the reason and new job assignment was explained to each individual. This change served multiple purposes—it made the flow of material through the department smoother and more efficient, it made the personnel feel that they were carrying only a fair part of the work load, and it unified the finance department as a functional working group rather than as two opposing groups.

With this success, John again talked to all finance personnel. Again, the interviews began with Mary. She rather reluctantly stated that they did not trust management. All the older employees had lost the bulk of their retirement when the present company took over. Under the terms of the merger, the company assumed no responsibility for prior service and would only administer the retirement plan in effect at the takeover until such time as it put its own plan into effect. This would result in a loss to everyone, and the older employees would have very few service credits under the new plan. However, three years after the takeover, the pension plan seemed as remote as ever. Mary further stated that she and the others felt that wages were low. Bonuses paid at midyear and Christmas, amounting to about two weeks' pay, were immediately discontinued when the company had been taken over. In addition to the loss of bonuses, which had been considered as earned pay, the supervisors sent in by the company were authoritarian and demanding and had instituted more restrictive rules governing employees, but fewer advantages. These complaints by Mary were echoed almost verbatim by all Finance personnel. The employees felt overworked, underpaid, and degraded by the new "regime." John also learned that there had been a fairly fast turnover of employees.

John discussed the matter with other supervisors and found that their personnel had the same general feelings. Some time later, Gary, who worked in assembly, came to John on a payroll matter. Through several meetings, John and Gary developed a mutual friendship and respect for each other. While resolving problems, John inquired about the feelings of plant production personnel and learned that they coincided pretty much with that of office personnel. They felt that the new management was interested only in the company and not in the employees. Gary said that soon they would have a union to help with company dealings and preserve their rights.

John was not too surprised when one afternoon Gary and a group of fellow workers were just outside the company property line passing out union organization literature. Within a period of six months an election was held under the guidance of the National Labor Relations Board, the employees overwhelmingly voted for union representation, and Gary was elected president of the local. A contract was negotiated that called for an 11 percent increase in pay the first year, a 12 percent increase the second year, two additional paid holidays, and company participation in the insurance program. A pension fund was created in the second year of the contract in which the company paid 5 cents per hour worked into a union-administered retirement fund. The manufacturing employees now felt they had someone to represent them. The deep resentment of past treatment was reflected in the fact that, during the first year of the union contract, eighty-nine grievances were filed by union personnel that required arbitration; nineteen of these required the services of a federal mediator. The second year of the contract was much the same.

The gains won by the union for production workers were reflected in gains given to office personnel in slightly higher rates of pay and increased holidays and insurance to meet those of the union members. Several employees in the office were heard to comment "I feel that I should pay Gary and his union monthly dues, as all I have ever gained under this new company can be attributed directly to the union contract."

QUESTIONS

1. Did the complaints center around motivators or hygienic factors?
2. Which can the union provide?

PART III A NEW PARENT COMPANY

Two years later there was an announcement that the company was to be sold to a medium-sized manufacturer of equipment. The immediate reaction of both union and nonunion personnel was "maybe things will be better—certainly they can't be worse!" The company was to be operated as a separate corporation.

The new parent company replaced the president and general manager with its own men and announced that in the near future there would be sweeping changes in personnel, personnel policy, line of machinery manufactured, and so on. It announced that "people are our most important asset—we take care of our people." An announcement also was made that work was beginning on a pension plan for office personnel that would be at least equivalent to that already enjoyed by the union. However, to enjoy these new benefits it also was stated there must be some sacrifices. The following personnel rules, along with others, were introduced in a six-page booklet governing personnel:

1. All personnel, regardless of status, except corporate officers, must keep daily attendance cards.
2. Persons arriving at their work station after 8:00 A.M. must register with the security guard. Three violations within one month will result in a three-day suspension. Three suspensions within the calendar year will result in dismissal.
3. No electrical appliances are allowed—coffee pots, radios, and so on.
4. Parking in an area not assigned to the individual will, upon the third offense, result in suspension of parking privileges on company property.
5. Paid sick leave will be limited to forty hours per calendar year, and each occurrence must be verified by a certificate from your doctor.

QUESTIONS

1. How will the employees react to the new situation?
2. Will they make the necessary sacrifices?

PART IV NO IMPROVEMENT

These and similar rules served only to antagonize the clerical staff as well as plant production personnel. The quality of equipment and efficiency of production began to deteriorate drastically, reaching the point where many machines shipped to customers were inoperable. With the drop in quality and work performance, the new management became more demanding and authoritarian. The traditional morning and afternoon coffee breaks were abolished, with instructions "you may go to the vending machines and make your purchases and return to your work area for break, but there will be no idling in the lounge area." Top management and staff began frequent trips through the work areas stopping to interrupt any conversation that appeared to be casual and reminding the employees to "keep at it." The clerical staff also became less efficient, and resentment increased as morale deteriorated. Complete distrust of the company and its supervisors abounded.

After two years, the promised pension plan and general betterment of conditions had failed to materialize. Personnel turnover surpassed the 100 percent mark, and the general manager was required to spend much of his time in the mediation of grievances filed by the union and office personnel.

Finally as an act of desperation the company contracted with a consulting firm to conduct a confidential survey of all personnel to determine causes of discontent and to make recommendations to restore harmony, and improve efficiency and production. The Opinion Survey revealed:

1. Management of the firm is poor and lacks overall objectives.
2. Present products are considered by employees to be only of average quality, being manufactured on obsolete, worn equipment.
3. Job security is considered good, but working conditions and climate are poor, with very little training offered and virtually no chance for advancement.
4. Wages and fringe benefits are considered to be poor.
5. Employees are dissatisfied with the company in general.

QUESTIONS

1. What would you suggest to top management?
2. What changes can be made immediately? What changes will be long-run in nature?

PART 11

GROUP BEHAVIOR

CHAPTER 7

Interpersonal Behavior

LEARNING OBJECTIVES

When you have finished this chapter, you should be able to:

- *Cite the parts of the personal system and give their role in human behavior.*
- *Understand how the self concept operates and is protected.*
- *Understand how interpersonal needs, orientations, and attraction may affect behavior.*
- *Explain how one evaluates the consequences of interpersonal behavior.*
- *Give three kinds of behavior demonstrated in groups and examples of each.*
- *Understand how transactional analysis provides a framework for understanding communications between people.*

In this chapter we undertake an examination of interpersonal relations. Previously, the individual has been the focus of our attention, but now our concern will be interpersonal interaction between two or more persons. While the preceding individual concepts are relevant, an expanded frame of reference must be developed to understand interpersonal relationships. Consequently, a model of interpersonal behavior is given to point out some of the more relevant variables that influence interpersonal associations.

To clarify the factors contained in the interpersonal model, we will be examining the following topics:

1. the personal system—goals, beliefs, competencies, and values
2. the self-concept
3. interpersonal mechanisms
4. interpersonal awareness
5. interpersonal needs
6. interpersonal orientations

Because the consequences of interpersonal interactions influence subsequent behaviors of participants, we will present a framework for appraising interpersonal consequences using exchange theory, which outlines how one weighs the rewards and costs of a relationship.

We will examine group roles and behaviors by looking at task behaviors and maintenance behaviors and the kinds of roles associated with each. In addition, we will look at self-oriented behaviors and their impact on group interaction.

Finally, we will examine the communication process in interpersonal relationships, using transactional analysis as a framework for analyzing clear and blocked communications.

INTERPERSONAL BEHAVIOR: A MODEL

Interpersonal relations are "the whole range of human conduct between individuals who interact as they are involved in relationships of communicating, cooperating, changing, problem solving, and motivating."[1] In such relationships each individual is trying to influence and modify the behavior of the other to satisfy his or her own needs. Interpersonal behavior can be illustrated as shown in Figure 7-1.

The diagram shows how interpersonal interactions are influenced by an individual's personal system, self-concept, and other individual predispositions. The resulting behavior in turn interacts with the activities from other persons to produce an action–reaction series of events or interactions. Finally, the interactions produce definite consequences for the individual. The self-concept may be confirmed or threatening in varying degrees. If the interchange is satisfying, the individual will continue or perhaps increase his or her interactions with others. Conversely, if the interchange is dissatis-

Figure 7-1

A Model of Interpersonal Behavior

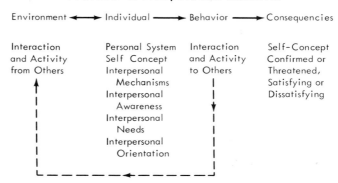

Environment ⟷ Individual ⟶ Behavior ⟶ Consequencies

Interaction	Personal System	Interaction	Self-Concept
and Activity	Self Concept	and Activity	Confirmed or
from Others	Interpersonal	to Others	Threatened,
	Mechanisms		Satisfying or
	Interpersonal		Dissatisfying
	Awareness		
	Interpersonal		
	Needs		
	Interpersonal		
	Orientation		

fying, the individual will seek to modify or terminate his or her interactions with others. Behavior is a function of its consequences.

Much of the following material is devoted to examining the relevance of the personal system, the self-concept, and other interpersonal tendencies for interpersonal behavior.

THE PERSONAL SYSTEM

In previous chapters we examined the basic ingredients of the personal system, focusing on the influence of beliefs (or assumptions), values, needs, and the self-concept on perception and behavior. Elements of the personal system were developed separately, but now each must be drawn into one framework—the personal system. Basically, the personal system is comprised of four parts.[2]

1. goals and needs
2. assumptions or beliefs
3. competencies—skills and abilities
4. values

Being a system, these parts are interdependent and exert mutual influence on one another.

Goals

Personal goals are the things or conditions we strive for to meet our basic needs.[3] As noted, needs are the energizers of goal-directed behavior. Some goals are long range and are best attained by seeking short-range goals. For example, if you wish to achieve a leadership position in an organization, a series of intermediate goals is necessary. These may range from making a high test grade to obtain a good course grade, a college degree, and a position in a certain promising organization. In other words, one's shorter-range goals are a means to attaining more distant, ultimate goals. In career planning, individuals are encouraged to establish professional goals each year and examine how well they move one to his or her ultimate goals. Such goals provide direction, purpose, and meaning to one's activities.

Competencies

An examination of personal goals is likely to raise questions of competency. Competencies are the knowledge, abilities, and skills that are relevant for coping with various roles. While our primary concern is occupational goals, one may be concerned with one's competency as a husband, wife, father, or mother and even in interpersonal relationships. One may have the abilities necessary for handling his or her job but lacking in his or her role as a parent.

Some competencies are limited or constrained by inherited capacities that set a ceiling on some activities. For example, a lack of depth perception may preclude one from being a good draftsman. Successful occupational adjustment requires that one analyze personal strengths and weaknesses to determine which are fixed and which can be changed. You can compensate for those weaknesses that can be changed and concentrate on improving those that are more easily remedied. For example, one may evaluate his or her administrative knowledge and ability, technical competence, leadership ability, ingenuity and creativity, oral and written communication skills, and so on. This kind of an analysis reveals one's most important strengths, principle fixed weaknesses, and correctable weaknesses. Weak competencies can be improved through various experiences, training, and education. Insights gained from such an examination are necessary for the formulation of realistic goals.

Assumptions and Beliefs

Assumptions and beliefs are the ideas that individuals have about other people, work, and society in general. Such beliefs not only affect perception but also behavior. One may believe that others are lazy and indolent (Theory X assumptions) or that others are capable of self-direction and self-control (Theory Y assumptions). One may believe that the economic system rewards the competent or exploits the worker. As previously shown, stereotyping and expectancy or self-fulfilling prophecy, are perceptual mechanisms used to ensure that beliefs and assumptions are confirmed.

Values

Values are the conditions that one would like to see prevail above all others, that is, factors that are important and basic to the individual. As noted in Chapter 2, traditional values are expressed as hard work pays off, competition encourages excellence, a strong person controls his or her own life, doing any job well is important, honesty is the best policy, and so on. Such values are standards that guide actions and decisions and thereby provide coherence and unity to one's life.

While many of the previous comments about the personal system related to one's career, the components of the personal system influence interpersonal interactions. For many persons their most rewarding associations are found among those in similar careers. People having similar personal systems are more likely to be compatible and experience rewards from their interactions whether on the job or off. Conversely, individuals with highly divergent personal systems are less likely to find their interactions mutually satisfying. Other factors contributing to the outcomes of interpersonal experiences will be discussed in the following paragraphs.

THE SELF-CONCEPT

The nucleus of the personal system exists in the self-concept. How one sees himself or herself is interrelated with his goals, competencies, beliefs, and values. Mankind is unique in that a person becomes an object to himself or herself, that is, his or her self-concept. One has the capacity for thinking about his or her behavior and appearance to others. Furthermore, each person has a set of beliefs and feelings toward himself or herself. This comprises the self or self-concept. A person has an attitude toward himself or herself consisting of three aspects—beliefs, feelings, and behaviors.[4] The belief component represents the content of the self. This is illustrated by such thoughts as "I am intelligent, ambitious, honest, gregarious, overweight," and the like. The feeling component about one's self is reflected in feelings of self-worth or in general as I'm O.K. or I'm not O.K. Finally, the behavioral component is the tendency to act toward one's self in a self-deprecating or self-enhancing manner.

The self-concept is a reflection of all one's past experiences and includes characteristics and qualities that distinguish the person from others. From one's experiences with other persons, an inner self is formed that represents one's most central characteristics and most important attitudes toward himself or herself. Once the self-concept is established and specific patterns of behavior are adopted, it tends to resist being changed.

The self-concept is characterized by a degree of stability that prevents an individual from regarding himself or herself as worthless at one moment and worthy at the next. Since the activities of an individual are organized and integrated in relation to the self or self-concept, each person develops a relatively consistent life-style. One has a characteristic way of relating to others, communicating, dealing with conflict, thinking, and so on. The personal system and its unifying force, the self-concept, strongly influences one's behavior and interpersonal relationships.

Maintaining an Interpersonal Environment

An individual achieves a stable interpersonal environment by maintaining a consistent relationship between his or her self-concept and his or her beliefs about how others behave and feel toward him or her with regard to his or her self-concept.[5] An individual actively uses certain mechanisms for maintaining his or her interpersonal environment so as to maximize congruency or harmony. These stabilizing interactions are as follows.

1. Misperception: When the actual expectations of others are not congruent with the person's self-concept or behavior, an individual may simply misperceive how others see him or her to achieve congruency.
2. Selective interaction: A person elects to interact with those persons with whom he or she can most readily establish a congruent state.
3. Selective evaluation of the other person: A person maximizes congruency by favorably evaluating those who behave congruently toward him or her and devaluates those who do not.
4. Selective evaluation of self: A person maximizes congruency by altering the values placed on various aspects of his or her self-concept so that the aspects that are in agreement with his or her perceptions of his or her behavior and those of others are most highly evaluated.
5. Response evocation: An individual intentionally or unintentionally behaves in a way that results in others' behaving toward him or her in a congruent fashion. A person in interaction controls the cues provided others to ensure that he or she will be categorized in certain ways and not in others.

The mechanisms given here convey some of the means used to achieve a balance in one's interpersonal activities and personal adjustment. One's use of such mechanisms not only protects one's self-concept but also will influence awareness in interpersonal relationships.

Awareness in Interpersonal Relations

In Chapter 2 reference was made to the self-concept's hiding behind facades or having a content that is neither known to the individual nor known to others. This is varied, however, depending on the openness of the personal self. The dynamics of the known and unknown to one's self and to others is shown by the ''Johari window'' in Figure 7-2.

Figure 7-2

The Johari Awareness Model of Interpersonal Processes

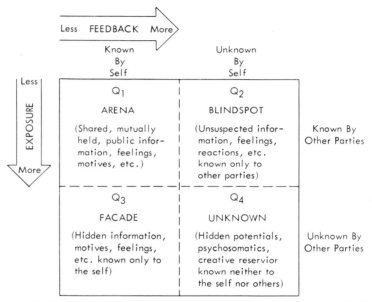

Source: Jay Hall, ''Interpersonal Style and the Communication Dilemma. II: Utility of the Johari Awareness Model for Genotypic Diagnosis,'' *Human Relations* 28 (October, 1975): 716.

Quadrant I is the arena, which represents the ''public self.'' Information about the self—behavior and motivation—is shared and mutually held by the self and others. Quadrant II is a blindspot to the self but is known to others. Quadrant III, the facade, is the private self, which is known by the individual and is not revealed to others. Finally, quadrant IV represents that part of one's self that is unknown by the individual or others.

If quadrant I is very small, there is very little free and spontaneous interaction. On the other hand, if I expands, one is freer to be more like himself or herself and to perceive others as they really are. Quadrant III, the private self, or facade, shrinks as quadrant I expands. As one's facade decreases, it becomes less necessary to hide or deny things one knows or feels. The blindspot, or quadrant II, takes longer to reduce because ego-defensive and protection mechanisms are involved.

Growth in quadrant I, the public self, is affected by exposure and feedback in interpersonal relations. These two variables are shown as two large arrows in Figure 7-2. Exposure is shown on the left and feedback at the top of the figure; each one is shown to range from less to more. Exposure ranges between closedness (less) and openness (more); both involve rewards and costs. Being open offers the possibility of self-understanding, growth, and better interpersonal adjustments, but it may result in learning things about one's self that are painful. On the other hand, being closed avoids being exposed and hurt, but it prevents personal insight and development. Too much openness may be as harmful as too little. The aroused anxiety can be detrimental to one's self-concept and difficult to cope with or assimilate.

Exposure, however, is related to and influenced by the feedback that one receives or solicits. The feedback given by others may be of no value or it may be helpful. Constructive feedback is more likely if the communication about behavior and reactions has the following characteristics.[6]

1. Intended to help the recipient.
2. Given directly, with real feeling, and based on a foundation of trust between the giver and receiver.
3. Descriptive rather than evaluative.
4. Specific rather than general, with good, clear, and preferably recent examples.
5. Given at a time when the receiver appears to be in a condition of readiness to accept it.
6. Checked with others to be sure that they support its validity.
7. Includes only those things that the receiver might be expected to be able to do something about.
8. Does not include more than the recipient can handle at any particular time.

When openness is coupled with effective feedback having the characteristics just noted, an individual has an opportunity to develop his or her interpersonal awareness. Interpersonal learning means that a change has taken place so that Quadrant I, the shared self, is larger and one or more of the other quadrants has grown smaller. Several principles of change summarize some of what has been presented on this topic.[7]

1. A change in any one quadrant will affect all other quadrants.
2. It takes energy to hide, deny, or be blind to behavior that is involved in interaction.
3. Threat tends to decrease awareness; mutual trust tends to increase awareness.

4. Forced awareness (exposure) is undesirable and usually ineffective.
5. The smaller the first quadrant, the poorer the communication.
6. Working with others is facilitated by a large area of free activity or expression, that is, quadrant I. This means that more of the resources and skills in the relationship can be applied to the task at hand.

OTHER DETERMINANTS OF INTERPERSONAL BEHAVIOR

As we have seen, interpersonal behavior is influenced by one's personal system and self-concept. However, other factors do affect interpersonal relationships. Interpersonal needs, interpersonal orientation, and interpersonal attraction are concepts that further assist one in describing and explaining the variations found in interpersonal behavior.

Interpersonal Needs

People need people, but in what ways? An interpersonal need is satisfied only through the attainment of satisfactory relations with other people. Schutz maintains that there are three interpersonal needs—inclusion, control, and affection—that cause one to establish and maintain relations with others.[8] These needs are defined as follows:

1. inclusion—the need for interaction and association.
2. control—the need for control and power
3. affection—the need for love and affection

Individuals differ, however, in the strength of their interpersonal needs.

For each interpersonal need, there are two behavioral aspects—expressed and wanted. Expressed behavior is the behavior that we initiate toward others, whereas wanted behavior is the behavior we want or prefer from others toward us. Table 7-1 illustrates both wanted and expressed behavior for each interpersonal need.

Compatability is a property of a relationship between two or more persons that leads to the mutual satisfaction of interpersonal needs and harmonious coexistence. Each individual desires a certain optimal relationship between himself or herself and others in each need area. For a dyad (two persons) this means that one person wants to act in a certain way toward the other and wants to be acted toward in a certain way. If what is wanted and what is expressed is equal for both interacting persons, mutual needs are satisfied. For example, those who wish to dominate and control activities work well with those who want to be controlled or directed. However, if both parties want to dominate, some degree of conflict may be expected.

Table 7-1

Interpersonal Behaviors

Expressed Behavior	Need Dimension	Wanted Behavior
I initiate interaction with people	Inclusion	I want to be included
I control people	Control	I want people to control me
I act close and personal toward people	Affection	I want people to get close and personal with me

Source: William C. Schutz, *The Interpersonal Underworld* (Palo Alto, Calif.: Science and Behavior Books, 1966), p. 59.

Interpersonal relations may be associated with some amount of anxiety. Such anxiety arises because one may anticipate a nonsatisfying event, that is, being ignored, dominated, rejected. Also, one may fear the exposure, to himself and others, of the kind of person he or she really is; that is, one's self-concept may be threatened. In perceiving the self, the need for inclusion is to feel that the self is significant and worthwhile; for control, the need is to feel one's self as a competent and responsible person; for affection, the need is to feel that the self is a lovable person.

Interpersonal Orientations

Individuals vary greatly in how they relate to and influence others. Three basic types of persons have been identified—the tough battler, the friendly helper, and the objective thinker.[9] These three styles and associated behaviors are outlined in Table 7-2.

The interpersonal orientations are shown in terms of extremes, but they are familiar and descriptive of personal behavior. Many people are more oriented to one style than another and feel more comfortable with its associated behaviors. While one's style is related to his or her personal needs and self-concept, a style can be overdone and distorted. Each style

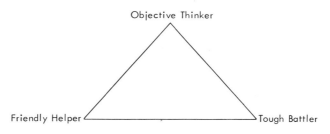

Table 7-2

Three Interpersonal Orientations
and Associated Behaviors

	Tough Battler	Friendly Helper	Objective Thinker
Emotions	Accepts aggression Rejects affection	Accepts affection Rejects aggression	Rejects both affection and interpersonal aggression
Goal	Dominance	Acceptance	Correctness
Judges others by	Strength, power	Warmth	Cognitive ability
Influences others by	Direction, intimidation, control of rewards	Offering understanding, praise, favors, friendship	Factual data, logical arguments
Value in organization	Initiates, demands, disciplines	Supports, harmonizes, relieves tension	Defines, clarifies, gets information, criticizes, tests
Overuses	Fight	Kindness	Analysis
Becomes	Pugnacious	Sloppy, sentimental	Pedantic
Fears	Being "soft" or dependent	Desertion, conflict	Emotions, irrational acts
Needs	Warmth, consideration, objectivity, humility	Strength, integrity, firmness, self-assertion	Awareness of feeling, ability to love and to fight

Source: Cyril R. Mill and Lawrence C. Porter, "An Expanding Repertoire of Behavior," *Reading Book,* 1972 ed., of the NTL Institute for Applied Behavioral Science, associated with the National Education Association, p. 15.

reflects behaviors that, in varying degrees, are ineffective in some situations. Most of us fall somewhere within the triangle shown on page 204. Note where you think you are and then get the opinion of a close friend. Do you agree on this?

The Tough Battler would relate better to others if he or she were more sensitive to others, could accept his or her own inevitable dependence on others, and recognize that some situations will not yield to pugnacity. The Friendly Helper would be more satisfied if he or she could stand up for his or her own interests and face conflict. Likewise, the Objective Thinker could relate to others more effectively if he or she were more aware and accepting of his or her own feelings and those of others. One does not have to assume that his or her behavior is fixed or impossible to control. Expanding one's repertoire of behavior requires experimenting within a framework that elicits feedback as to its effectiveness.

Interpersonal Attraction

An individual is not passive in his or her interpersonal interactions with others but seeks to structure these relationships. An individual elects to interact with others whom he or she can most readily establish a harmonious relationship. For example, if one regards himself or herself as very intelligent, that person will interact with others who respect his or her intelligence or allow him or her to use it. By choosing such persons as friends, an important and durable source for harmonious interactions is created. People interact most frequently with those who are perceived as confirming their self-concept to the greatest extent. A great deal of strain is avoided that might be placed on an individual's self-concept if one were to interact with just anyone.

As a result of past experience, an individual becomes dependent upon others for information about the environment. This information is used to confirm and extend one's impressions of his or her perceptions. The individual needs support from others for his or her attitudes and beliefs. When one encounters another with different attitudes, a state of strain arises, especially if the other person is liked. Such strain is uncomfortable, and the individual seeks to resolve it by finding agreement with others. This is the need for *consensual validation,* which means that people attempt to validate their attitudes through seeking agreement with others.[10]

The greater the importance and common consequences of an object for two people, the greater the attraction between both persons. An object may refer to any focus of perception—including physical objects, symbols, the other person's self-concept—or to one's own self-concept. This relationship is depicted in Figure 7-3.

Figure 7-3

Interpersonal Attraction

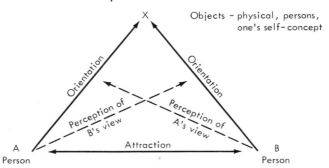

The attraction of A towards B is affected by the similarity between A's attitude toward X and his or her perception of B's attitude toward X. Furthermore, A's own attitude toward X and his or her perception of B's attitude are influenced by the degree to which he or she is attracted to B. For example, assume that A, who is attracted to B, discovers a difference between his or her and B's attitude toward their supervisor, X. A likes the supervisor, but B does not and holds many unfavorable views of him. Since A is attracted to B but holds divergent views, a strain is created that must be resolved. Return to a state of balance may take several forms.[11]

1. A shift in A's perception of B's attitude may occur. A may decide that he or she was mistaken in attributing to B a negative attitude toward the supervisor. If B actually does have a negative attitude, this would be a misperception.
2. A might change his or her attitude in the direction of B's and develop a negative attitude toward the supervisor.
3. A might try to convince B that B is mistaken about the supervisor. If B is attracted to A and is also experiencing a strain, B might be susceptible to such persuasion.
4. A might restore balance to the relationship by reducing his or her attraction toward B.

These actions indicate how people seek to validate their attitudes through seeking agreement with others—consensual validation.

When a group begins to interact and acquire information of others' views and attitudes, bonds of attraction form most strongly between those who hold similar views toward things that are important and relevant to both. Also a person likes others who have the same feeling toward him or her as that person has toward himself or herself. This reinforces one's self-concept and facilitates interpersonal relations.

EVALUATING THE CONSEQUENCES OF INTERPERSONAL BEHAVIOR

Exchange Theory of Attraction

Since behavior is a function of its consequences, we must examine how such consequences may be evaluated by the individual. The exchange theory of attraction offers an explanation of how the consequences of interpersonal interaction may be appraised. Basically, the theory consists of four concepts: reward, cost, outcome, and comparison level. Reward is any activity on the part of one person that contributes to the gratification of the needs of another. For example, consensual validation about the world as well as about one's self is a kind of reward. Affection, love, formal courtesies, and friendship are other rewards. In other words, any activity on the part of one person that contributes to the gratification of another person's needs can be considered a reward from the standpoint of the latter person. The second term used in exchange theory is cost, which is considered to include punishments incurred and deterrents in interacting with another person such as fatigue, anxiety, and fear of embarrassment as well as rewards foregone because of the interaction.

The third term in this theory is outcome, which is rewards less costs. If the outcome of an interaction is positive, it may be said to yield a profit; if it is negative, a loss. The reward–cost outcome must be at least slightly above some minimum level of what the person feels is his or her due. Finally, evaluation of the outcome is achieved by the use of a comparison level, which is a standard against which satisfaction is judged.

In evaluating the acceptability of outcomes, two standards for evaluation can be identified—comparison level and comparison level for alternatives.[12] The comparison level (CL) is the standard against which an individual evaluates the attractiveness of the relationship or how satisfactory it is to him or her. This reflects what the person feels he or she deserves or is entitled to. The comparison level is influenced by past experiences in the relationship and/or in comparable relationships and perceptions of what others like one's self are obtaining. Outcomes that fall above CL would be relatively satisfying and attractive, whereas outcomes falling below would be unsatisfactory.

The second standard for evaluating outcomes is the comparison level for alternatives (CL alt). This is the lowest level of outcomes that an individual will accept in light of other available alternative opportunities. Consequently, when outcomes drop below CL alt, the individual will leave the relationship. Alternative relationships with which the present one is compared in developing the CL alt may include other dyads, more complex relationships, joining no group, or being alone. The formation and survival of a relationship depends largely upon whether or not the jointly experienced outcomes are above each member's CL alt.

The two standards of evaluation reflect two different forces. While CL reflects *attractiveness* of a personal relationship, individual, or group, CL alt indicates *dependency*. An individual may be greatly dependent on another without the relationship's being attractive or satisfying. For example, one's dependency on a group, and therefore its power over him or her, is not necessarily highly correlated with his or her attraction to the group or satisfaction from belonging to it. In other words, more attractive associations are not available to the individual; the individual is dependent on whatever satisfactions are attainable in the existing membership or relationship.

Figure 7-4 diagrams the evaluative process. Notice the potential kinds of rewards and costs associated with an interpersonal relationship. The outcome or ''profit'' reflects the consequences of the relationship, which are determined by the comparison level (deserved satisfaction) and the comparison level for other associations.

Figure 7-4

A Diagram of Interpersonal Exchange

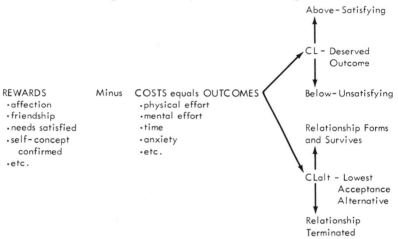

Changes in the costs and rewards in a person's experience in relations with others may stem from any of five sources.

Changes in Costs and Rewards

Any change in an outcome experienced can be analyzed as either a change in costs or a change in rewards.[13] Changes in the costs and rewards in a person's experience in relations with others may stem from any of five sources.

1. Past experiences that shift reward–cost values: As each person continues to exchange rewards, the behaviors may become increasingly costly due to fatigue, loss of alternatives, rewards, and so on. Also, the value of the reward may decrease as the relevant needs of each person become satisfied.

2. Changes in the characteristics of the two members: Such changes frequently happen as a result of experiences in other relations, new opinions, attitudes, training, and education. Also, other kinds of needs emerge and new goals are accepted. Such changes alter the reward and cost values of both parties.

3. Changes in external circumstances that introduce new rewards and costs and therefore modify the values of previous ones: One example is, the increase in attraction toward an expert when the situation demands his or her skills and knowledge.

4. Sequential factors in the relationship itself: An individual experiencing profitable interactions becomes increasingly motivated to ensure the continuation of such interaction by increasing the profit of the other. This can work in the reverse direction when a person whose reward–cost outcome is adversely affected reduces the profits experienced by the other who retaliates in the same manner.

5. Association with other behaviors having different reward–cost values: Behaviors of each person that were neutral become rewarding or costly through associations with other behaviors. For example, a person may become fond of his or her work group because of off-the-job social activities.

Changes in Comparison Level

In addition to changes in rewards and costs, the comparison level may be affected in interpersonal relationships. Change may occur not only because of the reward–cost experiences noted but also because of changes in perception of others' experiences in similar relations and the evaluation of alternative situations. The comparison level will gradually rise as the outcomes become progressively better or decline as they become worse. As the relationship develops, increasing profits for both members, the comparison level itself (what one deserves) also rises, making the increase in profit less than if the comparison level remained constant, for example, the experienced decline in satisfaction that one experiences after the initial glow of some relationships in their early stages. Similarly, the comparison level falls as profits in the relationship decline. The decline in what one feels he or she is entitled to or deserves explains why persons frequently find satisfactions in situations they never thought possible. Finally, the comparison level for alternatives determines the durability of the relationship. A relationship may persist even though outcomes are low because the potential for satisfaction from other sources is even lower.

GROUP ROLES AND BEHAVIOR

Additional insight into interpersonal behavior can be achieved by examining interactions in a group setting. Increasingly, organizational life takes the form of group meetings of one kind or another. Many jobs contain required activities that include group discussions, meetings with other groups, or committee assignments. Numerous organizational issues are so complex and the interdependencies of groups are so extensive that the specialized expertise of numerous individuals and groups must be pooled. The time and expense involved provide an incentive to focus on group meetings and their effectiveness.

Behavior in groups can be viewed in terms of its purpose or function. Three functions are clearly evident.[14]

1. Task behavior to achieve a goal or objective.
2. Maintenance behavior to keep the group working together smoothly and effectively using each member's resources.
3. Self-oriented behavior to meet some personal need or goal without regard to the group's problems or goals.

Several forms of behavior are expressive of each category of group behavior.

Task Behaviors

Task behaviors are conducive to getting the task accomplished. The types of behavior that are helpful in achieving the group's *tasks* are as follows.

Initiating: Proposing tasks or goals, defining a group problem, suggesting a procedure or ideas for solving a problem.

Seeking information or opinions: Requesting facts, seeking relevant information about a group concern, requesting a statement or estimate, soliciting expressions of value, seeking suggestions or ideas.

Giving information or opinions: Offering facts, providing relevant information about a group concern, stating a belief about a matter before the group, giving suggestions and ideas.

Clarifying and elaborating: Interpreting ideas or suggestions, clearing up confusions, defining terms, indicating alternatives and issues before the group.

Summarizing: Pulling together related ideas, restating suggestions after the group has discussed them, offering a decision or conclusion for the group to accept or reject.

Consensus testing: Asking to see whether the group is nearing a decision, sending up trial balloon to test a possible conclusion.

Maintenance Behavior

Maintenance behaviors are conducive to maintaining a climate for task activities, reducing hostilities, and soliciting everyone's contribution. These behaviors are described as follows:

Harmonizing: Attempting to reconcile disagreements, reducing tension, getting people to explore differences.

Gate keeping: Helping to keep communication channels open, facilitating the participation of others, suggesting procedures that permit sharing remarks.

Encouraging: Being friendly, warm, and responsive to others, indicating by facial expression or remarks the acceptance of others' contributions.

Compromising: When one's idea or status is involved in a conflict, offering a compromise that yields status, admitting error, modifying in interest of group cohesion or growth.

Standard setting and testing: Testing whether the group is satisfied with its procedures or suggesting procedures, pointing out explicit or implicit norms that have been set to make them available for testing.

A work group needs to have both task and maintenance behaviors to effectively achieve its objectives. If the task behaviors are not adequately expressed, the group will tend to flounder about in an ineffective manner. The quality of its deliberations and goal attainment are impaired. A group may need to examine which behaviors are missing or inadequately demonstrated in its activities. Likewise, the maintenance behaviors must be expressed when necessary to avoid destructive conflict and to repair ruptured interrelationships. Individuals may withdraw from the group's activities or may need some encouragement to contribute what they have to offer to the group's effort. An adequate balance of both categories of behavior must occur if the group is to function efficiently.

If you are functioning as a group to discuss the text cases or in any manner, your group may find it worthwhile to analyze its task and maintenance behaviors. Are any of the behaviors missing? Overdone? Do these behaviors seem related to the group's effectiveness or difficulties? As an individual, what behavior(s) do you display most often? Should you try to expand your role behaviors?

Self-oriented Behavior

Not all group behaviors are of the task and maintenance variety. Some behaviors are highly individualized or personal. Personal needs and emotional issues may interfere with effective group functioning. Not only is the group's activity impaired, but the individual fails to grow when his or her behavior is based on self-oriented needs. The emotional issues center around the following kinds of problems.

Identity: Who am I in the group? Where do I fit in? What kind of behavior is acceptable here?

Goals and needs: What do I want from the group? Can the group goals be made consistent with my goals? What have I to offer to the group?

Power, control, and influence: Who will control what we do? How much power and influence do I have?

Intimacy: How close will we get to each other? How personal? How much can we trust each other? Can we achieve a greater level of trust?

The behaviors resulting from such problems are seen in the following activities.

Dependency–counterdependency: Opposing or resisting anyone in the group who represents authority.

Fighting and controlling: Asserting personal dominance, attempting to get one's way regardless of others.

Withdrawing: Trying to remove the sources of uncomfortable feelings by psychologically leaving the group.

Pairing up: Seeking out one or two supporters and forming a kind of emotional subgroup in which the members protect and support one another.

An effective group can recognize such behaviors and try to identify the issue. Subsequent efforts will focus on finding ways that permit these emotional energies to be directed toward the group's effort. Most groups do not have the insights or skills necessary to cope with such individuals, and outside assistance or a consultant will be required. With such help and training, the group can become adept at handling emotional issues.

COMMUNICATION IN INTERPERSONAL RELATIONS

Interpersonal relations provide a setting in which people influence one another; this is achieved primarily by communication. Communication can be the source of harmonious, gratifying interaction or the source of anxiety and conflict. Transactional analysis provides a means for analyzing and understanding the quality of communications between individuals.

A transaction is an exchange between two people. A conversation is a series of transactions, one exchange after another.[15] Transactional analysis provides a framework for understanding such exchanges by emphasizing (1) the "selves within" a person and (2) the interaction or transactions between people as they involve these "selves."[16]

The "selves within" each person consists of three parts—Parent, Adult, and Child. These are illustrated as shown. All people have these three "persons" within, all of which are technically known as ego states. Each ego state reflects habitual ways of thinking, feeling, and reacting that occur together. The division of a person's personality into three parts and the associated functions are developed in the following paragraphs.

Three Parts of the Ego: Parent, Adult, and Child

Parent

The Parent in you feels and behaves in the same ways as you perceived the feelings and behavior in your parents, teachers, and authoritative figures. All the do's and do not's, should's and should not's are recorded in this part of one's self. Parent functions can be nurturing or critical and are reflected in activities that

1. set limits
2. give advice
3. discipline
4. guide
5. protect
6. make rules and regulations about how life should be
7. teach how-to's
8. keep traditions (God, mother, apple pie)
9. nurture
10. judge
11. criticize

The functions of the Parent are neither positive nor negative. One needs to discover and be aware of his or her Parent and then sort out what makes sense and what doesn't in terms of present realities. It is important for one to update one's attitudes, behaviors, and feelings in terms of what is appropriate for him or her rather than what is appropriate for his or her parents.

Adult

The Adult is the part of you that figures out things by looking at the facts. It is the nonemotional, rational, logical part of the personality. Adult functions are

1. data gathering on the Parent and Child, that is, determining how the Child feels and what he wants; what the Parent says, feels, or reacts to; what the memories of past decisions in the Adult have to say; and what the external situation in the here and now supports.

2. sorting out the best alternatives from this data collection, that is, the Adult computes, if a decision is needed, which data to use or decides that the data are insufficient for making a decision.
3. planning steps in the decision-making process, that is (a) results wanted, (b) best way to go after them, (c) first step to get a result, (d) action or alternatives if desired result is not achieved, (e) recycling process.

Child

The Child in you is what you were when you were very young. It records one's early experiences and one's response to such experiences. When a person is experiencing feeling, he or she is in the Child ego state. While in the Child state, one may be either free or adapted in his or her behavior:

1. The natural or free Child may be loving, spontaneous, creative, carefree, adventurous, joyful.
2. The adapted Child reacts to all the things "parent figures" have said that children must do and is compliant or comforming.

An individual is all three persons; all three are important. No ego state is better than any other. However, the situation and the Adult determine what is appropriate. The Adult needs to be functioning all the time to be aware of the Parent, Child, and the situation so as to help with decisions.

An Analysis of Transactions

Transactions are the interactions between two people and between the three selves within each. Actually, this means that six ego states are involved in communication. The nature, quality, and effectiveness of communication are determined by the various ego states that are involved.

The simplest communication consists of a stimulus and a response. Transactions are diagrammed by showing an arrow from the ego state that is in charge in the *first person* to the ego state for which it is intended in the second person. Likewise, the response is shown by an arrow from the ego state in charge of the *second person*. For example,

First Person　　　　　　　Second Person

Transactions can be parallel, crossed, or ulterior. If there is to be useful communication, the lines must not cross.

Parallel transactions

A parallel transaction occurs when a message sent from a specific ego state gets the predicted response from the same ego state in the other person.

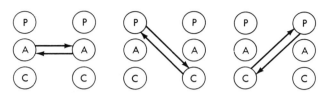

In other words, the response is appropriate and expected and follows the natural order of healthy human relationships. For example, two people may transact Parent–Parent when discussing family values and traditions, Adult–Adult when solving a problem, and Child–Child when having fun together. If the transaction is parallel, the lines of communication are open and the people can continue transacting with one another.

1. First Student: There must be some variables we haven't considered in this experiment.

2. Second Student: You are probably right. Let's go back and check our procedure step by step.

Crossed transactions

A crossed transaction occurs when an unexpected response is received. An inappropriate ego state is activated, and the lines of transacting between people are crossed.

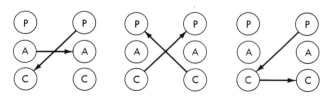

When this occurs, people may withdraw, separate, or change the topic of conversation. The person initiating a transaction expects a certain response but does not get it. Such transactions are a source of irritation and/or pain between people.

1. Boss: What time is it?
2. Secretary: Why don't you get yourself a watch?

Ulterior transactions

Ulterior transactions are complex since they involve more than two ego states. When an ulterior message is sent, it is disguised under a socially acceptable transaction. Take for example, the question, "Would you like to come up to see my etchings?" The Adult is saying one thing while the Child by means of innuendo is sending a different message.

If a salesperson says to a customer, "This is our finest television set, but it may be too expensive for you," the message sent may be heard by the customer's Adult or Child. If the customer's Adult responds, the customer may say, "Yes, you are right, considering the financial obligations I now have." However, if the Child responds, the customer may say, "I'll take it. It's just what I want." In this example, the salesperson's transaction is Adult–Adult on the social level, but the ulterior message is Adult–Child. The latter response of the customer indicates that his or her Child has been "hooked."

One can become acquainted with his or her own P-A-C by listening to these three different voices within himself or herself and by spotting them in others. This is revealed not only in verbal communication but in nonverbal communication as well. One's vocal tone, posture, facial expressions, and body gestures speak loudly. If a verbal message is to be completely understood, the receiver must also consider the nonverbal aspects as well as the spoken word. Table 7-3 illustrates some of the nonverbal cues for each ego state.

One of the goals of learning transactional analysis is to understand what part of the individual is "coming on." Many organizations have given training sessions to make participants more aware of the ego states involved in communications and improve their interpersonal relationships. The potential range of applicants and the effectiveness of transactional analysis has been well documented. Employee–customer and superior–subordinate relationships, to mention only a few, have been improved dramatically with such training.[17]

Table 7-3

Nonverbal Cues of the Three Ego States

	Parent Ego State	Adult Ego State	Child Ego State
Voice tones	Condescending, putting down, criticizing, or accusing	Matter-of-fact	Full of feeling
Words used	Everyone knows that... You should never... You should always... I can't understand why in the world you would ever...	How, what, when, where, why, who, probable	I'm mad at you!... Hey, great (or any words that have a high feeling level connected with them)
Postures	Puffed-up, supercorrect, very proper	Attentive, eye-to-eye contact, listening and looking for maximum data	Slouching, playful, beaten down or burdened, self-conscious
Facial expressions	Frowns, worried or disapproving looks, chin jutted out	Alert eyes, paying close attention	Excitement, surprise, downcast eyes, quivering lip or chin, moist eyes
Body gestures	Hands on hips, pointing finger in accusation, arms folded across chest	Leaning forward in chair toward other person, moving closer to hear and see better	Spontaneous activity, wringing hands, pacing, withdrawing into corner or moving away from laughter, raising hand for permission

Source: Thomas C. Clary, "A Roadmap to Better Human Relations by Using Transactional Analysis," (Washington, D.C.: National Training and Development Service for State and Local Government), p. 2.

SUMMARY

A model of interpersonal relationships provided a framework for evaluating several factors that influence interactions in varying degrees. The model also noted the consequences of interpersonal behavior for one's self-concept and level of satisfaction. Whenever an individual interacts with another, his or her personal system consisting of goals, beliefs, competencies, and values is involved in the interaction. The personal system is unified and given consistency by one's self-concept. An individual protects or maintains his or her self-concept by the use of interpersonal behavioral techniques or mechanisms such as misperception, selective interaction, selective evaluations of others, and selective self-evaluation. These protective techniques influence interpersonal awareness. Interpersonal awareness is also influenced by the extent to which one is willing to reveal his or her true self or to be open in interactions with others. Openness when coupled with constructive feedback from others about one's personal behavior becomes the means for developing self- and interpersonal awareness.

Additional determinants of interpersonal interactions are interpersonal needs, interpersonal orientations, and interpersonal attractions. Interpersonal needs of inclusion, control, and affection strongly influence interactions between people. These needs affect both expressed behavior toward others and the amount of behavior wanted from others. Individuals also have interpersonal orientations that may be broadly labeled as Tough Battler, Friendly Helper, and Objective Thinker. Each interpersonal orientation is associated with personal goals, emotions, needs, values, and behaviors. Finally, interpersonal interactions are affected by the interpersonal attraction between two persons. Such attraction is determined by the extent to which each views important objects—persons, things, one's self-concept—in a similar matter. Agreement supports each member's attitudes and beliefs, thereby providing consensual validation. Consensus may be achieved by one or both changing their attitudes toward or their perceptions of the other's attitude. If agreement is achieved, interpersonal attraction will continue or increase; if not, attraction and interaction will diminish or cease.

Since behavior is influenced by its consequences, the exchange theory of attraction was presented as a framework for evaluating interactions. A reward–cost outcome (profit) determination is made by interacting persons. The outcome of the association is appraised in terms of what the individual feels that he or she deserves or is entitled to (the comparison level) and also the lowest level of outcomes that an individual will accept in view of other available alternatives. Continuation of the relationship is dependent upon the assessment of these two comparison levels.

Behaviors in a group setting may consist of task roles for accomplishing the group's objective or maintenance roles for keeping the group working harmoniously. Both kinds of behaviors are necessary if a group is to be effective. Self-oriented behaviors block the group's progress toward goal attainment.

Transactional analysis was used as a framework for examining communications between people. An exchange may be initiated from one's

Parent, Child, or Adult ego state. If one gets the predicted response from the same ego state in the other person, communication is open and continues. When an inappropriate ego state is activated, communication becomes difficult and may cease. The consequences of interpersonal relations are greatly influenced by personal communications.

QUESTIONS FOR STUDY AND DISCUSSION

1. Interpersonal behavior is affected by its consequences. What does this statement mean?

2. What are the parts of the personal system? How are interpersonal relations affected by the personal system?

3. How may one protect one's self-concept?

4. How can one's interpersonal awareness be increased? What advantages and risks are involved? How may the risks be minimized?

5. What is consensual validation? How is this achieved when some disagreement arises between two persons?

6. How can the exchange theory of attraction be used to evaluate the consequences of interpersonal behavior? Can you give an example of this from personal experience?

7. What is the difference between task and maintenance behaviors in a group setting? Why is each kind of behavior important?

8. What is a parallel transaction? How are interpersonal relations affected by a parallel transaction?

NOTES

[1]Knowles, Henry P. and Borje O. Saxberg, *Personality and Leadership Behavior* (Reading, Mass.: Addison-Wesley, 1971), p. 1.

[2]Cohen, Allan R., Stephen L. Fink, H. Gadon, and Robin D. Willis, *Effective Behavior in Organizations* (Homewood, Ill.: Irwin, 1976), pp. 127–137.

[3]McCaskey, Michael B., "Goals and Directions in Personal Planning," *Academy of Management Review* 2 (July, 1977), pp. 574–462.

[4]Secord, Paul F. and Carl. W. Backman, *Social Psychology* (New York: McGraw-Hill, 1964), pp. 579–580.

[5]*Ibid.,* pp. 580–591.

[6]Anderson, John, "Giving and Receiving Feedback," in Gene W. Dalton, Paul R. Lawrence, and Larry E. Greiner, eds., *Organizational Change and Development* (Homewood, Ill.: Irwin, 1970), pp. 339–346.

[7]"The Johari Window: A Graphic Model of Awareness in Interpersonal Relations," Reading Book, 1972 Edition, of the NTL Institute for Applied Science, Associated with the National Education Association, pp. 13–14.

[8]Schutz, William C., *The Interpersonal Underworld* (Palo Alto, Calif.: Science and Behavior Books, 1966), pp. 14–33. See also. Liddel, William W. and John W. Slocum Jr.,

"The Effects of Individual—Role Compatability Upon Group Performance: An Extension of Schutz's FIRO Theory" *Academy of Management Journal* 19 (September, 1976), 413–426.

[9]Mill, Cyril R. and Lawrence C. Porter, "An Expanding Repertoire of Behavior," in *Reading Book, op. cit,* pp. 15–16.

[10]Secord and Backman, *op. cit.,* pp. 247–248.

[11]*Ibid.,* p. 253.

[12]Thibaut, J. W. and H. H. Kelly, *The Social Psychology of Groups* (New York: Wiley, 1959), pp. 9–30.

[13]Secord and Backman, *op. cit.,* pp. 262–265.

[14]*Reading Book, op. cit,* pp. 29–31.

[15]Clary, Thomas C., "A Roadmap to Better Human Relations by Using Transactional Analysis" (Washington, D.C.: National Training and Development Service for State and Local Government.)

[16]Anderson, John P., "A Transactional Analysis Primer," John E. Jones and J. William Pfeiffer, eds., in *The 1973 Annual Handbook for Group Facilitators* (Iowa City, Iowa: University Associates, 1973), pp. 145–149.

[17]Jongeward, Dorothy, *Everybody Wins: Transactional Analysis Applied to Organizations* (Reading, Mass: Addison–Wesley, 1973), pp. 73–239.

cases cases cases

Case Study: The Donnybrook

Middle management is composed of two types of individuals. The first is the talented high school graduate who has worked his or her way up in the plant by demonstrated leadership and technical proficiency. After twelve years it is possible for such exceptional persons to become a shift or area supervisor, a process engineer, and, in rare instances a department supervisor. No further advancement is permitted.

The second type of individual is the college graduate who starts in the staff area rather than on the production line as in case of the noncollege individual. Promotion on the basis of ability occurs as upper-level positions become available. The college graduates are younger and short on practical experience, whereas the noncollege supervisor personnel are much older and have a minimum of twelve years with production processes.

On each Thursday afternoon at 1:30 P.M., a scheduling meeting is held in the maintenance supervisor's office. The purpose is to schedule production changes that will be made during the next week. Members present include the following:

1. Production Planning representative (college graduate)
2. Forming representative (noncollege)
3. Process Control representative (college graduate)
4. Maintenance representative (noncollege)
5. Fabricating representative (noncollege)

At one of these meetings the following discussion took place.

Production Planning Representative: Next week we will have six product changes. The timing for these changes will be as follows: A and D will be changed on Tuesday and . . .

Forming Representative: Wait a minute. We just made that change two weeks ago and you want us to change back next week. Can't you people in production planning get anything straight? Why do my efficiencies have to pay for your mistakes?

Production Planning Representative: We just received a rush order for this material and we don't have any in inventory.

Forming Representative: I don't give a damn about your problems, or what the customer wants—my problem is to push those pounds out, and with all these changes our operating efficiencies just go to pot. You make me look bad to my boss with your stupid mistakes.

Later during the meeting.

Process Control Representative: The following product improvement testing trials are to be run next week. Trial A is to begin on Wednesday and will involve maintenance changes that . . .

Maintenance Representative: I don't think there is any way that we will be able to run all those trials. Our maintenance personnel are overworked now anyway. With all those production planning changes that will have to be made, trials with their second priority will probably be out in left field.

Forming Representative: That's good, those trials mess me up so the fewer the better. We're running all right with the present setups. Things should be left as they are. Anyway, 90 percent of those trials fail to pan out. Most of the time the trial has either been run before or is so far out in left field that there is no way for the thing to work. I've been here for twelve years, and you process engineers are all just rookies. When you have any experience you'll be able to see that those far-out lame-brain ideas you college boys are always dreaming up just won't work out here in the real world. They ought to get rid of all useless process engineers anyway.

Fabrication Representative: It wouldn't matter anyway, that trial can't be run anyway. Our in-process material has the maximum number of runs on it now. Unless some shuffling is done with the present distribution of materials, we won't be able to handle any trials next week.

QUESTIONS

1. What interpersonal orientation seems prevalent in this meeting?
2. What task behaviors do you see in this episode? Maintenance behaviors? Self-oriented behaviors?

3. In terms of transactional analysis, what ego state(s) are reflected in this meeting? Results.

4. What other factors may explain the behaviors demonstrated in this meeting?

cases cases cases

Case Study: A Clouded Career

PART I A NEW JOB

Tom Gandy was hired as a management trainee soon after his graduation from college. Gandy was only twenty-two years old, and the job was his first real business experience. The training program was designed to develop administrative managers but included only brief views of the company's manufacturing facilities.

At the end of his training period, Tom Gandy had to pick from several job offers within the company. He remembered the corporate controller's comment, "The Customer Service Division is our most profitable and best-run division at the present time. There are some real experienced heads running that division." He had also noticed that there were few young men in the division and that there were no college graduates in any of the manager positions. In his interview with the director of Customer Service, Ed Moultrie, it was emphasized that Gandy would be the only young man and the only college graduate reporting to him. He hinted that the division had rapid advancement plans for the young man if he took the job. The talk convinced Gandy that the job was the one he should take, and he accepted a position as the assistant manager of the Operations Reporting and Control Department.

PART II A COLD START

Bert Palmer was the department manager. He had been in the position since the department was organized and had held a similar position for several years prior to that time. Palmer was fifty-two years old and had been with the company twenty-seven years. Starting as a company mail truck driver, he had slowly worked his way up to a manager's job. In his position he reported to Ed Moultrie. Carol Mann directed the functions designed to maintain controls on the finished production and unfilled orders. She had been a supervisor for eight years in the department, with the company for twenty-six years, and had acquired invaluable experience in the reporting and control functions. In her supervisory position she had responsibility for the performance of nine people carrying out the bulk of the department's work. Liz Ginn, supervisor of scheduling and controlling of outside processing area, had also been with the company for twenty-six years. Five employees reported to her. The job, assistant department manager, that Tom Gandy assumed was a new position with unclear responsibilities. He and both supervisors reported to Bert Palmer.

Tom Gandy entered the Operations Reporting and Control Department anxious to learn its functions and to assume some responsibility. The first few weeks on the job produced some strong initial impressions. Bert Palmer, the department manager, seemed to play a largely inactive role in running the department. He relied on his supervisors, Carol Mann and Liz Ginn, to see that all work was carried out. He did use his experience in data processing to solve unusual problems. However, he let the supervisors run the department and handle the employees' job problems. Gandy heard the comment about Palmer from several of the women that "He doesn't bother us, but of course he doesn't help us either." The women in the department seemed to respect Palmer's knowledge. They also seemed to enjoy his lack of participation in supervising their work. But at the same time there were hints of resentment at his inaction on their problems. Gandy saw immediately that the supervisors did a good job of running the department. The reports and controls were subject to many deadlines, but the supervisors made sure that the work was completed on time. He also discovered that the work activities were more complex than he had originally thought. The experience of the women in the department and Palmer's easy-going style disguised the complicated nature of most of the reports and control figures created in the department. Most of the reporting output resulted from punch card input into the Data Processing Center. Because so much of the work was built into computer programs, Gandy found it difficult to follow the flow of work. Another distinct impression was that there was no place and no real need for him in the department.

Tom Gandy's work, or lack of it, began to bother him more and more as the months passed. He had picked up several small duties from Ed Moultrie who seemed to like his work and asked for his help more frequently on special projects and reports. These tasks helped fill part of his time and took his mind off of his uncertain situation. But the fact was still painfully clear to him that he was taking no part in the department's functions. Everyone was nice, but they never involved him or advised him about their work. Bert Palmer was doing the same thing. Gandy had initially hoped that Palmer would work with him to build up his knowledge of the department. He had assumed that Palmer would want an assistant, but Palmer ignored him in much the same way as the rest of the department. In fact, Palmer had never even introduced him or explained to the department what his job was to be. Tom Gandy felt the situation on a very personal level. He began to feel that in some way he was not trying to be part of the department, that perhaps his efforts to learn were not enough.

Two conversations that occurred several months after he entered the department, when Tom Gandy was going through a period of self-doubt, helped him begin to see his situation more clearly. One morning during a conversation with Palmer's secretary, one of the few people in the department who had accepted him readily, she told him in a confidential tone that, "Carol Mann thought she deserved the position you were hired for, and she sure didn't like it when you were hired above her. I think she still resents your being in the department." The second conversation that enlarged Gandy's view of the situation was with Bert Palmer. One evening, when the two men were alone in the department, the conversation turned to education. Palmer was talking about the need for a college education to get a good job. He said, "Tom, with your education you have a bright future, but, with just high school, I've had to work hard to get where I am. Nowadays, I probably wouldn't be so lucky. The bad thing is, I know I'll never be able to get a better job." This conversation made him realize that Palmer probably felt he was protecting his job by not training him in the department. He could see how he presented an unintended threat. But Tom Gandy's increased understanding did not seem to improve his relationships with Palmer as the weeks wore on. He tried to work with Palmer on many occasions but was always given a short answer or loaded down with some trivial detail work.

For a person who wanted so much to assume responsibility, the situation was very frustrating. The work he did for Ed Moultrie began to take more and more of his time. Tom Gandy was confused as to what his job was supposed to be. The work he did for Moultrie was enjoyable and challenging but gave him no increased responsibility. It did not help him at all in better understanding the Operations Reporting and Control Department. With eight months on the job he had little more responsibility than when he entered the department. As he left for a week of vacation in August, Gandy was more dissatisfied than ever with his position. He had decided to assess his future outlook during the week off and to have a talk with Ed Moultrie upon his return.

PART III A NEW DEAL?

Several days after Gandy returned from vacation, Ed Moultrie asked him to come by his office for a talk. During the conversation between the two men, the subject of Gandy's future in the division came up. Moultrie again emphasized the great opportunities that were open to a smart young man. He praised the work Gandy had been doing and said his progress was excellent. As the conversation continued, Moultrie hinted that he had plans to give him more responsibility in the Operations Reporting and Control Department and that Bert Palmer might move up to another position. The talk ended with Moultrie's encouraging Gandy to keep up the good work but without any definite plans or suggestions being mentioned. Gandy left the meeting feeling hopeful but still uncertain about his future. The fact that he was ignorant about what really went on in the department bothered him a great deal. He was beginning to wonder if he was ready to assume more responsibility without first gaining more knowledge.

As he approached completion of his first year in the department, Tom Gandy was still busy trying to learn everything he could about the department on his own. Moultrie had not mentioned the subject of advancement again. Bert Palmer continued to run things alone. The women in the department had begun to make Gandy feel more relaxed, but he felt useless and unneeded in helping them with their jobs. With nearly a year of experience behind him, Tom Gandy remained confused about his management role, and he was once again becoming disheartened about the whole situation surrounding the job.

QUESTIONS

1. What were Tom Gandy's goals, values, beliefs, and assumptions when he took the job?

2. What has happened to Gandy's self-concept?

3. What does Gandy have in common with others in his department? How is this affecting interpersonal relationships?

4. How "open" have Ed Moultrie and Bert Palmer been with Tom Gandy?

5. Upon returning from his vacation and talking with Ed Moultrie, why didn't Tom Gandy expess his doubts and feelings? Should Tom press for a clarification now? Why?

6. Does role ambiguity help explain what is happening in this case (see Chapter 4)?

CHAPTER 8

Work Group Behavior

LEARNING OBJECTIVES

When you have finished this chapter, you should be able to:

- *Understand the interaction between the formal and informal organization.*
- *Diagram and use a work group model.*
- *Cite the cohesive and differentiating factors that may exist in groups.*
- *Explain the three informal structures that can exist in groups.*
- *Understand the possibilities and limitations of managing the informal organization.*

The typical work group engages in task activities that are structured by management as part of the formal system and in emergent or informal activities that develop around the required job duties. To understand the interactions of the formal and informal systems, we will look at a social systems model that outlines the variables contained in each system. Since the informal organization often complicates the work group's activities, we will examine the reasons for its existence.

A work group may be better understood by evaluating the influence of two different factors—cohesive and differentiating. Cohesive factors contribute to unity and solidarity; differentiating factors stem from characteristics or conditions that emphasize differences among group members. A work group's activities may also be understood by analyzing its informal but overlapping friendship, power, and communication structures. Finally, since the informal system is a fact of organizational life, its management is considered.

FORMAL AND INFORMAL WORK ARRANGEMENTS

The Formal Organization

Organizations are complex social entities designed to produce goods or provide services. Such objectives are achieved by blending the efforts of individuals and groups with other resources. Goods and services must be produced efficiently if organizations are to survive or justify their existence. Consequently, organizations are designed, built, and managed with such objectives in mind. Whatever the objective, a structure must be provided that groups tasks into jobs and jobs into appropriate administrative units. This is achieved by specialization in task activities with organizational members performing jobs that are reduced to manageable components and performed repetitively. The organizational blueprint reflects the social, psychological, and administrative assumptions of its designers, whether realistic or not.

The best-known version of a formal organization is the bureaucratic model formulated by Max Weber. Bureaucracy was considered the most efficient form of social organization. The bureaucratic model has structural characteristics that are most effectively used in complex organizations to meet the needs of modern society. Weber describes bureaucracy as having the following characteristics of organizational design.[1]

1. a well-defined hierarchy of authority
2. a division of work based on specialization
3. a system of duties designating the rights and duties of position incumbents
4. a system of procedures for dealing with the work situation
5. impersonality of interpersonal relationships
6. selection for employment and promotion based on technical competence

Such an organization is logical or rational, and members must adopt its rationality as their own. There is no room for individual differences in value and attitude or for expression of feeling or emotion. Organizational members are taken for granted.

Much of the subsequent work by writers and researchers have demonstrated that the bureaucratic organization is not a model of efficiency. Unintended, detrimental consequences have been found to accompany the use of rules and procedures. Specialization has led to monotony and fatigue rather than to efficiency in many instances. The employee is not passive or motivated only by economic incentives. Finally, it has been demonstrated that the network of job relationships within an organization is definitely not impersonal. With all the new insights, however, the organization has not become personalized. Seldom is an organization designed to accommodate the employee; the individual must adapt to the organization. The basic elements of the bureaucratic model are still found in varying degrees in most organizations and may be functional or dysfunctional, depending on the situation.

The Informal Organization

Organizations never function as intended and planned. The formal organization is supplemented by the informal organization, which is the "unplanned, informal set of groups, friendships, and attachments that inevitably develop when people are placed in regular proximity to one another."[2] In other words, the formal organization provides the setting from which the informal organization emerges; as systems the two are interdependent.

However the behaviors and activities of the informal organization have no place in the formal plan. Officially, they do not exist; they certainly are not found on any organizational chart. Yet informal organizations have a profound impact on an organization's activities.

The informal organization serves to meet the personal needs of its members that are not fully satisfied by the formal organization. In this respect, it supplements or compensates for the lack of satisfaction experienced in the formally designed structure. Security, belonging, and recognition needs are met within the informal system as it protects and controls many of the activities of its members.

The well-known Hawthorne studies launched in 1924 at the Western Electric Company first demonstrated the power of the informal organization.[3] Initially, the experiment was designed to study the effects of illumination on worker productivity. The light intensity under which the operators worked was varied systematically. Both the test group and the control group that worked in constant light intensity increased in productivity. Even when the light intensity was decreased to an uncomfortable level, the test group increased its productivity. The experimenters concluded that illumination had no predictable effect on productivity and also that something else caused the improved performance.

The "something else" led to additional better-controlled experiments. Two well-known experiments, the relay assembly test room and the bank wiring observation room, provided insights into the social situation of the workers. Some of the findings underlined the role played by the informal orgnaization such as[4]

1. the spontaneous, unplanned development of stable relationships based on personal attraction or mutual dependency.
2. the development of standards of acceptable behavior, and
3. the enforcement of these standards by an informal leader.

Research since these early studies has verified these findings and has extended our knowledge of the informal organization. Understanding the informal organization and its relationship to the formal organization is crucial for an understanding of organizational behavior.

MODEL OF WORK GROUP BEHAVIOR

Any overview of group behavior must reflect the behavior as structured by the formal organization and the behavior that emerges over and above that which is required. Homans has developed a framework for analyzing group behavior that is applicable to all groups.

The Elements of Group Behavior and Basic Model

The Homan model describes group behavior in terms of three behavioral elements.[5]

1. Activity: This refers to what an individual does, such as operating a machine or making a computation.
2. Interaction: This behavioral element notes what is taking place between two individuals. The flow of work may necessitate two persons' coordinating their activities. Communication is a contact between persons that is initiated by one and responded to by another.
3. Sentiment: This element includes ideas, beliefs, and feelings about work or work associates. Unlike activities or interactions, sentiments are subjective and must be inferred from what is said or done.

These three elements are interrelated and are descriptive of both the formal and informal organization.

The work group model includes four parts that reflect a cause-and-effect sequence. Basic elements of the model are shown in Figure 8-1.

Figure 8-1

Overview of the Work Group Model

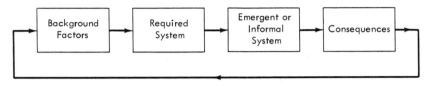

The model indicates that background factors are instrumental in shaping the required system. Both these parts comprise the formal organization and provide the foundation from which the emergent or informal organization evolves. The required and emergent systems are described in terms of activities, interactions, and sentiments as will be shown later in this chapter. Finally, interaction of the required and emergent systems results in outcomes or consequences that impact on the group, individuals within the group, and the organization. The model denotes a complex system with the background factors being analogous to inputs and the consequences analogous to outputs.

THE OVERALL WORK GROUP MODEL

The Homan's conceptual scheme for understanding group behavior has been extended to a version of the model shown in Figure 8-2, which is relevant for all work groups.[6] A close examination of this figure shows that the parts of the model have been numbered 1 through 8. This notation will designate that part of the model being considered.

Background Factors (1)

The formal system is shaped by numerous background factors. Some of these factors are historical, having evolved over a period of time. None the less, these factors shape and determine how an organization operates. Management related background factors are

1. management assumptions and practices
2. leadership behavior
3. organization structure

Figure 8-2
Work Group Behavior

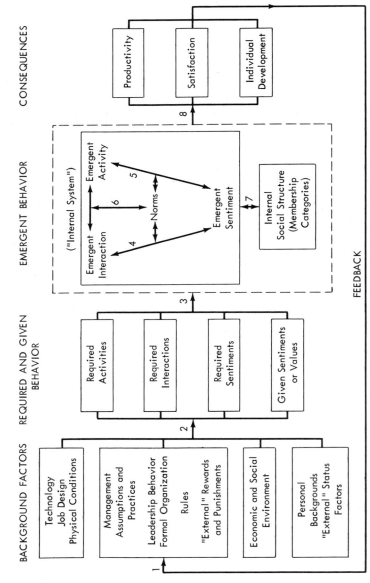

Source: Paul R. Lawrence and John Seiler, *Organizational Behavior and Administration*, rev. ed. (Homewood, Ill.: Richard D. Irwin, 1965), p. 158. © 1965 by Richard D. Irwin, Inc.

4. rules and procedures
5. reward system

Such factors interact in the context of a technology appropriate for achieving the organization's objectives. In turn the job design and physical working conditions are shaped by the technology itself.

As open systems, organizations are imbedded in an economic and social environment. This environment provides inputs not only of a material nature but also knowledge and values.

Finally, an input of a different nature enters the organization, the individual. The individual brings with him or her his or her own unique background, personal system, and an external status or position. Obviously, the entire personal system is not relevant to the position to be filled, but these elements are part of the person. Directly and indirectly, they will influence the formal and informal systems.

Required Behavior as Determined by Background Factors (2)

To achieve its objectives, an organization must divide the total effort into jobs for individuals. This leads to the designation of required activities and required interactions for each position. The task activities are designed by management and may be stated in job descriptions. Less tangible are the required sentiments (ideas, beliefs, and feelings) pertaining to the job, co-workers, and the supervision. The employee must have certain sentiments to perform the task as assigned. For example, such required sentiments are reflected when the employee is required to take a preventive measure to avoid a breakdown of equipment, to exercise creativity, or to be innovative.

Finally, the required system is affected by given sentiments that work group members bring to their jobs as part of their backgrounds outside the organization. Such sentiments may be reflected in their feelings about authority or supervision, what constitutes a fair day's work, whether hard work pays off, the desirability of unions, and so on.

Emergent Behavior (3)

The behavior that emerges in work groups is usually quite different from that which is required. Ways of thinking and behaving develop that vary as to what is required to perform the job. Purely social activity takes place, more or less work may be done, or the work may be performed in ways different from that prescribed by management. Such emergent behaviors may facilitate or hinder effective task performance. From the background factors and required system, there is formed an emergent system or informal organizatioan with its "own" activities, interactions, and sentiments. These are related to but different from the required system.

As noted the sentiments that a worker brings into an organization may affect the required system. These sentiments also influence the emergent system. First, the status that a group member brings from the external environment or community affects his or her status and rank in the emergent social system. If outside status is high, status, at least initially, is likely to be high in the informal system. Second, the ideas, beliefs, and feelings that a person brings to the work group has a strong influence on interpersonal relations. The more such given sentiments are similar to those of the work group's sentiments, the more likely the individual will become an accepted group member.

Interaction and Sentiment (4)

The required behavior of the external system makes up the starting point for subsequent interactions. Emergent interactions are more likely between persons required to interact to do their jobs and between those whose jobs place them near one another. Interaction and interpersonal sentiments are closely related as we saw in the previous chapter. In general, favorable sentiments are likely to emerge between persons who interact frequently. Likewise, frequent interaction takes place between members who like each other.

Activities, Sentiments, and Norms (5)

Unfavorable sentiments will be directed toward group members who do not share or who violate group norms. Such sentiments are often accompanied by activities that punish those violating the norms. Defensive or aggressive reactions by the violators set up a circular situation in which both have their sentiments about the other reinforced by their reciprocal activities.

Activities, Norms, and Interactions (6)

Whenever a member violates a norm, interaction toward that person will increase as efforts are made to get him or her to conform. If such efforts fail, the norm violator will be the recipient of increasingly unfavorable sentiments and decreasing interaction. Punishment for persistent norm violation is isolation from regular group membership. For example, "slackers" or "rate busters" are the object of hostility and subsequent low interaction with other members for violating the group's output norm.

Social Structure and Membership Categories (7)

Informal activities, interactions, and sentiments serve to preserve group norms. These patterns of behavior protect the group against outside threats and pressures that are perceived as menacing activities that the group finds relatively satisfying. Group membership is based upon the extent to which individual members support the group's activities. Membership falls into three categories.

1. Regulars: Regular members are the recipients of favorable sentiments and are frequent interactors; their activities conform closely to the group's norms. Regulars include the informal leader or leaders who tend to be frequent initiators of interaction for group members. The leaders are especially careful to live up to group norms because they have the most to lose by violating them.

2. Deviates: These individuals interact relatively frequently among themselves and even with the regulars. However, they are denied regular membership because of unwillingness or inability to accept the group's dominant norms and values.

3. Isolates: At the other extreme of regular members are isolates whose interaction with other members is infrequent. Usually, they will have adapted to this situation and will express little interest in regular membership or in observing the group's norms.

In general, social standing in the group will depend upon faithfulness or adherence to the group's norms. Those who violate group norms pay the price of exclusion in varying degrees. Interpreting the behavior of individual members is assisted by knowing their membership classification.

Consequences (8)

The external and internal systems interact to produce consequences that are both material and human. Productivity will be affected not only by the formal system but also by group output norms. In most groups, output norms emerge that specify the quantity and quality of work expected, and pressure is exerted to ensure conformity to such norms.

The network of emergent interpersonal activities will strongly influence the social satisfactions that group members derive from their work experience. If there is relatively frequent interaction, members like one another, and the social structure is relatively stable, satisfaction will likely be high. This may be so whether productivity is high or low. Not to be overlooked is satisfaction derived from the task or the work itself. Task satisfaction may or may not be associated with social satisfaction. As we saw in Chapter 6, the lack of job satisfaction may be expressed in absenteeism and turnover.

In addition to productivity and satisfaction, individual development is influenced by work group behavior. Groups may encourage or limit their members' needs to learn, grow, and develop. The pattern of interaction, sentiment, activity, and norms define the extent to which members are able to achieve their potential and attain important personal goals and rewards. Individual development may be facilitated by high productivity, but only if individual contribution to the task does not conflict with required sentiments or group norms. The individual may have to choose between the group's rewards of acceptance and belonging and management's rewards of pay and promotion that usually reflect growth and development.

The job activities of many work groups consist of simple, repetitive tasks and dead-end jobs that have no promotion potential and thwart individual development. Consequently, satisfaction is derived almost entirely from emergent social activity rather than from accomplishment of the formal task. While satisfying needs for social interaction and stability, many groups do little to satisfy needs for self-esteem and personal development.

The Group Model as a Framework for Analysis

The group model provides a framework for organizing complex formal and informal organizational information and for observing their interdependence. Consequently, the understanding, prediction, and influence of group phenomena is facilitated. To this end, the background factors and resulting required systems may be viewed as inputs that may be varied. Such changes work through the overall system and influence the consequences, which are the resulting outputs. As noted in Figure 8-2, the consequences provide feedback to parts of the overall system. If the consequences reflect a potential problem, the appropriate input(s) may be altered to achieve different results. The cause-and-effect relationships inherent in the model serve to remind one of the many ramifications that will be set into motion once a given factor is modified.

WHY THE INFORMAL ORGANIZATION

As we have seen, the required system provides only the bare minimum of group behavior. The emergent behavior is infinitely more complex and varied. Why do groups complicate their lives by developing interactions, activities, and sentiments that are not required?

The Satisfaction of Employee Needs

Most people work with the expectation that certain of their personal needs will be satisfied. As we saw in Chapter 3, these needs may range from the physiological to self-actualization. After being hired, most people become aware that their work activity places definite limits on the needs that are met and the satisfactions that are experienced. However, most employees usually become members of an emergent system or informal organization. Individuals eventually find some kinds of satisfaction from both the required and the emergent systems, but these satisfactions are not necessarily the same. For example, the required system may satisfy economic and achievement needs, whereas social needs are primarily satisfied through the emergent system. In some work settings, the emerging system is a means for compensating for poor working conditions, monotonous or repetitive jobs, or the lack of social interaction. Human needs are satisfied despite the limitations of the required system.

A Protective Security Function in the Emergent System

The individual employee often feels subjected to continuous pressures for productivity by the organization.[7] At the same time, there may be strong forces within the worker for minimal productivity because of the lack of intrinsic interest in the job itself. The worker is in a position of being considerably less powerful than the organization. At the same time there are strong forces in the group to establish a basis for greater equity. Very frequently a productivity norm emerges that has several purposes. First, such a norm defines a "fair day's work," which allows workers to increase their control over the work environment. Often a group will agree on what percentage of production is permissible beyond the amount set by management. Second, a productivity norm prevents additional output that may cost some of the workers their jobs. The norm is perceived as protecting their wage-earning prospects. Finally, the output norm protects the slower, but respected, workers and prevents competition among group members. This serves to protect group unity and solidarity.

COHESIVE FACTORS IN GROUPS

Cohesiveness is defined as the strength of member attraction to the group. Cohesiveness is shown in the friendliness that members feel toward one another; they usually enjoy being together. Individual members feel free to express their opinions and make suggestions. Also group members are usually enthusistic about what they are doing and are willing to make personal sacrifices for the good of the group. They are willing to assume responsibility for their share of the activities and for meeting obligations. Such activities demonstrate unity, closeness, and mutual attractiveness of group members.

Factors Contributing to Cohesiveness

Group cohesiveness is facilitated or increased by several conditions.[8]

Common values and goals

Frequent interaction is no guarantee that camaraderie among persons will occur or that a cohesive group will develop. Such results are more likely to take place, however, if group members have similar attitudes, values, and goals. As noted, these constitute the personal system that members bring to the group. Similar attitudes and values facilitate interpersonal attraction, consensual validation, and the personal rewards of association. Group cohesion is more likely under such conditions. The common characteristics of individual personal systems have a strong influence on both the formation and cohesion of a group.

Success in achieving goals

A cohesive group is characterized by success in achieving its goals. The attainment of important goals increases group unity, satisfies member needs, and makes the group more attractive to its members. After all, who likes being associated with a weak, ineffective group?

High-status groups

The degree of cohesiveness will also be influenced by the position of the group in relation to other groups within the organization. High-status groups are more attractive to members. Both success in achieving goals and high status evoke pride and satisfaction, although they are not necessarily related.

Resolution of differences

The cohesiveness of a group depends on its ability to keep its members in effective interaction with one another. When members disagree on matters of significance to the group, harmony requires a resolution satisfactory to all members. Unresolved differences or solutions acceptable to only a few members reduces interpersonal attraction and liking and may impair goal attainment.

Conformity to norms

A major fact of group life resulting from interaction is the development of group norms and pressures for conformity to these norms. Group members develop shared ways of looking at the world or shared frames of reference. Broadly viewed, group norms include[9]

1. the frame of reference in terms of which a given relevant object is viewed,
2. prescribed "right" attitudes or behavior toward that object,
3. affective feelings regarding the "rightness" (sacredness) of these attitudes and the violation of norms, and
4. positive and negative sanctions by which proper behavior is rewarded or improper behavior is punished.

Norms aid group stability by facilitating the predictability of behavior within the group. The operations of a group are made more automatic and less effortful.[10] Many group functions that would otherwise require time-consuming efforts or decisions are made more efficiently through resort to norms that establish expectations for behavior.

Conformity to norms contributes to cohesiveness for several other reasons. Norms are accepted as a means for protecting and maintaining the group. If group members do important things differently, there is less probability that the group will remain friendly and cohesive; conflicts and dissensions are more likely to arise. Second, conformity to norms facilitates the achievement of the groups' goals. Norms emerge that establish preferred ways of attaining group purposes of security, social interaction, output levels, and the like.

The extent to which a group can exert pressure on its members to conform to a norm is limited by the cohesiveness of the group.[11] As seen previously, cohesiveness is determined by the attractiveness of membership or the rewards experienced through membership. In other words, this means that the strength of negative sanctions is limited by the strength of the forces that hold members in the group. Members of high-cohesive groups are more willing to accept influence than are members of low-cohesive groups.

Some Results of Cohesiveness

Several research studies indicate that membership in a cohesive group helps to increase job satisfaction and reduce absenteeism and turnover. In a study of a group of textile workers who were required to adapt to frequent changes in work methods,[12] it was observed that while turnover rates were very high, workers who were members of cohesive groups quit at a much lower rate than did those who were not. The cohesive groups, however, had strong antagonistic feelings toward management. Another study[13] demonstrated a lower rate of absenteeism among white-collar workers who had a sense of group belongingness and solidarity than did their blue-collar counterparts.

The effects of cohesive work groups on the adjustments of members among work groups in a large, heavy machinery manufacturing company was also investigated.[14] Cohesiveness was indicated if the members perceived themselves to be part of a group, preferred to remain rather than to leave the group, and perceived their group as better than others in compatibility, relying on one another, and sticking together. Members in cohesive groups generally experienced fewer work-related anxieties (tension) than did those in less cohesive groups.

The effect of cohesive groups on productivity appears to be mixed. Even the classic Hawthorne investigation produced conflicting results. In the relay assembly test room, a tightly knit group seemed to be responsible for the steadily increasing productivity. However, in the research conducted in the bank wiring observation room, different results were found. The wiremen established norms for production and each employee consistently produced the proper amount of work. Significantly, the group maintained a level of production lower than its members could have easily achieved and consequently received lower pay than necessary under the wage-incentive system.

In the textile study, the more cohesive groups provided greater support to members who opposed the management's innovations in work methods, whereas the heavy machinery manufacturing study found that workers in cohesive groups were no more or less productive than were those in noncohesive groups. However, the workers in the cohesive groups were more uniform in their output; that is, they all produced about the same amount.

DIFFERENTIATING FACTORS IN GROUPS

Coincident with cohesive forces making for unity and solidarity, other factors present in a group serve to make members different from one another.[15]

Factors Contributing to Differences among Group Members

Each group member has a rank or standing within the social structure. While the ranking system is not as explicit as that in the formal system, which uses titles and status symbols, ranking structures do exist in the informal organization. Describing the internal social structure depends upon understanding the factors that members use to ascribe high, low, or the same standing to one another. High-status members are more likely to demonstrate one or more of the following characteristics than are low-status members.[16]

1. high degree of conformity to group norms
2. assisting in goal achievement of the required and/or emergent system

3. assisting group members in their personal system goal achievement
4. having access to scarce resources
5. having access to important communications and/or information
6. high formal rank due to the job or group position
7. having high external status in the eyes of group members

These characteristics are usually reflected in high-status members' having a wide range of interactions and initiating interactions with other members. Differentiating group status factors are expanded in the following material.

External status

Each individual comes to a work group having a status in the outside community. If that status is high, his or her internal group status is likely to also be high. The group, however, must value the role or activity from which the external status is derived. Furthermore, the individual must establish his or her standing on the basis of what the group deems important to its objectives and activities. One's external status influences only his or her initial position within the group's informal structure.

Status congruence

Many factors are determinants of a person's status within the informal system. Age, sex, education, marital status, ethnic origin, race, and so on are influential factors in assigning status. Three different sources of status within a work group have been identified: production performance in terms of speed or skill, interpersonal skill, and the job that an individual holds.[17] Several of these status factors are attained by work and ability. Other status factors are due to birth (sex, race) or simply living (age).

However, a person may be high, low, or mixed on the characteristics to which status accrues. The degree of consistency on status factors is called "congruence." Consequently, individuals may be high across all status factors—high-status congruence—or low across all status factors—low-status congruence. Finally, some group members may be high on several status factors but low on others—status incongruence. The lack of status congruency generates some anxiety in each member regarding his or her own status and the kind of behavior that he or she can expect in others. In other words, status congruency facilitates interaction because members are sure of where they stand with respect to each other. This increases general satisfaction in the group, stimulates nontask activity, and increases conformity with group production norms. However, where group norms specify a high level of productivity, high-status congruency can be expected to lead to high output.[18]

Conformity to norms

As we have seen, norms are the prescribed attitudes and behavior shared by group members. Norms facilitate the attainment of group objectives, protect the group against external pressures, promote group stability, control member behavior, and so on. Obviously, norms are perceived by group members as central to their effective functioning. Consequently, it is quite understandable why conformity to the group's norms will strongly influence an individual's standing or position within his or her work group. The membership categories—regular, deviate, and isolate—reflect individual acceptance and conformity to the group's norms.

However, not everyone may be able to go along with all the group's norms. For example, employees from rural areas often feel that their employer is entitled to a fair day's work, a view that often conflicts with a group's norm of limited output. An individual's goals, values, and beliefs may vary so significantly from those of the group that he or she cannot go along with the groups' objectives and activities. For such a person, the rewards of group membership and acceptance are less than the costs of relinquishing personal integrity.

Role Behavior

The stability of an individual's self-concept and behavior rests on consistencies in his or her interpersonal environment. The social structure is one source of stability. Because a person occupies a certain position in a social system or group, that person is seen by others and sees himself or herself in the terms required by the role that he or she occupies. People learn the behavioral expectations belonging to a position and also the personal attributes associated with it. By occupying certain positions, they are consistently defined by others and consequently define themselves in terms of traits associated with the role.

Once an individual has entered a group, his or her participation is partially determined by the conditions and processes that control the group. The social structure contributes to stability in individual behavior because[19]

1. it determines the frequencies of interaction between an individual and other persons,
2. it places the individual in various role categories, and
3. it controls the behaviors of others toward the individual.

However, to a certain extent an individual can influence each of these factors and thereby shape his or her interpersonal environment. In interactions with this environment, the individual strives to establish relations that are consistent with his or her self-concept and behavior.

INFORMAL STRUCTURES

The cohesive and differentiating factors in groups are reflected in patterns of relationships. These patterns are seen in informal structures of friendship, power, and communication.[20]

Role Relationship: A Basis for Informal Structures

Task differences require different activities and interactions among members. The task roles specify the connection between two people and may be one of several types. Two individuals can do the same task but work independently. Other workers can work on separate but sequential steps of the same task so that the output of one provides the input of the other. Finally, the task connection may be complementary or reciprocal so that work activities are simultaneously linked together. These tasks affect the degree of dependence that persons have on one another in their work activities.

The role relationships provide the centerpiece around which various but interrelated informal structures evolve. From the context of required task relationships, there emerges a friendship structure, a communication structure, and a power structure. The overlap and interdependence between these structures is illustrated in Figure 8-3. Within the framework of task relationships, a complex network of structures evolve.

Figure 8-3

Informal Structures in a Work Group

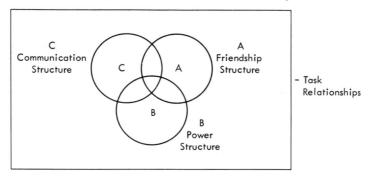

Friendship Structure

Any group observed over a period of time will exhibit regularities of association. Observation will disclose the informal leaders, regulars, deviates, and isolates. As noted, conformity to the dominant norms determine members' positions in the social structure. However, within this social structure, a friendship or affect network will develop. This will definitely be related to required tasks that determine the proximity of persons in the work area.

However, the friendship structure of a work group is influenced by additional factors. In Chapter 7, interpersonal behavior, we pointed out some of the factors that have a bearing on personal associations. The friendship structure may be shaped by any or all of the following factors:

1. similarity in values, beliefs, and goals (personal system)
2. similarity in views of members' respective self-concepts
3. compatability of interpersonal needs
4. reward–cost outcome of the association
5. consensual validation

The friendship structure will influence and be influenced by the communication and power structures.

Power Structure

The roles within a group can be described in terms of the relative power or influence of each role. In a formal group, management designates to each role its position in an authority hierarchy and its superordinate or subordinate relation to other roles. Power differences are likely to be equally prominent although less explicitly defined in informal groups.

Power is the potential influence of one person on another. There are five bases of power: (1) reward power; (2) coercive power; (3) legitimate power, such as the right of a chosen leader to direct the actions of others; (4) referent power, based on one's liking or identification with another; and (5) expert power, based on knowledge or "know how."[21] In informal groups, members differ in their relative influence. The more influential or powerful members are central in helping the group to attain its goals and to have access to scarce resources such as information, know how, or other things important to the needs of members. Friendship or affect relations between members have power potential to the extent that one is attracted to another, or the group, or to the extent that valuable rewards can be provided or withheld.

Formal leaders hold positions in the required system that convey authority and status, whereas, the informal leader often holds no formal position, having "earned" his or her ability to influence others. The informal leader's influence or power depends on the willingness of group members to accept his or her leadership or directions. Although the informal leader does not have the use of formal sanctions, he or she is often as influential, and sometimes more so, as the formal leader in directing the activities of group members. Informal authority may come from the personal qualities, abilities, or charisma of the individual. Additionally, it may also stem from knowledge, status, role, skills, age, or seniority. Consequently, the informal leader influences others through the use of personal power.

The informal leader must have been a strong supporter of the group's norms, perhaps even being influential in the formulation of such norms. Having achieved a leadership position, however, the informal leader may initiate new norms. Such activity must be perceived as helpful rather than as detrimental to the attainment of group objectives. Group members expect the informal leader to initiate change so as to maintain or enhance the group's position. Some deviation from existing norms and the establishment of new ones are consistent with group expectations.

Above all, the informal leader is one who is instrumental in helping the group to achieve its objectives. Individual members are assisted in attaining various needs as the informal leader initiates structure, solves problems, and fills the breach in group activities and interaction. Often the leader maintains a balance between group need satisfactions and achievement of the group's task.

Communication Structure

A group's communication structure is a pattern of communication links utilized during group activity. The direction and pattern of communication are important for the informal group's activities, interactions, and satisfaction. Information may flow primarily through the informal leader, through all members, or one to one. Such networks usually develop without group design or even an awareness of how they operate. Some members have access to important information and therefore assume an important role in the communication structure. High-status or influential (powerful) members initiate and receive more communications than do lower-status members. Access to critical communication and/or information, a resource, may then be the source of an individual's power.

MANAGEMENT OF THE INFORMAL ORGANIZATION

Whether informal groups oppose or support organizational goals and objectives may mean the difference between effectiveness or ineffectiveness or even perhaps success or failure for the organization. Groups can direct the efforts of their members in opposition to organizational goals just as readily as they can lend support to these goals. The question for students of organizational behavior is, How can one effectively utilize the informal group?

Supervision

The Hawthorne research studies had shown that management was a social skill that requires an understanding of the social structure of the firm and of the work groups. Informal groups have an impact on goals and objectives as well as on group member satisfaction. An understanding of group dynamics, such as presented in this chapter, suggest the following possibilities for mobilizing the energies of an informal group.[22]

1. Encourage employees to function as a social unit, both formally and informally, by strengthening team work and group solidarity.
2. Promote group activities on the job and recognize group members for work performed collectively.
3. Apply group incentives when appropriate.
4. Assist in the development of a common purpose while working under a minimum of supervisory pressure.
5. Encourage the group to develop its own means for internal self-control.
6. When practical, respect the standards, norms of behavior, and values that the group believes are proper.
7. Identify and cooperate with informal group leaders to minimize conflict and assure the informal leadership that it is promoting organizational objectives.

These actions are consistent with Likert's principle of supportive relationships.[23]

The leadership and other processes of the organization must be such as to ensure a maximum probability that in all interactions and all relationships within the organization each member will, in the light of his background, values, and expectations, view the experience as supportive and one which builds and maintains his sense of personal worth and importance.

Participation

Since the thrust of informal group activities may be against management, participation has been proposed as a means of "bringing workers into management."[24] The purpose, of course, is to minimize the conflict of managerial objectives and group values. However, the character of participation can vary widely. The range of participation may extend from solicitation of ideas to consultation or an interchange of ideas and to group decision making. Depending on the overall situation, any of these may be appropriate, and each gives some degree of influence over work-related matters.

The potential benefits that result from participation provide insights into why it is a promising approach to working with groups. Participation provides group members with a means for satisfying needs of self-determination, independence, and power. Additionally, it gives the group an opportunity to affect work-related matters in ways consistent with their own interests. The needs and interests of the group are taken into account so that the managerial decisions are less likely to seem arbitrary. It adds some of the qualities of the managerial role to employees' jobs thereby bringing, to some degree, workers into management. Conflict and opposition may be replaced by more cooperative activities as group and managerial objectives merge.

Structural Changes

As noted, informal emergent activities are often a means of compensating for dull, repetitive, monotonous, required activities. While informal activities provide satisfaction for the group, they also frequently curtail productivity and effectiveness. Several methods of mitigating the source or need for such emergent activity were presented in Chapters 4 and 5. Job redesign is an approach that builds motivators into jobs that make them more satisfying and challenging. This is a possible solution to the underutilization of employees and increasing the various rewards from task performance.

Also the utilization of sociotechnical work systems provides a possible means for eliminating unchallenging work. The simple elements of jobs previously distributed among workers are combined and assigned to self-regulating work teams that perform relatively whole operations. The objective is to establish a cohesive social unit of workers that is integrated with meaningful technological arrangements. Organized in this manner, the work group has autonomy and responsibility as a group for the total task.

Limitations

The emergent system arises from the spontaneous interaction of employees, and it is unlikely that the informal group can be eliminated. Furthermore, it is doubtful if it would be desirable to do so. The suggestions for supervision, participation, and structural changes are not designed to eliminate the emergent, informal organization but, rather, to obtain an effective liaison with it.

However, these working guidelines are not without limitations. Effective leadership and supervision are difficult to define and implement. The supervisor's role is constrained by his or her superior who may well negate the social skills required to work effectively with a work group. No amount of training will overcome "human relations" skills that are not reinforced or are incompatible with the organization's climate. Leadership and climate are the topics for chapters 10 and 15.

Participation is also subject to many questions. Inherent in participation is the critical assumption of a substantial commonality of interests between employee and employer. Relevant forces in the supervisor, the group, and the situation itself must be examined before deciding upon the appropriate degree of participation. These factors will be examined in chapter 10 on leadership.

Finally, structural changes are not feasible in many organizations. Technology, the flow of work, and the employees themselves are only a few of the constraining factors that might be involved.

SUMMARY

Because the mutual interdependence of the formal and informal organization has been shown to complicate and enrich work group behavior, we presented a work group model to identify the elements of this social system and to show how they are related. The basic components of this model consist of background factors, required activities, the emergent or informal organization, and consequences. Such a total systems model enhances one's ability to understand, predict, and influence work group activities.

A work group is shaped by two contrary sets of factors—cohesive and differentiating. Cohesiveness was shown to be increased by common values and goals, success in achieving goals, group status in the organization, and conformity to group norms. Differentiating factors in work groups were shown to consist of unequal contributions to group activities, external status, status congruence, and the degree of conformity to important group norms.

Job or role relationships were shown to be the focal point around which a friendship structure, power structure, and communication structure may develop. These informal structures overlap and are interrelated in varying degrees with group cohesive and differentiating factors.

Since the work group may facilitate or impede the attainment of formal goals and objectives, management of the informal group was examined. Supervisory actions, participation, and structural changes were considered as possible approaches to obtaining work group support. However, each strategy has its limitations.

QUESTIONS FOR STUDY AND DISCUSSION

1. Do you know of any organization that does not have the elements of Weber's bureaucratic model? How is it different? Why do you think that it is different?

2. Can you apply the work group behavior model to a work group in which you were a member? How was the required and emergent behavior related? What were the consequences?

3. Why does the informal system appear?

4. What factors contribute to the cohesiveness of groups? Does any one factor appear to be more important than another? If so, which one? Why?

5. What characteristics are very likely to be associated with high-status group members? Can you relate this to any personal group experiences?

6. Can you identify any informal structures in groups with which you have been associated? Were these informal structures interrelated? How?

7. Should the informal system or organization be eliminated? Why? How would you proceed to abolish an informal organization?

8. How can the informal organization be managed? What are some of the difficulties that you can expect to encounter?

NOTES

[1]Dessler, Gary, *Organization and Management* (Englewood Cliffs, N.J.: Prentice-Hall, 1976), pp. 30–32.

[2]Tannenbaum, Arnold S., *Social Psychology of the Work Organization* (New York: Wadsworth, 1976), p. 1.

[3]Roethlisberger, F. J. and William J. Dickson, *Management and the Worker* (Cambridge, Mass.: Harvard University Press, 1940).

[4]Tannenbaum, *op. cit.,* p. 25.

[5]Homans, George C., *The Human Group* (New York: Harcourt Brace Jovanovich, 1950), pp. 33–40.

[6]Turner, Arthur N., "A Conceptual Scheme for Describing Work Group Behavior," in Paul R. Lawrence et al., eds., *Organizational Behavior and Administration,* rev. ed. (Homewood, Ill.: Irwin-Dorsey, 1965), pp. 154–164.

[7]Jacobs, T. O., *Leadership and Exchange in Formal Organizations* (Alexandria, Va.: Human Resources Research Organization, 1971), pp. 199–200.

[8]Cohen, Allan R., Stephen L. Fink, H. Gadon, and Robin D. Willits, *Effective Behavior in Organizations* (Homewood, Ill.: Irwin, 1976), pp. 53–58.

[9]McGrath, Joseph E., *Social Psychology* (New York: Holt, Rinehart, 1965), p. 105.

[10]Jacobs, *op. cit.,* p. 198.

[11]Secord, Paul F. and Carl W. Backman, *Social Psychology* (New York: McGraw-Hill, 1964), pp. 337–338.

[12]Coch, L. and J. R. P. French, Jr., "Overcoming Resistance to Change," *Human Relations* 4 (1948): 512–533.

[13]Mann, F. G. and H. G. Baumgartel, *Absences and Employee Attitudes in an Electric Power Co.* (Ann Arbor: Survey Research Center, University of Michigan, 1952).

[14]Seashore, S. E., *Group Cohesiveness in the Industrial Work Group* (Ann Arbor: Survey Research Center, University of Michigan, 1954).

[15]Cohen et al., *op. cit.,* pp. 63–72.

[16]Coffey, Robert E., Anthony G. Athos, and Peter A. Raynolds, *Behavior in Organizations: A Multidimensional View* 2nd ed. (Englewood Cliffs, N.J.: Prentice-Hall, 1975), pp. 101–104.

[17]Whyte, William F. et al. *Money and Motivation* (New York: Harper and Row, 1955), Chap. 4.

[18]Secord and Backman, *op. cit.,* pp. 384–385.

[19]*Ibid;* pp. 592–594.

[20]McGrath, *op. cit.,* pp. 77–86.

[21]French, John R. P., Jr., and Bertram Raven, "The Bases of Social Power," in Dorwin Cartwright, ed., *Studies in Social Power* (Ann Arbor: Research Center for Group Dynamics, Institute for Social Research, University of Michigan, 1959), pp. 150–167.

[22]Heinen, J. Stephen and Eugene Jacobson, "A Model of Task Group Development in Complex Organizations and a Strategy of Implementation," *Academy of Management Review* 1 (October, 1976), 98–111.

[23]Likert, R., *New Patterns of Management* (New York: McGraw-Hill, 1961), p. 103.

[24]Tannenbaum, *op. cit.,* pp. 98–102.

cases cases cases

Case Study: Do Your Own Thing

Miss Billings, director of nursing education, was concerned with the neglect and refusal by the hospital's orderlies to perform all the tasks as instructed and shown in their work descriptions. A careful check on the activities of the orderlies had disclosed that they refused to take T.P.R.s (temperatures, pulse, and respiration), make up beds, and remain on their assigned floors.

The full-time orderlies all had many years of experience working in hospitals. The demand for orderlies was great because, as many of the orderlies would say, "many will not and cannot do the type of work we do." Most of the orderlies had worked at the hospital for many years. Two of the orderlies had been employed for over twenty-five years and were about to retire.

The orderlies were instrumental to care at the hospital. Take for example, Herman Morton, who worked on the fourth floor, the orthopedic section of the hospital. As one nurse said, "Herman and a few of the older orderlies know the book on traction. Why, if Herman ever left, I don't know what I would do."

Each floor was characterized by the type of patients located there, and each orderly was assigned to a floor according to his interest and expertise. The major complaint among new orderlies was the isolation. One orderly was stationed on each floor. Sometimes several hours would pass before a situation occurred that required the services of an orderly. Most orderlies read or visited one another on their floors. Often, two orderlies would informally work together, covering both floors as a team. Friendships developed between the orderlies throughout the hospital. One orderly described the situation, "We work together here. Nobody wants to break his back lifting a patient. If I need help all I have to do is visit another floor and I'll get all the help I need. I expect it from him and he expects it from me. We work together here." Each floor in the hospital had a series of numbered lights. If an orderly was not found by the nurse, she pushed a button that rang a bell and turned on the light representing the floor. In the orderly room, she would leave a note with the job request. Sometimes, the orderlies did not see the light and a patient would be left in discomfort for a period of time.

The nursing staff and the orderlies had a high degree of cooperation. A typical statement heard from a nurse was, "The orderlies only do the work that we are not allowed to do and that we are not physically capable of doing. Why, if I had to lift some of those heavy patients, it would break my back. You know, I admire these men because they often work twelve hours a day to support their families. They are always ready to help when asked, but don't ever ask one to make up a bed because he will only shake his head. I guess they think that's women's work, but its no problem with me." On the other hand, the following comment by an orderly was also typical: "You don't make up beds or take T.P.R.s. The nurses and their aides do that. Why, if you had to do all that, you would feel like death at the end of the day."

Upon reviewing the job description and work environment of the orderlies, Miss Billings wondered what changes should be made concerning the orderlies.

QUESTIONS

1. Why are the orderlies departing from their job description?
2. Are the results of performing the job different from what was intended? Helpful? Detrimental? For whom?
3. Is there a conflict between the personal needs of the orderlies and the hospital's objectives?
4. Do the orderlies have any power? What kind? From what?
5. What would you advise Miss Billings to do?

cases cases cases

Case Study: An Effective Group

PART I A NEW OPERATION

The Process Control Computer Section functions to monitor plant conditions, monitor the plant's start-up and shutdown, and control certain devices in the plant. Computers for this function are bought from the manufacturer and brought to the general office. They are programmed to perform specified functions and then are taken to the plant site for installation.

The initial computer group was formed with four members. John Alfonsetti, a young engineer, had received company training after being hired. His first few years were spent training in the plant's functions. After working in results testing, he was sent along with Roger Armfield, Hal Croft, and Joe Wickers for computer training by the manufacturer.

Joe Wickers was an engineer, thirty-five years of age, who was working in the control department before transferring to the computer section.

Hal and Roger were high school graduates who had worked at other jobs in the plant. Hal was twenty-seven and had been in the plant for three years. Roger had served in the military for ten years before joining the company. Hal and Roger scored very well on an aptitude test for programmers, so they were transferred to the computer group.

The four worked closely on the computer under adverse conditions. The computer was late in shipment, so the initial programming had to be done without an opportunity to test the programs. Some pressure was present in as much as this was a proving ground for future computer installations. With the help of the manufacturer's and group's close working relationship, the results were rewarding. The schedule was met with minor revisions as in-house people were familiar with the computer and changes or additions could be made readily with minimum cost and time.

The computer monitor and control systems were considered a necessity in the new, modern plants. John Alfonsetti was appointed director of Computer Applications and was given responsibility for obtaining an efficient working computer team to serve the new plants' functions. John set out to staff for this purpose, and additional personnel were hired to meet future demands. He followed a procedure of hiring people who were trained in the plant and had an aptitude for programming and college graduates in engineering or computer science.

The group was formed with six engineers just out of college and ten programmers that only had training through ranks. Functional areas were developed, and each was headed up by a project director. In addition to overall coordination of system progress, the project director worked as a member of his function application group.

Considerable interaction was required since group members had to exchange ideas on solutions to plant problems concerning the computer as well as on future program design. Group members were forced to share computer time for testing and the practice developed of having the computer ready for the next person at a specified time. Each member had a concern for production and a sense of pride. Output was high, and production schedules were often completed ahead of time.

The members of the group worked well together and engaged in outside social activities as well as in leisure-time interaction at work. Once or twice a month the members of the group would schedule a basketball game or go out to a club for the night. Steve Farris, an engineer, seemed to initiate these activities, and the others would follow his suggestions of places for the outing.

Several members of the work group lived in the same housing complex. Over half the group lived in the same community outside of town, and they formed a carpool to ride to work.

There was also group interaction during the lunch hour. The members would gather for a card game. Before the game the group would draw straws to see who would go get the drinks. A set procedure was used to determine who kept score for the card game. The low points on the first hand kept score and the low player for the game contributed a nickel for a new deck of cards. The coffee machine was also refilled by different people.

A meeting was scheduled every Monday afternoon with John presiding. The purpose of the meeting was to keep everyone informed and to discuss matters that required future decisions. Any problem that bothered members of the group was also discussed. John was always available and willing to discuss any problem.

PART II EMPLOYEE EVALUATIONS

The following comments were from members of the computer group. Roger Armfield, who had been with the group since the start, offered the following comments: "This group works together. Of course, we kid the college graduates about having just the piece of paper. But that is not true. They know more of the theory and the way textbooks say to do it. We depend on each other to get the job done. I really look forward to coming to work in the mornings."

Ted Hiott was another noncollege graduate who, like some of the other programmers, received his training in the plant. "The reason that we are productive is that we respect one another. On development of new programs or solving a problem in the field, we work as a unit because we do not have time to waste. We have a lot of new programs to write. We compliment each other by little pats on the back. No one tries to take the credit for another person's ideas."

Hal Croft and Bob Tomko related the following story: "Hal and I were at the construction site checking out the computer. We knew it was about time for our six-month progression review. You know that John and Joe drove all the way down after work to talk with us. They met with each of us separately in the motel and discussed our progress. We talked about our strong points and areas for improvement. He also let me participate in my review and evaluate his leadership. I really appreciate that."

Hal Croft added, "They did not have to come down that night. We could have discussed it next week. It made me feel real important."

Sam Kaminer liked the weekly meetings. "The meetings keep us together. We share ideas and announcements of what is going on. Everyone is allowed to participate in the solutions of our problems. John is a determined leader and holds to the objectives of the meeting. We all respect John."

Bob Mahon, an engineer with plant experience, explained, "Everyone is willing to share ideas with one another. Ted is an expert on plant sequence start-up, and Roger is an expert on monitoring alarms. They do not try to protect their knowledge but are willing to share with anyone who is interested. We cross-train in our functional groups so that everyone gets a piece of the action and within five years knows a complete system. We are beginning to standardize programs so that we may use the same program from system to system. It is very important to keep documentation and flowcharts updated—we stress that."

Larry Hough, a programmer with plant checkout experience, offered these comments about John. "John really fights for his workers. He's not afraid to stand up to management. He fought to get the ones without a college degree a pertinent computer title. He also fought to get a key to the building so that we may enter during the weekend. This is contrary to company policy, but he was able to do it. He also got us parking places assigned near the building, and parking is a real problem. Even some managers don't have parking places. These little things may not mean much, but it gives you a secure feeling to work for John. You know that he is fighting for you. This lets you concentrate more on job tasks and not worry about politics."

In one of the weekly meetings, John explained some of his views. "I do not believe in standing over anyone's shoulder. I expect you to take responsibility, formulate your project and production schedules, and achieve the common objectives of this group. I am an engineer myself and plan to contribute my part, but I do not plan to be a slave driver. I hired all of you to function as a group, to obtain the goals of the group. I stress sharing ideas among group members as to how work should be implemented. I hope that we can keep in mind the goals of the group and how these support the goals of the organization.''

QUESTIONS

1. Why is this a cohesive group?
2. In what ways is leadership affecting the group and the results obtained?

CHAPTER 9

INTERGROUP BEHAVIOR

LEARNING OBJECTIVES

When you have finished this chapter, you should be able to:

- *Describe three forms of group interdependence.*
- *Identify three sources of power in intergroup relationships.*
- *Summarize six factors that may influence intergroup interaction.*
- *Understand five ways of managing intergroup interaction.*
- *Outline and describe a model of management-union relationships.*
- *Describe the behavioral issues in union representation.*

In the previous chapter, we examined the formal and informal aspects of a work group and their interrelationship. Building upon these insights, the study of the behaviors and relationships between groups becomes the major concern of this chapter. In addition to different background factors, required interaction, and emergent behavior, intergroup behavior also is affected by intergroup stability, power, and the "orientation" of each group. Other factors that may influence intergroup relationships are unequal dependency, conflict of interests, difficulty in assigning credit or blame, dependency on common resources, communication barriers, and personal factors. After the elements pertinent to intergroup behavior have been developed, means of managing or directing their interaction will be considered. Finally, management–union relations will be explored as a special kind of intergroup interaction.

AN OVERVIEW OF INTERACTING GROUPS

Intergroup behavior refers to the behavior and relations that exist between groups. In an organization, some groups, like individuals, are required to interact to achieve specified objectives. The interacting groups may be in the same department, such as quality control and production, or in separate departments within the same organization, such as sales and personnel. In some instances, the interaction may be with an outside group, for example, management dealing with a labor union.

Whenever groups interact, numerous factors may influence the nature or quality of the relationship. An overview of several group characteristics, with the consequences of intergroup interaction, is given in Figure 9-1. A group, having its own characteristics, is required to interact with another group to attain task objectives. As with group behavior, emergent behavior or relationships develop; that is, behavior unintended by management takes place between groups. Some emergent behavior may be reflected in uncooperative behaviors or in unproductive conflict. Conflict will be examined in depth in Chapter 14. Finally, varied group attributes, required interactions, and emergent behaviors produce definite consequences. The consequences for the development and maintenance of the organization, intergroup relations, and the individual are shown on the right-hand side of the figure.

The first part of this chapter will present and clarify several of the factors outlined in the figure. Kinds of group interdependencies are explored first because this reflects the amount and direction of intergroup activity. Then we will examine the significance of intergroup stability, power, and group orientations for interacting groups.

KINDS OF GROUP INTERDEPENDENCE: REQUIRED INTERACTION

Although an organization is a system consisting of interdependent subsystems, this does not mean that each part depends on and/or supports every other part. The amount of intergroup interaction may range from zero to

Figure 9-1

An Overview of Two Interacting Groups

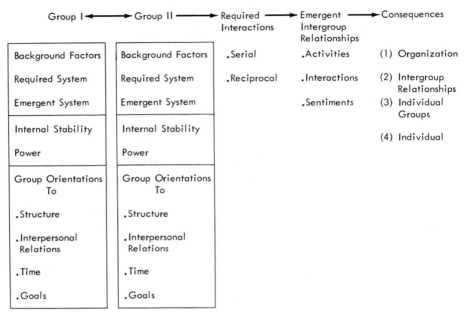

Group I ⟷	Group II ⟶	Required Interactions ⟶	Emergent Intergroup Relationships ⟶	Consequences
Background Factors	Background Factors	.Serial	.Activities	(1) Organization
Required System	Required System	.Reciprocal	.Interactions	(2) Intergroup Relationships
Emergent System	Emergent System		.Sentiments	(3) Individual Groups
Internal Stability	Internal Stability			(4) Individual
Power	Power			
Group Orientations To	Group Orientations To			
.Structure	.Structure			
.Interpersonal Relations	.Interpersonal Relations			
.Time	.Time			
.Goals	.Goals			

Source: Adapted from John A. Seiler, "A Systematic Way of Thinking about Intergroup Behavior," in Paul R. Lawrence and John Seiler, *Organization Behavior and Administration,* rev. ed. (Homewood, Ill.: Richard D. Irwin, 1965), p. 561. ©1965 by Richard D. Irwin, Inc.

very high and is reflected in the groups' interdependence. Three forms of interdependence—pooled, sequential, and reciprocal—are evident in intergroup relationships.[1]

In pooled interdependence, the units do not interact. An insurance company can have agencies distributed throughout a geographical area, but there is no interaction between these agencies. Each contributes to the welfare of the organization, but they are not related directly to one another. Pooled interdependence can be coordinated by standard routines and procedures.

Interdependence becomes more complicated when it is sequential. In this case, the work flow dictates that the output of one unit becomes the input of another. One group cannot begin its task until another provides inputs of the appropriate quantity and quality. An assembly-line operation in which a product moves from one station to the next is a classic example of such interdependence. Coordination is sought by planning or establishing schedules that dovetail the required output–input work flows. The potential for conflict is clearly present when one unit's activity is dependent upon another's output.

Intergroup relationships are most complex when there is reciprocal interdependence. The output of each becomes the input for the other as information or services are exchanged between the units. In the development of a new product, it is necessary for a research and development unit to work in conjunction with engineering units and the production division to ensure a product that is scientifically and economically sound. Coordination by mutual adjustment is necessary for such reciprocal interdependence and may be influenced by any of the antecedents to conflict that will be discussed later in this chapter.

To understand intergroup interaction, it is necessary to know the kind of interdependence that exists. The extent of dependency will influence organizational behavior and also the selection of methods to manage the interaction.

Intergroup Stability

Each group has its own unique characteristics. It is a social unit having a status within the organization and some degree of stability. Supervisors are admonished to encourage their subordinates to function as a social unit, both formally and informally, by strengthening team work and solidarity. Group activities on the job are promoted, and group incentives are applied when appropriate. However, stable units do not always emerge. The amount of intergroup stability is significant, not only for the group itself, but also for intergroup cooperation and conflict.

One study of a manufacturer of pharmaceuticals examined the interaction among the research, engineering and production departments.[2] Work flowed smoothly between these diverse organizational units having reciprocal interdependence. The company had an outstanding reputation for innovative products and the rapid development of ideas into mass-production items. Although the departments had opposing values of quality and economy, the conflict was not destructive. One of the primary causal factors was the internal social stability of each department.[3]

> Each of three departments represented a social unit in which members could find not only satisfaction for their needs to belong, but also job interest, promotion opportunity, and so on. Not one of these departments suffered from internal fragmentation.

Consequently, departmental time, energy, and effort were not spent on structuring a fulfilling work environment. The departments were free to focus on intergroup relationships. Intergroup stability is a basic requirement for effective intergroup relationships.

Power in Intergroup Relationships

If you have observed any form of organizational life or group activity, it may have become apparent that some individuals and/or groups exercise more influence in determining what is done and how than others do. This is called having clout or power.

Power stems from a dependent relationship that may range from none to complete and it provides the condition for one unit's exercising influence over another. Consequently, power is defined by many, and is used here, as the determination of the behavior of one social unit by another unit.[4]

Interorganizational dependency arises because an organization is an open system facing uncertainty but requiring some degree of certainty if it is to operate efficiently. Parts of the organization have as their primary task the coping with such uncertainty, for example, planning departments and research and development divisions. The division of labor within an organization creates interdependencies so that various units are fulfilling the requirements and needs of other units. In the process, units become dependent on and subject to the power of others.

Intergroup power has been associated with three factors: (1) the extent to which a subunit copes effectively with uncertainty for other subunits, (2) the extent to which a subunit's activities are substitutable or can be performed by others, and (3) the extent to which the activities of a subunit are linked to other subunits—centrality.

Absorbing uncertainty

Organizations allocate to various subunits tasks that vary in uncertainty, and those units by performing effectively reduce the impact of uncertainty on other activities and groups. For example, production units would be faced with uncertainty if the sales unit did not forecast demand and/or obtain a smooth flow of orders. Production would not know how many or what kind of products to produce. Coping with uncertainty may be accomplished by prevention, by information, or by absorption. In the example just given, forecasting by the sales unit is an example of coping by information; obtaining a smooth flow of orders is coping by prevention. Coping by absorption is evident when a drop in sales is countered by a promotional campaign. By coping effectively with such changes, other organizational units are provided a more certain or stable environment in which they can work. This coping confers power through the dependencies created.

Substitutability

Substitutability of a unit indicates the ability of an organization to obtain alternative performance of the activities of a subunit. The less the possibility of having a unit's work performed by other subunits, the greater the power of that unit within the organization. For example, in the newspaper industry typesetters occupy a crucial position. No other work group can perform this skilled job, and no paper is printed if this group should strike or "walk out." Such a strategic group is not replaceable; it has power. In some instances a department may hold onto power by retaining information that would enable others to do what it does. This prevents lowering the substitutability of the unit.

Centrality

The power of a group is also related to its centrality. The centrality of a subunit is the degree to which its activities are interlinked with those of other units. The degree to which a subunit may be interdependent was indicated in the previous discussion of pooled, sequential, and reciprocal interaction patterns. The centrality of an organization unit is also indicated when its activities cease. If the termination of work activities quickly and substantially slows the flow of work within the organization, it has considerable power.

However, the degree of interconnectedness with other units and the speed of impact on the work flow are not necessarily closely related. A finance department is connected to all other units through the budget system, but, if its activities were stopped, it would be some time before the effects would be felt. The typesetters in a newspaper are connected directly with only a few units, but a work stoppage by this group would immediately paralyze the organization.

While each of the factors contributing to dependency, and therefore to power, have been examined separately, it is their combination that is meaningful. For example, unless a unit has a minimum of centrality, coping effectively with uncertainty and substitutability cannot affect power. Such a unit is stuck out in left field all by itself, so to speak. Consequently, it is the interrelationship of all three factors that most accurately conveys the extent of organization interdependence or power. Collectively, these provide control of strategic conditions for other subunits and determines the amount of power that a subunit has.

A summary diagram of the determinants of power is shown in Figure 9-2. In the figure we see that coping effectively with uncertainty, substitutability of a unit's activities, and the centrality of a unit in work flows combine or "summate" to give control of strategic conditions for other organizational units. The number of conditions controlled determines the power a unit possesses to influence other units.

Different Orientations

A study by Lawrence and Lorsch of firms in the plastics, packaged foods, and standardized containers industries demonstrated that groups or operating divisions within these organizations developed different orien-

Figure 9-2

The Sources of Power of a Subunit

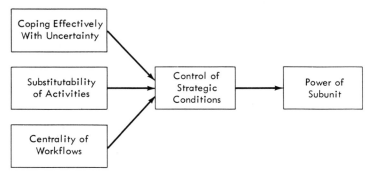

Source: Adapted from D. J. Dickson et al., "A Strategic Contingencies' Theory of Intra-organizational Power," *Administrative Science Quarterly* 16 (June 1971): p. 223.

tations or views.[5] In responding to a diversified environment, the sales subsystem is oriented to the market subenvironment, production to the technical-economic subenvironment, and research development to the scientific subenvironment. The environment for each subsystem varies in terms of the rate of change, the certainty of information at a given time about environmental conditions, and the time required for feedback on the degree of success in coping with the environment. The ranking of each subenvironments on a scale of 1 (least certain or longest in time span) to 3 (most certain or shortest in time span) along these three dimensions is shown in Table 9-1.

The table indicates that the scientific environment is less certain than are the other two environments. In other words, the research and development department is faced with more uncertainty in the scientific suben-

Table 9-1

Ranking of Subenvironments on Three Dimensions

Subenvironment	Certainty of Information	Rate of Change	Time for Feedback	Total
Science	1	1.5	1	3.5
Market	2	1.5	2	5.5
Technical economic	3	3.0	3	9.0

Source: Paul R. Lawrence and Jay W. Lorsch, "Differentiation and Integration in Complex Organizations," *Administrative Science Quarterly* 12 (June 1967:) p. 14.

vironment than is production, which is oriented to the technical-economic portion of organization's environment.

These investigators found that each subsystem develops particular attributes in coping with its segment of the external environment. The characteristics can be summarized as follows.

1. Subsystems having greater certainty in their environment have a more formalized structure, that is, use preexisting programs and controls.
2. Subsystems confronted with environments of moderate certainty will have personnel with more social interpersonal orientations; subsystems facing very certain or uncertain environments have members with more task-oriented interpersonal orientations.
3. The time orientation of subsystem personnel varies directly with the time required to obtain the results of its activities. Consequently, members may develop long, intermediate, or short time perspectives.
4. Personnel of a subsystem will develop a primary concern for the goals relevant to their particular part of the environment.

The significance of different orientations lies in their potential impact upon intergroup behavior. Whenever groups are required to interact with one another, each may see and evaluate issues differently. Their unique orientation toward structure, interpersonal relations, time, and goals will affect group interrelationships. Such divergent perceptions must be reconciled, or conflict in varying degrees may be experienced. Group differences must be managed appropriately for obtaining the objectives of the organization.

FACTORS BROUGHT TO FOCUS IN GROUP INTERACTIONS

The previous factors—intergroup stability, power differences, and differences in orientation—will definitely color intergroup interactions. However, there is another set of factors that has potential for influencing intergroup behaviors.[6] These factors are shown under required interactions in Figure 9-3 and will be examined for their potential influence upon group relationships.

Task dependency is the key variable in intergroup behavior. Dependency is the extent to which two parties depend upon each other for assistance, information, compliance, or other coordinative acts. Consequently, dependence can range from zero, to low, to high. Interdependence provides an incentive for collaboration and an occasion for conflict. In an organization, parties independent of one another are not likely to conflict over an issue.

Figure 9-3

Additional Factors Having a Potential Effect
on Required Interaction

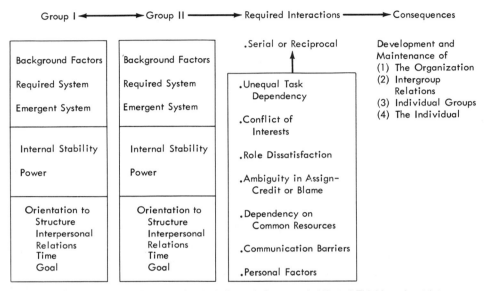

Group I ◄────► Group II ────► Required Interactions ────► Consequences

Group I	Group II	Required Interactions	Consequences
Background Factors Required System Emergent System	Background Factors Required System Emergent System	•Serial or Reciprocal •Unequal Task Dependency •Conflict of Interests	Development and Maintenance of (1) The Organization (2) Intergroup Relations (3) Individual Groups (4) The Individual
Internal Stability Power	Internal Stability Power	•Role Dissatisfaction •Ambiguity in Assign-Credit or Blame	
Orientation to Structure Interpersonal Relations Time Goal	Orientation to Structure Interpersonal Relations Time Goal	•Dependency on Common Resources •Communication Barriers •Personal Factors	

Source: Adapted from John A. Seiler, "A Systematic Way of Thinking about Intergroup Behavior," in Paul A. Lawrence and John Seiler, *Organization Behavior and Administration*, rev. ed. (Homewood, Ill.: Richard D. Irwin, 1965), p. 561. ©1965 by Richard D. Irwin, Inc.

Unequal task dependency

Dependency between two parties is seldom equal, and the more dependent party may be at a disadvantage in the relationship. Such an imbalance is frequently observed between line groups concerned mainly with providing the product or service and staff groups concerned with providing specialized assistance to the line. The staff is dependent upon the line for use of its expertise. Often, the line views such help as unwanted or disruptive of operations. Consequently, the line sees cooperation as having little value. The more dependent party may try to increase the incentive to cooperate by seeking to influence the relationship or interfere with the task performance of the more independent party.

As with occupations, departments or units within an organization are ranked according to prestige or power. When units interact, the more prestigious or higher-status unit initiates action for units having less status. For example, if engineering (high status) initiates action for production (lower status), the influence is legitimate, that is, from high to lower status.

However, if a lower-status unit initiates action for a higher-status unit, an illegitimate influence, the relationship between the two groups tends to break down and conflict may be generated.

Conflict of interests

Conflict tends to arise when each party has responsibility for only a part of the task and/or there is a conflict of interest or objectives. For example, staff units value change as a test of their innovative ability, but line units prefer stability. For one party to obtain what it desires means that the other must give up something and a conflict situation results.

Conflict is further stimulated when the reward system devised by higher management emphasizes the separate performance of the parties rather than their combined effort. A reward system that recognizes the separate performance of interacting groups may be replaced by a superordinate goal. A superordinate goal is one that can be achieved only by the collective efforts of both groups. Consequently, groups, not individual performances, are rewarded for their joint effort. This provides an incentive for cooperation and working together.

A conflict of interest may reflect values held by interacting groups. For example, long, economical runs of similar products are desired or valued conditions that are optimum for the operations of the production department. The sales department prefers product diversity and quick delivery that has the potential for disrupting the conditions desired by production and will be resisted.

Role dissatisfaction

Dissatisfaction with role requirements can be a source of conflict and may stem from a variety of sources. Blocked status aspirations of service and staff members has led to conflict with other units because these professionals felt the lack of recognition and advancement opportunities. Ambiguities in the definition of work responsibilities can also lead to offensive and defensive maneuvers as the parties seek to restructure the situation. On the other hand, when role definitions are clear, each party can expect a certain type of behavior from the other, and fewer opportunities for disagreement occur.

Ambiguities in assigning credit or blame

Difficulty in assigning credit or blame arises when it is difficult to assess the contribution of each party. For example, disputes have resulted between production and sales units when it could not be determined which department had made a mistake.[7] High variability and uncertainty of means to attain goals increase the potential of conflict for interdependent parties.

Dependence on common resources

Conflict potential exists when two parties depend upon a common pool of resources such as manpower, operating funds, equipment, capital funds, and so on. Competition for such scarce resources tends to decrease coordination and joint problem solving.

Communication barriers

Conflict will be greater when barriers to communication exist. Semantic difficulties, differences in training, and physical separation can impair the clarity of information required for interaction between parties.

Personal factors

A review of experimental studies found that personality attributes such as high authoritarianism, high dogmatism, and low self-esteem increase conflict behavior. Even personal differences in background, values, education, age, and social patterns have been found to lower the probability of parties' understanding one another. Such factors may also contribute to communication problems and role dissatisfaction.

The factors just examined, if present, do not necessarily lead to undesirable consequences. They may not be perceived as a significant irritant or not perceived at all by interacting interdependent groups. However, the potential disruptive influences of such factors must be considered when designing work structures and work flows as well as their subsequent management.

MANAGING INTERGROUP INTERACTIONS

Whatever the number and nature of variables affecting intergroup relationships, the groups must be managed to achieve the appropriate amount and quality of interaction. When groups interact to exchange ideas on plans, directions, services, or products, their activities must be directed and coordinated in some manner. Ways of managing group interactions are shown in Figure 9-4, under required interactions.

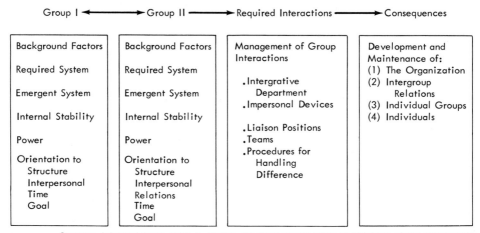

Figure 9-4

Managing Intergroup Interactions

Group I	Group II	Required Interactions	Consequences

Background Factors
 	
Required System
 	
Emergent System
 	
Internal Stability
 	
Power
 	
Orientation to
  Structure
Interpersonal
Time
Goal
	Background Factors
	
	Required System
	
	Emergent System
	
	Internal Stability
	
	Power
	
	Orientation to
	  Structure
	Interpersonal
	Relations
	Time
	Goal
		Management of Group
		Interactions
		
		. Intergrative
		  Department
		. Impersonal Devices
		
		. Liaison Positions
		. Teams
		. Procedures for
		  Handling
		  Difference
			Development and
			Maintenance of:
			(1) The Organization
			(2) Intergroup
			    Relations
			(3) Individual Groups
			(4) Individuals

Source: Adapted from John A. Seiler, "A Systematic Way of Thinking about Intergroup Behavior," in Paul R. Lawrence and John Seiler, *Organization Behavior and Administration,* rev. ed. (Homewood, Ill.: Richard D. Irwin, 1965), p. 561. ©1965 by Richard D. Irwin, Inc.

Approaches to Managing Group Interaction

Strategies for managing group interaction may take the form of several traditional approaches. Rules and procedures can be used to specify the required activities of interacting groups. Interaction is minimized and stabilized by resorting to standardized procedures when the activities are known in advance or are repetitive. Planning also facilitates coordinating group performance because the resulting goals and controls integrate the activities of interdependent groups. Such traditional approaches have been supplemented by other methods of directing intergroup performance as organizations have become more complex.[8]

Integrative departments

An integrative department may be used to coordinate several interdependent departments or functional units. Coordination by an integrative unit is more effective if its managing personnel have relatively high influence based upon expertise or knowledge. Coordinators whose influence stems primarily from the formal authority of their position or because of their closeness to top management have been found less effective. In addition, the more effective integrators were rewarded for the performance of all the interdependent activities that they were directing. They were evaluated and rewarded with other department managers on overall performance. Finally, interunit cooperation was more effectively achieved when the integrators openly confronted differences rather than smoothed them over or forced decisions on the groups.

Impersonal devices

These may be used to regulate certain kinds of intergroup activities. For example, sales and production may fight about the quarterly production schedule, but, once the schedule is finalized, it determines what is produced and when. The two parties are no longer at odds with one another on this issue. Also, inventories or buffer stocks may be used as an impersonal regulating activity. This is possible when one unit is dependent upon another for a product or service before it can begin or complete its work activity, that is, in the case of serial interdependence. If the product flow is disrupted, the dependent unit is prevented from meeting its scheduled work, and hostility or conflict frequently erupts between the two units. The placement of additional stock or inventory can prevent such delays while remedial measures are being taken to restore the normal flow of goods or services.

Liaison positions

Management of interacting groups may consist of using a liaison person to maintain contact and communication among several units. This provides the interacting groups with more timely information of real or potential problems and promotes a better understanding of each other's functions and responsibilities.

Teams

Teams consisting of representatives from each work group may be effectively used to facilitate the coordination of subsystem activities. Formal machinery for discussing and resolving mutual problems is provided by this arrangement. In some organizations a similar function may be performed by an individual. While such a person may also be called a liaison person, the role and setting in which he or she operates is different from the use of teams.

Procedures for resolving differences

Management of intergroup activities can take the form of establishing procedures for resolving conflict. Such a norm may be formal or, having evolved from precedent, informal. Basically, this approach is a tacit recognition that conflict has or will arise from group interaction. One approach is to insist that the parties in conflict resolve their own differences. Another tactic is to immediately toss the issue to the common boss of the conflicting units for resolution. While this provides an easy "out" for the parties, problem-solving abilities and procedures are never developed. A more promising approach consists of insisting that the parties resolve their own differences, only sending an issue to higher management as a last resort.

In summary, whenever groups are required to interact in the attainment of organizational objectives, management cannot assume that cooperation will take place or that performance will be adequate. Each group brings unique characteristics to the relationship that may facilitate or impair joint performance. An adequate understanding of organizational behavior must include insight into intergroup relationships and promising strategies for coping with such interactions.

MANAGEMENT–UNION RELATIONSHIPS

Management–union relationships represent a special case or kind of intergroup interaction. While not all employers deal with labor unions, union membership is high in many organizations, both public and private. A labor union is an association of employees for the primary purpose of influencing the employer's decisions about their conditions of employment. After examining an overview of several key variables involved in management–union interaction, we will consider some of the behavioral issues in union representation.

A Model of Management–Union Relationships

A simplified overview of some of the variables affecting management–union interaction and the consequences produced help us to understand this complex relationship. Figure 9-5 indicates that both management and the union bring to the required interactions their own unique background factors, that is, goals and value systems, views of the other party, and so on.[9] Required interactions stem from existing labor laws. The Wagner Act (1935) gave employees the right to organize a labor union and to bargain collectively with management through chosen representatives. Recognition of the union was to be settled by elections supervised by the National Relations Board to determine if employees desired to be represented by a union. Approval of the union is followed by the legal requirement that both management and labor bargain in good faith in seeking a contract governing wages, hours, and working conditions. The second required activity stems from the agreed contract, that is, the implementation and policing of contract provisions to confirm that they are being followed.

Figure 9-5 indicates the potential impact of several factors on the required interactions. Several external or environmental variables interact on the negotiation and administration of the contracts. Governmental influence is felt not only through existing labor laws but also through the intervention of federal mediation, if contract negotiations break down, and a cooling-off period, if a strike threatens the national welfare. Customers of the organization are also to be considered in contract negotiation, because negotiated wages and benefits will eventually be reflected in the price of products and services. Both management and labor must consider what the market will bear and the extent to which alternative competitive products are available.

Figure 9-5

An Overview of Management–Union Interaction Factors

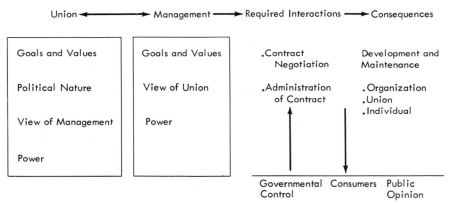

Source: Adapted from Leon G. Meggenson and C. Ray Gullett, "A Predictive Model of Union-Management Conflict," *Personnel Journal* 49 (June 1970): 502. Reprinted with permission. *Personnel Journal,* Costa Mesa, Ca. Copyright June 1970.

Public opinion is also a factor that may exert some influence upon the required activities. Disregard for the public welfare may result in pressure for governmental action and additional legislation. For example, the organization's product may be boycotted or pressure may be applied to institute legal compulsory arbitration that would eliminate strikes.

As shown in Figure 9-5, maintenance and growth of both management and the union are affected by the resulting required interactions. The union–management relationship may range from joint problem solving to a continual power struggle as a contract is negotiated and administered. The quality of this interaction will be influenced by the background factors of both parties. Moreover, growth and maintenance of the individual is affected by the management–union relationship.

Management-Union Background Factors

Both management and the union bring different background factors to the two required interactions shown in Figure 9-5. An examination of several of these will help to explain the behaviors and consequences that stem from these interactions.

Values and objectives

The union basically views its purpose as regulating the decisions of management in areas of activity that affect the working force. In terms of union interests, there is no limit to the subjects over which bargaining should take place. Basically, however, union objectives boil down to (1) higher pay; (2) shorter hours of work (daily, weekly, and annually); (3) improved working conditions, both physically and sociopsychologically; and (4) improved security, both of the person and the job.[10] The objectives center around the living standards and economic status of union members and the provisions of security against market fluctuations, technological change, and management decisions.

The quasi-political nature of unions

Union organizations are not economic entities in the sense that business organizations are. Rather, unions are concerned with promoting and maintaining solidarity within their ranks to be effective. To achieve this end, unions seek to shape labor relations laws that favor and do not threaten union gains and goals. Social legislation and public policy is promoted to shape a society in which unions can thrive.

Sometimes unity and cohesion within union ranks is generated by focusing on "unfair" and "unjust" behavior of some outside force, usually management. If management is acting in ways perceived as unjust by its employee, union leaders are likely to use such actions to coalesce the ranks of employees and generate support for its demands. Additionally, it may be necessary for union leadership to look for issues when none exists or create worker dissatisfaction in a reasonably peaceful environment.

Finally, members of the union structure are elected to their offices by the employees. To maintain their positions, they must demonstrate proficiency in helping their "electorate" in some capacity. The shop steward must prove his or her worth by processing grievances, the union president by obtaining wages and benefits comparable to what other unions have obtained, and so on. Concessions must be obtained from management even at the cost of long-run implications to the organization or management–union relationships.

View of management

The union will have a view of management that is significantly influenced by past relationships. Management may be seen as dedicated to union busting or to varying degrees of cooperation. Some unions are convinced that management occupies an economic and class position that conflicts with the best interests of the worker.

Power

Unions will have varying amounts of power, ranging from weak or ineffective to what some have called monopolistic. Some will lack the support of their own members; others will have not only member backing but the assistance of strong national unions with which they are affiliated. One union may represent an entire industry and negotiate on an industrywide basis, such as the Teamsters union.

For the union, power involves the extent to which it has a voice in the way in which management runs the organization. The question of whether the union can influence certain decisions has centered around management rights or prerogatives. Originally, the union had the legal right to participate in decisions relating to wages, hours, and work conditions. However, over the years the items over which the union and management must negotiate, if the other side desires to do so, has grown substantially through both the law and court decisions. For example, plant closedown and relocation, price of company meals, discriminatory racial policies, and the like may be items for bargaining.[11]

Finally, the union has demonstrated power by promoting consumer boycotts of an organization's product and strikes to enforce its demands.

Management Background Factors

Values and objectives

Management has its own set of objectives. Its task is the effective utilization of human and material resources to produce a good or service for its customers at a profit. Long-term profitability and success of the organization is viewed as depending upon freedom of action and maneuverability. Flexibility and change are viewed as necessary to achieve maximum economic welfare for both the organization and its employees. This position collides, of course, with the union's objective of maintaining a check upon management's unilateral action and maintaining and increasing the economic welfare of the same employees.

272

Management, while concerned with the welfare of its employees, has responsibilities to a number of groups. Among these are the public, consumers, and stockholders or owners. Both the union and management seek to achieve differing objectives through the same organization, whether this is a business firm or a public entity.

View of the union

Another significant background factor is management's view of the union. How legitimate is the union as to its ends and means? This involves recognition of the union and its methods of operation.

In the past employers' stands on unionism had a philosophical basis similar to the restraints placed by the constitution upon the invasion of the rights to life, liberty, and property. The right of free contract is basic to the enjoyment of property. Since the buying and selling of labor implies a contract, any restriction of the process is a violation of the liberty to contract and a violation of the rights of private property. The employee was conceded the right to seek employment and to acquire property in the form of wages, whereas the right to contract for services and freely operate a business was deemed a part of the property rights of employers. Organized labor, therefore, was viewed as a threat to the freedom to contract. When ownership was separated from managerial control, management often justified its position by insisting that its obligations to stockholders would not permit bilateral management unless the stockholders endorsed such action. Furthermore, management has considered it administrative folly to work cooperatively with a third party that would have no responsibility if control were shared.

A range of possible views toward a union is reflected in the following.[12]

1. A conflict philosophy:

    Managements' collective bargaining strategy is directed toward maintaining its unilateral power and resisting union demands regardless of merit.

2. A legalist philosophy:

    Management rigidly follows the legal requirements governing labor –management relations, but no positive advantages are perceived in employee representation or collective bargaining.

    In order to maintain its position of power and preserve its prerogatives, management endeavors to work around the union, even on matters that are of joint interest.

    Management works to build "company-mindedness" among employees and competes with the union for the loyalty of employees.

3. A cooperative philosophy:

Management deals willingly and frankly with authorized union representatives and with regard for the rights and responsibilities of the union.

Properly managed, responsible, and democratic unions are not incompatible with the American economic system; the union is accepted as a permanent factor in the operation of the organization.

Positive advantages accrue from bargaining with a strong and well-disciplined union.

Labor–management relations are a product of consultation and cooperation, and management separates the areas of conflict and nonconflict.

Employees' cooperation cannot be won if their union and representatives are under continual attack by management; therefore, management strives to secure and maintain the respect of both employees and their union.

It is possible for employees to be loyal to both the organization and their union.

These management views about unions will obviously influence the quality of relationships between the two parties. Management behavior is predisposed to conflict at one extreme and cooperation at the other extreme.

Power

Management has sought to reserve certain areas from bilateral determination with the union and retain them exclusively for itself. Due to labor laws and court opinions, nearly every former inherent management right has been challenged by unions. The ultimate determination of what can be restricted from negotiation depends upon the relative bargaining power of the two parties. The collective bargaining agreement reflects which rights and how much such rights and powers management has conceded or agreed to share with the union.

The power of management is also evident in its economic strength to withstand a long strike rather than to give in on an issue. Also the ability to shut down the plant or lock out employees may be used as a power strategy. Economic power is not unlimited, however, because prolonged strikes can lead to the loss of customers to competitors or the producers of alternative products. Also, the union may have access to strike funds that are used to provide some compensation to employees during a strike.

Consequences of Management-Union Interaction

The preceding background factors of management and the union, while not exhaustive, do provide some insight into what has been called required interaction, that is, contract negotiation and administration. The contract and its subsequent administration, however arrived at, have consequences for management, union, and the employees covered by the contract. Quite possibly, the parties may have achieved a relationship that holds promise of a higher level of cooperation and accommodation. Whatever the consequences, they become part of a collection of experiences or past relationships that influence subsequent interactions.

Finally, consequences of a different sort are produced indirectly in terms of governmental control, the public, and the consumer. While these parties are affected by union–management interaction, they also have an influence upon these interactions. Both management and the union are concerned about the impact of their activities upon these "outsiders" and their potential for stimulating change that may be to their disadvantage. This is another way of saying that even union–management relationships constitute an open system that is subject to environmental influences.

BEHAVIORAL ISSUES IN UNION REPRESENTATION

Why Workers Join Unions

Why do workers join unions? The reasons may vary or consist of multiple motives.[13] These reasons are noted in the following paragraphs.

Steady employment with adequate income

Probably the most basic desire of employees is for security, especially economic security. For many employees, job security takes priority over the amount of wages in determining job satisfaction. If employees perceive the union as able to provide steady jobs at a satisfactory wage, they may be inclined to join the union.

Fair personnel policies

Since an employee's security is based upon the organization's personnel policies, there is a concern that job assignments, transfers and promotions, discipline, layoffs, rehirings, and other rewards and punishments will not be handled equitably. This is a special concern if management is felt to act irrationally, discriminatorily, or prejudically. A hand in the determination and enforcement of such personnel policies may be achieved by union representation.

A voice in decisions affecting their welfare

Workers may gain a voice in affairs other than personnel policies by belonging to the union. A role in ones' own fate and self-determination may be achieved regarding automation, plant relocation, or the closing of the plant. The union can also provide a channel of communication for frustrations, feelings, ideas, and purposes that may influence management's decisions.

Protection from economic hazards beyond their control

Employees are subject to sickness, accidents, and eventually to retirement. Many workers feel that their employers are partially or wholly responsible for helping them cope with such adversities. Unions seek to deliver such benefits and increase their coverage during contract negotiations.

Recognition and participation

Peer pressure may cause workers to become union members. As we have seen, the need for acceptance and belonging is a compelling motive for many individuals. Also, recreational and social activities associated with unions provide an incentive for some employees.

Compulsion

Finally, some workers are compelled to join the union to obtain or hold a job. Legal union provisions such as the union shop requires that the employee join the union after a certain length of employment, usually thirty days. Labor laws enforce union membership in the thirty-one states that do not have right-to-work laws. Compulsory membership, of course, promotes union security and strength.

An implicit factor in joining the union

Permeating these reasons for joining a union is the perception by the individual that he or she is at a major disadvantage in bargaining with the organization or management.[14] This may invoke a feeling of powerlessness when it comes to a worker's determining what control he or she has over his or her job and job-related matters. The union is seen as a means for equalizing management's power and decreasing the uncertainty about wages, job security, job layoffs, and so on. While few, if any, would charge management with deliberate oppression, the union is perceived as a hedge or protection against exploitation based on position power. There is apprehension that management's power might be used in a discriminatory or arbitrary manner to decrease the individual's needs.

Dual allegiance

A union member is obviously a member of two vastly different organizations at the same time—the employing organization and the union. Does this create a problem for union members? The small amount of research available seems to indicate that employees can have favorable attitudes toward both the union and company, especially if a mature bargaining relationship exists.[15]

Many employers, however, see themselves as competing with the union for the loyalty of employees. Frequently, the personnel program is structured to contain all the means for satisfying employees' needs and securing their loyalty. Programs designed with this objective in mind have often failed. Some managers now hold the view that the employee as a union member need not feel antagonistic toward management or classified as pro-union or pro-management. Such a position exists at Raytheon Manufacturing Company. ''The company believes that employees can have dual loyalties, just as a foreman must have loyalty to his employees as well as to the management. This duality need not present serious conflict or create adversaries.''[16]

An examination of these reasons for joining unions reveals the prevalence of lower-order needs, that is, the needs for security and belonging. Unions have been successful in dealing with economic issues and basic rights that meet such needs. A survey by the University of Michigan's Survey Center disclosed that 84 percent of the employees questioned said that the union protects workers against unfair practices; 80 percent agreed that unions improve security; and 77 percent said that unions improve wages.[17]

However, unions have not been able to deliver on the higher-order needs. As seen in Chapter 3, these needs are job related and involve achievement, advancement, recognition, and psychological growth. In general, unions have opposed job-enrichment and other human resource development techniques for fear that their influence will be undermined or result in the worker's being exploited.

The union's unwillingness to influence the higher-order needs is indicative of not serving individual needs. Unions push for uniformity, equality, and standardization in contract negotiations with management. This results in benefits that are general and apply only to large groups. Individual differences and situations generally are ignored as unionwide or companywide standards prevail.

Why Workers Do Not Join Unions

Despite the compelling reasons for joining the union, many employees do not choose to belong.[18] Why?

Lack of a compelling reason

Many employees are not overly concerned about security and safety needs because they consider their wages, work conditions, and fringe benefits satisfactory. Many organizations are managed to promote such favorable conditions. To change by affiliating with a union may be perceived as risking the disruption of quite adequate conditions.

Identification with management

Many employees identify themselves with management. This is more likely with white-collar, scientific, technical, and professional employees who have aspirations for supervisory and managerial positions. Such occupational groups tend to think that they can make it on their own and do not wish to be tied to the standardized conditions characteristic of unions. For many, union membership is associated with blue-collar work and the view that to join a union would lower their social status.

Unions are not trusted

Many employees associate unions with socialism and the welfare state, which are seen as contrary to the free enterprise system and individual initiative. The results of public suffering and inconvenience from prolonged strikes are not considered worth the gains achieved or the issues involved. Distrust also is generated by evidence of corrupt labor leaders' stealing or mishandling employee health and welfare funds and the acceptance of or extraction of bribes from employers. Unions free of such malpractices are associated with the tainted ones.

A Choice: Expectancy Considerations

As seen, there are reasons for and against joining a union; this may put an individual in the position of having to make a decision. What is the motivation for making such a choice? Expectancy theory (Chapter 3) provides some insights here. The union will be peceived as associated with a variety of outcomes, each having an expectancy or subjective probability of happening.[19] Each outcome has valence or attraction for the individual because of the degree to which it satisfies personal needs. This may be diagrammed as shown in Figure 9-6. Notice that the second-level outcomes are not shown or developed or the valences assigned to the outcomes listed as this would depend on the worker.

In this hypothetical example, the expectancy of outcomes is based on the thoughts developed in the preceding material. The importance of each outcome (valence) will depend upon the individual. For example, an em-

Figure 9-6

Expectancy Considerations in Deciding Whether or Not to Join a Union

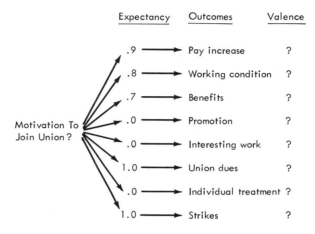

Expectancy	Outcomes	Valence
.9 →	Pay increase	?
.8 →	Working condition	?
.7 →	Benefits	?
.0 →	Promotion	?
.0 →	Interesting work	?
1.0 →	Union dues	?
.0 →	Individual treatment	?
1.0 →	Strikes	?

ployee having an instrumental orientation toward work may have a zero valence or attraction for interesting work and promotion. That is, work is valued only because it is a means to attain other important ends. Such an employee may be inclined to join the union. On the other hand, an employee of an organization having good working conditions, a high pay scale, and good benefits will not have a high need for these outcomes. Basically, such needs are already being fulfilled. Furthermore, the expectancy that the union can improve these factors may be low or zero. If this is the case and the union is perceived as unable to influence interesting work and/or promotion, which are important, the employee will be inclined to refrain from joining the union. The expectancy diagram provides a promising means for appreciating the thought process involved in choosing to join or refrain from joining the union.

SUMMARY

Organizations of any size are characterized by intergroup interdependencies made necessary to attain goals. Frequently, the interactions among groups fall short of achieving the cooperation necessary to achieving objectives effectively and efficiently. An understanding of the intergroup dynamics involved is necessary before appropriate remedial action can be taken.

Each work group has its own unique social system (background factors, required system, and emergent system) that strongly influences its internal stability and its orientation toward structure, interpersonal relationships, time, and goals. In addition, each group has power to the extent that it deals effectively with uncertainties affecting other groups, the ease or difficulty of replacing its work activities, and the degree of its involvement in the flow of work. Each of these factors has an influence upon intergroup relationships.

The quality of required intergroup interactions also may be affected by other factors that stem primarily from the way in which tasks are structured. Included are unequal task dependency, conflict of interest, ambiguity in assigning credit or blame, dependency on common resources, communication barriers, and personal factors.

An understanding of the potential factors that can influence intergroup relationships is of value in deciding how they may be managed. Managing group interactions may be achieved by integrative departments, liaison persons, teams, impersonal devices, and procedures for handling differences that inevitably arise between groups.

Finally, management–union interaction was shown to parallel intergroup relationships. Both parties bring their own goals, values, and power positions to their required interactions that have definite consequences for management, union, and employees. Workers may or may not join a union, and their choice is dependent upon expectancy considerations. The outcomes of union membership have different valences or significance to each person.

QUESTIONS FOR STUDY AND DISCUSSION

1. What kinds of group interdependencies are found in an organization? Which has the most potential for conflict and misunderstanding? Why?

2. Why is intragroup stability important for intergroup interactions?

3. How does power affect intergroup relationships? What determines the amount of power that a group has?

4. In dealing with different subenvironments, subsystems develop unique orientations. What are these orientations? How do they affect intergroup behavior?

5. Other than intragroup stability, power differences, and varying orientations, what additional factors can influence group interactions?

6. How may intergroup interactions be managed?

7. How are management–union relationships similar to intragroup relationships? Different?

8. Why are some workers inclined to join a union? What human needs are most likely served by joining? Why do workers fail to join unions?

NOTES

[1]Thompson, James D., *Organizations in Action* (New York: McGraw-Hill, 1967), pp. 54–57.

[2]Lawrence, Paul R. and John A. Seiler, *Organization Behavior and Administration*, rev. ed. (Homewood, Ill.: Irwin, 1965), pp. 583–585.

[3]*Ibid.,* p. 584.

[4]Hickson, D. J. et al., "A Strategic Contingencies' Theory of Intraorganizational Power," *Administrative Science Quarterly* 12 (June 1971): 216-227.

[5]Lawrence, Paul R. and Jay W. Lorsch, "Differentiation and Integration in Complex Organizations," *Administrative Science Quarterly* 12 (June 1967): 1-47.

[6]Walton, Richard E. and John M. Dutton, "The Management of Interdepartmental Conflict: A Model and Review," *Administrative Science Quarterly* 14 (March 1969): 73-84.

[7]*Ibid.,* p. 77.

[8]*Ibid.,* p. 77.

[9]Megginson, Leon C. and C. Ray Gullett, "A Predictive Model of Union-Management Conflict," *Personnel Journal* 50 (June 1970): 495-503.

[10]Megginson, Leon C., *Personnel: A Behavioral Approach to Administration* (Homewood, Ill.: Irwin, 1967), p. 62.

[11]Yoder, Dale and Herbert G. Heneman, Jr., eds., *Employee and Labor Relations* (Washington, D.C.: Bureau of National Affairs, 1976), p. 128.

[12]Milton, Charles R., *Ethics and Expediency in Personnel Management* (Columbia: University of South Carolina Press, 1970), pp. 130, 165, 205-206.

[13]Megginson, *op. cit.,* pp. 55-58.

[14]Jacobs, T. O., *Leadership and Exchange in Formal Organizations* (Alexandria, Va.: Human Resources Research Organization, 1971), pp. 199-200.

[15]Fossum, John A., Labor Relations (Dallas: Business Publication, 1979), pp. 123-124.

[16]Woods, Leslie E., "Ten Years of Labor Peace at Raytheon," *Personnel Series,* (1957): 37-45.

[17]*U.S. News & World Report,* "Labor Trends" May 14, 1979, p. 75.

[18]Megginson, *op. cit.,* pp. 58-59.

[19]Fossum, *op. cit.,* pp. 118-121.

cases cases cases

Case Study: Blue Book Interaction

The Blue Book Company is a large department store that is organized on a product line basis. Each department has its own items and a manager who is responsible for purchasing these products (see the organizational chart).

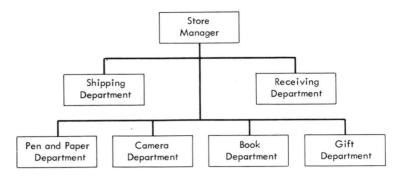

Since the success of the store depends on good service to its customers, everyone places emphasis on the needs of sales. From time to time, as necessary, people are borrowed from the Receiving Department to help cover the sales floor. All the department heads take care of their most important customers and the sales force handles the others.

Receiving and Shipping are service departments in the company. Items come into the Shipping Department, which takes the merchandise to the Receiving Department where the items are checked and priced. The Receiving Department then notifies the appropriate department so that it can take its merchandise to the floor or put it in stock. During the course of a work day, the department heads frequently interact with the Shipping and Receiving departments. For tasks such as moving stock or arranging for a pickup of supplies, the department heads contact Shipping.

The Sales Department managers often go to the receiving area to obtain items before they have been checked in and priced, claiming that they are desperately needed. Ted (Receiving Department manager) will occasionally allow them to take the items, although this is inconsistent with established procedures. He feels that by doing this, he can get more cooperation from the sales departments in removing their merchandise, which will provide space to process new incoming merchandise. When this fails Ted resorts to another tactic.

The following conversation was overheard:

Book Department Manager: Ted really gave me a hard time last week. I needed a book that had come in but had not been processed. He said that it had not been checked in because there was no room to work and that if I would claim the books we had received three days earlier, it certainly would help. Well, he just refused to give me the book and said he would bring it personally when I got those books moved out of his way. He seemed really angry about it and I don't understand why; there were a lot of other things around that were more in his way than my books."

Camera and Pen Department Manager: "I know what you mean. It seems like every day he bothers me about getting my stock out of his way. I told Ted the other day that I just could not leave the floor to get the merchandise, and he snapped back, "Well, if you can't get it put up, don't order the damn stuff." He was huffy.

Some of the problems noted with the work flow were as follows: If Shipping was busy, it would not bring the merchandise to Receiving immediately but wait until there was a large load to deliver. This caused Receiving to be idle at times, but, when the delivery arrived there was more work than the employees could handle. Ted had discussed this several times with the delivery person and, when this did not alleviate the problem, he talked with the store manager. After the store manager talked to the delivery section, the problem was alleviated for a while, but soon the practice of "wait to accumulate" became the procedure again.

Since the receiving room was rather small, it was important to process and remove the items quickly. The merchandise had to be checked in and removed by the proper departments in a steady stream to have room for other incoming items. Often, when the sales floor was busy, it was very difficult to find someone to move the checked merchandise.

Some of the feelings within the different departments of the store concerning the flow of work were as follows:

Shipping: We cannot be running up and down every time items come in just for receiving. Receiving thinks that it is the only department with work to do. We catch hell from floor personnel if we are not here to tell them how much shipping charges on an order will be or else we will catch hell from Sales or Receiving if we do not get the merchandise to them when it comes in. The sales people will ask us to take the items from Receiving after they have been checked in so that they will not have to leave the floor. I just do not have enough people to run this whole damn company, and I would like for you to tell me exactly what you expect from our department?

Receiving: All we want to do is keep the store supplied in an efficient and effective manner. What I want is for my workers to have work available for them when it's in the store. I do not want them to have nothing to do for four hours as happened the other day and then all of a sudden have two day's work staring them in the face. We need some cooperation from the other departments to do our job efficiently. We need Shipping to bring us a steady flow, and we need the departments on the floor to move their merchandise to the stock rooms for us to have room to work.

The Book Department manager summed up the various sales departments' thoughts when he said, "Our main job is keeping the customers happy. This means that we have to be on the floor most of the time. While we are busy with the customers, we do not have time to be getting the stock out of Receiving's way. We want to put the stock up so we will know where it is when we need it, but, when Receiving needs us, we are the busiest and just cannot do what it wants us to."

QUESTIONS

1. What kind of interdependence is there among the Shipping, Receiving, and Sales departments? Is this related to the problems observed? How?

2. What is the status ranking of these three groups? What is the direction of initiation of action?

3. When Ted's (Receiving manager) efforts to obtain cooperation by releasing items before clearing Receiving failed, what kind of power did he use? How effective was this? Why?

4. Do the objectives of the group differ? Does this contribute to the problem?

5. What would you suggest to the manager to improve performance?

cases cases cases

Case Study: Intergroup Conflict

A NEW PLANT

The A-E Chemical Company is jointly owned by two large parent companies, one located in Europe and the other in America. The board of directors of A-E is composed equally of representatives selected from both parent firms.

Originally, a chemical production company, A-E has expanded into the production of synthetic fibers. Having experienced considerable success, top management has decided to expand into the production of other synthetic fibers. Favorable market predictions and success of the previous expansion precipitated the decision to construct a nylon fiber manufacturing plant.

Since European Chemical operated a large nylon fiber plant, an agreement was made that its personnel would take part in establishing the new facility. Personnel from American Chemical and A-E Chemical also would be utilized in the new plant. Basically, the European Chemical contribution would be to

1. acquire and install equipment
2. provide the basic technology for producing nylon fiber from raw material to the finished fiber

The American Chemical contribution would be to

1. assist in implementing the European Chemical technology to produce a product that would be competitive in the U.S. market
2. provide research and development, marketing, and sales functions for the new fiber plant

The agreement also called for European Chemical and both American Chemical and A-E Chemical personnel to fill management positions at the new plant. A partial organizational chart of the new plant is as follows.

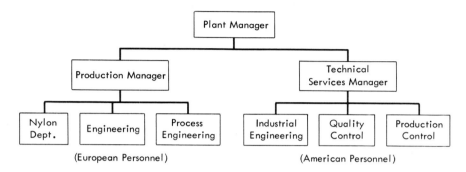

European Chemical Company's professionals were given extra benefits as an inducement to accept the new assignment. Benefits consisted of financial assistance for housing, expense-paid vacations back to Europe, and imported wine. These personnel were still under contract to the European Chemical Company and would return to jobs that would be determined by their performance at the new plant.

The European Chemical fiber plants were organized differently from their American counterpart's so that the Quality Control and other service functions were incorporated and subordinate to the Production Department. The production superintendent was responsible for both quantity and quality. Although all the European Chemical personnel had experience in nylon fiber production, this experience was recent. The bulk of their experience had been in the production of the raw chemicals for nylon fiber. The American professionals actually had more fiber-producing experience than the Europeans had.

A SLOW START

Initially, the European Chemical Company people had almost total authority and responsibility for plant activity. The American officials did not play an important role until after the production start-up began. Many problems had been encountered with the installation of the equipment, but the European Chemical "know how" had been successful in solving the problems before they became serious or costly. However, when it came to establishing processing conditions and actually producing fiber at normal production rates, serious difficulties arose. Conflicts between Quality Control and Production over processing conditions established by Production and Process Development resulted when the product failed to meet minimum quality standards.

The conflict resulted in slow machine start-ups and continued inferior quality. It was apparent that the Service and Production departments were not cooperating to solve these problems. The Production Department would continue to start-up machines under its own determined conditions regardless of quality reports. The Quality Control Department continued to downgrade all the products due to poor quality with no feedback to production other than yield reports. The plant manager spent most of his time arbitrating disagreements between the groups. It was apparent however that his lack of fiber technology weakened his efforts to resolve conflicts and establish areas of responsibility for each group. After eight months, virtually no change had occurred in the situation, and the problem had reached the crisis stage.

AN INVESTIGATION

The A-E Chemical Company had been very concerned over the lack of progress at its new plant and sent one of its vice presidents, Mr. Petri, to investigate the situation. Individual interviews were held with all the personnel from the Technical Services and Production departments. The following conversations convey the viewpoints of the various groups and individuals.

Plant Manager: We are really having a difficult time here as you know. The problems associated with putting a fiber plant into production are much more complex than are those associated with a chemical plant. These difficulties are going to take time to iron out. However, I do think these things could be accelerated if the Service group would assist the Production group more. This is where I have been spending most of my time. I think the production people have the technology to accomplish their goals. The good progress during the installation stage is an excellent example. Those European Chemical people really know a lot about synthetic fiber systems and equipment.

Technical Services Manager: To be frank, I really think that the company was sold a bill of goods when the decision was made for the European Chemical people to provide the technology for producing nylon. They are excellent chemical engineers, but their knowledge about producing synthetic fiber is inadequate. Sure, they know the basic procedures, but they have been producing fiber for European markets. The quality level for products there is generally less than it is in the States. The American market will not accept the product that we are producing here now. We have attempted to bring the quality level up by offering technical assistance and recommending better process conditions. None of these offers were accepted. Our responsibility is to ensure that A-E produces competitive nylon fiber. The plant manager will not allow us to shut down the equipment until process conditions are correct and quality is satisfactory. Therefore, we have no other choice but to reject the material during inspection.

Production Manager: We have been sent here to produce nylon fiber. We have the technology and experience to do this, and we are doing it. The fiber we have produced would be considered prime in Europe. I do not believe that the Service Department is using realistic standards to grade our product. The Service Department is attempting to usurp Production's responsibility for establishing process conditions by claiming that the present conditions are causing inferior quality.

Process Development Department Engineer: Although I have not worked here long, I have felt the bitterness that exists between the departments. I think that the groups in both departments go out of their way not to cooperate. It seems that the managers and superintendents make it a condition of acceptance not to cooperate with the so-called enemy. However, there is an interesting difference between the internal workings of the Service Department and the Production Department. There seems to be a lot more conflict within the Production Department. The various superintendents within the Production Department aggressively compete with each other. In fact I have seen conflicts between the heads of the nylon department and engineering that were as hot as any I have seen between the Service group and Production group. I think that the Service Department is much more united.

Mr. Petri decided to have samples of recent nylon production tested in the market for acceptability. Two users of synthetic fibers were contacted and asked to evaluate the yarn against the leading competition. Both organizations agreed that the product was inferior to that offered by the company's competitors.

QUESTIONS

Prepare a report for Mr. Petri that includes the following:

1. What is your diagnosis of the situation?
2. What remedial measures would you take and what objective is each measure intended to achieve?

PART III

ORGANIZATIONAL BEHAVIOR

CHAPTER 10

Leadership

LEARNING OBJECTIVES

When you have finished this chapter, you should be able to:

- *Describe the organization context of leadership.*
- *List and describe five bases of power.*
- *Summarize four leadership style studies and how they are related.*
- *List and describe the five leadership styles associated with the Management Grid.*
- *Summarize and contrast four situational leadership models.*

In previous chapters, we saw how informal leaders gained their positions of influence through the consensus of group members. In this chapter, attention is directed to the leader who is appointed to his or her position by the organization itself. While the emergent leader is responsible to the group of which he or she is a member, the appointed leader is fundamentally responsible to the organization. The organization selects and develops such persons for supervisory or managerial responsibilities. Traditionally, such managers are distinguished from nonmanagers by their involvement in the managerial process, that is, planning, organizing, directing subordinates, and controlling. Directing subordinates is the managerial activity that involves leadership.

We will use the generally accepted definition that leadership is the process of influencing the activities of an individual or a group in efforts toward goal achievement in a given situation.[1] From this definition, it is apparent that leadership is a process, not a person. Furthermore, three factors are involved in such a process: the leader, the followers, and situational conditions. In more detail, the factors would look as shown below. Interaction of these three variables determines the eventual outcomes of leadership: performance and job satisfaction.

This view of leadership has emerged gradually since the turn of the century as the study of leadership moved through three distinct phases:

1. determining the major traits of leaders
2. determining the major types of leadership behavior (i.e., leadership styles)
3. determining the situational variables that influence effective leadership

Each of these phases will be examined in Chapter 10. First, however, we will examine the organizational context or setting of leadership.

ORGANIZATIONAL CONTEXT OF LEADERSHIP

Organizations exist as hierarchical structures or arrangements of positions. Each position is assigned job duties, responsibilities, and some amount of authority that structures the behavior of the jobholder. Figure 10-1 presents an oversimplified view of such an organizational structure.

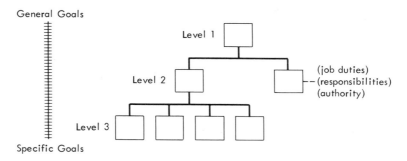

Figure 10-1

Organizational Structure

The number of layers between the highest and lowest levels in an organization depends upon the technology, complexity of the job, the number of persons required to produce a service, and so on. Whatever the number of levels, the structuring of roles is geared to achieve organizational goals. The goals at the highest level are general and broad; at the lower levels goals become detailed.

Authority

The supervision by one level of the activities of lower levels is achieved by defining the goals for lower or subordinate levels and by facilitating their accomplishment. These requirements serve as the basis of the authority that one position holder has over another and is a necessary arrangement for seeking organizational goals.

Authority is the right to enlist the assistance of specified other persons to perform one's task. The position incumbent obtains the legitimate right to take action because he or she has been given responsibilities to discharge. This legitimates control attempts by the position incumbent who also can use positive and negative sanctions in working toward goals.

Power

The provision of legitimate sanctions provides the job incumbent with power. Power consists of one person's capacity to get another to do something that he or she might not otherwise do. A power relationship is one of dependence in which one person is able to grant or deny the gratification of another's needs. If compliance is not forthcoming, the power holder may withhold benefits or inflict punishment.

Five different bases of power have been identified.[2]

Reward power. This derives from the capacity of one person to provide desired outcomes to another in exchange for compliance with the desired behavior. The use of reward power tends to cause the rewarding person to be more attractive to the complying person. Compliance can be achieved without direct supervision, especially when the results of compliance can be inspected.

Coercive power. This consists of the capacity to inflict negative outcomes on another; compliance is a means for escaping these negative outcomes. Compliance with coercive power, however, is not likely to occur without inspection and supervision. The outcome of using coercive power is frequently uncertain because the less powerful person may try to avoid the punishment rather than perform as desired. Consequently, coverups, false performance reports, and the like may be substituted for the desired behavior.

Legitimate power. This power results when the less powerful person believes that he should comply. The influence attempt is considered reasonable and appropriate behavior for one in such a position. Bases for legitimate power are found in cultural values and acceptance of the hierarchy of authority in an organization. Legitimate influence attempts, however, must be within the areas appropriate for the exercise of influence by the role incumbent.

Referent power. This power is based on a sufficiently high amount of attractiveness of the power figure so that the less powerful person identifies with the more powerful person and desires to please him or her by complying. Such compliance does not require supervision and may take place without one's being aware of being influenced. The use of reward power enhances the possibility of referent power.

Expert power. This power occurs when one has knowledge or ability in a given area that is not possessed by another person. If the expertness is relevant to the goals and needs of the less powerful person, compliance is likely to be achieved without supervision. However, expert power is limited to areas of demonstrated capability and will cease once another has acquired the needed knowledge and/or skills.

A review of studies on social power found evidence that[3]

1. coercive power induces greater resistance than does reward power, although overconformity to both may be comparable. However, coercive power is not very effective in producing compliance without inspection, because it does not result in attitude changes favorable to such compliance.
2. users of reward power are better liked than coercive power figures are.
3. conformity to coercive power increases with the strength of the potential punishment, whereas both conformity and liking for the power figure decreases as the strength of the resistance force increases.

4. as the legitimacy of a punishing act increases, conformity also increases, but liking for the punishing figure does not.

5. expertness on one task produces the ability to exert influence on a second, but only when the tasks are comparable.

Position Power and Personal Power

The foregoing examination of bases of power permit one to see two fundamental kinds of power: position and personal. Legitimate authority, reward power, and coercive power are determined by the organization for each formal leadership position; this is position power. On the other hand, expert and referent power depend primarily on the traits and behavior of one holding a position and is referred to as personal power; one may rely on personal power to influence subordinates.

Position and personal power have been used to explain successful versus effective leadership.[4] A leadership attempt may result in subordinate behavior that may be classified as successful or unsuccessful or somewhere between these two extremes (see Figure 10-2). If unsuccessful, the attempted leadership is inadequate. On the other hand, even if the leader's influence effort has been obviously successful, it must be further measured by two additional criteria: effective and ineffective. To be effective, the subordinate's performance must have occurred because he or she wanted to do it, found it consistent with his or her personal goals, and found it rewarding. The leader has made use of personal power although he or she has position power. Conversely, the leader's influence behavior is successful but ineffective when it has been attained only because the leader has control of rewards and punishments. The subordinate has performed as directed but only because of the leader's use of position power.

Figure 10-2

Successful and Effective Leadership Continuums

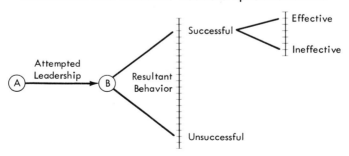

Source: Paul Hersey and Kenneth H. Blanchard, *Management of Organizational Behavior,* 3rd ed., 1977, p. 115. Reproduced by permission of Prentice-Hall, Inc., Englewood Cliffs, New Jersey.

The Mutual Dependence of Power

Power, however, is not a unilateral or one-way relationship. Rather, it is a mutual relationship in which subordinates often have substantial counterpower. The leader and subordinates are basically dependent upon one another. The subordinates are dependent upon the leader for promotion and pay increases, but indirectly they provide the same outcomes for the leader. If the work group performs well, the leader is recognized by the organization as an effective manager and is usually rewarded accordingly. However, the subordinates can also undermine the leader by withholding production, doing sloppy work, filing grievances, and so on. Given a high degree of mutual power between the leader and subordinates, there is potential for cooperation and mutual influence.

THE TRAIT APPROACH TO LEADERSHIP

The earliest approach used to determine leadership effectiveness consisted of studying the traits and characteristics of leaders. This was an outgrowth of the attention devoted to the role of "great men" of history, which assumed that some persons are natural leaders. Such persons were thought to possess certain endowed traits that enabled them to be successful leaders in any situation. The traits of clearly successful leaders were compared with the traits of unsuccessful leaders and nonleaders to identify the traits of natural leaders.

Studies were conducted to determine the intellectual, social, emotional, and physical qualities that distinguished the successful from the unsuccessful leaders. Such research yielded very little in the way of generally useful results. Summaries of numerous investigations failed to disclose any universal traits.[5] Traits associated with effective leaders in one study were different from those in other studies. Consequently, leader effectiveness could not be accurately and reliably predicted from leader traits.

The trait approach failed because it is the leadership situation— nature of the subordinates and the task—that determines what leader traits are essential for effective leadership. Such traits differ somewhat from situation to situation.

BEHAVIORAL STUDIES: LEADERSHIP STYLES

A second approach to understanding leadership has focused on the behavior of managers. Rather than look for trait characteristics of effective leaders, behavioral theories have concentrated on what the leader does and how he or she behaves in carrying out the leadership function.

Since leadership involves accomplishing goals with and through people, a leader must be concerned with both task and human relationships. These two concerns had previously been considered separately. In general, scientific management had emphasized a concern for task activities. On the other hand, the human relations movement stressed a concern for people. Finally, both the task and people dimensions were considered together as behavioral scientists began to focus on leadership after 1945.

Employee-Oriented and Production-Oriented Leadership Styles

Studies at the Survey Research Center at the University of Michigan were developed to determine what types of foreman behavior led to high levels of productivity and individual satisfaction in small work groups.[6] High- and low-productivity sections were compared to ascertain if there were any differences in supervisory behavior of such sections. The high- and low-productivity foremen had different relationships with their workers. Foremen of the high-production units spent more time in actual supervision and less time in production work, supervised less closely, had more interest in the off-the-job problems of their workers, helped them work toward better jobs, and reacted less punitively when they did a poor job. Such foremen were considered *employee oriented*. On the other hand, the foremen of the lower-production units tended to emphasize high productivity to the exclusion of other aspects of their job. Their crews were tools for the accomplishment of the job. Such foremen were designated as *production oriented*. Ironically, the employer-oriented foremen obtained the better performance levels.

The major findings of the Michigan research have been the identification of four general factors relating to productivity.[7]

1. Differentiation of supervisory role: Effective foremen engaged in unique functions that they alone could perform, leaving straight production work to their subordinates.
2. Closeness of supervision: More effective foremen supervised less closely by giving more freedom to their employees in determining how to perform their jobs.
3. Employee orientation: More effective foremen had a greater interest in work group members as individual people.
4. Group relationships: No general relationship was found between morale and productivity. However, satisfaction with the work group might have an influence on turnover and absenteeism.

The Michigan researchers originally felt, that as a foreman became more production oriented, he or she would become less employee oriented; that is, the two orientations were contradictory. An additional study indicated that such an inverse relation was not necessarily true.[8] A foreman could be high or low on either one or both orientations. The best foremen seemed to be high on both employee and production orientations.

Numerous studies by Likert and his associates have supported the thesis that the employer-centered leader is the most effective. However, in several instances employee-centered leadership was associated with low productivity and production-oriented supervision with high producing units.[9] The work situation contained factors that had not been accounted for.

Close and General Leadership Styles

While the employee- and production-oriented labels have been popularized by the Michigan studies, close and general styles of leadership were originally isolated and studied in the same setting.[10] General supervision includes such things as less frequent checking up on subordinates and permitting them to alter the ways in which they performed their jobs, that is, more self-direction and self-control. Close supervision is associated with tight controls and no freedom to exercise discretion in their work. A number of studies demonstrated that general supervision was associated with high productivity, whereas close supervision was associated with low productivity. Exceptions to these results have been found, however.

Authoritarian and Democratic Leadership Styles

One of the most popular and controversial distinctions of leadership style is that between authoritarian and democratic (participative) leaders. The Hawthorne studies, which initiated the human relations movement, had pointed to the effectiveness of participation in making decisions on work-related problems. The general distinction between these two styles is that the authoritarian leader makes extensive use of his or her authority and unilaterally makes decisions, whereas the democratic leader delegates authority to the work group and permits some involvement in making decisions.

One of the most frequently cited studies was done by Morse and Reimer that exposed work groups to either autocratic or democratic leadership.[11] The study was conducted in two clerical departments having approximately 500 employees and was continued for a year. In the two democratic groups, supervisors were trained to use more democratic methods and also to delegate more decision making. In the two autocratic groups, more of the decision authority was given the supervisors who also increased the closeness of their supervision. The increase in productivity as measured by cost reduction was higher for the autocratic than for the democratic groups.

However, the employees subjected to authoritarian leadership quickly became dissatisfied, whereas satisfaction increased and turnover and grievances decreased for the democratically supervised groups.

Not everyone responds favorably to participative leadership. There is evidence that participative leadership has positive effects only on employees having a high need for independence and strong nonauthoritarian values. Employees having a high desire for structure and low independence needs did not respond favorably to participative methods.[12]

Overall, however, there is a tendency for democratic leadership to be associated with high satisfaction, but its relationship to productivity is unclear.[13] Such findings have provided more impetus to the situational aspects of leadership, that is, contingency approaches.

Considerate and Structuring Leadership Styles

The leadership studies at Ohio State University sought to identify various dimensions of leadership behavior.[14] A questionnaire was administered to members of many different organizational groups so that they could describe their leaders. Two dimensions of leader behavior were found to exist: initiating structure and consideration. Leader behavior characteristics of each dimension are as follows.

Initiating Structure	Consideration
Assigning particular tasks	Explaining his or her actions
Specifying procedures to be followed	Treating subordinates as equals
Clarifying expectations of subordinates	Being friendly, approachable
Scheduling work to be done	Doing personal favors
Making sure his or her own role is understood	Looking out for workers' personal welfare
	Giving advance notice of change

Since these two factors are separate dimensions, the behavior of a leader could be described as a mix of initiating structure and consideration. Four combinations are shown in Figure 10-3.

Overall, high consideration has generally been found to be associated with employee satisfaction, low turnover, and low absenteeism, but the relationship to productivity was mixed or negligible. High-structure initiation frequently has been found related with higher productivity and lower employer satisfaction. Other studies, however, have obtained results in the opposite directions to those cited.[15] Such apparent contradictions have raised the possibility that crucial situational variables remain unexplored.

Figure 10-3

Combination of Initiating Structures and Consideration
(The Ohio State Leadership Quadrants)

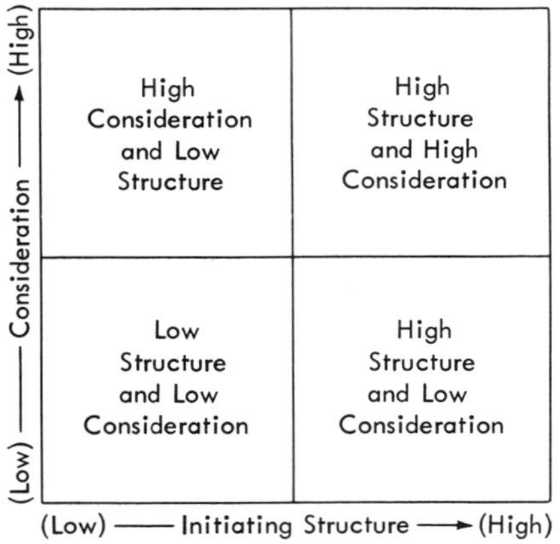

```
        (High)
          ↑    ┌─────────────────┬─────────────────┐
          │    │     High        │     High        │
          │    │  Consideration  │   Structure     │
          │    │   and Low       │   and High      │
Consideration   │   Structure     │  Consideration  │
          │    ├─────────────────┼─────────────────┤
          │    │     Low         │     High        │
          │    │   Structure     │   Structure     │
          │    │   and Low       │   and Low       │
          │    │  Consideration  │  Consideration  │
        (Low)  └─────────────────┴─────────────────┘
              (Low) ──── Initiating Structure ──→ (High)
```

Numerous studies have indicated that groups with leaders who score high on both dimensions are higher in overall effectiveness.[16] Group members generally want the leader to be high on consideration, while superiors want him or her to be high on initiating structure. The successful leader must balance the expectations of both for his or her group to be evaluated outstanding by both evaluators.

Synthesis of Leadership Styles

The leadership or behavioral styles previously discussed have been stated in terms of two extremes. These styles are noted here.

Employee centered	Production centered
Considerate	Structuring
General	Close
Democratic	Authoritarian

While these pairs of leadership styles have been researched and discussed individually, they overlap in many respects. One would expect, for example, that an employee-centered supervisor would probably be considerate, use a general style of supervision and also use participative and democratic methods. Several studies show that these behaviors are indeed interrelated to one another.[17] Consequently, there is some justification for placing employee-centered, considerate, general, and democratic styles into one category—a "people concern" category. The remaining styles—production, structuring, close, and authoritarian—would comprise a "task concern" category.

Whether one chooses to think of leadership in terms of pairs of opposite styles or as two broad encompassing "people" and "task" categories, there is the danger of thinking that they are mutually exclusive. The authoritarian leader may still show consideration toward his or her group. Likewise, the democratic leader may exert considerable control and may structure his or her subordinates' tasks.

As noted throughout the presentation of leadership styles, there are numerous positive but some negative findings as to their effectiveness. Consequently, one can not claim that a given leadership style is universally applicable. While the "people-oriented" styles increase the probability of obtaining higher employee satisfaction and possibly reduce turnover and absenteeism, the impact on productivity remains an uncertain outcome. Some of the uncertainty of the research findings is due to disregarding the leaders' qualities and traits, the personality and needs of the subordinates, and the nature of the work group's task. There is a need to take the total situation into consideration. As stated at the beginning of this chapter, leadership effectiveness is a function of the leader, the followers, and the situation.

THE MANAGERIAL GRID: FIVE LEADERSHIP STYLES®

Robert R. Blake and Jane S. Mouton have devised a managerial grid based upon a concern for production and a concern for people.[18] The emphasis is on the degree of concern for production and people by the leader because his or her actions are based upon personal attitudes toward these two factors. Production is not limited to things but may also include quality of policy decisions, number of creative ideas, quality of staff, and services. Concern for people can also be expressed in a variety of ways: accountability based on trust, self-esteem or personal worth of an individual, maintenance of good work conditions, maintenance of an equitable salary structure, and social relationships.

According to Blake and Mouton, a manager's management style is a product of five factors.[19]

1. manager's personality
2. the organization's practices or requirements
3. the specific day-to-day situation
4. the manager's values
5. chance (i.e., limited experience and learning opportunities)

The Managerial Grid

Figure 10-4 shows the concern for production and people and also five possible leadership styles. The horizontal axis indicates concern for production; the vertical axis indicates concern for people. Each is expressed on a nine-point scale of concern. The number 1 on each scale represents minimum concern, whereas the 9 stands for maximum concern. The degree of concern that a manager has for both production and people determines the way in which he or she acts. For example, a manager with a high degree of

Figure 10-4

The Managerial Grid

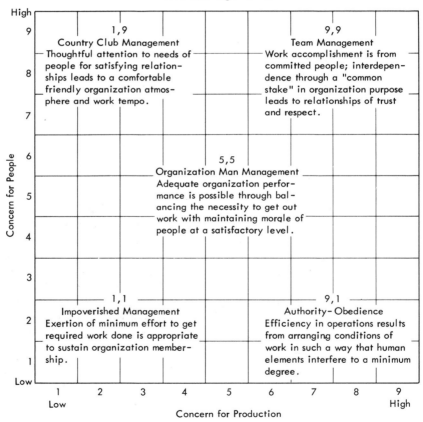

Source: The Managerial Grid figure from *The New Managerial Grid,* by Robert R. Blake and Jane Srygley Mouton. Houston: Gulf Publishing Company, Copyright ©1978, p. 11. Reproduced by permission.

concern for production and a low degree of concern for people will push production without regard for people.

Five basic leadership styles are shown on the grid. At the lower left is the 1,1 management style. This is a minimum of concern for both production and people. The 1,1 position is sometimes referred to as the impoverished or "do-nothing" manager.

In the upper left is the 1,9 management style. Here there is a minimum concern for production but a maximum concern for people. The 1,9 manager is often labled the "country club" manager.

In the lower right is the 9,1 management style. This is the "production pusher" who has a maximum concern for production but a minimum concern for human or people aspects.

In the upper right is the 9,9 manager or "team builder." In this position, concern for both people and production reaches a maximum.

Located in the center is the 5,5 manager who has an intermediate amount of concern for production and people. This is a middle-of-the-road position and is sometimes designated as "organization man."

Every manager has a basic leadership style that is utilized most of the time. However, one also has a backup style that is used depending on the situation and/or the people involved. For example a manager's predominant or most frequently used style may be 5,5 or the middle-of-the-road approach. However, if that style does not appear to be working, he or she may fall back and use the 9,1 style and become quite explicit about what is to be done and how.

To change one's style, the manager must learn

1. his or her management style
2. what is the best style
3. the behaviors required to move from his or her style to the preferred style
4. the ideal organizational culture necessary for the preferred style and how it is created

Which management style is best? Blake and Mouton are of the opinion that the 9,9 team builder is the most effective style. Research by the two grid authors shows that the 9,9 style is the one most positively associated with productivity and profitability, career success and satisfaction, and physical and mental health.[20]

MANAGEMENT SYSTEMS

No examination of leadership styles would be complete without considering the prevailing management systems of organizations. Leadership by an individual does not take place in a vacuum but is affected by the prevailing approach of working with and through people in the organization. The organization displays consistent patterns of behavior in utilizing its human resources that can be determined by a questionnaire developed by Rensis Likert. This measuring instrument is designed to gather information on the following operating characteristics of an organization: leadership, motivation, communication, decision making, interaction and influence, goal setting, and the control process used by the organization. Sample items from this instrument are shown in Figure 10-5.

Research by Likert has disclosed four management styles of organization that can be shown on a continuum from system 1 through system 4. The four management systems, from left to the right in Figure 10-5, are (1) exploitive authoritative, (2) benevolent authoritative, (3) consultative, and (4) participative group. The statements listed below each system are those operating characteristics associated with each system.[21] One need only check those conditions found in his or her department or organization to determine the kind of system it is.

The differing management systems are based on differing attitudes of trust and confidence in subordinates. For example, system 1, exploitive, is characterized by a lack of confidence and trust in people, use of fear and punishment, little interaction between superiors and subordinates, and centralized decision making at the top. System 4, participative group, is the opposite extreme and is characterized by trust, confidence, participation, extensive interaction, and so on. Systems 2 and 3 are intermediate stages between these two extremes.

Studies have tended to support Likert's contention that system 4, participative group, is an effective approach to management.[22] The more the management style of an organization approaches system 4, the more likely it is to have high productivity and employee satisfaction. The reverse, lower productivity and job satisfaction, obtains for system 1 (exploitive authoritative management systems).

SITUATIONAL LEADERSHIP MODELS

As will be recalled from the previous material, the study of leader effectiveness turned from an emphasis upon leader traits to an examination of their behavior, that is, leadership styles. However, no one style of leadership was found universally effective. The importance of situational factors for explaining leadership effectiveness became apparent. Consequently, effective leadership is now examined in light of the leader, his or her followers, the situation, and the interrelationship of these factors. These factors have been briefly alluded to previously, but now they will be explored in more depth.

Figure 10-5

Four Systems of Management

Organizational and Performance Characteristics of Different Management Systems Based on a Comparable Analysis

Operating characteristics	System of organization			
	Authoritative		Participative	
	Exploitive authoritative	Benevolent authoritative	Consultative	Participative group
	System 1	System 2	System 3	System 4
Organization variable				
Leadership processes used Extent to which superiors have confidence and trust in <u>subordinates</u>	Have no confidence and trust in subordinates	Have condescending confidence and trust, such as master has to servant	Substantial but not complete confidence and trust; still wishes to keep control of decisions	Complete confidence and trust in all matters
Extent to which superiors behave so that subordinates feel free to discuss important things about their jobs with their immediate superior	Fear, threats, punishment, and occasional rewards	Rewards and some actual or potential punishment	Rewards, occasional punishment, and some involvement	Econonimc rewards based on compensation system developed through participation; group participation and involvement in setting goals, improving methods, appraising progress toward goals, etc.
Extent to which immediate superior in solving job problems generally tries to get subordinates' ideas and opinions and make constructive use of them	Little interaction and always with fear and distrust	Little interaction and usually with some condescension by superiors; fear and caution by subordinates	Moderate interaction, often with fair amount of confidence and trust	Extensive, friendly interaction with high degree of confidence and trust

Source: Rensis Likert, *The Human Organization* (New York: McGraw-Hill, 1967), p. 4.

Continuum of Leadership Behavior

Often, the leader is perplexed as to whether he or she should be making the decisions or whether his or her subordinates should be involved in the process. The leader is torn between being autocratic or democratic in his or her decision-making behavior. Tannenbaum and Schmidt have proposed a useful framework for grappling with this dilemma.[23]

Figure 10-6 presents a range of seven possible leadership behaviors available to one making decisions. Each type of decision differs on the degree of authority used by the manager and the amount of freedom given subordinates in reaching decisions. The actions on the extreme left characterize the manager who maintains a high degree of control (boss-centered leadership); those on the extreme right characterize the manager who releases a high degree of control (subordinate-centered leadership).

Figure 10-6

Continuum of Leadership Behavior

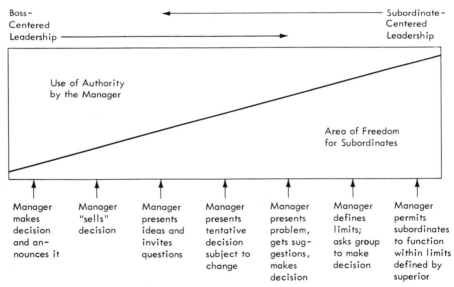

While Figure 10-6 shows the types of leadership that are possible, it does not indicate what type is practical or desirable. The appropriate kind of decision-making procedure depends upon (1) forces in the manager, (2) forces in the subordinates, and (3) forces in the situation.

306

Forces in the manager

The manager's behavior will be influenced by his or her own personality, background, knowledge, and experience. Some of the internal forces are

1. value system
2. confidence in subordinates
3. own leadership inclinations (i.e., directive or team role)
4. feeling of security in an uncertain situation, especially when operating on the right side of the leadership continuum

Forces in the subordinate

Before deciding on how to lead a group, one must consider the forces affecting his or her subordinates. Each employee is influenced by personality variables and expectations of how the boss should act in relation to him or her. Generally, the manager can permit subordinates greater freedom and involvement in decision making if they have

1. a relatively high need for independence
2. a readiness to assume responsibility for decision making
3. a relatively high tolerance to ambiguity (some employees prefer clear-cut directives)
4. an interest in the problem and feel it is important
5. an understanding and identification with organizational goals
6. the knowledge and experience to deal with the problem
7. learned to expect to share in decision making

The manager will probably tend to make more use of his or her own authority if the preceding conditions do not exist. At times there may be no realistic alternative to running a ''one-man show.''

Forces in the situation

In addition to forces that exist in managers and in their subordinates, characteristics of the general situation will also affect a manager's behavior. Important situational conditions are

1. type of organization—values and traditions that influence the behavior of people (i.e., this is the way we do it)
2. group effectiveness—shown by past experience, cohesiveness, mutual acceptance, and commonality of purpose
3. the problem itself—complexity that may require one person to work it out

4. the pressure of time—''immediate'' decisions that make it difficult to involve other people

The successful leader is one who is aware of those factors that are most relevant to his or her behavior at any given time. He or she accurately understands himself or herself, the individuals and group being directed, and the broader organizational environment. Furthermore, the successful leader behaves appropriately in light of these factors. If direction is called for, the leader is able to direct; if considerable participative freedom is appropriate, the leader is able to provide such freedom. The continuum of leadership behavior provides an excellent overview of the numerous factors relevant to effective leadership.

The Vroom and Yetton Model

The Vroom and Yetton model and the leadership continuum model are similar in some respects.[24] Both deal with only one facet of leadership behavior—the extent to which decision-making power is shared with subordinates. Both are contingency models that indicate that the way in which decisions are made should depend upon various situational factors. However, the Vroom–Yetton decision-making model provides a rational, step-by-step procedure for determining the optimal method for making a decision.

Table 10-1 shows the various decision processes that one can use. Each decision style is represented by a symbol (e.g., AI, GI, GII) that indicates the kind of decision process involved. In this ''shorthand'' notation, A stands for autocratic, C for consultative, G for group. The roman numerals following the letter note variations of that process. For example, AI and AII are variations of the autocratic process.

Table 10-1

Types of Management Decision Styles

AI: You solve the problem or make the decision yourself, using information available to you at that time.

AII: You obtain the necessary information from your subordinate(s), then decide on the solution to the problem yourself. You may or may not tell your subordinates what the problem is in getting the information from them. The role played by your subordinates in making the decision is clearly one of providing the necessary information to you, rather than generating or evaluating alternative solutions.

CI: You share the problem with relevant subordinates individually, getting their ideas and suggestions without bringing them together as a group. Then *you* make the decision, which may or may not reflect your subordinates' influence.

CII: You share the problem with your subordinates as a group, collectively obtaining their ideas and suggestions. Then *you* make the decision, which may or may not reflect your subordinates' influence.

GII: You share a problem with your subordinates as a group. Together you generate and evaluate alternatives and attempt to reach agreement (consensus) on a solution. Your role is much like that of chairman. You do not try to influence the group to adopt "your" solution and you are willing to accept and implement any solution that has the support of the entire group.

The decision-making model is presented as a decision tree in Figure 10-7. At the top of the figure are seven problem attributes, A through G, that are expressed as questions. These are situational variables that will influence the decision process used by the leader. The first three questions eliminate decision methods that threaten the *quality* of the decisions; the last four questions eliminate methods likely to jeopardize *acceptance* of the decision by subordinates.

To use the model in a decision-making situaion, one starts at the left-hand side and works toward the right, asking and answering each question. By responding "yes" or "no" to each successive question, a terminal point is reached. The number found at this point designates the kind of problem encountered and also the appropriate decision-making processes for coping with that kind of problem. For example, the terminal point noted on 1-AI indicates that this is problem type 1 having its own characteristics and can be handled by an autocratic decision style noted as AI. For the terminal point 3-GII, the "3" notes that this is a third kind of decision-making problem that a leader may encounter and the GII indicates the group decision-making style (see Table 10-1) appropriate for problem 3.

Application of the Model

To illustrate how the model works, put yourself in the position of a manager confronted with the following problem.[25]

The company has recently installed new machines and put in a new simplified work system, but, to the surprise of everyone, the expected increase in productivity was not realized. In fact, production has begun to drop, quality has fallen off, and turnover has risen. There is nothing wrong with the machines. Other companies using them are not having trouble, and the manufacturer of the machines report that they are all right.

While you suspect that some parts of the new work system may be responsible for the change, this view is not shared by your four immediate

Figure 10-7
Decision Process Flow Chart

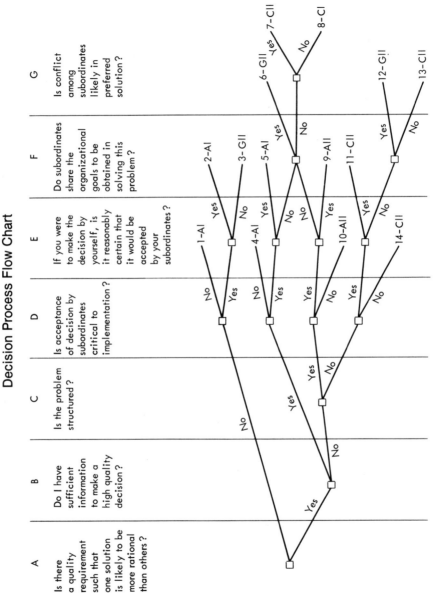

A
Is there a quality requirement such that one solution is likely to be more rational than others?

B
Do I have sufficient information to make a high quality decision?

C
Is the problem structured?

D
Is acceptance of decision by subordinates critical to implementation?

E
If you were to make the decision by yourself, is it reasonably certain that it would be accepted by your subordinates?

F
Do subordinates share the organizational goals to be obtained in solving this problem?

G
Is conflict among subordinates likely in preferred solution?

Reprinted, by permission of the publisher, from "A New Look at Managerial Decision Making," Victor H. Vroom, *Organizational Dynamics*, Spring 1973, ©1973 by AMACON, a division of American Management Associations, page 70. All rights reserved.

first-line supervisors, each in charge of a section, and your supply manager. The drop in production has been variously attributed to poorly trained operators, the lack of financial incentives, and poor morale. Clearly, this is an issue about which there are strong feelings among individuals and potential disagreement among your subordinates.

Your division manager has just expressed his concern in a phone call and would like to know within a week what steps you plan to take. The problem now is to decide what steps to take to rectify the situation.

Keeping the information given in mind, use the Vroom–Yetton model to determine the most appropriate decision style. Answer, in order, each question at the top of Figure 10-7. This moves you across the decision tree. What decision style should you use? Check your answer with the following analysis.

Questions	Answer
A: Quality?	Yes
B: Manager's information?	No
C: Structured?	No
D: Acceptance?	Yes
E: Prior probability of acceptance?	No
F: Goal congruence?	Yes
G: Conflict?	Yes

The appropriate decision process would be 12-GII; that is, you share the problem with your subordinates and arrive at a decision as a group (see Table 10-1).

Using brief cases like this one, Vroom and Yetton have started to validate their model using managers unfamiliar with the decision model. The results indicate that, if the manager's method of dealing with the case corresponded with the model, the probability of the decision being judged successful was 65 percent; if the manager's method disagreed with the model, the probability of its being deemed successful was only 29 percent. The authors of the decision model conclude that such results clearly support its validity.[26]

THE LEADERSHIP CONTINGENCY MODEL

According to a leadership contingency model developed by Fred E. Fiedler, the effectiveness of a group depends on the interaction between the leader and the situation.[27] This requires matching the leader's motivational structure as indicated by the goals given highest priority with the degree to which the situation is favorable or unfavorable to the leader.

The leader may be task motivated or relationship motivated. Leader motivation is measured by the least preferred co-worker scale (LPC), which asks the individual to think of everyone with whom he or she has ever worked. The individual is then asked to describe, on the measuring scale, the one person with whom he or she could work least well. This may be someone with whom the individual has worked years ago or someone with whom he or she works at the moment. Several of the items are shown here.

Pleasant __ __ __ __ __ __ __ __ Unpleasant
          8 7 6 5 4 3 2 1

Tense __ __ __ __ __ __ __ __ Relaxed
       1 2 3 4 5 6 7 8

An individual who described his or her LPC in negative and rejecting terms is showing a strong emotional reaction to such a person (a low LPC). When forced to make a choice, this individual would opt first for getting on with the task and worrying about interpersonal relations later; that is, this individual is task motivated.

Someone who described his or her LPC in relatively positive terms sees that person as having some acceptable, perhaps even admirable, traits. This is a high-LPC leader who sees close interpersonal relations as a requirement for task accomplishment; that is, he or she gives high priority to relationships and is relationship motivated.

At the base of Fiedler's theory are three situational conditions that determine whether task-motivated or relationship-motivated leadership styles are required.[28] The three situational conditions are

1. leader–member relations—the extent to which the leader "gets along" with his or her workers and the extent to which they have confidence in and are loyal to the leader
2. task structure—the routineness and predictability of the work group's task
3. position power—the degree to which the leader can reward and punish subordinates

These three conditions indicate the degree to which the leader has control and influence and can therefore determine the outcomes of the group's effort.

The most effective leadership styles for each of eight situational conditions are shown in Figure 10-8. The vertical axis shows the group's performance, poor to good. The horizontal base indicates eight combinations of leader–member relations, task structure, and leader position power. Each combination reveals how favorable or unfavorable the total situation is for the leader. The solid line in the center of the figure shows the performance of relationship-motivated leaders, and the broken line shows the performance of task-motivated leaders for various combinations of situational conditions.

Figure 10-8

The Performance of Relationship- and Task-Motivated Leaders in Different Situational Favorableness Conditions

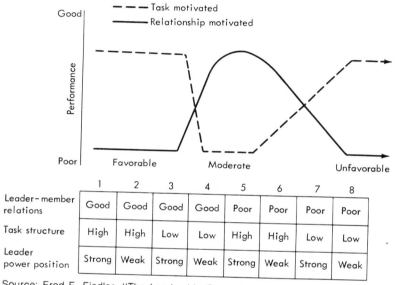

Leader–member relations	Good	Good	Good	Good	Poor	Poor	Poor	Poor
Task structure	High	High	Low	Low	High	High	Low	Low
Leader power position	Strong	Weak	Strong	Weak	Strong	Weak	Strong	Weak

The leadership implications of Figure 10-8 are that

1. relationship-motivated (high-LPC) leaders generally perform best in situations in which their relations with subordinates are good but task structures and position power are low *or* when relationships with subordinates are poor but task structure and position power are high (both situations of moderate favorableness).

2. task-motivated leaders (low-LPC) perform best when all three situational factors that define their control and influence are either high or low (i.e., favorable or unfavorable).

Fielder's model indicates that group performance can be improved either by changing the leader's motivational structure (basic goals) or by modifying the leadership situation. To change the motivation structure that is a part of personality, while possible, is a difficult and uncertain process. According to Fiedler, however, it is relatively easy to modify the leadership situation. A person can be selected for certain kinds of tasks and not others, assigned certain tasks (structured or unstructured), given more or less responsibility, or given leadership training to increase his or her power and influence. This amounts to engineering the work situation or changing the situation to match the leader.

PATH–GOAL THEORY OF LEADERSHIP

As we have seen, the impact of the leader in initiating structure and/or being considerate often produced mixed results when evaluated by performance outcomes and satisfaction. The reason advanced for this lack of clarity was seen as due to the failure to make allowance for important situational factors. The path–goal theory of leadership proposed by House examines some of the situational variables affecting leadership behavior.[29]

The leader's function is seen as a supplemental one. The leader provides subordinates with coaching, guidance, and rewards that are not found in the work situation but are necessary for effective performance. The leader is effective to the extent these things are provided. Additionally, the impact of the leader's behavior is determined by the situation in which the leader is operating and by dealing with the situation appropriately. Two crucial factors in the situation that the leader must consider are the characteristics of the subordinates and the task demands.

The characteristics of subordinates determine whether or not they view the leader's behavior as acceptable and/or the source of satisfaction. For example, subordinates with high needs for affiliation would see a considerate leader as a source of satisfaction. Those with high achievement needs would likely see initiating structure or behavior that facilitates task accomplishment as a source of satisfaction. If subordinates can accomplish their tasks effectively on their own, they will view leader directiveness as unacceptable.

The characteristics of the task with which subordinates must cope also determine effective leader behavior. Unstructured, nonroutine tasks can be more effectively handled if the leader initiates structure and removes role ambiguities. On the other hand, if the work methods are clear due to the routine nature of the job, the initiation of more structure and/or close supervision will be perceived by the subordinates as unnecessary. Also for unsatisfying tasks, consideration will be more important.

The research conducted by House and his associates and also other investigators suggests that the theory of leader effectiveness is useful.[30] The idea that effective leadership behavior is contingent on worker and task characteristics has been supported.

In summary, the situational models presented, with the exception of Fiedler, demonstrate that the effective leader must be able to adapt his or her leadership behavior to the needs of the situation and the followers. This also means that the leader must be aware of his or her own values, strengths and weaknesses, and leadership preferences. In other words, the leader must be sensitive to himself or herself, the work group, and the task situation.

Individuals in their role as leaders will differ in their ability to vary their leadership behavior or style. Some may be limited to a single leadership style; others may be quite flexible. Even the leadership situation itself will make different demands on adaptability. Some situations are stable and predictable, whereas other leadership situations are dynamic and unpredictable. This will require careful attention to the selection, placement, training, and development of leaders.

SUMMARY

This chapter may be summarized as it started, namely, that leadership is a function of the leader, the followers, and the situation. The path to this understanding of leadership has been long and filled with contradictions. However, significant insights have emerged and the leadership process has been brought into clearer focus.

The ''great man'' with unique traits is no longer considered a tenable approach to leadership. However, the leader's behavior, skills, knowledge, and values are known to be important factors in the overall leadership process. The demands made upon such characteristics vary from one situation to another.

The conclusion to be drawn from the studies of leadership style or behavior is that there is no one universal style. There is some evidence that the various styles are of two kinds: concern for people and concern for task. Additionally, because investigations of leadership style have failed to consider significant factors such as the task, the group, and the organizational setting, such omissions have frequently led to different interpretations of leadership effectiveness.

Finally, the examination of leadership has tended to focus upon the situation. There is no one right or best way of leading. Whether the leader is autocratic or democratic in decision making is dependent upon numerous factors. Each is appropriate under certain conditions. Whether one uses close or general supervision depends upon the workers and upon the nature of the task. The same conclusion holds for initiating structure or demonstrating consideration. The path toward a goal for a work group is made easier by the leader's behaving in a manner that provides what the situation dictates is necessary. This requires a high degree of sensitivity and flexibility on the part of the leaders.

QUESTIONS FOR STUDY AND DISCUSSION

1. Evaluate the statement that leadership is a function of the leader, group, and situation. What are some of the factors that would be included in each variable?

2. What are the five sources of power? Which ones do you think a supervisor should use most often?

3. What are the four leadership styles that have been the focus of leadership studies? How are they related?

4. Which one of the leadership styles of the Blake and Mouton Management Grid is most effective? Why?

5. What determines where a manager should be on Tannenbaum and Schmidt's continuum of leadership behavior when making decisions?

6. How are Vroom and Yetton's types of management decision styles related to those in Tannenbaum and Schmidt's continuum of leadership behavior? Which do you prefer?

7. According to Fiedler's leadership contingency model, what three conditions determine the appropriate leadership style? Under what conditions are relationship and task motivated leadership most appropriate?

8. How does the path-goal theory of leadership view the leader's function? What two factors must be considered?

NOTES

[1]Hersey, Paul and Kenneth H. Blanchard, *Management of Organizational Behavior,* 2nd ed. (Englewood Cliffs, N.J.: Prentice-Hall, 1972), p. 68. See also. Barrow, Jeffery, "The Variables of Leadership: A Review and Conceptual Framework" *Academy of Management Review* 2 (April, 1977), 231–251.

[2]French, John R. P., Jr., and Bertram Raven, "The Bases of Social Power," in Dorwin Cartwright, ed., *Studies in Social Power,* (Ann Arbor: University of Michigan Research Center for Group Dynamics, 1959). See also. Grimes, A. J. "Authority, Power, Influence and Social Controls: A Theoretical Synthesis," *Academy of Management Review* 3 (October, 1978), 724–735.

[3]Schopler, John, "Social Power," in Leonard Berkowitz, ed., *Advances in Experimental Social Psychology,* Vol. 2 (New York: Academic Press, 1965), pp. 177–218.

[4]Hersey and Blanchard, *op. cit,* p. 94.

[5]Mann, R. D., "A Review of the Relationships between Personality and Performance in Small Groups," *Psychological Bulletin,* 56 (1959): 241–270; Stogdill, R. A., "Personal Factors Associated with Leadership: A Survey of the Literature," *Journal of Psychology* 25 (1948): 35–71.

[6]Kahn, Robert L. and Daniel Katz, "Leadership Practices in Relation to Productivity and Moral," in D. Cartwright and A. F. Lander, eds., *Group Dynamics,* 2nd ed. (Evanston, Ill.: Row, Peterson, 1960), pp. 554–570.

[7]*Ibid.*

[8]Katz, D. and R. L. Kahn, "Human Organization and Worker Motivation," in L. R. Tripp, ed., *Industrial Productivity* (Madison, Wisc.: Industrial Relations Research Association, 1952), pp. 146–171.

[9]Likert, Rensis, *New Patterns of Management* (New York: McGraw-Hill, 1961), pp. 5–25.

[10]Katz and Kahn, *Group Dynamics, op. cit.*

[11]Morse, N. C. and E. Reimer, "The Experimental Change of a Major Organizational Variable," *Journal of Abnormal and Social Psychology* 52 (1956): 120–129.

[12]Vroom, Victor, "Some Personality Determinates of the Effects of Participation," *Journal of Abnormal and Social Psychology* 59 (1959): 322–327.

[13]Gibb, Cecil A., "Leadership," in G. Lindsey, ed., *Handbook of Social Psychology,* Vol. II (Cambridge, Mass.: Addison-Wesley, 1969), pp. 205–273.

[14]Stogdill, Roger M. and Alvin E. Coons, *Leader Behavior: Its Description and Measurement,* Monograph 88 (Columbus: Bureau of Business Research, Ohio State University, 1957).

[15]House, R. J., "A Path–Goal Theory of Leader Effectiveness," *Administrative Science Quarterly* 16 (1971): 321–338.

[16]Jacobs, T. D., *Leadership and Exchange in Formal Organizations* (Alexandria, Va.: Human Resources Research Organization, 1971), p. 31.

[17]Argle, M., G. Gardner, and F. Cioffi, "The Measurement of Supervisor Methods," *Human Relations* 10 (1957): 295–314; Hunt, J. G., "Organizational Leadership: Some Theoretical and Empirical Considerations," *Business Perspectives* 4 (Summer 1968): 16–24.

[18]Blake, Robert R. and Jane S. Mouton, *The Managerial Grid* (Houston: Gulf Publishing, 1964).

[19]*Ibid.,* pp. 13–14.

[20]Blake, Robert R. and Jane S. Mouton, *The New Managerial Grid* (Houston: Gulf Publishing, 1978).

[21]Likert, Rensis, *The Human Organization* (New York: McGraw-Hill, 1967).

[22]Hand, H., M. Richards, and J. Slocum, "Organizational Climate and the Effectiveness of a Human Relations Training Program," *Academy of Management Journal* 16 (1973): 185–195; Seashore, Stanley E., and David G. Bowers, "Durability of Organization Change," *American Psychologist* 25 (March, 1970): 227–233.

[23]Tannenbaum, Robert and Warren H. Schmidt, "How to Choose a Leadership Pattern," *Harvard Business Review* 36 (March–April 1958): 95–101.

[24]Vroom, Victor H., "A New Look at Managerial Decision Making," in Henry L. Tosi and W. Clay Hamner, eds., *Organizational Behavior and Management,* rev. ed. (Chicago: St. Clair Press, 1977), pp. 477–484.

[25]*Ibid.,* p. 483.

[26]Vroom, Victor H., "Can Leaders Learn to Lead?" *Organizational Dynamics* 4 (Winter 1976): 17–28. See also: Field, R. H. George, "A Critique of the Vroom-Yetton

Contingency Model of Leadership Behavior," *Academy of Management Review* 4 (April, 1979), 249–258.

[27]Fiedler, Fred E., "The Leadership Game: Matching the Man to the Situation," *Organizational Dynamics* 4 (Winter 1976): 6–16.

[28]Fiedler, Fred E., *A Theory of Leadership Effectiveness* (New York: McGraw-Hill, 1967), pp. 22–32. Fiedler, Fred E., "Validation and Extension of the Contingency Model of Leadership Effectiveness: A Review of Empirical Findings" *Psychological Bulletin* 76 (1971) 128–148.

[29]House, R. J., "A Path–Goal Theory of Leader Effectiveness," *Administrative Science Quarterly* 16 (1971): 321–338; House, R. J. and G. Dessler, "The Path–Goal Theory of Leadership: Some Post Hoc and a Priori Tests," in J. G. Hunt and L. L. Larson, eds., *Contingency Approaches to Leadership* (Carbondale: Southern Illinois University Press, 1974).

[30]Szilagyi, Andrew D., and Henry P. Sims Jr., "An Exploration of the Path–Goal Theory of Leadership in a Health Care Organization," *Academy of Management Journal,* 17 (December 1974) 622–634; Greene, Charles N., "Questions of Causation in the Path–Goal Theory of Leadership" *Academy of Management Journal* 22 (March, 1979) 22–41.

cases cases cases

Case Study: Leadership in the Accounting Department

A PROBLEM

Tom Fetcher, the industrial relations manager, had become quite concerned about the high turnover of personnel in the Accounting Department, particularly in the data processing group. Five positions in the department were now vacant, and a sixth would be added in two weeks as another resignation had just reached his desk. The Accounting Department was a service group to all departments in the plant through its extensive data collection routines and budgeting procedures, and this service was beginning to suffer.

Tom decided to approach his investigation in a two-pronged manner. He would talk to Keith Schultz, plant controller, and get his thoughts about the employment problem and would have Al Earles, the industrial relations supervisor, confer with lower-level management people from the Accounting Department. In addition to this formal, direct investigation, Al had been instructed to poll other departmental supervisors for comments that had come to them from accounting employees. The second approach was to be a review and summary of comments made by accounting employees during their annual performance reviews and comments made by ex-employees when given an exit interview.

Tom studied the personnel folders of people in the accounting section and made the following notes that would be used in the problem analysis.

Employee	Position	Service Time in Present Capacity	Prior Experience and Comments
Keith Schultz	Plant Controller	Two years	Had an engineering degree and two graduate accounting courses. Had been a group leader in spinning for three years, then moved to assistant plant controller. Six months later was made plant controller when the slot suddenly came open.
Lou Kaplan	Assistant Plant Controller	One year	Had an accounting degree and eighteen years' experience in another of the corporation's plants. Had moved to the present plant after making request to corporate office for transfer to warmer climate for health reasons.
Dan Corvinus	Data Processing Manager	Two years	College degree and five years' experience in data processing. Had been promoted from a position in one of corporation's plants to his present management position.
Rick Kirkland	Staple Account Supervisor	Six months	Accounting degree with a total of one and a half years' staple production experience, all at the present plant.
Bob Johnson	Operations Supervisor	Three months	Management degree with three years' supervisory experience in the plant's inspection and packing area. No data processing experience or background.

The twelve accountants all had degrees and from three to seventeen years' experience in accounting, most of which had been gained in the plant. The five programmers had college degrees, but the two trainees did not. Experience varied from four to ten years, mostly attained at the firm. These seven people reported directly to the data processing manager (see the organizational chart of the Accounting Department).

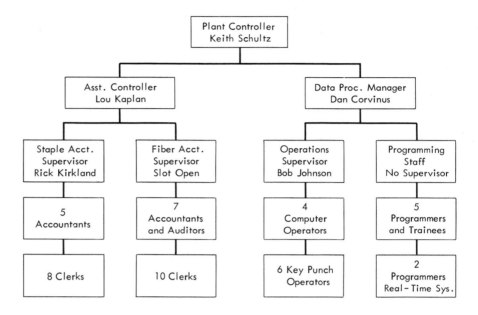

Some Opinions

Tom was now ready to confront Keith Schultz since he had told Al a problem solution was needed by Friday afternoon and it was now Wednesday morning. The discussion proceeded as follows.

Tom: We've got a tough problem in your department, Keith, with all these resignations, and a quick solution is certainly needed.

Keith: Yes, some complaints have come back from one production area, but a shifting of job assignments should take care of most of those problems.

Tom: How can you expect to handle the work load with five openings and a sixth on the way?

Keith: Well, we were slightly overstaffed and two more clerical functions will go on the computer in the next month or so.

Tom: Four of the openings are in the professional staff and that real-time programmer slot will be tough to fill.

Keith: Yeah, this austerity program we've been under for about eighteen months has hurt in giving decent raises.

Tom: I noticed in going through the personnel folders that the performance ratings have been lower this year than they were a year ago. What is the cause of this?

Keith: Lou and Dan may have been stricter this year, but I went along with them because I feel that the quality of work has dropped in the group lately.

Tom: Don't you feel that it's dangerous to give lower ratings when we already have an austerity program in effect?

Keith: Maybe so, but, if the work is poorer, we should penalize the people for it.

Tom: What is causing the poor performance?

Keith: I'm not sure; Lou and Dan handle the work assignments. But we've decided to crack down and improve the efficiency.

Tom: OK! Thanks, Keith. I'll be back in touch after Al and I can get our thoughts together and formalize a plan to get at the root of the problem.

Tom became involved with conferences during the remainder of Wednesday, but he and Al met again on Thursday.

Al: Well, the accounting guys tell me that the austerity program is a real bear and that they're losing people because of it. However, the "grapevine" in the plant says the accountants and D.P. fellows are as upset about the "people they work for" as they are about the lack of raises. Seems that the recent promotions of people from production areas to accounting management have really set off the feelings they have about Keith, Lou, and Dan.

Tom: I've been wondering why no recommendations of accounting people were made when those last two promotions came up.

Al: I checked the records, and Keith said that none of his people were ready for the responsibility.

Tom: That's possible, but I wonder. Do we have any of the accounting fellows in your management training programs?

Al: Only one; most of the participants are production supervisors. Jack (a programmer) is the only person that Keith has suggested for our training program though.

Tom: That seems to ring a bell. Let me see. Yes, just as I thought, Jack worked for Keith in the spinning area a couple of years back. Then he moved to the programming group. What about performance review comments and exit interview statements?

Al: Well, everybody is unhappy about the austerity program, but they really griped about the performance ratings. A brief synopsis of the reviews could be

Keith sits in his ivory tower and runs off to meetings all the time with reports we've generated. How does he know what we are doing?

Lou doesn't know what's going on here and he must be just a hatchet man.

Dan came under the gun from all the programmers and some of the accountants as presenting little leadership. To quote them, "He is always in the computer room operating the computer rather than being a manager." The real-time programmers are really upset because Dan doesn't even know what their computer is doing and doesn't seem to care.

Tom: Thanks, Al. I have a pretty good picture of the situation and I want to get it down on paper. I'll also draft a proposal as to what should be done.

Before the proposal was drafted another member of the accounting staff quit his job. The following is a summary of how he saw the situation.

1. The manager appears to feel that members of the group have little ambition or desire for responsibility.

2. The managers seem unsure of themselves in uncertain situations and fear the threat of subordinates to their positions. This probably occurs because of general lack of experience by the managers in fields that they now found themselves. Despite this, however, they make most of the decisions, announce them, and say "Do it this way."

3. Accounting employees have no motivation to do their jobs. No growth is possible, responsibility is minimal, and recognition and achievement are almost nil.

4. Management is using penalties that do not work and are hurting management because work quality is deteriorating and that are detrimental to the employees because raises and job satisfaction are almost nonexistent.

QUESTIONS

1. Evaluate the leadership demonstrated in the accounting department?

2. What kind of leadership would be most appropriate for professional employees. How does this differ from the leadership shown in the case?

3. What relationship do you see between leadership and motivation in this case?

4. What theories or models of leadership presented help explain what is happening?

5. What theories or models of leadership suggest what might be done that would make the accounting department managers more effective?

cases cases cases

Case Study: The Business Education Department

LEADERSHIP SETTING

Shelby High School consists of the eleventh and twelfth grades. Miss Winthrop, chairperson of the Business Education Department, has been with the school nineteen years, has taught every business subject at one time or another, and became chairperson after nine years. Miss Winthrop has a

Master's degree; all other members of the department have Bachelor's degrees.

Other than Miss Winthrop, only two teachers have been in the department more than two years—Mrs. Adams, eight years, and Mrs. Moore, five years. All other members consult these two about departmental problems rather than go to Miss Winthrop. A pattern of informal grouping has developed around these two, with Mrs. Trego and Mrs. Evans joining them to exchange "good mornings" and general conversation, usually in Mrs. Adams's room. These four are frequently observed together during lunch and conference periods, working out details on course requirements or analyzing some student's problem. Miss Winthrop never joins in any of these gatherings.

Although a teacher is designated as chairperson of a department, little prestige goes with this appointment. The teacher is expected to attend infrequent impromptu committee meetings called by the principal. Although a department representative, the teacher has little authority over its operation. Most announcements concerning the departments are made in general faculty meetings. Reports, approval of classroom activities, and invited speakers are usually handled by the individual teacher and the principal or one of the assistant principals. There is no difference in pay between the chairperson and regular teaching positions. Miss Winthrop made the remark that "the only reason we have a department chairperson around here is to take departmental inventory!"

LEADERSHIP EVALUATIONS

Considerable criticism has been voiced about what Miss Winthrop does *not* do as expected by others.

One teacher commented: "When I came to this school as a new teacher in the Business Education Department, it was several weeks before I realized that Miss Winthrop was the chairperson. She never offered me any guidance about departmental procedures or classroom duties such as keeping attendance reports to be submitted to the main office every six weeks. Instead, two teachers on the staff answered my "what do I do about this" questions and checked my first reports to the office to be sure that I was following the proper procedures.

"This is still the way we operate. Whenever we get a new teacher in our department, someone (usually the teacher in the adjoining room or one who teaches the same subject) will "adopt" her and try to fill her in on those little things that should be done but never seem to be in any teacher's manual."

Teachers are seldom consulted on use of or preference for types of equipment before its purchase.

Mrs. Adams related the following incident: "Several times I have tried to talk with Miss Winthrop about teaching materials that I feel I need to effectively teach my shorthand students. I have requested the Gregg set of transparencies to use with my overhead projector for two years now. Every time I try to see Miss Winthrop she is "too busy." The only time she ever requests them is at the end of the year on our general department requisition for supplies. The transparencies invariably get deleted as being too expensive an item what with all the other things the department needs.

"Finally, this year I went to Mr. Peperdine (school principal) personally to ask that these be ordered because I overheard him say that the school had some extra funds if any department needed something. Apparently, Miss Winthrop knew about this money but had said nothing about it to anyone. I asked the others to see if she had! She always wants everything to go through her records but never lets us know anything like that.

"Well, Mr. Peperdine approved the purchase. Meanwhile I had given the ordering material to Miss Winthrop. Even after telling her that I had spoken to Mr. Peperdine, she still did not requisition the transparencies or give me back the material.

"About a week later, or maybe even longer, Mr. Peperdine came by my room to ask if I still wanted the set. If not, the money needed to be spent elsewhere. I assured him that indeed I did still want them.

"After telling Miss Winthrop of this conversation with the school principal, she told me she had decided that dictation tapes would be more useful and had told Mr. Peperdine's secretary to order them earlier in the week.

"What could I say!"

No formal lesson plans are required. Sometimes a brief description or course outline is requested at the beginning of a semester. It is requested only that a lesson plan that can be used by a substitute teacher be left in the teacher's desk drawer with class rolls and seating charts.

The main guideline is simply to be sure that the material in the book has been presented "from cover to cover." How the teacher manages this is his or her responsibility. Any coordination of classes is left up to the individual teachers.

Mrs. Moore commented: "This deal of working out your own material suits me fine. I don't like to be told every little thing to do. Classes vary and respond differently to presentations of material. An instructor needs flexibility. If Karen is involved in a traffic violation, why not discuss the section on traffic regulations in business law right then and there. The students are certainly more interested in that right then than in types of bailments or contracts. And what could be more natural than the following section on automobile insurance? Especially if Karen's traffic violation concerned an accident involving car damage.

"But I do feel that we lose some valuable reinforcement between subject matter presented in one class and that presented in another. Students don't seem to get the idea of the flow of office work. They don't 'carry over' from shorthand to typing or business English—word division rules are a typing nuisance but what do they have to do with shorthand?"

Teacher evaluations are submitted each year to the area office by the principal. Classrooms supposedly are visited for observation of teaching activities, presentation of subject matter, and general housekeeping. No visits by the principal or assistant principals could be remembered by any member of the department. The only mention that this evaluation was actually conducted was in a general faculty meeting; the evaluation had never been discussed with any member of the department.

QUESTIONS

1. How would you describe Miss Winthrop's leadership?
2. Why do you think that Miss Winthrop related to her department as she does?
3. How much direction is required by teachers? Does Miss Winthrop's leadership meet this need? Why?
4. What changes in the chairperson's role would you suggest to the principal? What do you expect to achieve by such changes?
5. Are there any other changes that you would suggest?

CHAPTER 11

COMMUNICATION

LEARNING OBJECTIVES

When you have finished this chapter you should be able to:

- *Outline and explain a model of the communication process.*
- *List and describe six barriers and five facilitators of communication.*
- *Explain three kinds of communication flows and how they can be made more effective.*
- *Understand informal communication and how it may be influenced.*
- *Describe how communication networks have been studied in the laboratory.*
- *Explain the problems inherent in superior-subordinate relationships and how they can be minimized.*

Communication ties an organization together. Planning, organizing, directing, and controlling require communication in their formulation or initiation as well as in their implementation. Due to its persuasive nature, communication is often considered as a causal factor for anything and everything that is done improperly in an organization. However, good communication cannot overcome managerial efforts that are poorly conceived or inadequate; communication is only a part of good management.

The present chapter focuses on communication and its improvement in an organizational context. As a foundation, we examine a model of the communication process and some of the barriers to and facilitators of communication. Then we consider the downward, upward, and horizontal flows of communication and how they may be improved. Since such flows provide an incomplete view of organizational communication, we must look at the role of informal communication or the "grapevine," after which we examine the possible role of a union in communication matters and the results of laboratory studies of communication networks. Finally, the communication linkage between superior and subordinate is evaluated on the basis of trust and its development.

THE COMMUNICATION PROCESS

Basic communication is the process of transmitting information between two or more persons. The three elements involved in communication are the source (or sender), the message, and the receiver. This can be represented as follows.

The sender, or source, in communication may be an individual, group, or organization. Obviously, the content of the message and its effectiveness will be affected by the characteristics of the sender. Needs, attitudes, values, and perceptions of the sender will be reflected in the message. The receiver also may be an individual, group, or organization for whom the message is intended. Like the sender, the receiver is subject to many influences (needs, values, etc.) that can affect understanding the message.

The intended receiver may not receive the message because the message was sent via an inappropriate channel. Additionally, the receiver may not be attentive to the message. Hence the admonition often given communicators: "Get the attention of the recipient." For whatever reason, if the receiver is not "receiving," communication has not taken place, and there is no communication process.

For a more complete understanding of the communication process, however, our model must be expanded. Figure 11-1 gives a more comprehensive overview of the communication process. The model has a sender and a receiver of the message, but attention must be directed to what is basically involved in each of these three elements.

Figure 11-1

A Model of the Communication Process

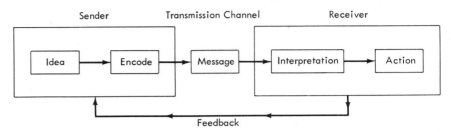

Sender

1. Ideation: The communication process begins with some idea, fact, meaning, or desired action that the communicator wishes to send. This forms the content and the basis for the message. This also means that there is a purpose that the sender has in mind. Furthermore, the sender must be explicit as to his or her purpose, not only for the clarity of the message but also to determine if the communication has been effective.

2. Encoding: After the sender has decided upon a message to communicate, its content must be put into a form that best conveys the message and that the receiver can understand. The message is structured in terms of a language whether words, math symbols, or diagrams or perhaps a combination of these. Communication of the message is facilitated when it is clear, concise, concrete, and correct. At this point the sender selects the most appropriate transmission medium because some are more effective for certain kinds of messages than others.

Transmission

1. The message may flow through the formal communication channels of an organization or through its informal channels. Additionally, the available medium used may be face to face, telephone, public address system, memo, bulletin board, and so on. Some messages may be sent via several media, as when complicated instructions are given orally and in writing.

Receiver

1. Interpretation (decoding): When the recipient receives the message, it is interpreted or "decoded"; the meaning of the message is sought. Understanding is the key to the interpreting process, but it can only occur in the receiver's mind. In other words, the meaning is not in the message but in the receiver. A sender wants the receiver to take from the message what was intended or sent; this may or may not happen.

2. Action: The interpretation is followed by action of some kind on the part of the receiver. Actions may range from storing the information provided, performing the task assigned, or simply ignoring the message.

Feedback

1. Since the receiver's understanding or action may not be what the sender intended, there always exists a need for feedback. Such feedback information may be verbal, nonverbal (facial expressions, written responses, gestures, etc.), or both. Simple compliance or observation of the receiver's behavior by the sender may also provide feedback. Whatever form the feedback takes, it is necessary to ensure that there has been understanding, acceptance, and/or compliance. The sender must determine if the purpose of his or her communication has been achieved. If not, further communication may be necessary.

The communication model shown reflects the complexity of the communication process and some of the potential difficulties at each step of the process. With the model as a background, specific barriers to communication and ways to facilitate communication will be considered.

BARRIERS TO AND FACILITATORS OF COMMUNICATION

Common Beliefs about Communication

Organizations require good communications to operate effectively, and it has been estimated that a manager spends from 80 to 90 percent of his or her time communicating in one way or another. In such a verbal environment, specific points of view about communicating have emerged that are highly questionable.[1] Some of these opinions are examined in the following paragraphs.

1. Communicating is transmitting facts and therefore is a logical process: This is only partially true. Facts must be interpreted, and interpretation may vary from person to person. There are also attitudinal and emotional elements to be considered.

2. Facts clearly understood secure conviction: This statement clearly ignores the possibility that the communication of facts may actually widen basic differences between two parties. Differences between labor and management, for instance, may rest upon real and substantial disagreement, and additional facts may not be enough to bridge the disparate positions of the parties on some issues.

3. If facts are presented one time and with sufficient clarity, this is sufficient to achieve mutual understanding: There are two assumptions in this statement. Rationality is assumed, and the imparting of facts is deemed sufficient to stimulate appropriate action. However, a person who has been told something may not understand what it is that he or she has been told. Furthermore, facts may be anchored to attitudes, values, and beliefs; these are the unseen part of an iceberg that may ultimately impair effective communications.

4. Communication is the art of telling management's story convincingly: This statement is only a half-truth. Communication is a matter of give and take. Persons on the receiving end of communication need to voice misgivings and opinions. Management must be as interested in understanding its employees as in getting its message across.

5. Communication primarily demands cleverness of presentation: This point of view requires a careful mapping of motives and a knowledge of the probable reaction of those who are to be influenced; in fact, it is a facet of applied psychology. In devising and implementing strategy in communications, a manager may run the risk of losing his or her personal touch and appear insincere. If this happens, it is usually obvious to subordinates. A manager who wishes to avoid the "hollow drum" effect should remember that there is no substitute for sincerity, understanding, and a willingness to work with people.

Beliefs about communications that have been described reflect in varying degrees the views of many communicators. The beliefs have a basic appeal because they are simplistic, partially true, and appeal to the rational side of one's nature.

Barriers to Successful Communications[2]

A fundamental problem in communications is that meaning and understanding are frequently hard to convey. Words are often a clumsy tool to move an idea from the mind of one person to that of another, and the sender of a message frequently discovers that the message sent is not the one that was actually received. Somehow in the process of communication the message has become distorted, leaving a gap in the understanding between the parties. Understanding is an elusive objective in communication, but many of the reasons for our inability to convey thoughts and ideas accurately have been discovered.

People hear what they expect to hear

What a person hears is largely shaped by his or her prior experiences. Instead of hearing what the communicator has said, a listener tends to hear what he or she expects the sender to say. There is filtering process that permits facts and ideas that are consistent with one's beliefs to pass through quickly, but those that a person does not accept or with which he or she disagrees are deflected or not received at all.

Each individual brings his or her own preconceptions into a communicating situation. Therefore what is heard is identified with similar experiences of the past, even though the similarity might be entirely superficial or even nonexistent. During an election campaign, the average newspaper reader or television viewer is likely to listen only to the information that supports his or her present position or views. In reading the company newspaper, an employee is likely to discount articles or stories with which he or she is in disagreement. When a person hears what he or she wishes to hear, it is because of filtering, distorting, or completely tuning out any idea that conflicts with his or her own ideas, preconceptions, or stereotypes.

Differences in perception

Because each person has a different background and has accumulated different experiences, it is understandable that the same communication will elicit varying interpretations. Take the case of a company's annual report that has been distributed to employees. This effort to provide knowledge and insight into the financial condition of the company as reflected in profits, productivity, and capital investment may not accomplish its purpose. Facts and figures that management sees as proof of a successful year, assuring the job security of employees, and permitting further progress of the organization may be viewed by the workers as evidence of exploitation and proof that they did not get their fair share. Such a situation can be explained by the fact that management and employees may live in different worlds and attach different meanings to the same facts. For example, the way that a company vice president and a laborer think about profits is hardly the same.

A person's perception is not only influenced by background and experience but also by his or her reference group—the group with which the individual identifies. Individual attitudes, values, and behaviors are shaped and strongly influenced by such groups. If an individual's associates are committed to maintaining high standards of quality and quantity, that person is likely to share the same commitment, because the individual wants their respect. Otherwise, the person would incur their resentment and hostility and perhaps be ostracized from the group.

Evaluation of the source

A person evaluates what is heard not only in terms of background, experience, and reference group but also according to his or her opinion of the sender of the communication. When an employee is given information by the company or by his or her superior, the employee asks, is it objective, is it reliable, is it trustworthy?

If the answers to these questions are negative, the individual simply will not accept the information regardless of its accuracy. For example, if employees consider the company newspaper simply a management propaganda sheet, they tend to disregard its stories no matter how truthful or objective their point of view. When a company refuses to accept a union's demand for a wage increase or a fringe benefit, employees may attribute this refusal to nonexistent motives. Furthermore, during the heat of collective bargaining or the conflict of a strike, both labor and management accuse each other of having selfish, or even sinister, objectives. In such situations the battle of words can become so intense that the real positions of the parties are obscured. In circumstances of this kind, neither labor nor management can objectively separate what may be factual in the arguments of the other from their feelings about the other.

Conflicting information

Understanding is frequently not achieved because of inconsistencies in communication. If a communicator says something that runs counter to what he or she said previously, the inclination of the listener may be to discount as untrustworthy the information received. Furthermore, if a person thinks that he or she detects a difference between what the communicator said and what the communicator actually does, a credibility gap will emerge. To illustrate, if a company makes a policy statement that promotions will be based on ability and demonstrated performance, but an employee is convinced by personal observation that favoritism is a significant factor in promotion, that employee simply disregards the company's policy statement and considers it insincere. In short, information that does not fit or coincide with what has been previously said or done will most likely be rejected.

The meaning of words

Semantic problems cause difficulty in communications. Words do not necessarily convey the meaning to the listener of what the speaker intends, and this may cause misunderstanding. Words suggest different things to different people; meaning is in the mind of the listener. To the scholar, the word "discipline" may mean a branch of learning, while to the worker in a plant it may connote a punishment of some kind. When management says that automation is essential for future growth and development, management means that it can increase efficiency, lower operating costs, stabilize employment, and eventually prevent layoffs. However, automation is a dreaded word to employees in certain industries. To them, it means loss of jobs, downgrading of skills, or even premature retirement. Therefore, when a company tells its employees about the need for automation, its message may be falling on deaf ears. Employees, convinced that their security and future are in jeopardy, will resist the change because automation means something quite different to them.

The force of emotions

Emotions are an important factor in communications. The emotional attitude of a person is a determinant of how he or she will react to specific information at any given time. If an employee feels insecure, stories in the company newspaper that will get his or her attention first are probably those articles on pending economic recession, automation, or labor trouble. Problems of this kind threaten people's security and frighten them. Thus items on such subjects are immediately scanned. However, under normal conditions topics of this nature should seem no more important than usual and would receive no greater notice than would any other news item.

Communications barriers explain why people frequently fail to understand each other and why it is sometimes difficult to transmit orders and information. The difficulties are aggravated when one assumes that providing accurate information will achieve mutual understanding. The oft-repeated statement, "give the people the facts and they will come up with the right answer," is a perfect example of this type of wishful thinking. People will come up with an answer, but their answer will be predicated on each one's interpretation as influenced by self-interest, group membership, prejudices, and beliefs. When a manager is sensitive to the barriers that may cause blocks in the flow of communications, that manager is in a position to deal with such obstructions constructively and to eliminate or at least minimize them.

Eliminating Barriers to Communication[3]

Is it possible to free a communications system from the common blockages that have been discussed? The answer to this question cannot be a simple "yes" or "no." Perfect communication is seldom attained because of the complexities involved. Also improving communication depends upon what one expects to achieve. The objectives of achieving, understanding, agreement, and compliance or cooperation are difficult to attain because of divergent goals, values, and interests. Good communication does not necessarily result in agreement. However, much can be done to improve the communication process, as we shall see.

In essence, feedback is the determination of how well the sender is getting his or her message across to the receiver. For example, managers want to know how well subordinates understand the information they are receiving and their reaction.

Feedback cues may vary from a nod or a facial expression to a question seeking clarification or additional information. Figure 11-2 shows some of the cues and methods that are appropriate for obtaining feedback.

Figure 11-2

Feedback Cues in Communication

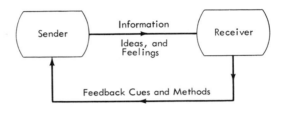

Visual-facial expressions, gestures, posture.
Auditory-tone of voice, listening.
Verbal- "Is that clear?" "What do you mean?"

Feedback gives an indication of understanding and may be visual, auditory, or verbal. In a face-to-face situation, a manager can observe comprehension, resentment, or anger on the faces of subordinates. A person's facial expression may show feelings or attitudes that he or she may be unwilling or reluctant to express in words, especially in a superior–subordinate relationship. When visual feedback indicates that communication is not effective, questions can be used as a verbal lever to ascertain whether the receiver understands the information or if further clarification is necessary.

Listening is an essential means of securing feedback information. The tone of an employee's voice in responding to an order may belie his or her verbal response. An effective manager listens with what has sometimes been called a "third ear." Such a person knows that it is necessary to "tune in" on the employee's comments and determine what the employee is really saying, what the employee is trying to say, and what the employee's silence really means. The use of listening skills is valuable because it permits one to understand not only what another says but how he or she is reacting. Listening with understanding will be discussed later in this chapter.

Because feedback is so essential to the operation of an efficient organization, many managers prefer to use oral instead of written methods in giving orders and instructions. A face-to-face encounter provides feedback so that one may judge if the received information equals what was sent. In personal encounters, it is also possible to determine whether or not spoken words mean the same thing to both parties. A manager has the opportunity to explore conflicting information and different perceptions. If the manager is a skillful listener, he or she can use these exchanges of information with subordinates to improve communications and prevent communications barriers from arising. Moreover, when the manager talks to subordinates personally, he or she is more likely to discover and address emotional problems that otherwise might color or influence what is heard.

Obviously, there is no guarantee that all communication barriers can be removed by feedback, but face-to-face conversation increases the possibility of reducing them. Therefore, many managers make personal communication of facts, ideas, and feelings with subordinates an integral part of directing people.

Sensitivity to the point of view of the employee

If a manager is to "get through" to employees, the manager must be sensitive to their viewpoints and realize that they may be very different from his or her own. The employees are often limited in their outlook because they tend to view company policies and practices according to how they are personally affected. A manager is inclined to regard company problems in terms of the organization as a whole, whereas an employee is concerned primarily about his or her individual interests and perhaps only secondarily about the company. If this difference is understood and accepted, a manager has a better chance of reaching an understanding with subordinates.

A manager may be unaware of the extent to which the difference in background and experience of employees affect their point of view, especially as this relates to the manager's communications. Furthermore, there are differences in education, power relationships, and even social distance that compound the problem of achieving understanding. Such variables make it imperative that a manager take the initiative to bridge the understanding gap that sometimes exists with subordinates.

A basic step toward the development of mutual understanding is for a manager to know his or her subordinates as individuals. With this knowledge the manager acquires insight and knows how to tailor communications to the attitudes, beliefs, and needs of each employee. This is helped by sensitivity to the view of subordinates as they are reflected in outlook, needs, and personal concern.

The use of language in communications

A communicator must pay careful attention to the language of his or her message, whether it is written or oral. The attainment of mutual understanding depends on clear, intelligible communication, but clarity is a matter of personal perception. A common rule of communications is to use direct, simple words and in most instances to avoid multisyllable or erudite language. It is also helpful to refrain from using words to which possible symbolic emotional meanings may be attached. Sentences should be of manageable length and subtle implications avoided. The primary objective of communication in an organization is to create understanding through concrete and intelligible language.

Repetition

In addition to using simple, direct language, there are occasions on which it is desirable, even necessary, to repeat certain kinds of information several times to make sure that it is fully understood. However, constant repetition can become monotonous. The manager who repeats the same instructions over and over again in exactly the same words risks the possibility of irritating his or her subordinates. Television commercials that are too repetitive sometimes have this effect. Even the boss's pet peeves are finally ignored if they become too familiar. However, originality and the use of example and illustration enable a manager to repeat his or her instructions several times and still retain the attention of subordinates. Originality and novelty in presentation can enhance communications, but a careful balance between redundancy and surprise should be maintained. However, if a communicator stresses originality of presentation too much, the message may be lost because employees become more interested in the methods than in what is said.

Actions to reinforce words

"Actions speak louder than words" is an old adage, but it explains why employees judge a company by its practices rather than by its written policies. The manager who reinforces his or her words with concrete and constructive action greatly increases the possibility that employees will accept communications at face value. For example, a manager increases the reliability of his or her communication by indicating that there will be periodic checkpoints in an activity and then follows up as promised. However, if the manager fails to follow up as stated, future communications may be ignored. One cannot say one thing and do another if he or she expects to be a successful communicator. Accuracy and dependability in communications can be achieved only if actions are consistent with the message.

In summary, we have noted that the complexity of communicating is often oversimplified when considered as the transmitting of facts that initiates a logical process and terminates in mutual agreement. We outlined the factors that complicate communications and suggested ways in which to eliminate or minimize them. Figure 11-3 summarizes some of the key factors involved.

Figure 11-3

Barriers and Facilitators in Communication

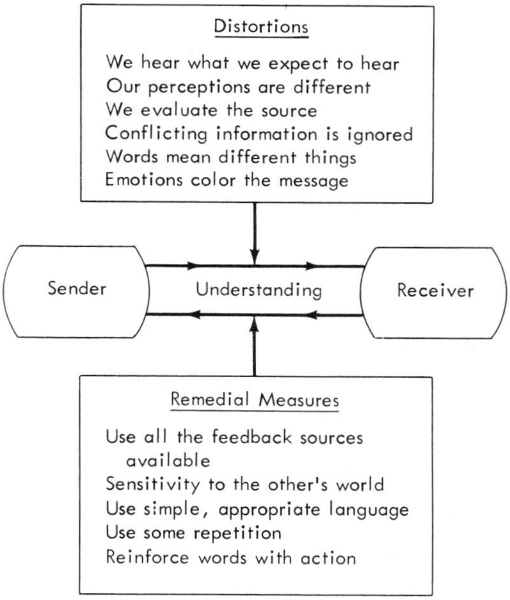
Distortions
We hear what we expect to hear
Our perceptions are different
We evaluate the source
Conflicting information is ignored
Words mean different things
Emotions color the message
Sender
Understanding
Receiver
Remedial Measures
Use all the feedback sources available
Sensitivity to the other's world
Use simple, appropriate language
Use some repetition
Reinforce words with action

COMMUNICATIONS FLOWS

Communications flows refer to the nature and direction of information movement. The basic concern is with communication needs; that is, what information is needed, where it is needed, and what methods facilitate movement in the desired direction.[4] In organizations there are three directions of communication flow: downward, upward, and laterally. Lateral communication may be horizontal or diagonal. Figure 11-4 illustrates these flows.

Downward Flows

The downward flow of communication tends to follow the chain of command or line of authority, that is, from positions at the organization's top to its lower levels. Much of the information needed to manage or direct

Figure 11-4

An Example of Communication Flows

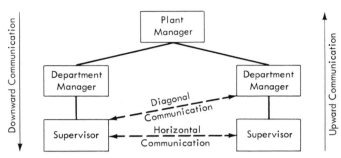

an organization originates at the upper levels and must be transmitted to the appropriate lower level. Consequently, objectives, policies, procedures, orders, requests, and the like are disseminated throughout the organization. The importance of such directives and instructions has often led managers to assume that communication is essentially getting management's message across to the lower levels; that is a half-truth at best.

Obviously, the more levels in an organization, the greater the potential difficulty of communicating with the employees at the lowest level. Distortion and filtering can occur at each level to modify the original message. Orders and instructions become more detailed and specific as they pass through each level. Managers at each level act as a filter in determining how much of the information from upper levels should be passed on to subordinates.

The media used most often in downward communication are face-to-face meetings, telephones, and written directives. Other media include handbooks, newspapers, bulletin boards, and employee letters.

Managers tend to overestimate the effectiveness of their downward communication, as was demonstrated by Keith Davis in a study of a large manufacturing plant.[5] Top management held a meeting with its middle managers and informed them of a change in the parking lot and tentative plans for the layoff of personnel. The middle managers were instructed to relay this information to their foremen who would convey it to the assistant foremen. The resulting downward communication was interesting. The study indicated that the layoff information was passed to 94 percent of the foremen and to 70 percent of the assistant foremen. The parking information was passed to 38 percent of the foremen and to 15 percent of the assistant foremen. This was a classic example of filtering. Parking information being less important and not related to production received more filtering than did the layoff information.

Gaps in downward communication were reflected in the study of a public utility.[6] Ninety-two percent of the foremen said that they always or nearly always told workers in advance about changes that would affect them or their work. In contrast, only 47 percent of the workers stated that they were nearly always informed about impending change. Similar results were found at the top of the organization. In this case, 100 percent of the top managers stated that they always or nearly always informed the foremen about changes in advance; only 63 percent of the foremen, however, agreed with their bosses. These results point to the need for periodic surveys of employees at each level of the organization to determine if they feel downward communication to be adequate.

Improving Downward Information

Filtering of downward communication can be minimized by utilizing appropriate media. Messages that are complex and need to be elaborated should be communicated orally. Furthermore, this provides an opportunity to obtain feedback and increase understanding. On the other hand, written media are more appropriate for communications that are simple and straightforward at the one extreme and lengthy and detailed at the other extreme. Often, a combination of both oral and written media is desirable. Complex problems can be presented orally to an individual or group to maximize feedback benefits and followed up by written information that can be further studied and/or used as a reference.

Sometimes insufficient downward communication occurs because a manager is not sensitive to the subordinate's needs. Minimal communication needs of subordinates may be met by clarifying job requirements, providing instructions in job procedures, and giving relevant job performance feedback. Inadequacies in meeting these needs may be disclosed through an employee opinion survey, the personnel office, or performance reports. Management education can be provided to stress the kind and importance of employee information needs and methods to reduce such role conflict (Chapter 4).

A manager may also block communication by withholding information from subordinates because he or she feels insecure and wants to maintain control.[7] Subordinates are kept dependent for instruction and guidance, and bright, upcoming employees are kept in their places. Information also can be a vehicle for wielding power that can be used to reinforce the manager's leadership style. Attitudes of the manager must be changed if downward communication is to be improved. Leadership training and sensitivity training may be used in this change effort.

Upward Flows

As seen in Figure 11-4, upward communication flows from lower to higher organizational position. As with downward communication, upward flows usually move through the chain of command but from subordinate to superior. The basic function of upward communication is to obtain information about the performance and activities of the lower levels. Much of this information is related to control and signals the accuracy of plans as well as an understanding and response to other downward communications. One will find that budget proposals, requests for assistance, opinions, and recommendations comprise other upward communications. Filtering also occurs in upward communication as information is integrated and summarized and then passed upward through successive levels.

Media for most upward communication are face-to-face meetings, written reports, and the telephone, but also may include the grievance procedure, questionnaire survey, suggestion programs, or special meetings with employees.

One manager has observed that perception downward is poorer than perception upward.[8] In other words, subordinates "read" their bosses better than the bosses "read" their subordinates. This occurs because employees in a subordinate position develop a keen understanding of the true motives, character, and personality of those in positions of power over them to survive and succeed. This often explains why upward communication is diluted, edited, or eliminated entirely.

Support for this observation was found in a study of supervisors, engineers, and both white- and blue-collar workers in eight companies designed to determine why subordinates fail to speak out. A large majority felt that their bosses were not interested in their problems and that they would become involved in a lot of trouble if open with their bosses.[9] Other studies indicated upward communication as least likely to be accurate when subordinates (1) are ambitious for advancement, (2) perceive their bosses to have substantial control over their retention, promotion, and pay increases, (3) do not trust their bosses, and (4) feel insecure.[10]

Improving Upward Communication

Some observers of the American scene note that people below the top level in organizations have become increasingly separated from decisions affecting their well-being. As a result, they feel frustrated, powerless, and exploited. The results have been a challenge to authority and a demand for more involvement in decision making. One possible response to such trends by organizations is upward communication.

With this premise in mind, Fenn and Yankelovich sought to determine those upward communication devices or approaches that have been used with reasonable success.[11] Since these devices vary from the traditional approaches, they will be outlined here.

1. "Speak up" or "feedback": Employees may telephone a special number to raise questions or voice concerns, or write notes to a designated person on company-prepared forms. There may be certain times of the month when top executives are available for phone calls. In some cases, time limits on responses are set; in other cases, answers are sent to employees directly and then printed in the company newsletter.

2. "Councils": Managers and/or employees get together regularly to talk about their problems. A formal agenda is submitted by both management and workers and then distributed to everyone. The subsequent disposition of each item is also publicly listed. The main council may be reinforced by subcouncils of employees built around work groups that provide inputs.

3. Cracker-barrel meetings: Conducted on a regular basis by first-line supervisors, the meetings are designed to move information downward to nonmanagement personnel and to pass ideas and complaints up the line to management.

4. Employee annual meetings: Modeled after regular stockholders' sessions, the president and other top officials report to employees on the state of the company and future plans. Then they are available for questions from the employees.

5. Nonmanagement task force: An attitude survey is used to determine the issues that most concern the work force. High-priority problems are selected and a special group of nonmanagement personnel seeks to resolve them. This process is given widespread publicity so that everyone knows the problems being studied and who is involved. Typically, the task force is allotted a certain amount of company time for investigation and report preparation. In turn, management must respond in a specified length of time and its comments are publicized.

6. Junior board of directors: The board is made up of middle managers and others below that level who make policy recommendations to the corporate board and present arguments on which the suggestions are based.

7. Corp of counselors or ombudsmen: Employees can make suggestions or criticisms to such persons with a guarantee of anonymity and then the counselors take responsibility for doing something about such grievances.

8. Existing mechanisms: Complaints that are not within the traditional jurisdiction of existing committees become a new responsibility. For example, a safety committee will permit discussion of a wide range of questions raised by employees at its management–labor safety meetings. Since the work force knows the employee members of the committee and sees them on safety matters in their work area, they are readily accessible to anyone who has something on his or her mind.

These plans must be modified to fit an organization's needs, but even then any one plan taken separately is likely to be inadequate. This is so because employees require two responses from a communications system. First, they need information to understand what is going on and why; these needs are served by information-handling devices or mechanisms. Most question-and-answer programs are of this nature and provide an opportunity to obtain information on policies and practices that are confusing or annoying. Second, employees need action on the things that trouble them. Since information-handling devices do not have a built-in capacity to achieve change, other systems designed to produce action and change must be used. For example, employee and management councils are specifically designed to produce action and change. Action programs focus on altering existing practices by directing attention to issues, making recommendations, and calling for a specific management response. Both information-handling and action systems are required for a balanced communications program.

One author has outlined his organization's approach for achieving a balanced communication system.[12] The upward communication program consists of (1) private lines (via mail or telephone), (2) task teams of employees, and (3) an interdepartmental team of first-line management personnel. The program has demonstrated its effectiveness in responding to employee concerns and has been reflected in productivity.

Since the filtering of upward information by employees at all levels is a potential problem, even in the best-managed organizations, information from alternative sources may be developed.[13] Quality-control inspectors, investigators, and financial auditors are used to determine performance, detect mistakes, and uncover improper conduct. Such alternative sources of information should offset attempts to cover up mistakes and problems. In essence an incentive is provided to reveal unfavorable information to the boss rather than to have it revealed from another source.

Finally, employee opinion surveys can be used to evaluate upward communication. Top management's commitment to two-way communication by corrective action will facilitate the development of confidence in its motives and sincerity.

Lateral Flows

The lateral flow of communication serves as a coordination device for groups and departments and may be horizontal or diagonal (Figure 11-4). Communication between persons at the same level in the authority hierarchy is horizontal. If the communication is between persons at different levels having no direct authority over one another, the communication is diagonal. The pattern of lateral communication is closely related to the flow of work and occurs regularly among employees as a team, interdependent work groups, separate functional departments, and line and staff personnel.

The media used most often in lateral communication are face-to-face meetings, the telephone, written memos, job orders, and requisitions. Primary functions of lateral communication are coordination and problem solving. In Chapter 9, several methods of managing group interactions were presented that are instrumental in promoting lateral communication. Galbraith concludes that growing informational needs can be met by the creation of lateral channels.[14] The lateral processes shown below are given in a sequence determined by increasing ability to handle information and increasing cost to the organization.

1. direct contact between managers
2. creation of liaison roles
3. creation of task forces
4. use of teams
5. creation of integrating roles
6. change to a managerial linking role

These channels must be designed because neither the hierarchy of authority nor the informal organization are adequate to coordinate interdependencies.

Informal Communication

The communication flows in organizations include informal communication as well as formal communication. Informal communications do not coincide with the formal structure and occur outside prescribed channels. Such communication is often referred to as the grapevine and is carried out by face-to-face interaction and sometimes by telephone.

Some managers regard the grapevine as an evil force given to spreading rumors, destroying morale and reputations, and challenging authority. Others regard it as a safety valve and a rapid medium of communication. Actually, the grapevine may be or result in all these. A major function of informal communication is the maintenance of personal relationships and informal groups, that is, social relationships. However, informal communication also may be task related, as formal communication flows often fail to provide sufficient task information. In this case, informal communication emerges so that tasks can be completed, problems resolved, and objectives attained.

Although the grapevine cannot be controlled, it can be influenced and/or utilized. Management may use the grapevine to get a message disseminated quickly and to make unofficial announcements or off-the-record statements. Davis found that formal communication is often used to confirm what has already been communicated by the grapevine.[15] Such confirmation results partly because of the speed of the grapevine that formal systems cannot match, because of its unofficial function, and because of its transient nature. In other words, the formal system makes it official and puts it on the record.

The typical pattern of grapevine transmission is a cluster chain in which information is passed along by only a few people (see Figure 11-5). In the figure, person A tells three selected others; only one of the three, person D, tells two others; of these two, only person F, tells another. The person who passes the information on to several other people is a "liaison individual"; others who receive information but do not transmit are "passive receivers." One study found that a small number of persons always filled the liaison role.[16] However, the study by Davis indicated that different kinds of information were disseminated by different liaison individuals who acted in a predictable way. Information on an interesting job function or on a personal acquaintance is passed on as quickly as possible by a liaison person.

Figure 11-5

A Cluster Chain in the Grapevine

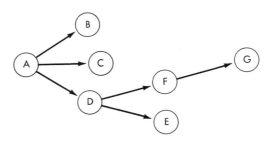

The study by Davis also revealed that managers at higher levels communicated more often and with more people than did managers at lower levels. The predominate flow of communication was downward or horizontal. An event at the bottom level usually reached a high level but by a single line of communication. From that point the information went downward and horizontally in the cluster chain as if it had originated at the top. Furthermore, staff personnel were more likely than line personnel to know about any company event. This happened because, in providing assistance to line people, staff personnel were involved in the chain of procedure and were more mobile since their duties required extensive contacts outside their offices. Finally, it was found that low-status people and those who were geographically isolated in the company were less likely to receive grapevine information, and, when they did, they were the last to do so.

Davis made the following suggestions based on his study.

1. Increase the number and effectiveness of liaison individuals if more communication is desired among managerial levels.
2. Rely more on staff managers than on line officials in spreading grapevine information.
3. Take steps to compensate for the fact that some groups are isolated from communication chains. This includes foremen who tend to be the last links in management communication chains, whether the chains are formal or informal.
4. Devote more attention to cross-communication, that is, between different departments. Procedures and social factors are more important than the chain of command in horizontal communication patterns.

While these elements are suggested only as starting points for action, managers should recognize the existence of the grapevine and attempt to use it constructively.

The Union and Communication

When an organization deals with a union representing part or all of its employees, the union may be used as a channel of communication. Whether or not the union is used or to what degree in communication will be determined by the prevailing kind of relationships. There are advantages and disadvantages involved. The union may distort, filter, or misuse the information for its own benefit. On the other hand, the union may represent a channel on which employees already depend and feel secure in using. Furthermore, a union's support of any information may increase employee acceptance of the communication.

If management intends to install an upward communication program (task teams of employees, employee annual meetings, etc.), participation of the union leaders may be important.[17] If the program is perceived as a way of decreasing the power of the union or its officials or as a union-busting device, opposition or sabotage can be anticipated. The ideal objective is to have union leaders support the effort and convey this to the union membership. Whether or not this is a plausible tactic will depend upon the prevailing management–union relationship.

COMMUNICATION NETWORKS:
LABORATORY STUDIES

Numerous studies have been conducted in the laboratory to test the influence of various networks on the effectiveness of communication. A network indicates the arrangement of information channels. The experimental laboratory permits the isolation and manipulation of one variable (independent) to show its impact on other variables (dependent). In these studies, the independent variable is the structure of the communication network, and the dependent variables are speed of communication, accuracy of communication, and the satisfaction of participants. The participants are usually placed into groups of four to six and are asked to perform a simple or complex task.

Typically, in such an experiment the following takes place: First, each individual is given certain information; second, the group's task is to assemble this information; and, third, the information is used to make a decision. Figure 11-6 shows three kinds of communication networks that have been examined and the results obtained from early research studies.

Figure 11-6

Communication Networks and Results

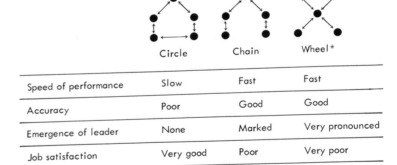

	Circle	Chain	Wheel*
Speed of performance	Slow	Fast	Fast
Accuracy	Poor	Good	Good
Emergence of leader	None	Marked	Very pronounced
Job satisfaction	Very good	Poor	Very poor
Flexibility to job change	Very fast	Slow	Slow

*Called a wheel because all communications pass through the center person, similar to the hub of the wheel

Source: Keith Davis, *Human Behavior at Work,* 5th ed. (New York: McGraw-Hill, 1977), p. 377.

Note that the wheel is a net in which the communications reduce the difficulty of organizational problems to a minimum. All information is directed toward the individual occupying the central position. The wheel is analogous to an organization having two levels that looks like the following.

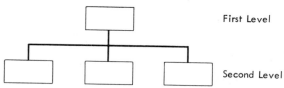

First Level

Second Level

The chain in Figure 11–6 is like an organization having three levels. In addition to the previous communication nets, some later research included an all-channel network, which is shown here.[18] The all-channel network permits direct communication among all members.

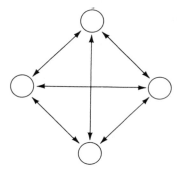

While research has produced conflicting findings, one investigator has drawn some definite conclusions from the many studies conducted.[19] Performance on simple tasks indicates that the wheel and all-channel are the best, and the circle network is the worst. However, morale of participants tends to be high in the circle network and generally low in the wheel network. When complex tasks are performed, the all-channel network is most effective.

The networks appear to maximize different variables. The wheel and chain networks give the best task performance but are low on flexibility to change and result in the lowest task satisfaction. This indicates that management may have to choose what it wishes to optimize. It also suggests that the wheel may be the best work structure to use in dealing with routine and repetitive problems characteristic of organizations that are operating in a tranquil, steady environment.[20] In contrast, the all-channel structure has the potential for dealing with the complexities associated with a turbulent environment. However, generalizing from controlled laboratory studies to real organizations in a complex, changing environment must be done with extreme caution.

SUPERIOR-SUBORDINATE COMMUNICATIONS

One of the most important communication relationships in an organization is that between the superior and subordinate. Such interpersonal communication is the focus of concern that follows. Managers are responsible for the attainment of organizational goals, and their communication skills will affect their success in doing so. Training may be required to attain the communication skills necessary to achieve such goals effectively and efficiently.

The Organizational Context

The nature of superior-subordinate communications will take place in the context of the total organization. As noted in Chapter 10, organizations display consistent patterns of behavior in utilizing their human resources.[21] The results are reflected in four different management systems; (1) exploitive authoritative, (2) benevolent authoritative, (3) consultative, and (4) participative group. Communication is one of the operating characteristics of these management systems and will influence the quality of communication between superior and subordinate. For example, the exploitive authoritative system of organization is characterized primarily by communication that is downward, initiated at the top, and viewed with great suspicion. There is little upward communication, and what there is tends to be inaccurate. On the other hand, the participative system of organization is characterized by communication that is downward, upward, and horizontal; initiated at all levels; and generally accepted or openly questioned. There is a great deal of upward communication that is accurate.

The Personal Context

In addition to the management system, each manager will have his or her own approach to leadership. While the management system will condition the superior-subordinate relationship, in most organizations there is some latitude for individual leadership practices. The leadership continuum of Tannenbaum and Schmidt presented in Chapter 10 not only reflects the subordinate's involvement in decision making but also his or her involvement in the communication process. For example, making a decision and announcing it involves one-way communication, whereas asking a group to make a decision on a specified problem represents two-way communication. Furthermore, the prevailing communication will be affected by the X or Y assumptions held by the manager. Such assumptions will influence the predominant direction of communication, one- or two-way, and also its quality, that is, the extent of openness and trust.

Authoritative Communication

The manager may overlook the requisite conditions for some forms of communication to be accepted as authoritative.[22] Four conditions must be present for a communication to be accepted as authoritative.

1. The communication must be understood. Unless a communication is interpreted accurately, it will have limited meaning and the recipient will disregard it or do anything in hopes that it is in compliance.
2. The communication must be compatible with the organization's purposes. Some communications may be considered more in the interest of the boss than in the interest of the organization. Also, some orders may conflict, which tends to paralyze the recipient and render compliance impossible.
3. The communication must be compatible with the recipient's personal interests as a whole. A communication to the detriment of an individual fails to provide any inducement for acceptance. Cases of voluntary resignation, malingering, or lack of dependability are typical responses.
4. The individual must be able to mentally and physically comply with the communication. If one is unable to comply, the communication will be disobeyed or disregarded.

While these considerations are especially relevant for communications having an instructive function, they are also relevant to other kinds of communication. Judicious use of feedback by a manager will facilitate detecting which condition(s) may be lacking.

Level of Trust

The superior-subordinate interrelationship will be affected by the respective positions of these participants, as revealed in several research studies that indicated a screening of information by low-status or low-power individuals to persons of high power.[23] Unpleasant information that reflected negatively upon the competence and therefore the security and/or progress of subordinate members is unlikely to be passed upward, especially if the subordinates desire to move up in the organization. In other words, the stronger the upward mobility aspirations of the subordinate, the less accurate his or her communication of problem-related information to the immediate superior.

With these studies as background, Read designed a study to determine the extent to which the subordinate's interpersonal trust of his or her superior and the perceived influence of the boss over career advancement affected the communication of upward information. The strength-of-mobility aspiration was determined by ten items each having two alternatives of a forced-choice nature. One alternative in each pair was the choice of a higher-level position, but with an unpleasant condition attached. Accuracy of upward communication was determined by the degree of agreement between superior and subordinate about the relative difficulty that the problem caused the subordinate. Low agreement was taken to indicate relatively poor or inaccurate communication. Fifty-two pairs of superior–subordinates from middle management were used in the study.

The results indicated the following:

1. The stronger the upward mobility needs of the subordinate managers, the less accurately they communicate problem-related information.
2. The less trust of their immediate superiors, the greater the tendency toward inaccurate information.
3. There was some indication that communication inaccuracy increased when superiors were perceived as high-influence persons and were, at the same time, not fully trusted.
4. Trust appeared to have the greatest single effect upon accuracy of communication.

Since trust appears to be central to superior–subordinate communication, the meaning of trust and its determinants must be examined.

Trust and Its Development

As seen in Chapter 7, relationships have the potential for confirming or denying an individual's self-concept. Depending on their quality, personal interactions have been labeled close versus distant and warm versus cold. Feeling supported, adequate, and worthy leads to closeness, warmth, and trust in a relationship. Trust is central to superior–subordinate as well as to all other kinds of human relationships. Trust is based on (1) confidence in another's competence and ability, (2) soundness of another's judgment, (3) another's willingness to be helpful, and (4) one's concern for another's welfare.[24] Trust is often cited as crucial in communication without specifying which factor is involved. Actually, trust may involve all of these, especially in superior–subordinate relationships.

For the supervisor, the ideal situation is to demonstrate behaviors in all these areas to his or her subordinates. This forms the basis for greater openness in communication. Theory X and Theory Y beliefs convey trust in others and are reflected in leadership methods and skills. Concern for the communication needs of subordinates—job requirements, job instructions, and job performance feedback—demonstrates a concern for the subordinate's welfare. The capacity to exercise influence upward on behalf of the subordinate also conveys a willingness to be helpful and a concern for the subordinate's welfare.

A trusting climate also is facilitated when the superior is nonpunitive and problem oriented about subordinate difficulties and mistakes. Rather than criticizing the subordinate when a mistake is made, the superior helps in solving the problem and in planning how to avoid mistakes in the future. Furthermore, the subordinate is evaluated on progress in learning to cope with job responsibilities over a reasonably long period of time rather than on short-term performance. However, organizations must establish an atmosphere and circumstances that enable, and even encourage, the supervisor to deal with subordinates in a manner that builds trust and opens communications.

Listening with Understanding

The major barrier to mutual interpersonal communication is our natural tendency to judge, evaluate, approve, or disapprove the statements of the other person.[25] Although these tendencies are common, they become heightened in situations where feelings and emotions are involved. Rather than finding a mutual element in the communication, there are two ideas, two feelings, and two judgments. On the other hand, communication occurs when we listen with understanding. This means understanding *with* a person, not about him or her. It means to see the expressed idea and attitude from the other person's point of view, frame of reference, and feelings about the matter.

How does one listen with understanding? This requires deliberate active listening with the purpose of drawing the other person out, discovering what he or she really wants to say, and providing a chance for free and full expression. This is especially difficult when the manager personally or his or her actions are the subject of direct or implicit criticism. The manager's ego is involved. Since most managers are action oriented, listening requires training and experience. Some general guidelines are as follows.[26]

1. Listen: This is to get the subordinate to talk freely, which requires the manager to refrain from talking. Listening is more than just not talking and requires an active effort to convey that you understand and are interested in what the other person is saying. An attentive but relaxed attitude is necessary. Comments such as ''I understand'' or ''Could you tell me more'' convey interest and encourage the person to continue talking.

2. Reflective responses: Active listening is supplemented by reflective responses to encourage the other person to talk. Feelings may be reflected or restated to help the person understand his or her own feelings and show that he or she is understood. Also, the content of what has been said may be restated without attempting to interpret, clarify, or evaluate. Comments such as ''You feel that the new procedure is unfair'' or ''The procedure interferes with your work'' are reflective. Both responses show that you are giving the person careful consideration and are being fair. Also,

they provide a chance to restate and elaborate if the person feels that you haven't grasped his or her point. Also, summarizing statements serve to pull important ideas and facts together, to establish a basis of further discussion, and to review progress.

3. Probes: After the person has had an opportunity to release his or her feelings and look at the facts more objectively, the manager may use probes to bring out information that the subordinate has not volunteered. By repeating certain statements or words from what the subordinate has said, the manager can indicate that he or she would like to hear more about a given area. This calls for directing the conversation but without forcing the subordinate into an area that he or she does not want to enter. This may be stating, "Could you tell me more about . . ." or "I am interested in what you said about . . .".

4. Solutions: After the facts have been disclosed, the subordinate is in a position to develop alternative solutions and select the best one. It is preferable to help the subordinate work out his or her own solution. For example, the performance appraisal may disclose areas of inadequate progress that require remedial action. Although the manager provides whatever support may be needed, the subordinate is responsible for developing a plan of action for improvement. The subordinate is capable of self-direction and self-control.

Depending on the nature and purpose of the conversation or interview, the manager may have to take action. If so, the manager will have to be firm and direct to ensure that the solution is consistent with the needs of the organization. For instance, the manager may listen with understanding to the subordinate's objections to a new change in procedures but still insist that they be maintained. The subordinate will not be happy with the results but at least has the satisfaction of presenting the issue and knowing his or her welfare has been considered.

The "listening with understanding" orientation is relevant when applied to any specific problem—performance evaluation, resistance to change, discipline, grievances, and so on. It is an orientation that the manager can apply with peers, subordinates, or the boss. It is a way of being ready to listen to another's point of view and taking this into account before taking action, if such is required.

Good communication does not occur by accident. It is the result of commitment by top management, and it then becomes the responsibility of every manager. This responsibility can be met by understanding the communication process, knowing the barriers to and facilitators of communication, planning for communication, and acquiring the skills necessary for good communication.

SUMMARY

In this chapter we examined the communication process as consisting of the idea, encoding, transmission, interpretation, action, and feedback. Next, we considered the barriers to communication and the means of facilitating more accurate communication.

The formal flows of communication in an organization are downward, upward, and horizontal. These flows were examined, and means for improving their effectiveness were considered. Additionally, the grapevine or informal flow of communication was seen as a means of supplementing the communication needs of individuals and groups within an organization.

For organizations that are unionized, the role of the union in communication is important. The extent of union participation in organizational communication was seen to depend on the quality of the relationship that exists between the union and management.

Laboratory studies of the influence of communication channels or networks on performance and satisfaction were shown to have implications for the structuring of work groups. However, generalizations of the findings from such controlled studies to real organizations must be at best suggestive.

Finally, we looked at communication between superior and subordinate. This communication is affected by the organization's system of management and the superior's approach to leadership. We concluded by examining the importance of trust in the superior–subordinate relationship and its development.

QUESTIONS FOR STUDY AND DISCUSSION

1. What are the steps in the communication process? Can you give an example of those steps from your own experience?

2. What would you suggest for eliminating each barrier to communication?

3. What does the statement "meaning is in the mind of the listener" mean to you?

4. Why is feedback important in communication? How do you obtain feedback?

5. Why does the downward flow of communication tend to dominate communication flows?

6. What are the "minimal communication needs" of a subordinate?

7. Of the methods given to improve upward communication, which two appeal to you the most? Why?

8. As a manager, would you use the grapevine for communication? Why? Would you use the union? Why?

9. How does an organization's system of management affect superior–subordinate communication? The superior's approach to leadership?

10. What is the basis for trust between two people? How can a supervisor develop a trusting relationship with a subordinate?

NOTES

[1]Sartain, Aaron Q., and Alton W. Baker, *The Supervisor and His Job* (New York: McGraw-Hill, 1965), pp. 302–308.

[2]Sayles, Leonard R., and George Strauss, *Human Behavior in Organizations* (Englewood Cliffs, N.J.: Prentice-Hall, 1966), pp. 238–246.

[3]*Ibid.,* pp. 246–258.

[4]Gray, Jerry L., and Fredrick A. Starke, *Organizational Behavior* (Columbus, Ohio: Charles E. Merrill, 1977), p. 181.

[5]Davis, K., "Success of Chain-of-Command Oral Communication in a Manufacturing Group," *Academy of Management Journal,* 11 (December, 1968), pp. 379–387.

[6]Likert, Rensis, *New Patterns of Management* (New York: McGraw-Hill, 1961), p. 52.

[7]Wexley, Kenneth N., and Gary A. Yukl, *Organizational Behavior and Personnel Psychology* (Homewood, Ill.: Irwin, 1977), p. 70.

[8]Harriman, Bruce, "Up and Down The Communications Ladder," *Harvard Business Review,* 52 (Sept.-Oct., 1974), pp. 143–151.

[9]Vogel, A., "Why Don't Employees Speak Up?" *Personnel Administration,* 30 (May-June, 1967), pp. 20–22.

[10]Wexley and Yukl, *op. cit.,* p. 67.

[11]Fenn, Dan H., and Daniel Yankelovich, "Responding to the Employee Voice," *Harvard Business Review,* 50 (May-June 1972), pp. 83–91.

[12]Harriman, *op. cit.,* pp. 147–149.

[13]Wexley and Yukl, *op. cit.,* p. 68.

[14]Galbraith, Jay, *Designing Complex Organizations* (Reading, Mass.: Addison-Wesley, 1973), pp. 110–111.

[15]Davis, Keith, "Management Communication and the Grapevine," *Harvard Business Review,* 31 (Sept.-Oct., 1953), pp. 43–49.

[16]Sutton, H., and L. W. Porter, "A Study of the Grapevine in a Governmental Organization," *Personnel Psychology,* 21 (1968), pp. 223–230. Also see Roberts, Karlene H. and Charles A. O'Reilly, III, "Some Correlations of Communication Roles in Organizations," *Academy of Management Journal,* 22 (March 1979), pp. 42–57.

[17]Fenn and Yankelovich, *op. cit.,* p. 90.

[18]Guetzkow, H., and H. R. Simon, "The Impact of Certain Communication Nets Upon Organization and Performance in Task Oriented Groups," *Management Science,* 1 (April-July 1, 1955), pp. 233–250.

[19]Burgess, Robert L., "Communication Networks: An Experimental Reevaluation," *Journal of Experimental Social Psychology,* 5 (July, 1968), p. 235.

[20]Nadler, David, A., J. Richard Hackman, and Edward E. Lawler III, *Managing Organizational Behavior* (Boston: Little, Brown, 1979), pp. 191–192.

[21]Likert, *op. cit.,* 225–227.

[22]Barnard, C. I., *The Functions of the Executive* (Cambridge, Mass.: Harvard University Press, 1938), pp. 165–166.

[23]Read, William H., "Upward Communications in Industrial Hierarchies," *Human Relations,* 15 (1962), pp. 3–16. Also see Roberts, Karlene H. and Charles A. O'Reilly, III, "Failures in Upward Communication in Organizations: Three Possible Culprits," *Academy of Management Journal,* 17 (June 1974), pp. 205–215.

[24]Cohen, A. R., S. L. Fink, H. Gadon, and R. D. Willits, *Effective Behavior in Organizations* (Homewood, Ill.: Irwin, 1976), pp. 177–178.

[25]Rogers, Carl R., and F. J. Roethlisberger, "Barriers and Gateways to Communications," *Harvard Business Review,* 30 (July–August, 1952), pp. 46–50.

[26]Sayles and Strauss, *op. cit.,* pp. 265–271.

cases cases cases

Case Study: Silent Communication

The researcher had been invited to take a look at the plant by its manager, Mr. A. C. Utsey, who was concerned about the effectiveness of his staff. His head foreman, Harvey Mills, had reported that some of the staff members were giving him the "cold shoulder" lately. Mr. Utsey wanted to find out why.

Mr. Utsey had been plant manager since the construction of the facility and previously had served as head foreman and assistant plant manager at another firm. He appeared to be self-assured, confident, and knowledgeable of all plant operations. Mr. Utsey went to his cabinet and pointed to several leather-bound loose-leaf notebooks. "In here you will find every position in the company and a detailed job description." Here is a partial organizational chart of the firm.

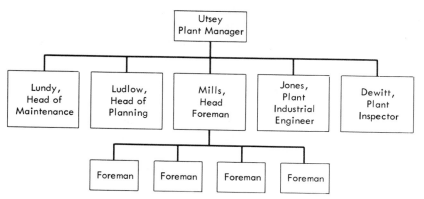

Researcher: What is your opinion of your staff?

Utsey (plant manager): Let me give you a rundown. Mills is the best head fore-man I have known. My job is to have him ready to assume my job when I get promoted. Dewitt has little experience. He has possibilities, but he needs developing. He needs to stand up on his own feet against Harvey Mills. A balance needs to be here. Ludlow is the best planning man in the plant. No one can doubt that with the job he has done. Jones is good. He is up for a promotion right now. I have discussed this with Mills since his replacement could very well be Mills's industrial engineer in a short time. Lundy is still developing. He will be outstanding one day, but he has to be brought along.

I make the decisions. However, once the decision is made, each department head is allowed to work to the end result by the method he feels is best. If I feel that he is wrong, I let him proceed anyway as long as the consequences are not too severe.

I need to know everything that happens within this plant. For this reason I have an excellent flow of information from the ground up. As long as a worker performs satisfactorily, he or she does not have to worry about his or her job. We have an excellent history of job security.

Researcher and Harvey Mills, Head Foreman

Harvey Mills: I am responsible for the manufacturing operations within the plant. My operating reports reflect the performance of my departments. The majority of costs incurred at this plant are in production. This is only logical due to the number of people and the amount of machinery within the departments. We employ approximately 180 people of whom 140 are in my departments.

I let a foreman run his shift as much as possible. The guidelines are set for him and he must work within them. I find it necessary to chew the foremen out every so often, either individually or as a group.

The other staff members and I work together to run the plant as efficiently and effectively as possible. As a rule, the other operations fluctuate around production since this is the most important function in the plant.

The researcher observed that a staff meeting was held each day at 9:00 A.M. in Mr. Utsey's office. Normally, all the staff members would leave except for Mills who would stay and talk with Utsey for thirty minutes or more. It became a joke among the other four staff members who called it "the real staff meeting." With the exception of Ludlow, Lundy, Dewitt, and Jones would gather in Jones's office for "their" staff meeting. Such sessions concluded in criticisms of Utsey and Mills. The researcher was present on several occasions and noted some of their comments.

"If there are to be 'fringe' benefits like leaving early, coming in late, going out to eat, having your grass cut, or your house wired, they ought to be available to all of us."

"Why does he say that my foremen only work three hours a day?"

Ludlow never took part in these meetings. He was invited to but declined. The researcher decided to make a few inquiries about such meetings.

Researcher and Dewitt, Plant Inspector

Researcher: Why do you have those extra staff meetings?

Dewitt: I feel stiffled. I can't seem to gain an advantage. For example, if scrap goes up, my people are scrapping good items. If scrap comes down, Mills is doing a good job. No one has ever gone up from my position, only sideways. The only change outside quality control is a lateral move to head foreman.

Researcher and Jones, Plant Industrial Engineer

Researcher: Why do you have those meetings in your office?

Jones: I have them as a form of protest for not knowing what's going on. Information in this plant is passed up not down.

Researcher: What do you mean?

Jones: As an example, I found out that I'm up for a promotion. Utsey hasn't said word one to me about it. I think he and Mills are in there talking about me.

Researcher and Ludlow, Head of Planning

Researcher: Why don't you attend the meetings in Jones's office?

Ludlow: I have too many problems in my department and don't have the time. Maybe I worry too much, but, if I mess up, this whole plant could be shut down.

Researcher: Where do you go from here?

Ludlow: Nowhere! This is as far as I go.

Researcher and Lundy, Head of Maintenance

Researcher: You never have a lot to say in Jones's office. Why?

Lundy: What's the point. All that hot air isn't going to solve anything.

Researcher: Solve what?

Lundy: The lack of recognition for doing a good job. If Mills didn't do it, then it isn't very good.

QUESTIONS

1. The plant manager feels that he has an excellent flow of information "from the ground up." Do you agree? Why?

2. Prepare a report for the plant manager consisting of a problem statement and corrective courses of action.

3. Evaluate the plant manager's leadership: his strengths, his weaknesses, his effectiveness.

cases cases cases

Case Study: Doers and Talkers

In 1973 the plant began to feel the economic pinch that seemed to be sweeping the country. Production layoffs followed within a very short time period, and the plant was running at approximately 45 percent of capacity. The plant, formally very resistant to unions, had another union make a bid for entry and obtained a majority vote.

There was a reduction of management personnel, and department heads and important salaried personnel voluntarily left for other jobs. The corporation filled these vacancies quickly with fairly competent people who went to work immediately trying to regroup their departments. Within two years, orders increased steadily, the various departments had settled down into a team, and the plant was well on its way to regaining its "most efficient" status. One exception to the return to normalcy was Maintenance and Plant Engineering. The change was so drastic that department heads and other plant personnel were often confused as to how to initiate projects for their departments.

The researcher was given permission to make a study of the Plant Engineering and Maintenance Department and then referred to Dick Cromer, the plant engineer who headed this department.

Cromer: The plant manager tells me that you want to make an in-depth study of my department.

Researcher: That's correct. I would like to study the operation and talk with some of your people.

Cromer: I can show you the operational procedures, let you talk to engineers, supervisors, or whomever else you wish to talk to. I can show you the theoretical chain of command (see the organizational chart), but I'll tell you right now that I don't believe in a formal chain of command, especially for this plant. I have some "doers" and some "talkers" in my department, and I try to give my "doers" room in which to operate regardless of their theoretical relationship to the "talkers."

Researcher: What do you mean by "talkers"? Have you tried to make them "doers"?

Cromer: My "talkers" are mainly guys who have worked their way up through the ranks, who were pushed up principally due to seniority, and who will never be able to rise any farther than they are now. They do their job sufficiently well to keep from being fired, but they don't have the drive or ambition that some of my other subordinates have.

Researcher: I understand that you have only been in the plant a little over a year. What do you think of it?

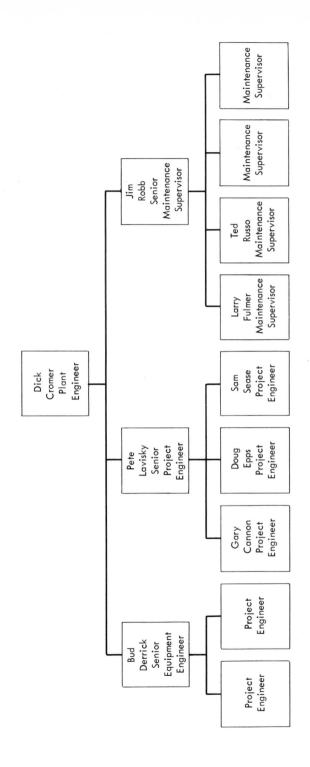

Cromer: To be honest with you, my past experience with the corporation has been in other divisions. I had never seen this kind of operation before I walked into this office, and I have been spending most of my time learning. From what I can see, this plant has a lot of potential, and I consider myself very fortunate to have a department that operates so smoothly.

Dick Cromer then introduced the researcher to Pete Lavisky, the senior project engineer. After a brief conversation, Cromer returned to his office.

Researcher: What is your job as senior project engineer? I see by the organizational chart that you have three other engineers under you.
Lavisky: As senior project engineer, I am supposed to coordinate all the projects and assign them to one of the three people that you mentioned. I must admit that I have been having a little trouble getting these three to work through me.
Researcher: In what way do they give you trouble?
Lavisky: They get projects straight from the department heads; then, after briefly discussing the project with Cromer, they light into them. Cromer is principally the cause of this, because in his attempt to develop these guys, he lets the formal structure slide. It is almost to the point where these three by-pass Cromer as well. Now don't get me wrong, these three are very good workers, but sometimes I get the feeling that they are waving their degrees at me.
Researcher: Do they openly defy you?
Lavisky: No, they just seem to ignore my position. All I know is that if Tom Whitehall was still here, he would never have allowed this to happen.
Researcher: Who is Tom Whitehall?
Lavisky: Tom was the plant engineer before Cromer. He left the plant about two years ago and took a fairly important job with another firm. This plant really suffered when he left.
Researcher: In what way did it suffer?
Lavisky: Tom was a smart engineer and he really ran this plant with an iron hand. He would lay out how every project was to be handled and you had better not change it without asking for his O.K. He would tour the plant several times daily and you never knew when he was going to show up. If he found a project not going according to his directions or found some of the maintenance mechanics having a bull session, you could bet your bottom dollar that someone was going to be raked over the coals. He may have been a little hot tempered, but he really kept things in line.
Researcher: Does Cromer check up on projects to any degree?
Lavisky: Cromer seldom goes into the production areas. This is one of the main reasons that the maintenance crews have gotten so slack.

Pete Lavisky then introduced the researcher to Gary Cannon, one of his young project engineers, and returned to his office.

Cannon: I understand you are doing an indepth study of our department; all I can say is that we need it.
Researcher: Why do you say that?
Cannon: Well, I've only been here approximately two years, but, in that length of time, even I can see that things need changing.

Researcher: What do you think needs changing?

Cannon: Mainly getting the incompetent people out of the way; not necessarily fire them because they have served the company for a long time, but move them to one side to improve the efficiency of the operation.

Researcher: Who do you think is incompetent?

Cannon: Take Pete Lavisky for an example. He is an excellent electrical engineer, and he has a good personality, but he is terrible as a senior project engineer. He does not like to make decisions. Often, I have a difficult time getting a straight answer to my questions concerning a project. Now that I think about it, he has never come right out and said that he didn't know the answer; he always gives you this "mumbo-jumbo" and you can't figure out what he said.

Researcher: Who else do you feel is incompetent?

Cannon: I think that most of the maintenance foremen are suffering from the same thing as Lavisky. They are very indecisive and don't know how to control their men. It has gotten to the point where the maintenance crews pull a slowdown during the day to get overtime at night. Project work and odds and ends used to be done by construction, but the maintenance crew complained so much about the poor quality of the work and the higher pay of the construction workers that the plant engineer began letting maintenance do the project work, mostly on overtime. Personally, I could never see any poor-quality work, and the higher pay for construction is reasonable for seasonal work.

Researcher: Do you think that having a union has helped bring about this difference in the maintenance crews?

Cannon: The three-year contract that we got is a fairly weak one. In fact it was so weak that the workers got mad enough to threaten to kick out the union. To answer your question, I don't think the union has influenced much of anything yet, but I do feel that, since they have their foot in the door, we might be hurting on the next contract in two years.

The researcher was then introduced to Doug Epps, another project engineer under Pete Lavisky.

Researcher: Doug, what do you think of the organizational structure of your department?

Epps: Theoretically it's fine, but somehow it seems to break down.

Researcher: How does it break down?

Epps: First, I get jobs from all directions. I get a job from anyone who wants to write a letter to Dick Cromer or myself with no priorities at all. It is left up to the project engineer to set his or her own job priorities.

Second, when I have a job going, I have to ride herd on the assigned maintenance crews to get it done. If I turn my back on them for a second, half the crew disappears. I don't think that it is my job to do this, but that is the only way that I can get the job done.

Researcher: How would you go about improving the situation?

Epps: I don't have any idea; I only know that, if things keep up like this, this plant is going to be in a lot of trouble.

The researcher next went to the office of Jim Robb, senior maintenance supervisor, who was in the process of working out the next week's maintenance schedule with his four maintenance foremen. The researcher was invited to sit in on the remainder of the meeting that went as follows.

Larry Fulmer: I need to put that cleaning of the number 3 combustion blower back on the schedule for next week.

Robb: I thought your mechanics were supposed to do that last week?

Fulmer: They were, but Sam Sease (another project engineer) pulled them off that job to fix an emergency, and I didn't even find out about it until several days later.

Fred Russo: I had similar trouble with Doug Epps' taking my electricians off to fix something and not saying a word about it.

The other two maintenance supervisors voiced the same complaint.

Robb: I'll say something to Dick Cromer about it again. Any other business? Meeting adjourned. Now, what can I tell you that you don't already know?

Researcher: I noticed that you said you would talk to Dick Cromer about this again. Have you said something about it before?

Robb: Yes I have, but all Cromer says is that the project engineers would not have to get the crews if the foremen were kept informed and knew when an emergency came up.

Researcher: How do you handle a project for these project engineers?

Robb: Essentially, we just turn over a crew, or whatever they say is needed, and don't look for the crew back until the job is done. Sometimes I wonder who is really running maintenance. Did you know that Cromer has given project engineers the authority to grant overtime? It used to be the general policy that only plant engineers could authorize overtime.

QUESTIONS

1. Evaluate the communication system of this organization.
2. Make an appraisal of Dick Cromer's comments on the chain of command. Do you agree? Why?
3. How is leadership related to problems seen in this case?
4. What recommendations would you make to the plant manager?

CHAPTER 12

CHANGE ANd iTS MANAGEMENT

LEARNING OBJECTIVES

When you have finished this chapter you should be able to:

- *Describe four ways organizations cope with changes in their environment.*
- *Give four basic factors that may be altered to modify the work environment of an organization.*
- *Outline and explain a model for analyzing change.*
- *List and describe the three phases in implementing a change.*
- *Understand why change is resisted and how to cope with such resistance.*
- *Outline and explain a model for behavior modification.*

The concept of change has been interjected into several of the previous chapters, but now we must examine the management of change more closely. If an organization is to survive, it must cope effectively and efficiently with change. In this chapter we will examine how organizations adapt to environmental complexities. Relating appropriately to the environment may require changes in the structure of the organization and the management system itself. After exploring adjustments to external factors, we consider individuals' adaptations to change. Whether change is externally or internally induced, people are invariably involved. Consequently, we investigate a general framework for diagnosing change, whatever its source or nature, providing a change model to guide remedial action. Then, we undertake an examination of the nature of change and the resistance frequently generated followed by a consideration of several common approaches to coping with change. Finally, we look at change by behavior modification as one of the more recent approaches to change management.

ENVIRONMENTAL CHANGE AND ORGANIZATIONAL ADAPTATION

Any organization, be it profit or nonprofit, is confronted with a varied and changing environment. The environment is not only economic but also political, social, legal and technological as well. Equally important, the environment is the source an organization's inputs—labor, materials, and so on—and also the recipient of its output(s). Faced with such dynamic complexities, one certainty of any organization is that there will be change. The amount of change will vary from organization to organization because each is confronted with a somewhat different environment. Obviously, an organization faced with an environment characterized as having little diversity and dynamics can design strategies, operations, and tactics to cope effectively with such conditions. Organizations enmeshed in a highly diversified and highly dynamic setting are faced with divergent and rapid changes that make planning complex and adjustments difficult.

Adaptation: Structural Adjustment

Lawrence and Lorsch[1] present evidence that an organizational structure must be properly adjusted to the environment if high production and performance is to be achieved. Organizations from three different industries —plastics, packaged foods, and standardized containers—were examined. The plastics industry operated in a rapidly changing, highly turbulent environment in which both the technology and the demands of customers were unpredictable. On the other hand, firms in the standardized container industry were in a highly stable environment. The packaged foods industry was confronted with an environment between these two extremes. The environment reflected three components: (1) the rate of change in environmental conditions, (2) the certainty of information at a given time about environmental conditions, and (3) the time required for definite feedback.

Two primary aspects of organizational structure—differentiation and integration—were examined. Differentiation is the division of the organization into subsystems, each of which develops particular attributes in responding to the requirements posed by its relevant external environment. The research, sales, and production divisions in these organizations were found to differ not only in structure but also in the terms of their members' orientations to interpersonal relationships, time, and goals. However, differentiation requires the integration of these subsystems to achieve unity of effort and the accomplishment of the organization's goals.

The researchers expected that the more turbulent environment would be associated with a greater degree of differentiation among the organization's subparts and also a correspondingly high degree of integrative effort. Likewise, an organization faced with a stable environment would have less differentiated subsystems and require fewer integrative procedures. The success of an organization would depend upon an appropriate amount of differentiation to cope with its environment and also the right amount of integrative or coordinating effort.

Lawrence and Lorsch tested the proposition that the fit between structure (differentiation and integration) and environment determined the performance of the organization. The plastic, packaged foods, and standardized containers organizations were separated into high performers, medium performers, and low performers. In each case the high-performing organizations were those that had a structure that best fitted the environmental demands. For example, in the plastics industry, faced with a turbulent environment, the high-performing organizations had the greatest differentiation and integration. In the standardized container industry, faced with a stable environment, the highest-performing organizations had the least differentiation and consequently the least need for integration.

Adaptation: Management Systems

Many changes within an organization are externally induced, and internal adjustments must be made by the management system. The thrust of twenty studies analyzed by Burns and Stalker is that the management system of an organization is related to the rate of environmental change.[2]

> If the form of management is properly to be seen as dependent on the situation the concern is trying to meet, it follows that there is no single set of principles for "good organization," an ideal type of management system which can serve as a model to which administrative practice should, or could in time, approximate. It follows also that there is an overriding management task in first interpreting correctly the market and technological situation, in terms of its instability or of the rate at which conditions are changing, and then designing the management system appropriate to the conditions, then making it work.

The appropriate management system for an organization is contingent upon its environment.

According to Burns and Stalker, a *mechanistic* management system is appropriate for stable conditions. An *organismic* management system is appropriate to changing conditions that give rise constantly to fresh problems and unforeseen requirements that cannot be handled by personnel in their usual job role. The characteristics of each management system is shown in Table 12-1.

Table 12-1

A Comparison of Mechanistic and Organismic Systems

Mechanistic Systems	Organismic Systems
1. Specialized, limited tasks	1. Continual adjustment of tasks through interaction with others
2. Subordinates pursue individual tasks with concern for narrow task completion	2. Generalized responsibility
3. Rigid chain of command	3. Commitment to organization as a whole
4. Interaction follows vertical lines along chain of command	4. Interaction laterally as well as vertically
5. Detailed and exhaustive job descriptions	5. Communication of advice and information rather than orders
6. Behavior is governed by superiors	6. Sanctions derived from peers and superiors with concern for the the whole organization
7. Emphasis is on narrow, specific knowledge rather than general, complete knowledge	7. A network structure of control, authority, and communication

Source: Adapted from William G. Ouchi and Reuben T. Harris, "Structure, Technology, and Environment," in George Strauss et al., eds., *Organization Behavior* (Madison: Industrial Relations Research Association, University of Wisconsin, 1972), 132.

The two forms of management systems represent opposite extremes, but intermediate stages between these two systems exist. An organization that oscillates between stability and relative change may shift between the two forms. Additionally, an organization can operate with a management system that includes both types to cope effectively with the environment. Each system should be appropriate to its own specific set of conditions.

The concept of organic and mechanistic systems suggests that organizations with highly predictable tasks (stable environments) will perform better by using highly formalized procedures. With highly uncertain tasks (unstable environments) that require more extensive problem solving, organizations that are less formalized, emphasize self-control, and member participation in decision making are more effective.

A study of four organizational units confirms these conclusions.[3] Two of the organizational units performed the relatively certain task of manufacturing standardized containers on high-speed, automated production lines. The other two were involved in the relatively uncertain work of research and development in communications technology. Each pair of units was in the same company and contained one highly effective unit and a less effective unit as determined by their company's management.

The objective of the study was to test the "fit" of the organization's characteristics and the job to be done. To make such a test, organizational characteristics were grouped into two sets of factors: (1) formal characteristics and (2) climate characteristics or subjective perceptions that individuals had about their work environment. These attributes were measured through questionnaries and interviews with about forty managers in each unit.

The principal findings of the study are best highlighted by contrasting the two successful organizational units. Table 12-2 illustrates some of the differences between these two units—Akron and Stockton.

Table 12-2

Differences in High-Performing Units

	Akron (task certain)	Stockton (task uncertain)
Formal characteristics		
Formal relationship (charts and job manuals)	Highly structured, precisely defined	Low degree of structure, less well defined
Pattern of formal procedures and control systems	Pervasive, specific, uniform, comprehensive	Minimal, loose, flexible
Climate characteristics		
Structural orientation	Tightly controlled behavior, high degree of structure perceived	Low degree of structure perceived
Distribution of influence	Perception of low total influence concentrated at upper levels	Perception of high total influence more evenly spread among all levels
Superior–subordinate relationship	Low freedom, directive type	High freedom, participatory type

The Akron unit involved in a certain task reflected many of the characteristics of a mechanistic system, that is, highly structured relationships, highly specific rules and procedures, and directive supervision, yet it was highly effective. Akron's highly structured formal practices fit its predictable tasks because behavior had to be rigidly defined and controlled around the automated, high-speed production line. Managers defined the job precisely and insisted that each person do what was expected. On the other hand, Stockton's highly unstructured formal practices made sense for the opposite reasons.

Adaptation: The Adaptive Subsystem

In addition to management systems' responding to environmental conditions, another organizational system has as its mission to cope with change and make recommendations for change to management. This is the adaptive subsystem, which is one of five subsystems in an organization.[4] These five basic subsystems are

1. production subsystems concerned with the work that gets done,
2. supportive subsystems of procurements, disposal, and institutional relations,
3. maintenance subsystems for tying people to their functional roles,
4. adaptive subsystems concerned with organizational change, and
5. managerial systems for the direction, adjudication, and control of the many subsystems and activities of the structure.

Of particular interest to us are the adaptive structures that develop in organizations to generate appropriate responses to external conditions. External changes in consumer taste, cultural norms and values, competitive organizations, and economic and political power, for example, reach the organization as demands for internal change. Failure to respond to such changes impairs the effectiveness and efficiency of the other subsystems. In most formal organizations, structures arise that are specifically concerned with sensing relevant changes in the outside world and translating the meaning of such changes for the organization. Structures that devote their energies wholly to the anticipation of change comprise the adaptive subsystem and bear such names as product research, market research, long-range planning, and research and development.

As one might expect, the role and structure of the adaptive subsystem in mechanistic and organismic organizations will differ.[5] For the mechanistic, hierarchical organization under stable environmental conditions, the adaptive subsystem will have a fairly simple structure. Information is usually plentiful and easily gathered. Experience dictates which parts of the environment to monitor, and fairly standard methods of adapting to change are developed. A high degree of environmental stability offers the mechanistic firm the opportunity to make long-range plans and capital commitments. On the other hand, for the organic organization facing a changing, often turbulent, environment, the adaptive subsystem has a complex task. The unpredictability of the timing, magnitude, and direction of environmental change makes monitoring and interpretation of the environment extremely difficult. Decisions about what goals and services to add, decrease, or completely drop and how much of each to maintain under varying sets of circumstances can become frustrating. The adaptability and flexibility of the organic organization, however, increases the probability of effectively coping with such change problems.

Adaptation: Protection of Core Technology

In addition to utilizing adaptive subsystems, organizations also strive to cope with change by sheltering their core technologies from environmental influences. Technology is the means whereby inputs are subjected to people and/or machine processes and subsequently become outputs for the organization. Three technologies have been identified as widespread in modern society.[6]

1. Long-linked technology: This technology involves serial interdependence in that activity Z can be performed only after the successful completion of activity Y, which in turn depends on activity X, and so on. The mass production assembly line is an example of the long-linked form of technology.
2. Mediating technology: The primary activity here is the linking of clients and customers who are or wish to be interdependent. The commercial bank links depositors and borrowers; the employment agency mediates the supply of labor and the demand for labor.
3. Intensive technology: This technology draws upon a variety of techniques to change some input or object. However, the selection, combination, and order of application of such techniques are determined by the needs or requirements of the individual case or project. For example the general hospital provides X-ray, laboratory, medical and pharmaceutical services but which services will be utilized and when is dependent on the patient's condition. In the construction industry the crafts required and the order in which they can be utilized depend on what is being constructed.

Whatever the nature of an organization's technology, it must be geared to input and output activities. The inputs must be of the appropriate kind and amount and available on time; the output must be disposed of in an orderly fashion. Not only are input, technological, and output activities interdependent, but both input and output activities are intertwined with environmental forces. Such forces can disrupt the required balance between these activities and affect effectiveness and efficiency. To prevent or minimize this possibility, organizations seek to protect their core technology from disruptive external influences.

Protection of the core technology is achieved by several methods.[7] Organizations seek to *buffer* environmental changes in both the input and output side of its operations. The objective is to have inputs flowing continuously, at a steady rate, and with specified quantity while the market absorbs the output in a continuous manner. A classic problem is how to maintain output inventories sufficient to meet all needs without incurring obsolescence as needs change. Buffering on the input side may be achieved by stockpiling materials acquired in an irregular market and their steady utilization in the production process. Buffering on the output side of long-linked technologies is often achieved by maintaining warehouse or distributor inventories. This permits the technical core to produce at a constant, efficient rate and distribution to fluctuate with changing market conditions.

While buffering absorbs environmental fluctuations, *smoothing* or *leveling* protects the technical core by reducing fluctuations in the environment. For example, electric, gas, water, and telephone utilities may offer inducements to customers who use their services during slack periods or charge premium rates to those who utilize services during periods of peak consumption. Retail organizations seek to cope with demand fluctuations by offering inducements in the form of special sales in slow periods.

When environmental changes cannot be buffered or smoothed, organizations seek to *anticipate and adapt* to such changes. A manufacturing firm can forecast demand for a specific time period and subsequently schedule the operation of its technical core at a steady rate. Production schedules for the next period may be modified on the basis of new forecasts. Most banks learn that local conditions and customs result in peak loads at predictable times during the day and week, and they schedule their operations to meet such shifts in demand.

Buffering, leveling, and adaptation to anticipated fluctuations are widely used devices for preventing interference with orderly, efficient operation, but there are occasions when these devices are not sufficient to ward off environmental disturbances. When this occurs, an organization may resort to *rationing*. Hospitals may ration beds to physicians by establishing priority systems for nonemergency admission. Manufacturers of popular items may ration allotments to wholesalers or dealers. The post office may assign priority to first-class mail and attend to lower classes only when the priority task is completed. While rationing is seldom the best solution, some system of priorities for the allocation of capacity is essential if a technology is to be effective.

The approaches to managing input and output activities for protecting an organization's technological core from environmental changes are summarized in Figure 12-1. Note that the potential results of protecting the technological core are better customer service, stable operations, and enhanced efficiency. Depending on the nature of the organization, other favorable results may be experienced. For example, electric utilities may be able to meet customer demand with less capital formation, plants, and generators.

Figure 12-1

Coping with Environmental Changes to Protect the Technological Core

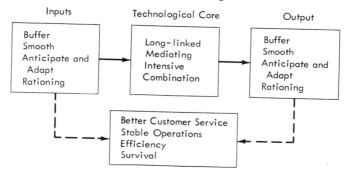

CHANGE AND INDIVIDUAL ADAPTATION

We have just examined some very broad responses that organizations make to a changing environment. Since the environment for most firms has become increasingly turbulent, organizational change is largely externally induced. To remain efficient and survive, there must be an appropriate adjustment. Whatever the nature of an organization's response, "it is people who must design, accept, and implement changes that are required to keep an organization in a healthy state."[8] Organizational adaptability is a function of its ability to learn and cope effectively with change, but in the final analysis it is the employees at all levels who must do this. Change will ultimately involve individuals, groups, intergroup interactions, and the total organization.

The Nature of Change

Work change refers to any modification of the work environment. However, to appreciate the complexity of change, we need to consider more closely what is included in the work environment. Actually, four factors are involved: task, people, technology, and structure.[9] Furthermore, as a system these factors are interrelated and interdependent; that is, a change in one produces alterations in one or more of the other work environment factors. Figure 12-2 depicts these four factors and their interdependent nature.

Figure 12-2

Factors in Organization Change

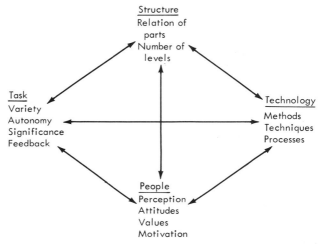

Source: Adapted from Fig. 1, p. 1145, Leavitt, H. J., "Applied Organizational Change in Industry: Structural, Technological and Humanistic Approaches", in J. G. March (ed), HANDBOOK OF ORGANIZATIONS, Copyright ©1965 by Rand McNally College Publishing Company.

Task refers to the job, which can vary in several ways or dimensions such as in variety, autonomy, task identity, feedback, and significance. *People* includes individuals who perform or fill various jobs within the organization. As we noted in Chapter 2, individuals vary in their attitudes, motivations, and values, which influence their perception and evaluation of change. This can complicate the implementation of change. *Technology* includes those methods, techniques, and processes that collectively convert inputs of the organization to its outputs. Finally, the structure embraces the job responsibilities and relationships of organizational members. *Structure* is reflected in the number of hierarchial levels, span of control (number of persons supervised), and the way in which parts are organized and related to one another. Communication, decision, and power systems are significantly influenced by such structural arrangements.

Organizational changes can be introduced through the alteration of any one of these four variables or a combination of these factors. One of the pitfalls of organizational change is focusing upon one of the change factors and failing to gauge its impact upon other factors, as they are all related. For example, the history of job design is filled with difficulties and other failures because the job was the primary or exclusive concern. The people factor and resulting social system have been ignored or inadequately appreciated in planning for change. Also, as we saw in Chapter 5, job redesign may affect not only the job and job incumbents but also influence technological and structural factors.

The results of change, as with many other phenomena, can vary considerably. Some changes are not resisted and may even be desired by employees. Other changes are trivial and routine and evoke little or no resistance. Lawrence and Lorsch have noted that change may call for slight or major behavioral change. Figure 12-3 shows some of the implications of different kinds of behavioral change.[10]

Figure 12-3

The Amount of Behavioral Change Required as the Target of Change Becomes More Complex

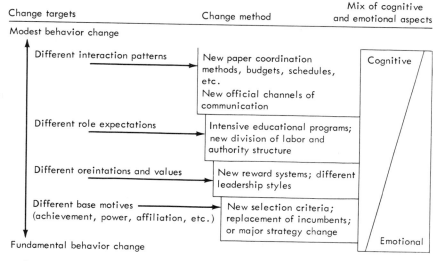

Source: Paul R. Lawrence and Jay W. Lorsch, *Developing Organizations: Diagnosis and Action,* ©1969, Addison-Wesley Publishing Co., Inc., Chapter 6, page 87, Figure 6. Reprinted with permission.

The amount of behavioral change, shown on the left, increases from slight to significant as one focuses on varied change targets, that is, interaction patterns, role expectations, values and orientations, and basic motives. The corresponding change methods suggest ways in which to modify the change target. Finally, the mix of cognitive and emotional aspects, shown on the right side of the figure, shifts from being primarily cognitive to being primarily emotional as the complexity of change increases. Change becomes more difficult to implement as the emotional aspects increase or predominate.

Framework for Analyzing Change Problem

Since the only certainty of organizational life is that there will be change, a conscious effort to shape such changes must be made by management. The deliberate planning of change has become a management responsibility in most organizations, and the management of change requires a systematic way for thinking about change. One of the most useful ways for conceptualizing change has been developed by Kurt Lewin who viewed activity or behavior as a dynamic balance of forces working in opposite directions.[11] In other words, the present condition of any system is a state of balance that is maintained by active driving forces and resisting forces. Resisting forces act to restrain, offset, or decrease the driving force. Equilibrium is reached when the sum of driving forces equals the sum of the restraining forces. For example, suppose that the production level of a work team fluctuates within small limits of around fifty units per day. Why? The driving forces tending to raise production are equal to the restraining forces tending to depress it.

The driving forces, restraining forces, and resulting equilibrium constitute a force field that may be depicted in diagram form once the various forces have been identified. For the work team whose output was fifty units, an analysis of the situation could be as shown in Figure 12-4.

Figure 12-4

Force-Field Diagram

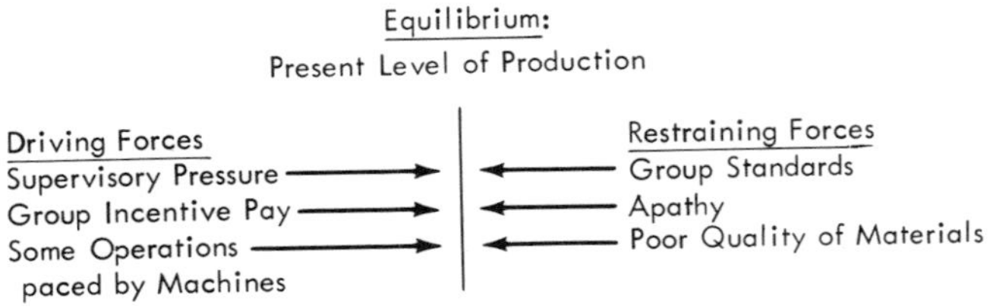

Equilibrium:
Present Level of Production

Driving Forces	Restraining Forces
Supervisory Pressure →	← Group Standards
Group Incentive Pay →	← Apathy
Some Operations → paced by Machines	← Poor Quality of Materials

The figure indicates the factors causing an equilibrium of fifty units of output. Supervisory pressure, group incentive pay, and some work operations whose speed is determined by the machines being utilized prevent production from falling much below fifty units. On the other hand, group output standards, apathy, and poor quality of materials restrain or prevent production from rising above fifty units. How may the situation be changed?

Since an equilibrium is involved, change will occur when there is an imbalance between the sum of the restraining forces and the sum of the driving forces. An imbalance may be achieved by (1) a change in the magnitude of any force, (2) a change in the direction of a force, that is, a restraining force may become a driving force, or vice versa, or (3) the addition of a new force.

An example of each strategy can be drawn from the force-field diagram of Figure 12-4. For example, supervisory pressure may be increased by even closer and more detailed supervision, which would increase the magnitude of the force. Apathy, a restraining force, may be countered by communicating the importance of the teams' output to the firm's overall efforts and its social significance. In this case, apathy may become a driving force because identification with the importance of the team's work will increase production. Finally, a new force, such as group participation or involvement to some degree in the decision-making process may be added.

Of the three means of creating an imbalance, changing the direction of a force from restraining to driving or from driving to restraining is extremely difficult in most situations. Consequently, most change strategies consist of increasing the driving forces, decreasing the restraining forces, or a combination of the two. In general, if *only* driving forces are utilized, there is a tendency to increase the tension level since restraining forces are not reduced. Higher tension levels create more instability and unpredictability and thereby enhance the likelihood of an irrational response to a change attempt. For example, in Figure 12-4, an increase in supervisory pressure with no effort to reduce any of the restraining forces might lead to sabotage of equipment, a walk out, or the team's seeking union membership.

A Change Model

Force-field analysis is a technique for diagnosing situations. Its proper use requires a careful and intensive analysis of variables creating any given level of activity. However, such a diagnostic effort is useful not only for examining the contributing factors involved but also for developing strategies for changing a given situation. Force-field analysis reveals factors that may become the focus for a planned change effort.

Kurt Lewin also conceptualized change as a process having three phases: unfreezing, moving, and refreezing.[12] In terms of the field-force diagram, change takes the form of unfreezing an existing equilibrium, moving toward a new equilibrium, and refreezing the newly achieved equilibrium. Planned change must manipulate situational forces to accomplish unfreezing, direct the movement in the desired direction, and maintain the new conditions so that the system does not regress to its previous level. How can these change processes be achieved?

Unfreezing

The purpose of unfreezing is to motivate and make the individual or group ready to change. The need for change must be seen, and this, of course, is no easy undertaking. Unfreezing occurs by means of disconfirmation, which is feedback that one's present behavior is ineffective or not as effective as it might be with reasonable effort, for example (1) objective measurements of physical production showing that one's intended level of production was not attained, (2) social comparison showing that one's performance is inferior to that of another comparable person, (3) information from important persons such as the superior, peers, or subordinates indicating subpar performance, and (4) criticism from important others emphasizing that one's behavior is seriously deficient compared with highly valued, ideal behavior.[13] These forms of feedback may produce feelings of shame or anxiety. Unfreezing is also facilitated by psychological support that leads one to feel that ineffectiveness is undesirable but can be remedied and that facing up to it is, in the long run, more useful and satisfying than is denying it. Psychological support provides assurance that change is possible and that one has the physical and mental resources to surmount the difficulties. Disconfirmation and psychological support increase readiness to accept new alternatives or change.

Moving or change

Once the individual or group has become more receptive or motivated to change, movement to a new level can begin. This is usually focused on the development of new values, new attitudes, and new behaviors. In essence, moving involves altering the magnitude, direction, or number of driving and resisting forces, thereby shifting the equilibrium to a new level. Many kinds of change occur by one of two mechanisms: identification and internalization. Identification occurs when models of behavior are provided from which an individual can learn new behavior patterns by identifying with them and trying to become like them. Internalization occurs when an individual is placed in a situation in which new behaviors are demanded to perform successfully and the individual modifies his or her behavior accordingly. In addition, change may be achieved by modifying the technology or structured tasks of the organization.

Refreezing

This is the process by which newly acquired behavior becomes permanent, thereby offsetting the regression toward the old pattern of behavior after the pressures toward change are relaxed. Numerous approaches facilitate refreezing. Confirmation that performance is effective aids in the stabilization process. It may come from task measurements, responses of others that verify a new level of effectiveness, social comparisons showing that performance has equaled or exceeded that of another comparable unit, or from one's own perceptions and interpretations. Confirmation may also involve rewards such as increased salary, bonuses, promotion, and greater responsibility.

Resistance to Change

No matter how efficient and organizationally sound the task or the technological or structural components of a change program, unless the people involved are considered, the change program will not materialize as intended. Management can plan and initiate change, but the employee controls the final decision to accept the change and is the one who actually makes the change. As agents of change, managers must appreciate why employees resist change and how their support may be obtained.

Resistance to change is distinguished by its protective function and describes the behavior that individuals or groups exhibit to protect themselves from either the real or the imagined effects of work change. Such resistance is found at the managerial levels as well as at the lower levels; it is just as evident in white-collar as it is in blue-collar workers. Whatever the level or type of employee, basic human needs are involved in the behaviors produced by change. Some of these need–fear linkages may be summarized as follows.[14]

1. Security

   Reduced wages and lower standard of living
   Demotion
   Unemployment
   Fear of the unknown
   Inability to perform adequately

2. Social

Breakup of the work group
New social adjustments
Isolation from friends
Fewer personal contacts with people
Reduced social status or standing

3. Self-esteem

Reduction of skills required
Difficulty and/or inability to relearn
Reduction in autonomy or increased controls
Greater specialization
Implication that present method is inadequate

Whether these evaluations of a situation by an employee are real or imaginary, they will influence his or her attitude and perception of impending change and also subsequent behavior. Such behavior may be either overt or covert. Overt resistance may take the form of employees' deliberately failing to do the things necessary for a successful change or simply being unenthusiastic about the change. The absence of overt resistance does not mean that resistance is not present, however, as resistance may be hidden from direct observation. Covert resistance can be more detrimental to change than open resistance because it is harder to identify and eliminate.

Common Approaches to Change

An appreciation of why employees resist change provides management with some invaluable insights into how change may be approached. As noted, security needs are aroused by fear of reduced wages, demotion, or perhaps even unemployment. Management has often sought to cope with such concerns by various *guarantees* to its employees. Such guarantees take the form of assuring employees that their earnings will not be reduced or that no one will lose his or her job because of the change. Although expensive, such guarantees are extremely useful in facilitating change. In some instances, management may be able to demonstrate that the change will actually improve the individual's economic prospects in the long run. The economic foundations of motivation are important and should not be underestimated in planning and implementing change.

Since fear of the unknown is a source of resistance to change, effective *two-way communication* is essential in the change process. Change cannot be implemented effectively by means of a one-way directive or a mimeographed instruction. Change information should explain what is to happen, why, and when. The principles of communication presented in Chapter 11 are especially relevant here. Opportunities for feedback should be provided to ensure that the information is understood. Doubts, fears, and misgivings should be vented and handled in a straightforward manner, as resistance is based upon emotions. Employees need to develop their own understanding of change, and free and open two-way communication is required to develop such insights.

Groups or work teams may also be involved in the change process. This can vary from providing management with inputs or ideas about an impending change to *group decision making* that involves employees in the process of planning and implementing the change. The extent to which employees are involved or excluded in change is largely a function of leadership. As one author has noted, there are three basic approaches to change that vary in the manner in which power is utilized.[15] At one extreme are unilateral approaches in which power is used to force change. For example, there is a "one-way" announcement from the manager that is passed on to those in lower positions. At the other extreme one finds delegated approaches that place almost complete authority for change in the group to be affected. Between these two extremes, power is shared; the manager allows employees to participate by influencing the change. For example, the group may select one of several alternatives advanced by their superior or simply influence the change by offering ideas or suggestions to their boss. By slightly altering Tannenbaum and Schmidt's continuum of leadership behavior discussed in Chapter 10 and also by applying the three alternative uses of power that we just examined, some appreciation of the varying degrees of group involvement in change can be achieved. The range of possibilities is shown in Table 12-3.

Table 12-3

Degrees of Group Involvement in Change and the Use of Power

Change	Approaches
Manager makes a change decision and announces it Manager "sells" a change decision Manager presents a change decision and invites questions	Unilateral
Manager presents a tentative change decision subject to change Manager presents a change problem, gets suggestions, and makes decision Manager presents change alternatives and the group selects one	Shared
Manager defines limits and asks group to make a change decision Manager permits subordinates to develop a change within limits defined by his or her superior	Delegated

As seen in the table, in the unilateral approaches the manager decides what changes are needed and how they will take place and then orders them to be made. While such approaches may be "sugar coated" by a sales pitch or improved by two-way communication, they are unilateral; influence by employees in the change decision is nonexistent. The shared approaches to change permit employees to exercise some influence on the change process. Their inputs can shape the change and provide some degree of control over their work environment. In the delegated approaches the group has almost complete authority for change. The group can identify change needs, make change decisions, and implement the changes.

An Experiment in Change Methods

When work methods are changed, employees are frequently dissatisfied, and their subsequent production reflects this. Believing that the problem of making changes in the work pattern was emotional rather than one of skill readjustment, Coch and French designed an experiment to test various methods for overcoming this emotional resistance.[16] In a garment factory, it was found that, when experienced female employees were transferred from one job to another, only 38 percent of them ever reached standard production again. This occurred despite the fact that the production standard on the new operation was based upon the same level of proficiency as on the old standard; 62 percent of the employees either became below-standard operators or quit during the learning period. Current employees who were transferred actually had much more difficulty with a given job than did new employees. In this setting, Coch and French put their plan for testing methods of change into effect when a modification was required in the method of inspecting, folding, and packing pajamas. The changes involved less than 10 percent of the total job, but this was sufficient to require the setting of new piece rates. Production records for four groups were maintained before and after the job change.

One group (thirteen employees) was handled autocratically. They were informed that the job had been changed and would have to be relearned, that bonus pay would be given during the relearning period, and that the new standard would be as easy to achieve as the old one. Results? Resistance emerged almost immediately in the form of aggression toward management, the methods engineer, and the supervisor and also in the form of filing grievances about the new piece rate. During the first forty days, 17 percent quit. Production took a sharp drop and never recovered.

Two other groups (seven and eight employees, respectively) were handled democratically. They were presented with the problem of the need to change the job layout to meet competition. Both groups participated in the planning of the change, including the new job layout, and worked with the time study expert as he studied the job and recorded movements. The discussions in both groups were lively and constructive. Results? There was no aggression and no one quit the job. Production recovered rapidly and reached a level that exceeded production in the previous job.

A fourth group was handled by a method part way between autocratic and democratic. All group members did not participate, but they were represented by two of their members. The two representatives participated with management in planning the change, and they discussed such developments with their group. Results? There was one act of aggression and no one quit. Production dropped sharply but recovered after two weeks and exceeded the production attained before the change was made.

The two groups handled democratically and the one group using employee representatives responded favorably to change. Output exceeded previous levels, and there was no turnover. In contrast, the autocratic management of change led to conflict, a high number of employee departures, and a level of production drastically below the prechange output level.

Organizational Change: How Durable?

Few efforts have been made to determine whether or not successfully planned changes survive as permanent features of the organization. Most change programs have been evaluated over a relatively short time span. One notable exception occurred in late 1961 when the Harwood Company purchased its major competitor, the Weldon Company.[17] Both companies made and marketed similar products, utilized similar equipment and manufacturing processes, had a similar volume of business and number of employees, and had histories of growth and a high reputation. Weldon, however, was losing money through high costs, high absenteeism, and high turnover. Harwood, the purchasing company, presented a sharp contrast to Weldon's performance.

Harwood had operated as a participative system with high value given to individual and organizational development as well as to effective performance. On the other hand, Weldon had managed with a highly centralized, authoritarian philosophy and with secondary concern for individual development and organizational maintenance. The two organizations were extreme examples on the continuum vaguely defined by the terms authoritarian versus participative. Quantitative assessments confirmed such differences.

The new owners embarked on a program to rebuild the Weldon enterprise according to the Harwood model. The ultimate aim was to make Weldon a viable and profitable firm in a short period of time. A strenuous and costly program of plant modernization, improved layout and flow of work, improved records and production control methods, product simplification, and changes in the human organization were undertaken. The change process incorporated the application of multiple and compatible change forces. The physical improvements in work resources and conditions were accompanied by appropriate information flows, enhanced motivation through rewards, and skill training.

At the end of 1964, after two years of change effort, there were improvements in employee satisfactions, motivations, and work performances. The organization had the characteristics of an adaptive, self-controlling, participative system. The firm moved from a position of loss to one of profit. The change program was successful, but would it last?

In 1969, four and a half years after termination of the program, follow-up measurements were made at Weldon. The earlier gains in satisfactions, attitudes, and optimism of the employees had been maintained or improved. There was also a rise in level of task orientation and production concern. Productivity itself could not be calculated, but it was estimated to have been stable. At the supervisory and managerial levels, the organization had progressed still further toward a participative organization system. Finally, the profitability of Weldon had made additional progress toward the organizational goals envisioned by the owners and managers in 1962.

Why did the change continue? No one knows for sure. So many factors were changed simultaneously that no one factor could be singled out as having produced such favorable results. However, the mutually reinforcing change actions of technical, structural, task, and people factors may have preserved the change characteristics and prevented regression.

CHANGE BY BEHAVIOR MODIFICATION

One of the most promising approaches to change for certain problems is behavior modification. Behavior modification is a practical procedure for shaping, improving, and motivating the behavior of organizational participants. The technique concentrates on a person's overt behavior rather than on the underlying causes of that behavior. Focusing on outward behavior allows the manager to realistically try to modify behavior. Managers need to have only the ability to observe and deal with overt behavior.

Behavior modification is derived from B. F. Skinner's theory of operant conditioning. An operant is learned behavior that operates on the environment to produce a consequence. Once such behavior appears, it may be effectively controlled or conditioned (strengthened, maintained, or eliminated) by the systematic management of the consequences of that behavior. If the consequences are pleasant, that behavior will tend to be repeated; if unpleasant, it will tend to disappear. There is a contingent relationship between the behavior and its environment, or an "if then" relationship. For example,[18]

> getting coffee from the office coffee machine is contingent upon inserting the proper coinage in the slot. *If* the proper coin is inserted, *then* coffee will come out. In this particular contingency we see an obvious behavior (putting in the coin) and an equally obvious consequence (coffee).

Antecedent environment conditions or cues also play an important role in contingencies. In the example the antecedent condition was the presence of a coffee machine. Basically, there are three major elements involved, which are frequently noted as A, B, and C. This is expanded and related to the coffee example in the following manner.

A (Antecedent Events) ⟶ B (Behavior) ⟶ C (Consequences)
Coffee Machine ⟶ Insert Coin ⟶ Obtain Coffee

Obviously, if one does not obtain coffee after a number of attempts, the behavior will cease. Behavior is a function of its consequences.

BEHAVIORAL CONTINGENCY MANAGEMENT

The overall approach to behavioral modification involves systematically identifying and contingently managing the critical performance-related behaviors of employees. The following steps may be used to structure and guide a problem-solving approach to behavioral change.[19] Look at Figure 12-5.

Step 1: Identifying the Behaviors

The behaviors that are to be changed must be carefully identified, selecting only those behaviors that have a significant impact on performance. Only observable and measurable behaviors are targeted for change.

Step 2: Measuring the Behaviors

The frequency of the behavior(s) identified in step 1 are recorded and then transferred to a chart. Such behavior is measured under existing conditions and is called the baseline period. Often, the frequency of behavior is plotted on the vertical axis of the chart, and time is recorded on the horizontal axis.

Step 3: Conducting a Functional Analysis

This step analyzes and attempts to identify the antecedent cues that precede the behavior and the consequences that follow and maintain the behavior. As we noted, this is shown as A (antecedent), B (behavior), and C (consequence). Understanding these relationships is necessary for developing a successful change strategy. However, A (antecedent event) does not cause the behavior; it only serves as the occasion for the behavior to occur. Although behavior is a function of its consequences, it can be influenced by antecedent events. An example of controlling antecedent events would be to enrich the job so that desirable employee behaviors would more likely occur.

Step 4: Developing an Intervention Strategy

Devising an intervention or change strategy consists of (1) considering environmental variables, (2) selecting and applying the appropriate strategy, (3) measuring the frequency of response after the change, and (4) maintaining the desirable behavior.

Environmental variables affecting intervention strategies must be considered if the program is to be successful. Decision making, communications, and control processes contribute to the success or failure of an intervention strategy. Technology may also facilitate or limit the applicability of certain change strategies. Finally, the impact on other members of the work group and also other work groups must be considered. Individually and collectively, these factors influence the outcome of the change strategy.

When selecting an intervention strategy, five basic options are available: positive reinforcement, negative reinforcement, punishment, extinction, or a combination of these strategies. *Positive reinforcement* consists of using some reward—money, attention, or feedback—to accelerate or increase the desired behavior. *Negative reinforcement* also increases performance—through withdrawal of some unpleasant condition; for example, one may work harder to get a nagging, pushing boss off his or her back. The use of *punishment* to decrease behavior is discouraged because of undesirable side effects; not only do people get upset but the behavior tends to be only temporarily suppressed. *Extinction* occurs when nothing happens to the person as a result of his behavior; for example, the door-to-door salesperson who repeatedly finds no one at home ceases to call. Extinction is used to eliminate behavior and involves simply ignoring the undesirable behavior; that is, the work environment is structured so there are no reinforcers to maintain the behavior.

Finally, after the strategy is selected and applied, there is continued measurement to ensure that the change is having the intended impact. This requires replotting the frequency of the behavioral response. By comparing this performance with that measured in step 2, before the intervention, the manager may determine whether or not the problem is solved. If the problem isn't solved, additional study must be made of the total work performance, step 1, and a new program developed. In some instances a reexamination of environmental factors is appropriate.

On the other hand, if the problem appears to have been solved, the desirable behavior must be maintained. Appropriate schedules of reinforcement can be employed to achieve this purpose. Initially, the steady support of continuous reinforcement (each successful response rewarded) may be needed, especially if the response is weak. As the behavior increases in frequency, that is, gains in strength, intermittent reinforcement should be used. The ultimate goal is to have the employee become self-reinforced for performance improvement and goal attainment.

Step 5: Evaluating the Performance Improvement

Since the initial step in behavioral modification consisted of focusing on significant behavioral events, overall performance improvement must be evaluated. The purpose of the intervention is to improve objective, bottom-line performance, but, if this has not been achieved, then additional corrective action must be taken.

Figure 12-5 presents a summary work flow diagram of behavioral contingency management as discussed. The five-step model serves as a guide to the application of this form of change management.

The behavioral modification model has been specifically applied in a variety of organizations.[20] The results have been very encouraging. In a survey of programs in ten organizations, the results reported significant improvements in productivity, cost savings, absenteeism, and other measures.[21]

In summary, it has been shown that a person's performance or behavior is strongly influenced by the consequences that he or she suffers or enjoys as a result of that performance. The consequences may be positive or negative. Proper management of consequences is critical in maintaining the desired performance. The behavioral contingency management model provides a systematic approach for achieving and maintaining results that work to the advantage of the individual and the organization.

SUMMARY

Change must be managed successfully if organizations are to survive. The stimulus for change may be external, internal, or a combination of both. Organizations respond to external environmental variation by developing the type of management system appropriate to cope with the rate of change

Figure 12-5

Behavioral Contingency Management

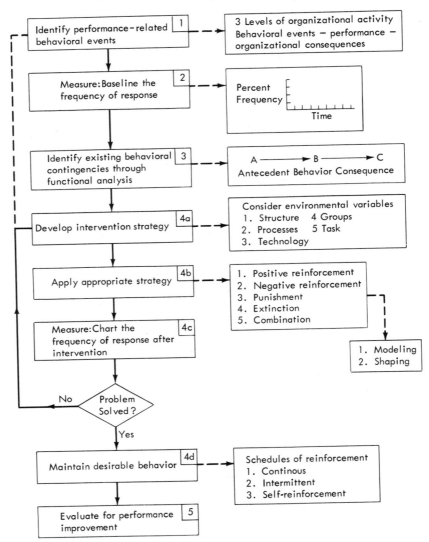

encountered. For dynamic environments, the organismic management system works best, whereas the mechanistic management system is best for a more stable environment. Adaptation to the environment is also facilitated by making structural adjustments. The more successful organizations achieve a good fit between their internal structural arrangements (differentiation and integration) and the kind of environment that they face.

Organizations also relate to the environment by the use of adaptive subsystems. An adaptive subsystem senses relevant external changes and interprets their implications for the organization. Adjustments are then made on the basis of such information. Finally, organizations respond to external changes by protecting their technologies. Inputs and outputs are stabilized to prevent the primary production process from being overwhelmed by fluctuating environmental conditions.

Whether caused by external or internal factors, change invariably affects people within the organization. Four interdependent factors—structure, task, technology, and people—are involved in change. The systems viewpoint dictates that a change in one factor will have an impact upon other factors. A force-field analysis, consisting of determining the driving and restraining forces producing a given situation, is one means of diagnosing a problem. Solving the problem itself can be handled by attending to the three phases of the change process: unfreezing, moving or making the change, and refreezing.

Finally, it was shown that certain problems could be handled by behavioral modification. The basic premise of behavioral modification is that behavior depends on its consequences. If the behavior is followed by pleasant, satisfying consequences, it will be repeated. If painful or unpleasant results follow one's behavior, it will be terminated. By managing the consequences of behavior, one can encourage behaviors that improve performance and output. Positive reinforcement of behavior by means of psychological and material rewards facilitates the attainment of individual and organizational objectives.

QUESTIONS FOR STUDY AND DISCUSSION

1. What are the differences between a mechanistic and an organismic system? Under what conditions is each appropriate?

2. What is an adaptive subsystem? Can you give an example of such a subsystem?

3. How can an organization protect its core technology? Why would it seek to do so? What are the results of protecting the core technology?

4. What are the four basic factors involved in change? Why is systems thinking important here?

5. Can you explain the concept of a force field? What does a force-field diagram look like? How can it be changed?

6. What are the three phases of a change process? What is involved in each phase?

7. Why do people tend to resist change?

8. What are some of the approaches to change?

9. What is behavior modification? What is a contingent relationship? How would you diagram a contingent relationship?

10. What are the steps in behavioral contingency management? What is involved at each step?

NOTES

[1]Lawrence, Paul R. and Jay W. Lorsch, *Organization and Environment: Managing Differentiation and Integration* (Boston: Harvard Graduate School of Business Administration, 1967).

[2]Burns, Tom and G. M. Stalker, *The Management of Innovation,* (London: Tavistock Publications Ltd., 1961). Also see Pierce, Jon L., Randall B. Dunham, and Richard S. Blackburn, "Social System Structure, Job Design, and Growth Need Strength: A Test of a Congruency Model," *Academy of Management Journal* 22, (June 1979), pp. 223–240.

[3]Morse, John J. and Jay W. Lorsch, "Beyond Theory Y," *Harvard Business Review,* 48 (May-June, 1970), p. 61-68.

[4]Katz, Daniel and Robert L. Kahn, *The Sociology of Organizations* (New York: John Wiley and Sons, 1966).

[5]Dodge, Delf, and Henry Tosi, "The Effects of Environments on Organization Systems", *In Organizational Behavior and Management,* rev. ed., Henry L. Tosi and W. Clay Hamner (Chicago: St. Clair Press, 1977), pp. 81–89.

[6]Thompson, James D., *Organizations in Action* (New York: McGraw-Hill) pp. 14–24.

[7]*Ibid.,* pp. 19-24.

[8]Argyris, C., *Management and Organization Development* (New York: McGraw-Hill, 1971), p. xi.

[9]Leavitt, H., "Applied Organizational Change in Industry: Structural, Technological and Humanistic Approaches," in J. March, ed. *Handbook of Organizations* (Chicago: Rand McNally, 1965), p. 1145.

[10]Lawrence, P. and J. Lorsch, *Developing Organizations: Diagnosis and Actions* (Reading, Mass.: Addison-Wesley, 1969), p. 87.

[11]Benne, Kenneth D., "Changes in Institutions and the Role of the Change Agent," in Lawrence, Paul R. and Seiler, John A. *Organizational Behavior and Administration,* rev. ed. (Homewood, Illinois: Irwin, 1965), p. 952-957.

[12]*Ibid,* p. 955.

[13]Zand, Dale E. and Richard E. Sorensen, "Theory of Change and the Effective Use of Management Science," *Administrative Science Quarterly,* 20 (December, 1975), pp. 532-544.

[14]Davis, Keith, *Human Behavior at Work,* 4th ed. (New York: McGraw-Hill 1972), pp. 163-164.

[15]Greiner, Larry E., "Patterns of Organization Change" *Harvard Business Review,* 45 (May-June 1967), pp. 119-130. Also see Lee, James A., "Leader Power for Managing Change," *Academy of Management Review,* 2 (January 1977), pp. 73-80.

[16]Coch, L. and J. R. P. French, Jr., "Overcoming Resistance to Change," *Human Relations,* 1 (Winter 1948) 512-532.

[17]Seashore, Stanley E. and David G. Bowers, "Durability of Organizational Change," *American Psychologist,* 25 (March 1970), pp. 227-233.

[18]Luthans, Fred and Kreitner, Robert, *Organizational Behavior Modification* (Glenview, Illinois: Scott, Foresman, 1975), p. 28.

[19]*Ibid,* p. 69-83.

[20]Zemke, Ron, "Performance Feedback & Positive Reinforcement", *Training* (December 1976), pp. 227-29. Also "Production Gains From a Pat on the Back," *Business Week* (January 23, 1978), pp. 56-59.

[21]Hamner, Clay W. and Ellen P. Hamner, "Behavior Modification on the Bottom Line," *Organizational Dynamics* 4 (Spring 1976), pp. 2-21. Also see Locke, Edwin A., "The Myths of Behavior Mod in Organizations," *Academy of Management Review,* 2 (October 1977), pp. 543-553.

cases cases cases

Case Study: Rejected Changed

Akron County Hospital is a 250-bed facility that has an emergency room operation, X-ray and pathology services, and a general and emergency surgery section. It is the only hospital in the county, and about 40 percent of its activities consist of care for indigent patients. The hospital is old and antiquated structurally, but is clean and functional.

Jim Schwartz is employed on a part-time basis by the hospital's business office because of his concurrent enrollment in a nearby junior college where he is pursuing a premedical curriculum.

After about two weeks of orientation and training in the In-Patient Admissions Office under the direction of Mr. Cato, the hospital's business manager, Jim was transferred to the Out-Patient Department. He was introduced to its employees (all female) and told to fully familiarize himself with the operation, as this was where he would probably stay. Mr. Cato told Jim that, if he had any suggestions as to how operations might be improved, he should feel free to discuss them with him at any time.

The out-patient operation consisted of admissions, cash receipting, filing of insurance claims, maintenance of out-patient accounts (receivables), delinquent account processing, and medical record maintenance. All these functions were housed in one room that encompassed approximately 150 square feet and was isolated from the rest of the business operation of the hospital.

Mrs. Metz was "somewhat in charge" of the Out-Patient Department. She had worked for the hospital for ten years, eight of which were in the Out-Patient Department. Jim was never told and it was never formally stated anywhere that Mrs. Metz was the department supervisor; it was just assumed by everyone because she had been in the Out-Patient Department longer than anyone else. She knew every phase of the operation but mostly concerned herself with keeping all the accounting ledgers, with their respective charges and payments posted on a monthly basis. These accounts, about 1,700, were divided into four sections, with a section being posted and a subsequent billing mailed out each Thursday of the month.

There was a very informal atmosphere among the out-patient employees, and everyone knew each other very well. They were constantly asking Jim questions about himself in an attempt to know him as they knew everyone else.

Within about six weeks Jim had learned the entire operation and was going upstairs with Mrs. Metz each Thursday to the Accounting Department to help on the weekly account posting and billing. Often, he relieved her on the posting machine, which was a fairly sophisticated machine to operate.

Jim began to feel comfortable with his job. He had been accepted by the group and began to know them very well. Jim also discovered that there were a lot of inefficiences in the operation and that a number of shortcuts taken to avoid problems and extra work actually caused more and greater problems in the long run. The department, and hence the hospital, was losing money because of such things as (1) inadequate information gathering at the time of admission to facilitate proper insurance billings and subsequent reimbursement for the services rendered—about 10 percent of the out-patient accounts bills were returned each month because of inaccurate addresses; (2) improper classification—about 30 percent of the accounts could be classified as delinquent and subsequently handled in a manner different from the regular ones; (3) slow filing procedures; and (4) shifting of accounts to an indigent category when bills hadn't been paid simply to make it easier to handle the account—indigent accounts were more easily handled than others.

In effect, the Out-Patient Department appeared to be operating smoothly on the surface, but only because many problems and complications were smoothed over by various shortcuts that prevented them from being noticed.

Jim brought this to Mr. Cato's attention who informed him that he was aware of it but, being physically separated from the situation, it was hard for him to do anything about it. He also felt that there wasn't anyone capable of taking complete responsibility for the operation. Mr. Cato told Jim that if he had any solutions or suggestions he should talk them over with the others, and, if all agreed to the suggested changes, to implement them.

After about three months things began to improve as indicated by a marked increase in account collections and insurance reimbursements. Most important, these improvements were made at the same time that they were confronting the many daily problems that arose. Problems were resolved immediately instead of avoiding or ignoring them as had been done in the past.

All this was accomplished because a few changes had been made, a few rules had been established, and a few overall directions and guidelines had been developed for the operation and the group. These improvements were initiated by Jim, and the group began to look to him for direction and answers; they also informally looked to him as their supervisor. An added factor that enhanced his emergent leadership was the first-name basis he enjoyed with Mr. Cato, which was not the case with the other department employees, including Mrs. Metz.

As a consequence of these developments, Mrs. Metz began a campaign to discredit and subvert Jim's emergent position within the group and in the eyes of Mr. Cato, so as to regain her status of "being in charge." As a result, the group began to polarize between Mrs. Metz and Jim. Within three weeks the operational improvements that had been attained were negated by conflict that hindered coordination and the needed integration of activities for an effective and efficient operation.

QUESTIONS

1. Evaluate Jim Schwartz's position.

2. Assume that you are Jim Schwartz. What strategies would you use in making changes now?

3. What would be your main concerns in making further changes?

4. Draw a field-force diagram of the situation that you are facing.

cases cases cases

Case Study: A Corrected Change

PART I: A QUICK CHANGE

All testing for the plant is accomplished in a single, centrally located lab with testers from the factory and the Quality Control Department using various types of testing apparatus. All testers are on four-shift operation as are the production operations. Factory testers report to factory shift supervisors on all shifts and receive only testing procedure and specification information from quality control. Quality control testers report to a quality control supervisor on days only and work without supervision on the weekends and second and third shifts. In day-to-day operations, there is very little actual supervision of the lab as a factory shift supervisor have perhaps one or two testers in the lab and twenty to fifty employees on the production floor.

The following problem was noted by the shift supervisors. Testers who required the entire eight-hour shift to complete their required tests were finding it increasingly difficult to do so due to the noise and confusion created by those testers who had completed their assignments and were taking breaks in the lab. Break consisted of eating, drinking, talking, and other nonwork-related activities.

Meetings were held by the supervisors to determine a means of effectively solving the problem of "breaking" testers' obstructing the completion of other testers' assignments. After much discussion, the supervisors determined that the following *rules* would provide adequate control:

1. All breaks will be taken in a break area outside the lab.
2. There will be no eating or drinking in the lab.
3. Individuals having idle time will go to a break area.

Enforcement required only that a supervisor *patrol* the lab at any time as any employee in the lab not working would be violating the rules and disciplinary action could be taken.

The rules were posted in the lab at 3:00 P.M. on a Friday afternoon.

QUESTIONS

1. Evaluate the manner in which the change was made? Strengths? Weakness?
2. What kind of leadership is reflected in this episode?
3. What will be the testers' reaction to the new rule?

PART II: A GRIEVANCE

On the following Monday morning, a grievance was delivered to management by a tester who was also a union steward. The grievance stated that the rules were "unfair":

> We, the lab testers, feel that the newly posted rules are unfair. They require us to live under more stringent rules than the rest of the plant as a substitute to supplying supervision...

QUESTION

1. How should management respond to the grievance?

PART III: A REVERSAL

Management determined that the grievance was valid and determined that it would take the following action:

1. The tester who initiated the grievance was to meet with the group of testers and draw up rules that they felt would be fair and improve the work environment so that all testers could complete their assigned tasks without interference.
2. The proposed list would be reviewed by management with a joint meeting of lab representatives and management, if necessary, to work out compromises.

Two days later, the following rules were submitted by the lab group:

1. All breaks will be taken in a break area outside the lab.
2. There will be no eating in the lab.
3. Coffee drinking in the lab will be permitted while working.
4. Individuals having idle time will go to a break area.

Management reviewed the new rules and approved them as written. The intent of the original rules was maintained with the only change being drinks allowed in the work area.

Following the agreement, management met with lab personnel to discuss the rules and made the following statement:

> Management feels that our testers and auditors do not require constant supervision. Our intent was and is to create a work climate in which you can best accomplish your various assignments. We are relying on you to help enforce the rules as we, management, and lab personnel, have agreed to.

QUESTIONS

1. Evaluate management's reaction to the grievance. How does this compare with the first change initiated?
2. How can similar problems be prevented in the future?

CHAPTER 13

ORGANIZATIONAL DEVELOPMENT

LEARNING OBJECTIVES

When you have finished this chapter you should be able to:

- *Define organizational development and understand its assumptions and values.*
- *Explain the role of a change agent.*
- *Outline and describe the stages in an organization development program.*
- *Recall four target groups of change and the change strategies used with each group.*
- *List and describe the eight steps in management by objectives.*
- *Explain the conditions for success and failure of organizational development.*

Coping with change requires sensitivity to changing external and internal conditions. If such sensitivity is coupled with appropriate adjustments, an organization will be more effective and efficient in attaining performance and human goals. A new discipline—organizational development—has emerged to assist in meeting the challenge of managing change.

The assumptions, values, and objectives of organizational development (OD) reflect a different manner of viewing an old problem. Furthermore, many of the OD methods used to cope with change are new approaches based on behavioral science knowledge and techniques.

DEFINITION AND BACKGROUND

Organizational development (OD) is a planned, long-range effort to improve an organization's effectiveness and its ability to adapt to change through the application of behavioral science knowledge and techniques.[1] The long-term time span required for planning and implementing change is necessary because OD is concerned with activities, interactions, attitudes, and values. Such changes demand time. Additionally, if improved conditions are to be maintained, improved performance must be reinforced by appropriate changes in the appraisal, compensation, training, staffing, task, and communications systems.

The changes are in response to three broad categories of problems.[2]

1. problems of testing—growth, identity, and revitalization
2. problems of human satisfaction and development
3. problems of organization effectiveness

The objective of OD is improvement in the problem-solving process of the organization and the revitalization of work activities of individuals and groups. Improving the problem-solving process of an organization means to enhance the way in which it diagnoses and makes decisions about the opportunities and challenges of both its external and internal environment. Revitalizing an organization, while related to problem solving, refers to renewal processes that make it possible for an organization to remain viable. This requires initiating and confronting needed change, adapting to new conditions, and learning from experiences.[3]

Organizational development has a very recent history, and the term itself was not used with any distinct meaning until the late 1950s. Two roots of OD, however, go back to the 1940s. One stem is laboratory training, that is, sensitivity training or unstructured small-group situations. The other stem is survey research and feedback methods.[4] This refers to a systematic collection of information about the organization and feeding such data back to appropriate groups throughout the organization for evaluation and planning. Applications of these two stems have been refined and the content of OD expanded.

Today OD efforts are international. Many of America's best-known firms have been involved in various OD programs. Applications have been numerous in public school systems, colleges, medical schools, social welfare agencies, police departments, churches, and governmental units at all levels.

Assumptions of Organizational Development

To understand the purpose of OD and its techniques for implementing change, note must be taken of its underlying assumptions. The assumptions relate to individuals, groups, and organizational systems as follows.[5]

Assumptions about people

1. Most individuals have drives toward personal growth and development, and these are most likely to be actualized in an environment that is both supportive and challenging.
2. Most people desire to make, and are capable of making, a much greater contribution to the attainment of organizational goals than most organizational environments will permit.

Assumptions about people in groups

1. Most people wish to be accepted and to interact cooperatively with at least one small reference group and usually with more than one group (e.g., the work group, the family group).
2. One of the most psychologically relevant reference groups for most people is the work group, including peers and the superior.
3. For a group to optimize its effectiveness, the formal leader cannot perform all the leadership functions in all circumstances at all times, and all group members must assist each other with effective leadership and member behavior.

Assumptions about people in organizational systems

1. Organizations tend to be characterized by overlapping, interdependent work groups. What happens to one subsystem (social, technological, or administrative) will affect and be influenced by other parts of the system.
2. The culture in most organizations tends to suppress the expression of feelings that people have about each other and about where they and their organizations are heading. Suppressed feelings adversely affect problem solving, personal growth, and job satisfaction.
3. Viewing feelings as data important to the organization tends to open up many avenues for improved goal setting, leadership, communications, problem solving, intergroup collaboration, and morale.

4. The level of interpersonal trust, support, and cooperation is much lower in most organizations than is either necessary or desirable.

5. "Win–lose" strategies between people and groups, while realistic and appropriate in some situations, are not optimal in the long run to the solution of most organizational problems.

6. Improved performance stemming from organizational development efforts needs to be sustained by appropriate changes in the appraisal, compensation, training, staffing, and task-specialization subsystem—in short, the total personnel system.

Values of Behavioral Scientist Change Agents

The assumptions inherent in OD provide a basis for understanding the values generally held by change agents.[6]

OD consultants tend to hold a comparable set of values.[7] A basic value is that the needs and aspirations of human beings are the reasons for organized effort in society. This means an opportunity for individual growth and self-realization for both the individual and the organization. OD programs are designed to improve the welfare and quality of work life for all members of an organization.

A second value that tends to be held by change agents is that work and life can become richer and more meaningful and organized effort more effective and enjoyable, if feelings and sentiments are permitted to be a part of an organization's culture. This includes relationships built on trust and openness and also direct confrontation of conflict.

A third value is the democratization of organizations. Emphasis on a democratic, participative way of work life is not intended to reduce or neutralize the influence of owners or managers. The goal is to utilize human resources more effectively by increasing the involvement and influence of everybody. This provides more self-direction, self-control, and identity with organizational goals.

Finally, there is a commitment to an action research change model. The action research model consists of gathering data from the system by the change agent, discussing these data with the client group, joint action planning by the change agent and the client, taking action, and evaluating the degrees of success attained. This approach will be discussed in greater detail later in the chapter.

The assumptions and values of organizational development convey an intent to change, if necessary, the activities, interactions, and values of an organizaton's members. The direction of some of these changes are as follows.

From		Toward
Meaningless work	⟶	Personal development from work
Denying feelings	⟶	Expressing feelings
Suspicion of others	⟶	Trust of others
Avoiding conflict	⟶	Facing conflict
Competition with other groups	⟶	Collaboration with other groups
Unilateral direction	⟶	Participation
One-sided problem solving	⟶	Shared problem solving

Assumptions and values provide the guidelines and directions for what will be undertaken in an OD program. Such a program is not value free. Change agents should make their values and beliefs known to their clients if trust is to develop and learning is to occur.

The assumptions and values of organizational development also indicate that OD is oriented to producing a definite kind of organization with specific characteristics. Such an organization resembles a Theory Y model (McGregor), with its emphasis on self-direction and self-control.[8] It also has the dimensions of confidence and trust, participation and shared decision making of Likert's System IV organization.[9] Finally, it has the attributes of an organic system that we examined in the previous chapter.[10]

> For many if not most OD theorists and practitioners, OD is development toward an organization characterized by wide employee participation in decision making and goal setting, individual and group self-direction and self-control based on jointly decided goals and objectives, and creative resolution of conflict between and across hierarchical levels—a setting which is expected to provide the opportunity for individual growth and fulfillment while at the same time removing barriers to effective performance.

In much of the remaining portion of this chapter, we will examine the ways in which OD seeks to obtain such changes in organizations.

Change Agents

Change does not automatically occur because someone in the organization has decided that an OD program would be helpful. Implementation depends largely on a change agent. A change agent is one who initiates, stimulates, or facilitates a change program; the agent may be an executive, a member of the organization, or an outside consultant. There are two kinds of change agents: external and internal.[11] An external change agent is someone not previously associated with the organization—a person who has been invited to assist with a problem. Being an outsider, the external agent or consultant sees organizational phenomena from a different viewpoint and more objectively. He or she has an independent attitude, not being dependent on the organization's reward system, which facilitates taking risks and confronting organization members when necessary to do so.

On the other hand, an internal change agent is a member of the organization and may be a top executive, a personal or industrial relations officer, or an organization member who initiates change. Some large organizations have established positions whose responsibilities consist of implementing change programs. These positions are found in the personnel, industrial relations, or planning departments, and those holding the position report directly to the president of the organization. The internal change agent has firsthand knowledge of how the organization operates formally and informally, the communication network, the decision-making system, and the distribution of influence or power among organization members. In contrast, the external agent will be unfamiliar with such facets of the organization's system and also its technology. Conversely, the internal change agent may lack objectivity, have biases, and be oblivious to some of the organizaton's inadequacies. Furthermore, the internal change agent is subject to the power structure and sanction system of the organization; consequently, he or she may be reluctant to confront influential managers or to raise sensitive issues. As a result, the internal change agent might not be as effective in moving the organization toward self-renewal, growth, and change as might an external agent.

Some organizations have utilized an external–internal consulting team to facilitate change programs. The advantages and strengths of one member offset the disadvantages and weaknesses of the other. In this complementary resources arrangement, the external change agent brings expertise, objectivity, and new insights; the internal change agent brings knowledge of the organizaton's power, social, and technological systems and an awareness of its strengths and weaknesses. Since the internal change agent is usually not as well trained in OD techniques as the external agent, the more successful OD consultants have worked upon the development of their internal change agent counterparts.[12] This facilitates dividing the change program work load and sharing the diagnoses, plans, and strategies. Furthermore, the external–internal consulting team achieves greater continuity over the entire OD program. Because an external consultant is involved in other outside activities, he or she is generally available to the organization for a few days a month. The internal agent, on the other hand, is a continuing point of contact for problems that arise and provides continuing support for maintaining the momentum of the OD program.

Considering change agents of all varieties, there are two basic types: the expert and the catalyst. The expert is brought in to solve a specific problem; the expert decides and acts. Since the expert takes control of the problem and its solution, the client does not develop problem-solving skills or self-sufficiency. Examples are the doctor or the management consultant. A catalyst-type consultant operates on the premise that the client unit—person or work group—has the capacity to cope with its own problems. The change agent's role is therefore to help create an interpersonal situation in which problem awareness and capacity awareness can occur. His or her role is limited to freeing up or speeding up a "natural" capacity for constructive change. This makes for independence, self-direction, and self-renewal.

The expert and catalytic roles are not mutually exclusive. Both roles are effective and interrelated and may be used at various times to meet changing client system needs. For example, the change agent may start out with a diagnosis that points to the need for job enrichment but shift to an expert role in teaching the client system how to use this technique. Some change strategies such as the managerial grid and survey feedback are "consultant centered" in that the change agent recommends and prescribes the treatment and plans and outlines the intervention, but does so with the agreement of the client.[13]

STAGES IN AN ORGANIZATIONAL DEVELOPMENT PROGRAM

An OD program usually proceeds in a stepwise fashion; there are definite stages from the beginning to the end.[14]

Stage 1: Problem Awareness—Need for Change

First, the organization must perceive the need for change if it is to cope effectively and efficiently with external or internal conditions. Sometimes this is described simply as "someone in the organization is hurting." In some instances it is recognition that things could be better or improved.

Stage 2: Entry of a Change Agent

A change agent is invited into the organization to explore the problems. The change agent may be an internal or external change agent. This stage of an OD program may be initiated by top management—a vice president or some concerned department manager within the organization. Whatever the point of entry, it must have the approval of top management. A relationship develops between the change agent and the client system at this point, which is crucial for the success of an OD program. The expectations and obligations of each party must be developed and understood. Issues dealing with responsibility, objectives, and the like must be clarified and defined.

Stage 3: Diagnosis

After the change agent has developed a working relationship with the client, a diagnostic effort begins that has several steps. First, there is data gathering. Information is collected to provide both the organization and the change agent with a better understanding of the problem. Although some data of an operational nature (e.g., production, absenteeism, etc.), are available, it will usually present an incomplete picture. Consequently, a decision must be made as to what kinds of data are to be gathered, where in the organization the data are to be collected, and how the data are to be obtained (i.e., by interview, questionnaire, observation, or some combination of these methods). The second step is the feedback of collected data to the client group. The change agent and client together analyze the information to identify problem areas and causal factors or relationships. A force-field analysis will be of value at this point. The problem as originally perceived may not be the real one confronting the organization. Also, an inaccurate diagnosis of the collected data can lead to a costly and ineffective program. Finally, a determination must be made of the exact problem(s) that need a solution. If several problems are found, priorities may have to be assigned so that the more serious one is treated first.

Stage 4: An Action Plan

Given an exact problem and its causal factors, an action plan must be developed for its solution. This will usually require a series of interventions, activities, or programs aimed at resolving the problem. Most action plans must include procedures for unfreezing and refreezing the client system. Additionally, the action plan must include objectives to be achieved. Goals and objectives facilitate checking the accuracy of the diagnosis and/or the effectiveness of the change strategy.

Stage 5: Implementation

A step-by-step action plan will greatly facilitate implementation of the change program. Each step is monitored to determine member reaction to the change effort. Continuous feedback will disclose whether the change effort should be modified, continued, or discontinued. Previously established goals will help to evaluate the accuracy of the problem definition and the selected change strategies. If found inadequate or ineffective, diagnosis may have to be started again. If the problem is corrected, new behavior must be stabilized, that is, refrozen, to prevent regression to previous conditions.

Stage 6: Termination of the OD Program

The final stage is the disengagement of the internal or external change agent's activities. If the client system has become more independent and demonstrates a self-renewal capacity, termination of the relationship is easily accomplished. On the other hand, if the client system has become too dependent upon the change agent, termination can be difficult and awkward.

Figure 13-1 outlines the steps in an OD program from problem awareness to termination. Note that the entire process is influenced by the assumptions and values of OD. The broken line running from the implementation stage back to the diagnostic stage indicates that the monitoring process may disclose unanticipated difficulties, inaccurate diagnoses, or the selection of an ineffective change method. Implementation may also reveal a need for "fine-tuning" of steps in the action plan, which is also indicated by a dashed line.

Figure 13-1

Steps in the Development of an OD Program

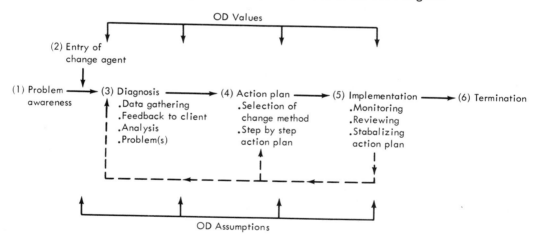

INTERVENTIONS AND CHANGE STRATEGIES

Whenever an external or internal change agent contacts a client system, an intervention has taken place. Intervention in this sense refers to entering among members or groups of an organization. As we saw in stage 2 of an organizational development program, such an intervention occurred when the change agent explored the possibility of helping to solve a problem. Collecting data by whatever method—interview, questionnaire, or observation—is also an intervention. More specifically, however, intervention refers to planned activities that are intended to produce change and achieve specific purposes. Frequently, such interventions are called change strategies or simply change methods.

OD interventions or change strategies structure the activities of selected target groups so that learning and change can take place. A classification of OD interventions based on target groups is shown in Table 13-1. As indicated, the target groups parallel the development of your text (i.e., individuals, teams and groups, intergroup relations, and total organization). The interventions on the right are designed to improve the effectiveness of these target groups.

Table 13-1

OD Interventions Based on Target Group

Target Group	Types of Intervention
Individuals	Life- and career-planning activities Role analysis technique Coaching and counseling
Teams and groups	Team building T-group (sensitivity training) Process consultation
Intergroup relations	Intergroup confrontation Organizational mirroring (three or more groups)
Total organization	Confrontation meetings Grid OD Survey feedback Management by objectives

Source: W. L. French and C. H. Bell, Jr., ORGANIZATION DEVELOPMENT: Behavioral Science Interventions for Organization Improvement, 2/e, ©1978 p. 112. Adapted by permission of Prentice-Hall, Inc., Englewood Cliffs, New Jersey.

TYPES OF INTERVENTIONS

The material that follows includes a brief description of the interventions available to a change agent. Prior to the intervention are some of the questions that a change agent may have asked in his or her diagnosis before deciding that the problem existed in a specific target group. The following presentation is based extensively on the French and Bell text, *Organizational Behavior* (see note 1).

Individuals as the Target for Change

Typical information sought

Does the individual perform according to the organization's expectations? How does the individual view his or her place and performance? Do certain kinds of problems typically arise? Does the individual meet the standards and norms of the organization? Does the individual need particular knowledge, skills, or ability? What career development opportunities does he or she have? want? need? What dissatisfaction is the individual experiencing?[15] Appropriate interventions are described in the following paragraphs.

Life and career planning

This consists of activities that enable individuals to focus on their life and career objectives and determine how they might go about achieving them. Structured activities lead to the development of life and career inventories, discussions of goals and objectives, assessments of capabilities, necessary additional training, and areas of strengths and deficiencies.

Role analysis technique

This intervention is designed to clarify role expectations and obligations of individual team members and to improve individual and team effectiveness. Four steps are involved: (1) A job incumbent describes his or her job, its place in the organization, the rationale for its existence, and its place in achieving overall organizational goals. The specific duties and behaviors are listed on a chalkboard and are discussed by the team; duties are added and deleted until the group and job incumbent are satisfied that the job has been completely defined. (2) The job incumbent lists his or her expectations of other members that most affect the incumbent's performance, and these expectations are adjusted and agreed upon by the group. (3) The members of the group describe what they want and expect from the job incumbent; these expectations are modified, if necessary, and agreed upon by the group and job incumbent. (4) The job incumbent makes a written summary of his or her role as it has been defined in the three previous steps; the incumbent's role profile is reviewed by the group before another individual's role is analyzed.

Coaching and counseling

These activities require the change agent or other organization members working with individuals to help them (1) define working goals, (2) learn how others see their behavior, and (3) learn new modes of behavior to see if these help them achieve their goals. Two features of this type of activity are the nonjudgmental feedback given by others to the individual and the joint exploration of alternative behaviors.

Teams and Groups as the Target for Change

Typical information sought in the diagnostic phase is as follows. What are the norms of the group? What are the attitudes, opinions, and feelings of group members toward compensation, group goals, supervision, and top management? What is the group climate—open versus closed, authoritarian versus democratic, repressive versus developmental, trusting versus suspicious, cooperative versus competitive? What are the major problems of the team? How can team effectiveness be improved? What do people do that gets in the way of others? Are member–leader relations those that are desired? Do individuals know how their jobs relate to group and organizational goals? Are the groups' working processes (i.e., the way in which they get things done as a group) effective? Is good use made of group and individual resources? Interventions that are relevant for coping with problems uncovered by these questions are given in the following paragraphs.

Team-building activities

These activities are designed to enhance the effectiveness of work groups or teams. Such interventions may relate to task problems or process problems. Task problems are concerned with the way in which things are done, the needed skills to accomplish tasks, the resource allocations necessary for task accomplishments, and so on. Process problems relate to the nature and quality of the relationships between the team members or between members and the leader. Attention is directed to communication processes, leadership processes, problem-solving processes, and the like. Various team-building activities for family groups (work teams) and special groups (temporary task force teams and newly constituted teams) are shown in Figure 13-2.

Team building tends to emphasize interventions that are either diagnostic or focused on various aspects of team building such as task activities, team relationships, and team processes. Frequently, a diagnostic meeting may precede a team-building session.

In a team *diagnostic meeting,* a manager and his or her immediate work group conduct a general critique of their performance. The manager may start by suggesting categories in which he or she wants to collect information. These can include how we are working together, the group's relations with others, what the group does best, what the group does worst, planning, and so on. This procedure helps to disclose and identify problems so

Figure 13-2

Various Team-Building Interventions

Source: W. L. French and C. H. Bell, Jr., ORGANIZATION DEVELOPMENT: Behavioral Science Interventions for Organization Improvement, 2/e, ©1978 p. 119. Reproduced by permission of Prentice-Hall, Inc., Englewood Cliffs, New Jersey.

that they may be worked on. The group then decides what change steps, if any, it wants to undertake. Taking action is generally an activity for a subsequent team meeting.[16]

Team building has as its goal improving the group's effectiveness through better management of (1) task demands, (2) interpersonal relationship demands, and (3) group processes (goal setting, decision making, etc.). The group looks at its performance, behavior, and culture for the purposes of eliminating inadequate behaviors and strengthening functional behaviors. Such a team-building session usually requires two days and should be held away from the workplace, if possible, to prevent distractions.

The typical procedure is to have a third party or consultant to interview each group member and the group leader prior to the meeting. They are asked what their problems are, how well the group functions, and what obstacles prevent better group performance. These interview data are grouped in topical areas or themes by the consultant who presents these to the group at the beginning of the meeting. The issues are examined and discussed by the work group and are then ranked in terms of importance. Solutions to the problems are considered, and action steps are established to bring about desired changes. A follow-up meeting is usually held to determine if the action steps were taken and whether or not they had the desired effects.

T-group (sensitivity training). A T-group is an unstructured, agendaless group session for about ten to twelve members and a professional "trainer" who acts as catalyst and facilitator for the group. The data for discussion are the data provided by the interaction of the group members as they strive to create a viable society for themselves. Actions, reactions, interactions, and the concomitant feelings accompanying all these are data for group discussion. Typical things learned in a T-group are interpersonal relationships, self-awareness, how others react to one's behavior, and group dynamics.

Process consultation. The purpose of this type of intervention is to help work groups improve their functioning by becoming more aware of their own processes such as (1) communication, (2) member roles and functions, (3) problem solving and decision making, (4) group norms and group growth, (5) leadership and authority, and (6) intergroup cooperation and competition.[17] The group, with the help of the change agent, learns to initiate its own solutions to process problems.

Intergroup Relations as the Target for Change

Typical information sought in the diagnostic phase is as follows: How does each subsystem see the other? What problems do the two groups have in working together? In what ways do the subsystems get in each other's way? How can they collaborate to improve the performance of both groups? Are goals, subgoals, areas of authority, and areas of responsibility clear? What is the nature of the climate between the groups—open versus closed, trusting versus suspicious, cooperative versus competitive? What do the members want it to be? Potential interventions for coping with problems disclosed by these questions are summarized as follows.

Intergroup confrontation. To reach a state of mutual understanding and cooperation (1) the two work groups, meeting separately, make three lists: how we see ourselves, how we think that the other group sees us, and how we see the other group; (2) the groups meet together, a spokesman from each group presents his or her group's list, but under the ground rules that no rebuttal is permitted, only clarifying questions; (3) the groups meet separately again to discuss differences in perception of each other and react to the feedback given; and (4) subgroups are formed consisting of members from both groups who agree on interface problems, solutions, action plans, and follow-up activities.

Organization mirror. This is a meeting that allows an organizational unit such as a staff or service (drafting, engineering, personnel) unit to obtain feedback from parts of the organization that use their output or service. First, the unit seeking feedback invites several guests, usually key people, from each of the invited groups. Next, a change agent interviews the "invited guests" to obtain data on the nature of existing problems. At the meeting itself, the outside guests and change agent discuss the collected data while the inside group listen. Afterwards, the host unit is allowed to ask questions of clarification but not to rebut. Subgroups, consisting of both host and invited people, identify problems and means for improvement that are then presented to the total group. Task teams are then assigned to work on the disclosed problems.

The Total Organization as the Target for Change

Prior to the selection of an intervention, information of the following kind is obtained. What is the organization's culture (i.e., norms, sentiments, beliefs, attitudes, values)? What are the attitudes, opinions, and feelings of the organization's members toward compensation, organization goals, supervision, and top management? What is the organization's climate—open versus closed, authoritarian versus competitive? How well do key organizational processes, such as decision making and goal setting, function? What kind and how effective are the organization's "sensing mechanisms" to monitor internal and external demands? Are the organization's goals understood and accepted? Several interventions for coping with problems disclosed by this line of questioning are outlined briefly in the following paragraphs.

Confrontation meetings

The confrontation meeting is a means for diagnosing problems when there is limited time for problem-solving action, but a need for rapid improvement, and when management is sufficiently cohesive and committed to ensure resolving organizational problems. After presenting the group rules for the meeting, information is collected by the formation of small groups from different functional areas and managerial levels. Bosses and subordinates are not in the same group, and top management generally meets as a separate group. The groups work on identifying problems. This information is then presented on a chart pad to the total group. Next the entire list of items is categorized into problem areas. The participants are then regrouped into functional work teams reflecting the organization's structure and headed by the top manager in that area. Each group then proceeds to identify problems important to their own area, assigns priorities to these problems, and develops action plans for solving the highest-priority items. The groups also select the issues to which they believe top management should assign the highest priority. Each group shares its outlines and action plans with the total group. Later top management reviews these inputs and develops a set of follow-up action plans that are then communicated to all the confrontation members. Progress reviews are held periodically to examine the outcomes of the action plans.

Survey feedback

In this intervention, data on facets of the organization's operations and culture are collected and serve as a basis for change. The following steps usually occur: (1) Data are collected from all organization members, (2) the data are given to the top management team and then are sent down the hierarchy to functional teams, and (3) each superior presides at a meeting with his or her subordinates who discuss and help interpret the data. Chapter 6 developed the survey feedback approach in considerable detail as monitoring the organization.

Grid OD

Grid organization development is based on the concepts of the management grid developed by Blake and Mouton.[18] As noted in Chapter 10, the grid identifies two variables of managerial behavior: concern for production and concern for people. Grid OD has as its objectives the development of a 9,9 (team-building) way of managing and the development of an ideal organization. In a six-phase program lasting from three to five years, an organization can move systematically from the stage of examining managerial behavior and style to the development and implementation of an "ideal organization model."

Phase 1: The Managerial Grid

In this phase all managers are given a grid seminar. The managers assess their individual managerial styles and also their organization's work culture by applying the grid framework. Attention is given to problem solving, communication, and team skills.

Phase 2: Teamwork Development

In this phase actual work teams apply grid concepts to developing effective teamwork within the company. This is achieved by an analysis of team culture (i.e., their way of life, the development of planning, objective setting, and problem-solving skills) and feedback to each manager about his or her team behavior.

Phase 3: Intergroup Development

While team development is designed to deal with problems within each team, intergroup development is designed to develop the basis for sound problem-solving relationships among teams (i.e., sections, departments, and divisions). The dynamics of intergroup cooperation and competition are examined, and interfacing teams identify those things that would be present in an ideal relationship. Action plans are formulated for moving the two groups from their actual state of intergroup relations to the ideal state.

Phase 4: Designing an Ideal Corporate Model

The object of this phase is to learn the concepts and skills of corporate logic necessary to achieve corporate excellence. This is done by the top management team. The ideal model is developed by an examination of six elements of corporate strategy: financial objectives, nature of the business, nature of the markets, corporate structure, policy, and development requirements. Using the comparisons of the ideal model versus what the organization is in reality facilitates recognizing what must be changed to achieve excellence.

Phase 5: Implementing the Ideal Model

To achieve the ideal model the organization must be reorganized (i.e., the present systems must be disassembled and put back according to the model). This is approached on a parts basis—profit centers, geographical areas, product line—by a planning team for each organization part that seeks to move toward the ideal model.

Phase 6: Systematic Critique

In the final phase the total effort, phases 1 through 5, is reviewed and progress assessed to consolidate results and plan the next steps of development.

Grid OD is one of the most thorough programs of organizational development. It is directed at creating and supporting a 9,9 work environment that promotes productivity, creativity, mental and physical health, and personal satisfaction. Blake, Mouton, Barnes, and Greiner evaluated the results of a grid OD program involving 800 managers and technicians of a large petroleum company.[19] Significant improvements were found on measures of profits, productivity, costs, and waste. There also was an increased emphasis on team work and problem solving and a definite shift toward 9,9 values. The managers themselves felt that their own effectiveness and that of the corporation had improved as a result of the program.

Management by objectives

Management by objectives or results is an approach to management planning and evaluation in which objectives are established for the organization and each manager. These objectives are used as guidelines for operating organizational units and assessing the contribution of each organization member. The following steps, taken from Raia's *Managing by Objectives,* are involved in most MBO programs.[20]

Step 1: Formulate long-range goals and strategic plans

Long-range goals are structured in light of the basic mission of the organization, that is, what is the present purpose of the organization or what it should be. After the mission is clarified, long-range goals are developed that are the product of analyzing the external environment and assessing its internal resources or capabilities. The process is shown as follows.

Long-range goals become a desired future condition; they are broad but provide direction. Strategic plans describe how the organization intends to cope with its total environment—external and internal—and reflect the means for survival and growth, for attaining long-range goals. An example of this is as follows:

Goal:

To increase return on investment to 15 percent after taxes by the end of five years.

Strategic Plan:

(1) To increase the firm's share of the market penetration and the introduction of a medium-priced product and (2) to reduce the average cost per unit to increase competitive advantage.

Step 2: Develop specific overall organizational objectives

To translate long-range goals into actions, short-range organizational objectives, usually one year, are developed. Such objectives express desired accomplishments or end results. To become operational, an objective must be specific, and its attainment must be capable of being measured.

To establish objectives, key result areas are identified, and the expected performance in each area is specified. Key result areas are those activities vital to the success of the organization. For a business organization, some key result areas would likely include profits, productivity, competitive position, and public responsibility. For a hospital, key result areas would probably include patient care, education and training, and research. The following is an example of several business goals.

1. Increase sales volume to 100,000 units next year.
   a. Increase product A by 70,000 units.
   b. Increase product B by 30,000 units.
2. Expand existing production facilities to produce 100,000 units at no additional cost per unit next year.

Note that these objectives are stated as results to be achieved and by when; some objective statements will also include the cost of attaining the goal.

Step 3: Establish departmental objectives

After the organization has established key result areas, derivative objectives can be formulated for divisions or departments. For example,

Organization Goal:
Increase sales volume to 100,000 next year.
Marketing Department:
1. Increase sales volume to 100,000 units next year.
   a. Increase eastern sales by 35,000.
   b. Increase southern sales by 65,000.
2. Increase share of market to 15 percent next year.
Production Department:

Expand existing facilities to produce 100,000 units.
a. Improve production scheduling.
b. Increase work force by twenty-two workers.

Step 4: Set individual objectives

Once departmental objectives have been established, an individual can formulate his or her objectives in a meaningful manner, that is, effect an integration of individual and organizational goals.

1. There should be an agreement between the superior and subordinate on tasks and responsibilities. What should the subordinate be doing? Perceptions may differ on this. The subordinate may be doing the wrong things, or the boss may not recognize the importance of the things being done.

2. The subordinate proposes goals and standards of performance. This starts with an identification of key result areas, that is, those aspects of a manager's job that contribute most directly to meeting his or her unit's objectives and are within the limits of delegated authority and responsibility. This leads to an identification of major job responsibilities. Objectives are set for each key result area, and levels of expected performance are established for each objective. Job objectives may be of several kinds. Some objectives may be *administrative* or *routine* but involve key result areas. Other objectives may be of a *problem-solving* nature, which stem from special problem areas that need correction, or they may be *creative objectives,* which represent innovations and completely new ways of doing things. Finally, but equally important, are *personal development* objectives that may pertain to interpersonal skills, technical skills, or advancement preparation. The purpose of such objectives is to combat managerial obsolescence, prepare for increased responsibility, and increase on-the-job competence.

3. After the subordinate has established his or her objectives and expected levels of performance, they are reviewed and discussed with the boss. The objectives may be modified or new objectives may be added, but an agreement is reached by the superior and subordinate, and the objectives are put in writing.

Step 5: Formulate action plans

The objectives agreed upon by both superior and subordinate reflect desired end results; they do not specify the means for attaining objectives. Action planning is required that specifies the activities required to reach an objective. After the major activities have been enumerated, the relationships between the activities are established to facilitate coordination of each activity. For example, certain activities may have to be completed before others can be started. Also, if other persons or departments are to be involved, their role and responsibility in achieving the objective must be clarified. Time requirements for each major activity and subactivity must be determined. Finally, requirements for additional resources and their cost must be made before an action plan is complete and acceptable.

Step 6: Implement corrective action

When the action plan for attaining an objective is implemented, one can not assume that all will work out as intended. External and/or internal changes may alter the situation so that corrective adjustments must be made if objectives are to be realized. This requires standards against which to measure performance and progress information to facilitate self-control by the subordinate.

Step 7: Review progress toward objectives

Systematic reviews designed to assess progress and performance in terms of previously established objectives are fundamental to MBO. The review involves the individual and his or her immediate superior and is generally intended to remove obstacles, identify problems, solve problems, plan for and take corrective action, revise existing objectives, establish new objectives, and review performance.

Step 8: Appraise overall performance

The final step represents an opportunity to realize many of the payoffs of an MBO program. Individual performance reviews involve an appraisal of current performance and the assessment of future potential. The performance appraisal may also include performance in areas other than MBO. There are several reasons for this—MBO performance may be due to luck or misfortune, all aspects of one's job cannot be expressed in tangible and verifiable terms, and the focus of MBO is on end results and does not assess management methods and processes (planning, organizing, and control). In addition to evaluating performance, the appraisal process provides a basis for assessing potential for advancement. The individual performance appraisal provides inputs into other systems—manager training, manager compensation, and career and labor planning. Finally, the performance appraisal provides the spring board for setting objectives for the following year; the whole MBO process begins again for both individuals and organizational units. Figure 13-3 summarizes the appraisal process and its relationship to other MBO activities.

Figure 13-3

Performance Appraisal and Related MBO Activities

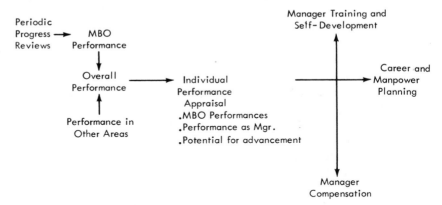

Source: From *Managing By Objectives* by Anthony P. Raia. Copyright ©1974 by Scott, Foresman and Company. Reprinted by permission. p. 116.

The MBO framework presented is a model. There is no one best design for an MBO system; the program must be adapted to suit the organization. Whatever its final form, MBO can be a stimulus for increased participation, effective leadership, motivation of members, and changing an organization's culture and values. An MBO program can also be a unilateral, autocratic means for achieving management's objectives. If so, the values of organizational development are obviously missing, and it cannot be considered a valid OD intervention.

CONDITIONS FOR FAILURE AND SUCCESS

Conditions of Failure

A basic condition for failure is present when the value system of an organization differs too greatly from those inherent in OD. A highly autocratic firm may be too rigid and inflexible to benefit from the self-directive and participatory objectives of OD. To a lesser degree, similar unfavorable results may be obtained when the values and beliefs of managers involved in change do not correspond with their actual behavior. For example, top management decides that it wants a more participative management style exercised within the firm but implements this decision in an authoritative manner. An additional condition for failure exists when a program of change activities is established without the guidance of long-range objectives. Such an OD program may also fail to tie in with other change efforts in the personnel and information areas. In other words, the system implications of OD are ignored.

Management has a short time perspective; that is, most managers are results oriented. If results do not occur in a short time, they lose heart and abandon the program. A realistic time frame for many OD efforts is from two to five years. A short time orientation also can lead to an overrealiance on "cookbook" solutions. Quick, simple, and easy solutions for improving organizational effectiveness are sought rather than carefully designing the change approach to the problem.

Conditions for Success

A setting conducive to success exists when there is pressure for change, when some strategic person or persons (usually at the top) are concerned and initiate a diagnosis of the problem. Under such conditions the required resources for the OD effort are more likely to be adequate. The probability for success is also enhanced by managerial values and benefits that correspond to those of organizational development.

The likelihood of success is improved when there is a realistic, long-range time perspective. Even when such a perspective exists, success of the OD effort is increased by tangible, intermediate results. Finally, success is facilitated when those involved are rewarded for their efforts to make long-range changes and improvements as well as for short-term results.[21]

DOES ORGANIZATIONAL DEVELOPMENT WORK?

As noted at the outset of this chapter, OD is a new discipline and must prove itself. Whether or not OD efforts are generally successful is not clear at this time. One author comments that OD has generated a few successes that are prominently displayed plus a large number of failures that are not.[22] Evaluating OD has been a difficult task; problems of controlled research studies have challenged the best investigators. As we have noted, OD is a long-range program, and evaluation studies must continue over the entire length of the effort. Under such conditions, controls and performance evaluation are difficult at best. Numerous studies however of a longitudinal nature are being conducted.[23] Case study evidence has supported the effectiveness of the managerial grid, survey feedback, and team building. While the case approach to evaluation admittedly fails to provide adequate controls, it is almost impossible to deny the major performance improvements that have resulted.[24]

French and Bell in their review of the status of this discipline conclude that OD can have a positive effect on individuals, work groups, and organizations in terms of attitude and behavioral and performance change. Evidence is accumulating that OD is a successful strategy for improving individual and organizational effectiveness.[25]

Despite its present limitations, OD represents a promising way to improve organizational excellence. It is a response to the needs of both individuals and organizations for improved strategies that will bring individual aspirations and organizational objectives together. Such a need always exists.

SUMMARY

Organizational development is a response to change that has humanistic assumptions and values. As a new discipline, it depends heavily upon the social sciences for its concepts and techniques. To promote organizational health and efficiency, OD seeks to modify the prevailing organizational culture—activities, sentiments, beliefs, values. Change agents play a catalytic role designed to develop the client system's self-direction and self-renewal.

An intervention or change program is based upon a careful diagnosis in which the change agent and client system collaborate in determining the problem and action plan. The action plan will be based upon one or more interventions to correct the problem.

Interventions described in this chapter were grouped according to their relevance for effecting change in target groups of different sizes.

1. Individuals: Life- and career-planning activities, role analysis technique, and coaching and counseling

2. Teams and groups: Team building and process consultation

3. Intergroup relations: Intergroup confrontation and organizational mirroring

4. Total organization: Confrontation meetings, grid OD, survey feedback, and management by objectives

At present, the effectiveness of organizational development has not been tested extensively and thoroughly. Preliminary evidence indicates that OD is a promising approach for improving the health and effectiveness of all levels in an organization.

QUESTIONS FOR STUDY AND DISCUSSION

1. What is organizational development? What are the objectives of organizational development?

2. Evaluate the assumptions of OD. Which assumptions do you question? Why?

3. OD is oriented to produce organizations that resemble the Theory Y model and Likert's System IV. What does this mean? Check Chapters 3 and 10 if necessary.

4. What is a change agent? What are the advantages of using an external change agent or an internal change agent? Both?

5. Can you give the stages in an organizational development program? What is involved at each stage?

6. What is an intervention?

7. What conditions would have to prevail for you to consider team building as a change method?

8. Why is management by objectives considered a total organization intervention?

9. Can you outline the steps in an MBO program? What is involved at each step?

10. What conditions increase the likelihood of failure for an OD program? Success?

NOTES

[1]French, Wendell L. and Cecil H. Bell, Jr., *Organizational Development,* 2nd ed. (Englewood Cliffs, N.J.: Prentice-Hall, 1978), pp. 14–15.

[2]Bennis, Warren G., *Organization Development: It's Nature, Origins, and Prospects* (Reading, Mass.: Addison-Wesley, 1969), p. 12.

[3]French and Bell, *op. cit.,* p. 15.

[4]*Ibid,* pp. 20–27.

[5]French, Wendell, "Organizational Development: Objectives, Assumptions, and Strategies," *California Management Review,* 12 (Winter 1969), pp. 23–46.

[6]Connor, Patrick E., "A Critical Inquiry into Some Assumptions and Values Characterizing OD," *Academy of Management Review,* 2 (October 1977), pp. 635–644.

[7]French and Bell, *op. cit.,* pp. 36–37.

[8]McGregor, Douglas, *The Human Side of Enterprise* (New York: McGraw-Hill, 1960).

[9]Likert, Rensis, *The Human Organization: It's Management and Value* (New York: McGraw-Hill, 1967).

[10]Miles, Raymond E., "Organization Development," in George Strauss, ed., *Organization Behavior: Research and Issues* (Madison: Industrial Relations Research Association Series, University of Wisconsin), p. 170.

[11]Harvey, Donald F. and Donald R. Brown, *An Experiential Approach to Organization Development* (Englewood Cliffs, N.J.: Prentice-Hall, 1976), pp. 75–76.

[12]Huse, Edgar F., *Organization Development and Change* (New York: West Publishing, 1976), p. 316.

[13]*Ibid,* p. 314.

[14]Harvey and Brown, *op. cit.,* pp. 51–54.

[15]French and Bell, *op. cit.,* pp. 54–57.

[16]Fordyce, Jack K. and Raymond Weil, *Managing With People* (Reading, Mass.: Addison–Wesley, 1971), pp. 99–100.

[17]Schein, Edgar, *Process Consultation: It's Role in Organization Development* (Reading, Mass.: Addison-Wesley, 1969).

[18]Blake, R. R. and J. S. Mouton, *Building a Dynamic Corporation Through Grid Organization Development* (Reading, Mass.: Addison-Wesley, 1969).

[19]Blake, R., J. S. Mouton, L. B. Barnes, and L. E. Greiner, "Breakthrough in Organization Development," *Harvard Business Review,* 42 (November-December 1964), pp. 133–55.

[20]Raia, Anthony P., *Managing by Objectives* (Glenview, IL: Scott, Foresman, 1974), pp. 28–126.

[21]Beckhard, Richard, *Organization Development: Strategies and Models* (Reading, Mass.: Addison-Wesley, 1969), pp. 93–97. Also see White, Sam E. and Terence R. Mitchell, "Organization Development: A Review of Research Content and Research Design," *Academy of Management Review,* 1 (April, 1976), pp. 57–73.

[22]Bowers, David G., "Organization Development: Promises, Performances, Possibilities," *Organizational Dynamics,* 4 (Spring, 1976), pp. 50–62.

[23]Pate, Larry E., Warren R. Nielsen, and Paula Bacon, "Advances in Research on Organization Development; Toward a Beginning," *Academy of Management Proceedings '76,* pp. 389–94.

[24]Miles, Raymond E., "Organization Development," *op. cit.,* pp. 181–182. Also see Porras, Jerry I. and Berg, P. O., "The Impact of Organization Development," *Academy of Management Review,* 3 (April 1978), pp. 249–266.

[25]French and Bell, *op. cit.,* p. 226.

cases cases cases

Case Study: An Unfinished Change

During eight years of operation, business had gradually increased, and additional production and technical personnel were added to the organization. As a result, management decided to streamline the operating organization and assigned Mr. Ash to the newly created position of director of planning and operations. Previously, both the planning supervisor and the operating supervisor reported directly to the manager of coordination (see the diagram of the new organizational arrangement).

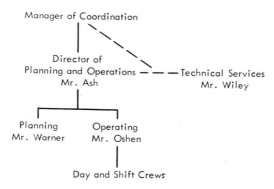

The researcher asked Mr. Ash for permission to study the effect of restructuring the operating group. Mr. Ash agreed and offered the following: "This has been a very challenging assignment. When I reported to the manager of coordination two years ago, he told me that I was expected to achieve several improvements and placed special emphasis on reducing tension and friction, improving morale, and increasing production through better coordination. I spent my first month being briefed and observing my two predecessors. The planning supervisor, Mr. Warner, has been assigned to the group since its start-up and expressed an optimistic opinion of the likelihood of success of the revised organization structure. Mr. Oshen, the operations supervisor, was openly resentful of having to now report to a younger man who would have more responsibility than he had previously. He told me that his relationship with the whole technical group had been unsatisfactory, but he was particularly derogatory in his comments about the technical supervisor, Mr. Wiley."

The researcher asked, "How did you proceed to introduce changes?"

"I began with the most obvious problem first. Mr. Oshen was clearly carrying a disproportionate share of the operating responsibility. I arranged to have another supervisor assigned to the operating building and kept soliciting tasks for him from Oshen. Under the guise of increasing my understanding of shift operations, I instructed the shift foremen to call me instead of Oshen when they had problems on second and third shifts. I received only a few calls because I encouraged the foremen to make decisions that they were qualified to make. It was then possible for Oshen to keep his work current and devote more time to planning and coordinating. I spent much of my time in the operating building so that Mr. Warner, back in the office building, had to use his initiative and judgment to deal with contracts under negotiation. When he needed to consult me, I encouraged him to come to the operating building, and, through firsthand observation, he gained a better insight into the way that his planning influenced daily operations. Nearly every change in responsibility or authority that I proposed to my boss was approved, but these changes were initiated only after discussions with the people affected had produced their suggestions that the change be made. Some problems were discussed many times before I received the recommendation I had decided to accept!

"The most beneficial change that we have been able to achieve is a significant improvement in operator morale through job enrichment. This work group had been so rigidly ingrained with Theory X attitudes that it took many months to change it. The turnover rate of the operators had been the highest of any group in the department, but now we haven't lost an employee in over fourteen months. We broke the old pattern by talking over our operating problems with each shift crew and asking for suggestions of improved techniques or equipment. At first, they were hesitant and even reluctant to express themselves, but after a while we started getting and adopting good suggestions. We tell the operators about contracts under negotiation and any new business as soon as it has been scheduled. Over half of our operators declined promotions that would have necessitated their transfer to another operating group."

The researcher commented, "It certainly sounds like the change was entirely successful."

Ash quickly replied, "No, that just isn't true. We haven't made much progress in eliminating friction between the operating people and the 'technicals.' This was an area of contention prior to my assignment and it still is.

"The technical group serves two important functions in the way that we conduct our business. They study the technical aspects of our operations; their concurrence is required on all significant operating decisions, and their approval is required in all work procedures. Mr. Wiley has this assignment and spends nearly full time in the operating building.

"They also study draft contracts from prospective customers and recommend revisions and techniques; they even veto contracts. Years ago, when our level of business activity was much lower, my predecessor customarily gave them sixty days to study a draft contract. Very frequently we cannot tolerate a delay of thirty days at present. They prefer to research each detail at their own pace. A common tactic now is to find some discrepancy in the submitted data and insist on a written correction, which often takes several days to achieve. Here is a typical example: This memo refers to a contract that stated an element thickness of 0.60" when the reference engineering drawing showed 0.06". It was patently a 'typo' in the contract, and any engineer who knew anything about the product would agree that 0.60ʺ was obviously an impossible dimension. Their request for written correction so infuriated Mr. Warner that he stormed at me with the announcement that he refused to write a letter to the contractor over such a trivial matter. The technical group finally agreed that we could telephone the contractor and, if he agreed, the contract dimension could be corrected.

"I tried a few scheduling meetings where Oshen and Warner joined me in conference with the entire technical group. I stopped convening such gatherings because of the raucous arguments that frequently developed."

QUESTIONS

1. Evaluate the change approach used by Mr. Ash. Successes? Limitations?
2. What factors are contributing to the difficulties being experienced between technical and operating personnel?
3. What organizational development intervention(s) would you suggest that Mr. Ash consider for solving the hostility between the technical group and the planning and operating groups. Outline your approach. Why do you prefer this intervention?

cases cases cases

Case Study: Volunteer Services in Confusion

Because the administrator and trustees of a new hospital realized the importance of expanding the dimension of personal concern and human warmth in total patient care, a department of volunteer services was established and a director appointed. Volunteer workers could lighten the load for busy hospital personnel and add to good patient care. They could supplement, complement, amplify, and extend or enforce services provided by salaried staff and also initiate services that might later require paid staff. These workers would provide some services not feasible or possible for paid staff to provide, but they would not supplant or displace paid personnel.

In the drive for volunteers, contact was made through radio, newspapers, church bulletins, speeches, and letters to civic organizations and school groups; there were personal appeals as well. All volunteers were carefully screened and interviewed, and there was a general orientation by way of movies, slides, and filmstrips. On-the-job training or further orientation was to be the responsibility of the department to which the volunteer was assigned. A position description was developed as follows.

POSITION DESCRIPTION

TITLE: Patient Care Assistant

PRIMARY FUNCTION: To provide assistance to nursing personnel in extending "extra" services to patients and also helping, whenever needed, with routine basic tasks.

EXAMPLES OF WORK:

1. Deliver fresh ice water
2. Obtain newspapers for patients who so desire
3. Visit patients
4. Help check menus and collect these
5. Help serve trays and nourishments
6. Make unoccupied beds

Each volunteer was provided with a handbook of volunteer policies and procedures. One hundred and twenty-five volunteers (seventy-five adults and fifty teenagers) were assigned to the following areas of the hospital: information desk, escort service, family service, X-ray, emergency room, medical records, patient care, purchasing, inhalation therapy, and physical therapy. Assignments were made on the basis of requisitions from any department or nursing unit during a given shift. Every volunteer was to be primarily responsible to the director of volunteers but under the immediate supervision of the department head for whom he or she worked.

Although nursing units had been provided with specific lists of duties that might be performed by volunteers working directly with the patients on the floors, complaints began coming to the director of volunteers office that the volunteers did not feel needed or were not being "kept busy" on the nursing units. Sometimes specific duties delegated to volunteers such as filling water pitchers had already been performed when the volunteer reached the floor. Few staff members seemed to take the responsibility for supervising and giving proper on-the-job orientation to the volunteers, and sometimes they were found sitting idly in lobbies on the patient floors—apparently awaiting some word of direction or encouragement from the nursing staff. To compound the problem, student nurses began their irregular field placement work shifts. The volunteers felt uncomfortable and unwanted.

Other complaints from the volunteers in the transportation services such as X-ray and physical therapy indicated that they were being requested to help lift and transport patients on stretchers with intravenous setups (both prohibited for volunteers). The volunteers were confused.

From the visitor control desk came the reports that the volunteers working there were being blamed when there was more than the allotted number of visitors in the patient rooms and were even being asked to request the visitors to leave. The volunteers were angry.

In the surgical waiting area, the volunteer acting as hostess for families of patients in surgery was refused coffee for these people on more than one occasion because she had to secure it from the nurses' lounge (the authorized place) and the supply was running low. The volunteers had their feelings hurt and felt insulted.

Teenage volunteers reported instances of having been asked to perform unauthorized duties (not listed in their handbooks). They were frightened and overwhelmed by such responsibility.

Soon, there was rapid attrition and assignments were vacant; hospital personnel labeled volunteers as "unreliable."

QUESTIONS

1. What has gone wrong with the volunteer services program?
2. Could this have been prevented? How?
3. What should be done now? What kind of intervention would you suggest? Outline a program of action.
4. As director of volunteers, who is seeking to manage by objectives, establish two general objectives for the year. What would you do to achieve each goal? Who would be involved? How would you know that the goal was achieved?

CHAPTER 14

CONFLICT AND ITS MANAGEMENT

LEARNING OBJECTIVES

When you finish this chapter you should be able to:

- *Recall the characteristics of a conflict situation.*
- *Contrast two views of conflict.*
- *Outline and describe a model of the conflict process.*
- *List three basic sources of conflict and understand the methods for coping with each source.*
- *Understand the dynamics of conflict for the individual.*
- *Describe the nature of interpersonal conflict.*
- *Outline and describe a model of intergroup conflict.*
- *Describe five personal styles for dealing with conflict.*

Since there are numerous definitions of conflict, a broad view of this topic will be used for the material that follows. Conflict may be defined as "all kinds of opposition or antagonistic interaction."[1] Such a definition is flexible enough to embrace incompatible goals, different value structures, divergent interests, and interactions that are covert or overt. The characteristics of a conflict situation help to clarify this phenomenon.[2]

1. At least two parties (individuals or groups) are involved in some kind of interaction.
2. Mutually exclusive goals and/or mutually exclusive values exist, in fact or as perceived by the parties involved.
3. Interaction is characterized by behavior designated to defeat, reduce, or suppress the opponent or to gain a mutually designated victory.
4. The parties face each other with mutually opposing actions and counteractions.
5. Each party attempts to create an imbalance or relatively favored position of power over the other.

Having defined conflict and noted its characteristics, the terms "competition" and "cooperation" must now be put in perspective.[3]

Conflict and competition are often used as synonyms or similar terms, but are they? All competitions are not conflicts. For example, there is no need for opposition or antagonism when departments are competing for the monthly safety award. Two employees can compete for the "Salesman of the Year" award without conflict. Although competition does not necessarily result in conflict, it may if the competition is based on scarce or limited resources. In this case one will gain at another's expense. Consequently, competition may exist without conflict, or, on the other hand, it may precipitate conflict. Any manager seeking to improve efficiency or productivity must project the consequences of his or her program if competition is to be employed.

Another relationship that is frequently misunderstood is that between cooperation and conflict. Is cooperation the opposite of conflict? The answer is "no," but managers have sought to develop cooperation as a means of eliminating conflict. As Robbins has pointed out, the opposite of conflict is no conflict, whereas the opposite of cooperation is no cooperation.[4] The elimination of conflict does not assure cooperation. Two organizational units may not be in conflict but remain uncooperative because there is no incentive to cooperate or they do not perceive a reason for join effort. Some mutually attainable goal may be required to stimulate cooperative interaction. Conversely, there may be too much cooperation. In this instance, harmony and stability are valued so highly that basic issues, problems, and alternative approaches affecting performance are ignored or glossed over. Cooperation exists, but the price is high, perhaps even jeopardizing the viability of the organization.

TWO VIEWS OF CONFLICT

As with most complex concepts, there is no universal agreement about conflict. Value judgments tend to emerge that label conflict as good or bad, desirable or undesirable. Such evaluations generally lead to two diverse positions: (1) conflict should be eliminated or resolved (old view), or (2) conflict is desirable and therefore should be encouraged within limits (new view). Each position has its own background and history.[5]

Old View (Human Relations)

Many of us have been taught the value of getting along with others and avoiding conflicts. The home, school, and church have instilled anti-conflict values during the susceptible developmental years of the individual's life. Consequently, there exists a fear of conflict, disagreement, and antagonism. Conflict becomes something that should be eliminated, suppressed, or avoided. Early management writers took the position that conflict was destructive and should be purged from the organization. Later, the human relations approach maintained that conflict indicated a breakdown of normal and healthy interaction among individuals and groups.

New View

The newer view holds that conflict is inevitable and desirable and that it should be encouraged within limits. Advocates of this view maintain that the goal of management is effective goal attainment, not the creation of harmony and cooperation. The elimination of conflict is neither realistic nor desirable. Rather, a climate should be maintained that supports conflict. Constructive conflict is necessary for new challenges, the stimulation of ideas and problem solutions, successful adaptations to change, and survival. One writer has made the following observation.[6]

> The absence of conflict may indicate autocracy, uniformity, stagnation, and mental fixity; the presence of conflict may be indicative of democracy, diversity, growth, and self-actualization. If conflict is managed properly, it must be stimulated as well as resolved.

A minimum level of conflict is optimal. Robbins maintains that the intensity of conflict can be considered as a continuous range—from no conflict to completely destructive conflict.[7] The desirability or undesirability of conflict is determined by evaluating its present intensity. Any intensity beyond the level sought will be destructive and should be contained by appropriate conflict resolution methods. On the other hand, if conflict intensity is below the level necessary for achieving the organization's objectives, conflict should be stimulated. Since no instrument exists for measuring the organization's conflict intensity temperature, one must use his or her own perception of the situation. Robbins's conflict management model is highly dynamic and requires the continual adjustment of the existing level of conflict within the group or organization to the desired level of conflict.

The two extreme positions on conflict have been summarized as follows.[8]

Old view (human relations) assumptions

1. Conflict, by and large, is "bad" and should be eliminated or resolved.
2. Conflict is not inevitable.
3. Conflict results from breakdowns in communication and lack of understanding, trust, and openness between parties.
4. The environment plays a major role in shaping behavior. Thus, any inappropriate or "bad" behavior, such as aggressiveness or competitiveness, results from circumstances in the environment that can be altered.
5. Man is essentially good; trust, cooperation, and goodness are given in human nature.

New view assumptions

1. Conflict is good and should be encouraged; conflict must be regulated, however, so that it does not get out of hand.
2. Conflict is inevitable.
3. Conflict results from (a) a struggle for limited rewards, be they food, status, responsibility, or power and (b) to a lesser extent, from innate aggressive and competitive instincts in people.
4. The importance of the environment has been overplayed; there are many determinants of behavior, including genetic and physiological, that program individuals to act aggressively.
5. Men and women, if not essentially bad, are nevertheless driven by aggressive, self-seeking, and competitive instincts.

Evaluation of the Two Approaches to Conflict

Old view (human relations)

The human relations approach to conflict has alerted the practitioner to important psychological processes and conditions affecting the relationship between parties in conflict.[9] Typically, this view has focused on (1) misunderstandings, (2) insensitive and nonsupportive relationships, (3) failure to communicate openly and honestly, (4) a climate of distrust, unreasonable pressure, or competition, and (5) the parties' perception of each other. Numerous conflict resolution techniques suggested by the human relations approach have been successfully used in many situations. Some of these approaches will be examined later in this chapter.

Although many processes and conditions in conflict situations have been identified, others have been ignored. The most significant oversight is the realistic basis for some conflicts. For example, scarce resources lead parties to compete, which can result in a more appropriate allocation of scarce means of production. Additionally, the conflict resolution methods are based upon values of openness, flexibility, and trust. Such values are counter to many cultural and organizational values. Competitiveness is considered normal and healthy, and a high value is placed on aggressiveness by many people and organizations.

Finally, the human relations emphasis on eliminating conflict tends to (1) promote excessive conformity and rigidity, (2) emphasize the desirability of adapting individuals and groups to existing structures, and (3) eliminate the discipline and clarity of thought promoted through the conflict of ideas. Despite these limitations, the human relations approach to conflict has had, and continues to have, an enormous impact on thinking about conflict and its resolution.

New view

As noted, the newer view holds that conflict is an inevitable and desirable form of human interaction if managed properly. The general validity of this view is evident in the free enterprise system and the American political system with its checks and balances. Also, there is a growing amount of research that indicates the advantages of conflict. Studies have shown that intragroup conflict and rivalry in sports teams contributes to team effectiveness and provides a stimulus for achievement. Research and development scientists were found to be most productive in organizations having intellectual conflict.

On the other hand, it is obvious that conflicting interests and viewpoints do not always lead to desirable outcomes. Dissension can reduce effectiveness and the attainment of goals. Differences between persons and groups can become ritualized and overdramatized to the point that conflict resolution is difficult to achieve. Furthermore, keeping conflict within healthy bounds is an unknown and unpredictable art at the present time.

Finally, the new view maintains that the parties should have roughly equal power. Not only is this difficult to promote in many situations, but it ignores the perception of power. Perceptions of relative strength are important in determining the quality of the relationship between parties.[10]

Research evidence suggests that perceptions of power inequality can undermine trust, inhibit dialogue, and can decrease the likelihood of a constructive resolution of conflict. Inequality tends to undermine trust on both ends of the imbalanced relationship, directly affecting both the party with the perceived power inferiority and the party with perceived superiority.

One reason that the power advantage undermines trust is the tendency for power to be used by those who possess it. On the other hand, the weaker party expresses more negative attitudes toward the stronger party as the power differential increases. The power-advantaged party is very likely to interpret cooperative behavior by another as compliant rather than volitional, which reduces its trust of the weaker party.

THE CONFLICT PROCESS

Conflict can best be understood if it is viewed as a dynamic process. A conflict between two parties—individuals, groups, or organizations—can be seen, described, and analyzed as a sequence of conflict episodes. The episodes tend to unfold in the manner shown in Figure 14-1.

Figure 14-1

The Conflict Process

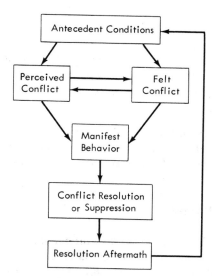

Source: From INTERPERSONAL CONFLICT RESOLUTION by Alan C. Filley. Copyright ©1975 by Scott, Foresman and Company. Reprinted by permission. p. 8.

The six steps shown in Figure 14-1 are briefly described as follows.

1. Antecedent conditions are the characteristics of a situation that generally lead to conflict, although they may be present in the absence of conflict as well (phase 1).
2. Perceived conflict is a logically and impersonally recognized set of conditions that are conflictive to the parties (phase 2-A).
3. Felt conflict is a personalized conflict relationship, expressed in feelings of threat, hostility, fear, or mistrust (phase 2-B).
4. Manifest behavior is the resulting action—aggression, competition, debate, or problem solving (phase 3).
5. Conflict resolution or suppression has to do with bringing the conflict to an end, either through agreement among all parties or the defeat of one (phase 4).
6. Resolution aftermath comprises the consequences of the conflict (phase 5).

In the material that follows, each phase of the conflict is described in more detail.[11]

Antecedent Conditions of Conflict: Phase 1

Antecedent conditions are characteristics of a situation that increases the likelihood of conflict. In Chapter 9 we examined many of the potential antecedents to conflict.[12]

Unequal task dependency
Different objectives and values
Role dissatisfaction
Ambiguities in assigning credit or blame
Dependence on common resources
Communications barriers
Personal factors

One researcher has condensed the long list of sources of organizational conflict into three basic types: (1) competition for scarce resources, (2) divergence of subunit goals, and (3) drive for autonomy when one party seeks to exercise control over another.[13]

Perceived Conflict: Phase 2-A

The antecedent conditions noted above may or may not lead to conflict. They must be perceived as threatening if conflict is to develop. Perceived conflict is an impersonally recognized set of conditions that are harmful to the parties. However, as noted in Chapter 2, perception is a highly individualized and subjective process; it may provide accurate or inaccurate evaluations of existing conditions. The parties may accurately see the situation as threatening a potential loss. On the other hand, the parties may fail to identify potentially disruptive conditions, which prevents conflict from developing. Finally, conflict conditions may be perceived when none actually exists. This may occur when one party does not understand the other's actual position or when each has a limited knowledge of the facts.

The perception of conflict need not result in conflict between the parties. The situation may be ignored if it is seen as minimally threatening or having a low potential loss. This is a conflict-avoiding process. However, the parties may choose to attend some conflict situations. Those most likely to be acknowledged and dealt with are ones that have established and readily accessible procedures for their resolution. For example, disagreement may focus on issues that can be handled by the existing grievance system. Issues that are novel, highly explosive, and not susceptible to routine resolution procedures may be suppressed.

Felt Conflict: Phase 2-B

Perceived conflict may, but not necessarily, lead to felt conflict. However, if feelings are generated, they tend to influence perception of the conflict (see Figure 14-1). Felt conflict is a personalized conflict relationship, expressed in feelings of threat, hostility, fear, or mistrust. Conflicts become personalized when the whole personality of the individual is involved. If the other party is "evil and diabolical" and the feelings are personalized, one feels threatened. However, if the party feels that "we believe different things," the relationship is depersonalized.

Like perception, feelings and attitudes may create conflict when none really exists. Such a condition may stem from the characteristics of the individual personality. High sensitivity and low self-esteem may cause one person to personalize many situations that others would see as neutral or nonthreatening.

Feelings and attitudes about the mutuality of the relationship may also play a part in avoiding conflict. When the parties value cooperation and the attainment of mutual needs, the situation is less conflictive than if the parties feel that only one can win. Such attitudes affect the perception of the situation and also the feasibility of solutions. Likewise, trusting attitudes can strongly affect the outcome of a potential conflict situation.

Manifest Behavior: Phase 3

Manifest behavior is the action resulting from perceived and/or felt conflict (see Figure 14-1). Such overt behavior may be conflictive or problem solving. When there is a conscious, though not necessarily deliberate, attempt to block the goal achievement of the other party, the behavior is considered conflictive. Such behavior may range from covert sabotage or defensive alliances to more open forms of aggressive behavior. On the other hand, the manifested behavior is problem solving when the parties seek to achieve the goals of both by supportive efforts.

Conflict Resolution or Suppression: Phase 4

After behavior has occurred that clearly indicates conflict, the next step in the conflict process is to resolve or suppress the conflict. Conflict resolution is the termination of manifest conflict between individuals or groups. The termination may leave the parties with different reactions to the resulting agreement. How the parties feel about the settlement will depend upon the strategy used to resolve the conflict. Three basic strategies for dealing with the conflict are the win–lose strategy, the lose–lose strategy, and the win–win strategy. These strategies will be examined in detail in this chapter.

Resolution Aftermath: Phase 5

Efforts to resolve or suppress conflict have a definite impact on the conflicting parties. The resolution aftermath is the consequence of the conflict resolution method employed, which will affect the future relations of the parties. If the conflict is genuinely resolved to the satisfaction of all participants, the basis for a more cooperative relationship has been structured. On the other hand, if the conflict has been suppressed or smoothed over, the latent conditions of conflict may be aggravated and lead to an explosion or simply persist and contaminate relationships. Resolution methods obviously differ and may increase the probability of future conflicts or contribute to future harmony and cooperation.

In summary, the conflict process has been shown to consist of five phases; each phase and its interrelationship to other phases can be of value in predicting and influencing conflict outcomes.

SOURCES OF CONFLICT AND RESOLUTION METHODS: A FRAMEWORK

An overview of conflict sources and an outline of possible conflict resolution methods are shown in Figure 14-2. Following the model of Robbins, conflict sources are divided into three broad categories: communication, structural, and personal and behavioral.[14]

Figure 14-2

Sources of Conflict and Resolution Methods

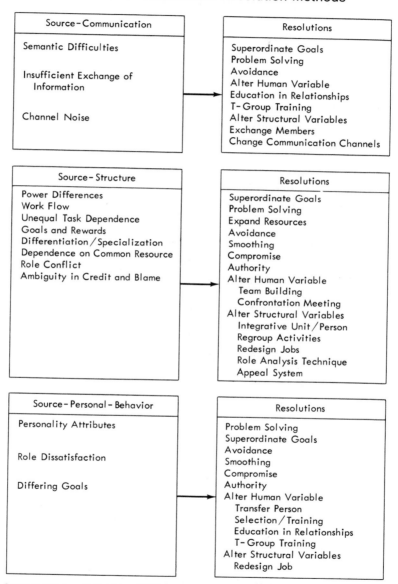

Source – Communication	Resolutions
Semantic Difficulties Insufficient Exchange of Information Channel Noise	Superordinate Goals Problem Solving Avoidance Alter Human Variable Education in Relationships T–Group Training Alter Structural Variables Exchange Members Change Communication Channels

Source – Structure	Resolutions

Power Differences
Work Flow
Unequal Task Dependence
Goals and Rewards
Differentiation/Specialization
Dependence on Common Resource
Role Conflict
Ambiguity in Credit and Blame
	Superordinate Goals
	Problem Solving
	Expand Resources
	Avoidance
	Smoothing
	Compromise
	Authority
	Alter Human Variable
	  Team Building
	  Confrontation Meeting
	Alter Structural Variables
	  Integrative Unit/Person
	  Regroup Activities
	  Redesign Jobs
	  Role Analysis Technique
	  Appeal System

Source – Personal – Behavior	Resolutions

Personality Attributes
 	
Role Dissatisfaction
 	
Differing Goals
	Problem Solving
	Superordinate Goals
	Avoidance
	Smoothing
	Compromise
	Authority
	Alter Human Variable
	  Transfer Person
	  Selection/Training
	  Education in Relationships
	  T–Group Training
	Alter Structural Variables
	  Redesign Job

Source: Stephen P. Robbins, MANAGING ORGANIZATIONAL CONFLICT: A Nontraditional Approach, ©1974, p. 99. Adapted by permission of Prentice-Hall, Inc., Englewood Cliffs, New Jersey.

Sources of Conflict

Communication as a source of conflict includes all factors that impair the transmission and understanding of information, thereby retarding collaboration and stimulating misunderstanding. Such sources of conflict include semantic difficulties, insufficient exchange of information, and noise.

Structural sources of conflict refer to barriers and roles created by management in seeking to structure and coordinate organizational activities. The organization's structure for achieving objectives is often poorly planned and/or implemented so that conflict is generated. Structural sources of conflict can include unequal task dependence, power differences, role conflict and work flows.

Finally, there is some potential for conflict anytime that individuals are brought together to achieve specific goals, even in the best-designed organizations. Personal–behavioral sources of conflict are due to individual attributes, values, and expectations.

Several additional comments about the sources of conflict shown in Figure 14-2 are necessary. First, the sources of conflict shown do not exhaust the potential sources; there are others. Second, the sources of conflict may interact or reinforce one another. For example, a behavioral–personal conflict (personality attributes) may find expression in communication activities and be reinforced by power inherent in the structural arrangement. In such a case, detecting the real source of conflict may be difficult.

Conflict Resolution Methods

By focusing on sources of conflict, insight can be gained into resolutions available to cope with each source. In Figure 14-2 sources of conflict and potential resolution methods are brought together. The conflict resolution methods shown do not imply that they are the best, only that they may be used. Some are obviously short-run solutions or are win–lose or lose–lose. Other resolution approaches are win–win solutions and have the potential for resolving the conflict permanently and to the satisfaction of both parties. The advantages and disadvantages of win–lose, lose–lose, and win–win strategies are developed in the following paragraphs.

Win–lose methods

In the win–lose strategy, one party fails to achieve his or her objective. The loss may be caused by the exercise of authority and/or power that are used to reward or punish. *Majority rule* creates a minority group through the voting process. When a minority continuously loses, it may consider such losses as a personal defeat. *Minority rule* also has the same potential for creating a win–lose feeling as does majority rule. One or two influential persons may dominate a meeting or railroad an issue through the group.

Lose–lose methods

When neither side obtains what it wants or each side gets only part of what it wants, a lose–lose strategy is operating. This strategy is usually based on the assumption that getting something is better than nothing or that avoidance of conflict is preferable to personal confrontation. When two parties reach a settlement to a dispute and announce a *compromise,* a lose–lose situation exists. Although compromise is often necessary, it is second best to a win–win strategy. Another lose–lose strategy is the submission of an issue to a *neutral third party,* as for example, when two department managers may ask their common superior to decide an issue or a labor dispute may be submitted to arbitration. In both examples, the parties have avoided further confrontation and problem solving in hopes of a favorable decision. Of course, the third party can decide the issue totally in favor of one side and create a win–lose situation. On the other hand, a "middle-ground" decision provides something of value to both disputants, but it is likely to be unsatisfactory to both sides.

Perhaps the most natural response to conflict is *avoidance,* as when one party withdraws from the arena of confrontation. Although the issue has not been resolved permanently, avoidance may be a successful short-run solution. An employee who finds himself or herself at cross-purposes with a superior on most issues can use the avoidance approach.[15]

Suppression is another form of avoidance. As with avoidance, suppression does not become a win–lose situation. No side wins, but no side completely loses either. In the final analysis, suppression only conceals differences between parties and is a short-run solution at best. The employee and boss who are always at cross-purposes may not be able to avoid one another, but they can withhold beliefs and feelings when interacting.[16]

Smoothing is the process of playing down differences that exist between parties while emphasizing common interests. The smoothing process, like suppression, avoids differences, but it is different in that similarities are discussed. By focusing on issues on which similar views are shared, positions are seen as less polarized and relationships may be improved. Union and management representatives use such an approach to explore an issue on which there is a common goal or interest such as job safety. However, smoothing is a superficial and short-term solution. Differences that were never confronted will inevitably rise to precipitate conflict at a later time.

Win–win methods

The win–win strategy focuses on an acceptable gain for all parties. Two related forms of the win–win strategies are consensus and integrative decision making.[17]

The *consensus strategy* consists of seeking a solution that is mutually acceptable to all. Goals of the parties are defined so that they can proceed to find an alternative that satisfies the needs of both. This does not mean that both parties must seek the same objective but that a solution exists that achieves everyone's goals. Consequently, there is no polarized conflict and little arguing about means and ends of solving the problem. To achieve consensus, the parties proceed in a manner that facilitates their interaction. Suggested consensus-achieving processes are to (1) focus upon defeating the problem rather than each other, (2) avoid voting, trading, or averaging, (3) seek facts to avoid dilemmas, (4) accept conflict as helpful, provided that it does not elicit threats or defensiveness, and (5) avoid self-oriented behavior when it portends the exclusion of others' needs or positions.

Integrative decision making differs only slightly from the consensus strategy. Integrative methods are more concerned with sequencing the decision process through a series of steps and is particularly useful when the parties become polarized around a few solutions. At this point the parties pool their goals and values before attempting to move toward a mutually acceptable solution. Elements in the integrative decision-making process are

1. review and adjustment of relationship conditions
2. review and adjustment of perceptions
3. review and adjustment of attitudes
4. problem definition
5. search for solutions
6. consensus decision

The first step is designed to compare the objective conditions of the parties' relationship with conditions known to promote cooperation. Then, perceptions and attitudes are explored to determine the extent to which they match reality. If these three steps are handled properly, the parties are prepared to move on to a mutual problem definition, search for a solution, and reach a consensus decision. However, two parties may perceive that one party must gain at the expense of the other and that their perceptions are correct. In this case, it may not be possible to restructure the relationship so that it is nonconflictive.

As Filey notes there are a number of predisposing attitudes associated with the use of problem-solving and consensus methods.[18] There is a belief in the availability and desirability of a mutually acceptable solution, in cooperation rather than competition, in the legitimacy of others' position, in the willingness of others to cooperate, and so on. Such belief statements, while not complete, do indicate that they are based on cooperation and trust. It is questionable whether these beliefs are held by a majority of people and may account for the wide practice of win–lose and lose–lose strategies. In many organizations extensive team building might be necessary to develop the beliefs described here.

Other possible win–win methods of resolving conflict exist in the use of a superordinate goal, expanding resources, modifying the human variable, and changing the organization structure. Each of these strategies will be explained in the following paragraphs.

A *superordinate goal* is one that cannot be achieved by the parties' working separately. It is based on interdependency and must supersede other individual goals that the parties have. A superordinate goal reduces conflict by requiring the parties to work together in achieving the goal(s) that they mutually seek. Although superordinate goals are popular because each party can win, they are difficult to create. Individuals or groups often find it difficult to ignore the differences between themselves and to develop mutual trust and confidence in each other.

When conflict is based upon the scarcity of a resource, as in the case of a secretarial pool, conflict can be resolved by *expanding the limited resource*. Such a resolution is very successful because it leaves the conflicting parties satisfied. However, its use is limited because many resources may not be easily expanded.

In some conflicts, *altering the human variable* may provide a means for resolving differences. Some of the organizational development strategies cited in Chapter 13 are well suited to modify the parties' behavior. Education in relationship skills and T-groups (sensitivity training) may be used to alter individual behavior. At the group level, team-buiding and role analysis techniques may be utilized to cope with certain kinds of conflict. Confrontation meetings offer promise of resolving conflicts between groups. While such techniques are often slow and expensive, the results can be rewarding for all concerned parties.

Finally, the *formal organization structure* may be modified to reduce conflict. Members can be exchanged between organizational units when conflict is due to misunderstandings and lack of information. Employee exchange can be used to reduce conflict between production and sales when members of these two units switch jobs for a given period of time. Such exchanges can promote greater understanding and expanded perspectives and ultimately result in reduced intergroup conflict.

In conflicts between units, a *coordinator* or *integrator position* may be created. Usually, such positions are occupied by persons having experience in the units that require coordination. However, the integrator must still use methods for resolving differences between the conflicting units that maybe win–lose, lose–lose, or win–win. The more successful integrators have been found to make more use of confrontation or problem-solving techniques.[19]

Selection of the appropriate resolution method can become complicated. Selection must be guided by contingency reasoning, that is, by the evaluation of situational factors. For example, problem-solving and superordinate goal approaches, while preferable, may not be feasible because of hostility and distrust between the parties. Smoothing over the conflict may be the best immediate solution until disruptive conditions can be changed and a more promising long-run or win–win solution utilized.

In the following material, conflict will be examined at several levels of behavior. Individual conflict, interpersonal conflict, and group conflict will be explored. Each level has unique characteristics, and each is approached differently.

CONFLICT AT THE INDIVIDUAL LEVEL

Frustration as a Factor in Individual Behavior

A problem arises for an individual in a conflict situation when he or she is blocked from achieving a goal or objective. In some instances the individual may be able to get around the obstacle and attain the goal, or may even settle for a lesser goal. Such behavior involves problem solving, usually characterized by variability in thought and action. Variability in behavior may be relatively simple, or it may be creative. In both cases, however, it frees a person from old, ineffective ways of doing something.[20]

Whenever goals are blocked and substitute goals are not possible, the individual may avoid the obstacle or become frustrated. If one cannot escape the situation or chooses to remain, tensions build up inside the individual. One may become frustrated. If so, the individual's behavior undergoes a distinct change and may become highly emotional, unreasonable, stereotyped, and destructive.

Some of the major characteristics of frustrated behavior are aggression, fixation, and resignation. Aggressive behavior represents an attack and may be physical or verbal. One may attack another's reputation, gossip, or plant rumors about someone. The relationship between frustration and aggression has been experimentally established.

Fixation is to continue a kind of activity that has no adaptive value; the behavior is repeated over and over. Individuals may become blindly stubborn and unreasonable, although they may consider themselves persistent or cautious. Finally, one may become resigned when all forms of activity or alternatives seem closed. The resigned person is one who has lost hope of bettering his or her condition.

These symptoms have a common quality; problem-solving or goal-motivated behavior has become frustration-instigated behavior. Whether or not interference of goal attainment will produce symptoms of frustration depends on the individual's tolerance for frustration, the amount of frustration previously experienced, the pressure that the individual is under, and his or her interpretation of the situation.

Several methods exist for dealing with frustration in individuals, and each demands a constructive viewpoint. If one reacts to hostile aggressive behavior by striking back, an unpleasant situation is made worse. To avoid such a response, it is important to see the frustrated person as one who needs help. Such an approach encourages a problem-solving state of mind.

The most desirable procedure for dealing with frustration is to correct the situation that is causing the behavior. If an individual is frustrated by his or her failure to obtain a promotion due to inadequate performance, the situation may be changed by additional training and development. Many situations, however, cannot be modified because some degree of conflict and frustration are an inherent part of the situation or job.

Relief from frustration may also be achieved by catharsis or giving expression to one's feelings. For such expression to take place, a situation must be created so that the individual feels free to "blow off steam." Since frustration builds up emotional tension and diminishes the capacity for rational behavior, it is necessary to reverse this process. Counselors or supervisors who understand the emotions behind verbal attacks provide opportunities for harmless aggression such as "talk it out" or gripe sessions.

The Individual in a Conflict Situation

In conflict an individual may find himself or herself confronted with two mutually exclusive goals or motives. In this setting, there are three basic types of conflict situations.[21]

1. In approach–approach conflict, one must choose between two goals, each of which is positive or satisfies a need. If one has to choose between more pay or better hospital benefits, the choice will be between two positive goals.

2. In approach–avoidance conflict, both positive and negative incentives are associated with a goal. One is then in an ambivalent situation, being both pulled toward and repelled from something. For example, an employee trying to decide whether to work overtime or not may be attracted by more money but regrets the loss of leisure time. If these two forces are approximately equal, a difficult choice is presented.

3. In avoidance–avoidance conflict, one must choose between two unpleasant situations. This type of choice has no positive incentive, and the indi-

vidual must choose between the lesser of two evils. For example, an employee must elect to do an extremely unpleasant task or be layed off for three days.

Because choice behavior depends upon a person's needs, the behavior is oriented with reference to the self. However, when one satisfies his or her own needs by depriving others the satisfaction of their needs, social friction may be expected, and interpersonal conflict can result.

INTERPERSONAL CONFLICT

In the examination of interpersonal conflict, one focuses on the interaction patterns and behaviors between two or more individuals. Such conflict may take the form of *individual versus individual.* Two individuals may be competing for the same position, in which case the conflicting parties are at the same hierarchial level. This is sometimes referred to as lateral conflict. There is also a vertical dimension to interpersonal conflict; the best-known example is that between superior and subordinate.

Interpersonal conflict may take the form of *individual versus the group.* In Chapter 4 we saw how one worker might experience role conflict when he or she and co-workers held divergent expectations of how a job should be performed. Another example of individual versus group conflict was explored in Chapter 8, when it was shown how conflict may arise from an individual's efforts to promote personal interests by high production for more money and possible promotion when his or her work group had an output-restriction norm.

The material that follows will focus upon the individual versus the individual type of conflict.

A Model of Interpersonal Conflict

According to Walton,[22] there are four basic components in an interpersonal conflict: (1) the conflict issue or problem, (2) the circumstances that precipitate manifested conflict (trigger events), (3) the behavior or conflict acts of the participants, and (4) the consequences of the conflict. The model in Figure 14–3 shows these four elements of conflict.

As seen in Figure 14-3 interpersonal conflicts are cyclical. Two persons who are opposed are only periodically engaged in manifested conflict. At times the conflict is latent or hidden, although issues or problems exist. Then the conflict is brought out into the open by some triggering event. The subsequent conflict behavior eventually subsides, usually because of its consequences, and becomes less important for a period of time only to break out again. This iterative cycle of manifested conflict is indicated as episode 1, episode 2, and so on. The conflict is latent between episodes.

Figure 14-3

A Cyclical Model of Interpersonal Conflict

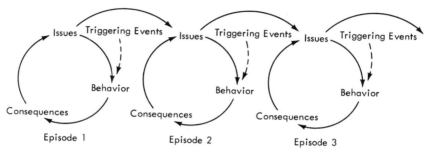

Source: Richard E. Walton, INTERPERSONAL PEACEMAKING: CONFRONTATIONS AND THIRD PARTY CONSULTATION, ©1969, Addison-Wesley Publishing Company, Inc., Chapter 5, page 72, figure 5.1.A, "Cyclical Model of Interpersonal Conflict." Reprinted with permission.

Each of the four elements of a conflict cycle suggest a target for conflict management.

1. Issues: An attempt may be made to eliminate or resolve the basic issues. While this approach to conflict resolution is straightfoward, it is often the most difficult to achieve.

2. Triggering events: Conflict may be prevented from igniting by understanding the triggering factors and subsequently avoiding or minimizing them when the symptoms occur. Although this will avoid conflict exchange, the conflict may go underground and become more explosive. On the other hand, it may provide a cooling-off period that will permit the implementation of other control efforts.

3. Behavior: Rather than attempt to prevent all conflict exchange, the form of conflict can be constrained by attempts to set limits on the tactics used. For example, conflicts may be resolved informally by a series of meetings between two people prior to a formal meeting so as to avoid direct conflict when they meet as members in a group.

4. Consequences: The costs of conflict acts can be minimized depending upon how the target person copes with them. This influences the psychological costs and the extent to which one creates new issues or initiates a new round of conflict. One coping response is to ventilate feelings to

a friend and thereby reduce tension and avoid direct or indirect retaliation. A second coping response is to develop sources of emotional support from one's colleagues that may serve to raise one's tolerance for conflict. Finally, while not resolving the issues, alternatives can be generated that make one's future less dependent on the other conflicting party.

Interpersonal conflict may involve either substantive or emotional issues. Substantive issues involve disagreements over policies and practices, competition for the same resources, and different conceptions of roles and role relationships. On the other hand, emotional issues involve negative feelings between the parties such as anger, distrust, resentment, and rejection. The distinction is important if a third-party is used to resolve the conflict.[23]

> Substantive issues require more mediation by the third party and more problem-solving and bargaining between the individuals in conflict. When the conflict is interpersonal and emotional, the feelings must be worked through to change the perceptions of the individuals involved, and the third party must be more conciliatory in his interventions.

Diagnosing conflicts requires determination of which issues, substantive or emotional, are basic and which are symptoms of a more basic problem. Frequently, a party will inject a substitute issue into the conflict because it provides a more legitimate, and therefore more acceptable, reason for the conflict. For example, substantive issues are often introduced into a basically emotional conflict. Another variation exists when substantive issues are not stated but underline the stated issues that convey a more legitimate basis for the disagreement. A frequently unstated issue is the competitive incentive of two persons who are being considered for the same promotional opportunity.

Many conflicts have both substantive and emotional issues. This is likely because of the proliferation of issues. Emotional conflict tends to create substantive disagreements that provide the parties with a more tangible basis for differentiating and separating themselves. On the other hand, substantive conflict may create emotional issues accompanied by hostility and lowered trust. For example, if I reject the position you take, I may develop attitudes of dislike and even hostility toward you. One of the purposes of dialogue between two persons is to allow identification of the more basic issues.[24]

> If the parties can individually or jointly gain an appreciation of how issues have been added on, they are better able to conceive the present conflict in its more essential, original terms. It becomes more apparent that part of the total conflict which exists between them is a result of a few essential issues.

CONFLICT AT THE GROUP LEVEL:
INTERGROUP CONFLICT

A work group may vary in size and number of components (i.e., section, department, and division). Whatever their structural characteristics, many work groups are interdependent and must cooperate if the organization is to achieve its goals. All too often conflict exists.

Intergroup Conflict: A Model

As noted in Chapter 9, the quality of intergroup interaction will be affected by the nature of the group interdependence (i.e., pooled, sequential, or reciprocal). Also the degree of intragroup stability will facilitate or impede intergroup cooperation. A group divided by internal conflict is not inclined to give very much attention to its relationships with other groups. Internal fragmentation occupies the group's attention and effort. Finally, interacting groups differ in power, which influences their interactions. These intergroup factors and several others examined in this chapter are shown in Figure 14-4. This overview of intergroup variables serves as a reminder of some of the factors in an intergroup setting. The management of intergroup activities and conflict takes place within such a context.

Looking at the Consequences

The consequences of group interaction are shown on the right side of Figure 14-4. In examining the consequences of intergroup relationships, several precautions must be taken before deciding if there is a problem. Both cooperation and conflict may have favorable and unfavorable results. As mentioned, cooperation can exist to an excessive extent and may result in the avoidance of change. Cooperation may prevail but at the expense of confronting and dealing with important issues. One must examine the quality of problem solving, the basis for positive attitudes, and so on to make sure that these are not a cover-up for outmoded forms of action. The quality of cooperation must be measured, when possible, against productivity when these are relevant considerations.

Conflict as a result of intergroup interaction must also be examined for its impact, that is, favorable or unfavorable. Conflict may be energizing or debilitating or possibly a mixture of both. For example, rigid, formal relations may lower adaptability to change but enhance stability in the system under certain conditions. Some degree of conflict may not lower productivity measures but may serve to increase them. The effect of a conflict relationship must be made on the basis of an analysis of the characteristics of the interaction and task requirements. Conflict may be evident but handled constructively so that the task objectives of the groups, and therefore the organization, are attained more effectively.

445

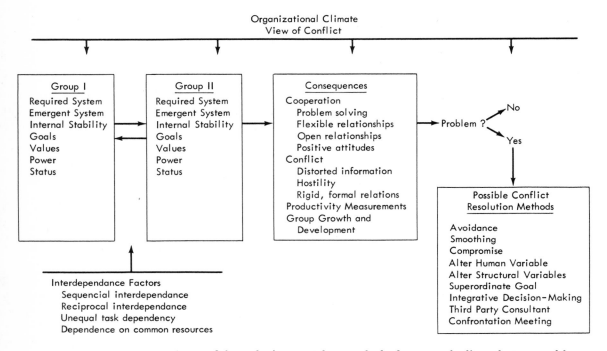

Figure 14-4

Overview of Some Intergroup Variables and
Conflict Resolution Methods

A careful analysis must be made before concluding that a problem does or does not exist. Cooperation between parties is no guarantee that there is no problem. Likewise, the presence of conflict is not irrefutable evidence that there is a problem in intergroup relationships.

Conflict Resolution Methods

If an analysis of the consequences of intergroup activities indicates that there is a conflict problem, some kind of conflict resolution must be used. The right side of Figure 14-4 lists some of the potential methods for resolving conflict. As seen, resolution methods vary in their win–win, win–lose, and lose–lose potential and therefore in their impact on future relationships (conflict aftermath). In the final analysis, selection of the most appropriate resolution method will depend upon the situation.

Management of intergroup conflict will be strongly affected by the view of conflict that permeates the organization. As we have seen, this may range from the elimination of conflict as an undesirable form of organizational life to its acceptance and promotion within limits. Organizations with a fear of conflict may seek to avoid or smooth over episodes of conflict. Another resolution tactic is to immediately toss the issue to the common boss of the conflicting units for resolution. While this provides an "easy out" for the disagreeing parties, problem-solving abilities and confronting procedures are never developed. Furthermore, this approach tends to invite a compromise solution rather than a settlement based upon facts and the merits of the situation.

On the other hand, organizations accepting conflict as a way of life and seeking to make it productive will be more inclined to use confronting procedures for resolving conflict. With such an orientation, intergroup confrontation (an organizational development technique), integrative decision making, or use of third-party consultants are more likely to be used.

The first two resolution methods—intergroup confrontation and integrative decision making—have been discussed; the use of a consultant as a third party requires some elaboration. This involves direct negotiations between representatives of the warring parties in the presence of a third-party consultant. The negotiating activity is structured to clarify the assumptions and motives of each party. Also the separation of substantive and emotional issues is sought so that the parties can focus on the basic problems dividing them. These activities force the confrontation of differences, set the stage for new learning, and can result in the ultimate resolution of conflict.

An integrative subsystem directed by a managerial official may be used to coordinate several interdependent departments or functional units. Research has shown that conflict resolution is more effective if the managing officials have relatively high influence based upon expertise or knowledge.[25] Officials whose influence stemmed primarily from the formal authority of their position or their closeness to top management have been shown less effective. In addition, the more effective integrative officials were evaluated and rewarded on overall performance measures embracing the activities of the department's being coordinated. That is, they were rewarded for the achievement, with others, of a superordinate goal. Finally, interunit cooperation was more effectively achieved when the integrators openly confronted differences rather than smoothed them over or forced decisions.

THE MANAGER'S ROLE IN CONFLICT

The manager's role in conflict will be significantly influenced by the view that he or she holds about disagreements.[26] As noted, two general positions may be taken: (1) conflict should be eliminated as an undesirable characteristic of organizaton life, or (2) conflict is a positive force for change that should be encouraged within limits. The viewpoint taken provides a perceptual framework from which conflict is analyzed and action is formulated. One's position will influence not only the resolution of conflict but also the organization's climate and effectiveness.

Managerial Styles of Conflict

Managers develop their own personal approaches for handling conflict situations. Blake and Mouton have modified their managerial grid (Chapter 10) so that it becomes a conflict grid for presenting personal conflict styles.[27]

Whenever an individual is confronted with a conflict situation, he or she has in mind at least two basic concerns. One is the people with whom he or she is in disagreement; the other is production of results or getting a resolution to the disagreement. The amount and kind of emphasis placed on various combinations of concern for people and productivity determine one's thinking in dealing with conflict. Five basic conflict styles are shown on the conflict grid in Figures 14-5. While no one conflict style is used to the complete exclusion of others, one conflict style usually dominates an individual's approach to disagreement.

The 9,1 conflict style. Conflict cannot be allowed; therefore it is controlled by suppression. The authority–obedience control formula is used to resolve questions or disagreements, that is, "Yours is not to question why." At best, this approach is subtle coercion. In an employment situation, this is a win–lose relationship; the boss wins, the subordinate loses.

The 1,9 conflict style. Positive, harmonious, and accepting relationships are sought by avoiding negative emotions and disagreements. The basic approach is to smooth over conflict by talking people out of it or glossing it over. Harmony is promoted by discussing only those topics on which there is widespread agreement. Real issues are never brought into focus but are put in such an abstract way that everyone can agree with them. Negative emotions, however, are not suppressed, and anyone under tension is given a chance to vent his or her feeling. With a little patience and listening, everything is all right.

The 1,1 conflict style. Conflict is handled by avoiding it. In this conflict-free style, disagreement is circumvented by withdrawal or, if this is impossible, by maintaining strict neutrality. By keeping one's eyes closed, the conflict is not seen. If a disagreeable situation is ignored, it will go away, given enough time. In essence this is a "see no disagreement, hear no disagreement, speak no disagreement" approach to conflict resolution.

The 5,5 conflict style. This conflict style leads to a middle-of-the-road solution to differences through accommodation and adjustment. Disagreement is settled through bargaining for a compromise solution. Compromising means agreeing so as to be agreeable, even at the expense of sacrificing sound action, that is, settling for what you can get rather than working to get what is sound in the light of the best available facts and data.

Figure 14-5

The Conflict Grid

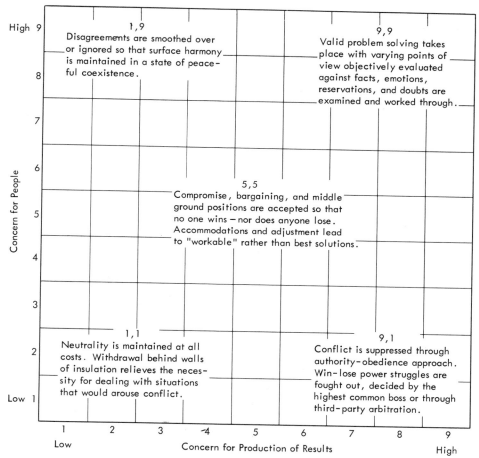

Source: Reproduced by special permission from *The Journal of Applied Behavioral Science,* "The Fifth Achievement," by Robert R. Blake and Jane Srygley Mouton, Volume 6, Number 4, p. 418, copyright 1970, NTL Institute.

Conflict is also resolved by talking to each party separately. Subsequently, a middle-ground decision is made that is given to each party separately. A similar approach is used in "group discussion" when each individual is contacted in private and concurrence is obtained on a course of action. In the "group discussion," the "seeded" solution is adopted and conflict is neutralized. Finally, permanent physical separation is used to avoid direct contact, or individuals are transferred to another department.

The 9,9 conflict style. Under the 9,9 approach, disagreement is valued as an inevitable result of the fact that many individuals have strong convictions about what is right. Since conflict is inevitable, but resolvable, it is managed by direct confrontation. Issues are faced, put on the table, and evaluated by the conflicting parties. The parties openly work through disagreements, identify steps of resolution, and follow up. This approach may be time consuming in the short run, but it is time conserving over the long term.

For each conflict style there is a basic, underlying approach to resolution. For the 9,1 style, it is suppression; for the 1,9 style, it is smoothing; for the 1,1 style, withdrawal or avoidance; for the 5,5 style, compromise; and for the 9,9 style, confrontation. The strengths and limitations of each of these methods from a win or lose perspective have been examined. Research indicates the 9,9 style, or confrontation, as the most effective approach to conflict situations. Have you been able to identify your personal conflict style from the grid?

SUMMARY

Conflict in one form or another is everywhere. Regardless of its prevalence, two opposite positions are taken about conflict. One view holds that conflict is an undesirable characteristic of organizational life and should be eliminated. The contrasting view maintains that conflict is a healthy stimulus for change and should be encouraged within limits.

Conflict is a dynamic process that tends to move through clearly discernible stages. Latent antecedent conditions for conflict are present in all organizations. When any of these antecedent conditions is perceived and becomes personalized, conflict usually appears in some behavioral form. At this point in the conflict process, various conflict resolution methods may be used, or the conflict may be suppressed. Whatever the approach to resolution, there are ensuing consequences (resolution aftermath). Such conditions depend upon how the conflict was handled. The conflicting parties may be satisfied in varying degrees, or the resolution may provide fuel for the next cycle of conflict.

Sources of conflict were grouped under three broad headings: communication, organizational structure, and personal. Potential conflict resolution methods for each source of conflict were described. Each resolution method also was classified as a win–win, win–lose, and lose–lose strategy for coping with conflict.

Conflicts among individuals and groups were examined, and the management of conflict by various means was considered.

Managers develop their own personal approach for coping with conflict situations. Conflict management styles take the form of avoidance, suppression, smoothing, compromise, or confrontation. These five styles reflect the two views of conflict: undesirable and eradicate or desirable and regulate.

QUESTIONS FOR STUDY AND DISCUSSION

1. What is conflict? What are the characteristics of conflict?

2. Contrast the two views of conflict. Whch one do you prefer? Why?

3. What are the phases of the conflict process? How are they interrelated?

4. What are the win–win methods of conflict? Why are they successful? Have you had any experience with a win–win method?

5. How does the interpersonal conflict model (Figure 14-3) resemble the conflict process model (Figure 14-1)? How are the two models different?

6. Why must one examine the consequences of intergroup conflict closely before deciding if cooperation or conflict actually exists?

7. What are the most promising intergroup conflict resolution methods? Why are they more likely to be successful?

8. What are the basic styles that managers use in coping with conflict? Which one is most likely to be successful? Why?

NOTES

[1]Robbins, Stephen P., *Managing Organizational Conflict* (Englewood Cliffs, N.J.: Prentice-Hall, 1974), p. 73.

[2]Filley, Alan C., *Interpersonal Conflict Resolution* (Glenview, Ill.: Scott, Foresman, 1975), p. 4.

[3]Robbins, *op. cit.,* pp. 25–28.

[4]*Ibid.,* p. 27.

[5]Nightingale, Donald, "Conflict and Conflict Resolution," in George Strauss, ed., *Organizational Behavior: Research and Issues* (Madison: Industrial Relations Research Association, University of Wisconsin, 1974), pp. 141–163.

[6]Rico, Leonard, "Organizational Conflict: A Framework for Reappraisals," *Industrial Management Review* (Fall 1964): p. 67.

[7]Robbins, *op. cit.,* pp. 93–97.

[8]Nightingale, *op. cit.,* p. 143.

[9]*Ibid.,* pp. 152–157.

[10]*Ibid.,* p. 153.

[11]Filley, *op. cit.,* pp. 9–30.

[12]Walton, Richard E. and John M. Dutton, "The Management of Interdepartmental Confict: A Model and Review," *Administrative Science Quarterly* 14 (March 1969): 73–84.

[13]Pondy, Louis R., "Organizational Conflict: Concepts and Models," *Administrative Science Quarterly* 12 (September 1967): 296–320.

[14]Robbins, *op. cit.,* p. 99.

[15]Robbins, *op. cit.,* pp. 68–69.

[16]Robbins, *op. cit.,* pp. 69–70.

[17]Filley, *op. cit.,* pp. 25–30, 92–93.

[18]Filley, *op. cit.,* pp. 60–72.

[19]Lawrence, Paul R. and Jay W. Lorsch, "Differentiation and Integration in Complex Organizations," *Administrative Science Quarterly* 12 (June 1967): 1–47.

[20]Maier, Norman R. F., *Psychology in Industry,* 3rd ed. (Boston: Houghton Mifflin, 1965), pp. 85–110.

[21]*Ibid.,* pp. 426–428.

[22]Walton, Richard E., *Interpersonal Peacemaking: Confrontations and Third Party Consultation* (Reading, Mass.: Addison-Wesley, 1969), pp. 71–75.

[23]Huse, Edgar F., Organization Development and Change (New York: West Publishing, 1975), p. 227.

[24]Walton, *op. cit.,* p. 88.

[25]Walton and Dutton, *op. cit.,* pp. 73–84.

[26]Thomas, Kenneth W. and Warren H. Schmidt, "A Survey of Managerial Interests With Respect To Conflict," *Academy of Management Journal,* 19, No. 2 (June 1976), pp. 315–318.

[27]Blake, Robert R. and Jane Srygley Mouton, "The Fifth Achievement," *The Journal of Applied Behavioral Science,* 6, No. 4 (1970), pp. 413–426.

cases cases cases

Case Study: Conflict at the Top

The corporation had experienced a very rapid growth between 1974 and 1978 and, during this time, had completed an extensive capital expenditure program. Sales volume had more than tripled. The number of employees increased from 60 employees in 1974 to 175 in 1978. The firm was primarily concerned with the design, fabrication, and erection of structural steel.

Although sales volume had shown a great increase, there was a sharp decline in profits, deteriorating quality resulting in backcharges from customers for corrections and repairs in the field, and contractual problems resulting from poor delivery performance.

As the organization chart shows, there were three key department heads under the president. The vice president of sales, the vice president of production, and the comptroller. The president, vice president of sales, and

vice president of production were graduate civil engineers; the comptroller was a graduate accountant. The president gave the necessary authority to his key people to effectively operate in their own areas of responsibility but often tolerated the efforts of some who sought additional authority outside their own areas.

The Sales Department had responsibility for maintaining a backlog of work on the books and did this through sealed bids to architects, engineering firms, owners, and contractors. Some negotiated work was booked that was more profitable. Basically, sales were on a sealed-bid basis, with the lowest bidder being awarded the job.

After the sale, the contract was then handled through the Production Department, with the contracts managers' handling the drawings and keeping customers advised of contract status. The required interaction between the Sales Department and the Production Department after a sale was limited because contracts managers handled the contract after the sale except for additions or change orders to the original contract. Interaction among the contracts managers, engineers, draftsmen, and the shop was heavy.

Because of the problems with the production quantity, quality, and delivery, customers were contacting either the president or vice president of sales because adequate solutions were not found at the level of the vice president of production. This led to conflict between the sales and production groups.

There was also considerable friction within the Production Division, between the contracts managers and the foremen and between the contracts managers and the vice president of production. This was often caused by contractual complaints from customers to contracts managers that weren't being solved by the foremen or the vice president of production. One problem was that the vice president of production, who scheduled production, would schedule the easy or heavy sections of jobs to meet production requirements in terms of raw tonnage. The tonnage report was a norm of the corporation, and, to meet the tonnages, customers were left ''to hang'' for the light or miscellaneous portions of the contracts. This often led to extended periods of very low production while the small pieces were formed and worked.

Work rules in the production shop were very informal and were left to the individual foremen. Although the foremen had no supervisory training other than on the job, the production vice president stated that they "knew what to do. They know how to get the most out of the men that they have working for them." Questions of production methods were handled by the vice president of production. When problems arose that required a decision, the decision could come from only one place.

There was considerable friction among the top four executives in the organization. The vice president of sales was concerned with how the Production Department had deteriorated and the effect that it was having on customers and future company sales. The vice president of production blamed all the problems on the Sales Department for not selling the work at a high enough price or not figuring enough hours for the job. There was much interaction between the comptroller and the vice president of production who claimed that the accounting department was generating "bum" reports. He often stated that "The accounting department is hosing me down." There was much free interchange at the top level, but most formal meetings never resolved anything. The president acted as referee, but the conflicts were never resolved. The vice president of production always insisted that he was right and would not cease to argue his point. At executive and production meetings, the vice president of production would always stress the point that "the Production Department was the most important department and everyone else was here merely to serve that department." This added fuel to the hostilities noticeably present.

QUESTIONS

1. What are the consequences of intergroup interaction in this case?
2. Evaluate the production department. Explain what is happening.
3. What changes would you make in this organization? What methods would you use to make the needed change? Why are you suggesting this method?

cases cases cases

Case Study: Conflict Follows Harmony

The Mayberry Mill gets most of its incoming raw material (yarn) from another plant and ships its finished product (cloth) to a third plant for further processing. Thus almost no one at the plant is involved with the final customers.

Mayberry has a reputation of producing a quality product at the lowest possible cost on schedule. Most of the accounting, engineering, research, marketing, and other staff functions are performed at the corporate offices. The staff groups at the plant serve as support to production and as liaison to the corporate offices but report to the plant manager.

The four clerks who are the focus of concern all have similar duties but report to two different managers (see the partial organization chart). Whenever one of them is ill or on vacation, the other three perform her duties in addition to their own.

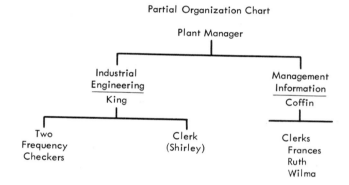

Partial Organization Chart

Name	Age	Years of Service	Dept.	Duties
Shirley	26	8	I.E.	Receptionist, telephone switchboard, keypunch and verify, posting sheets, time-study summary work
Frances	43	23	M.I.	Accounting, posting sheets, keypunch and verify, assist in supply room and general backup to Coffin
Ruth	28	8	M.I.	Posting sheets, typing, keypunch and verify, miscellaneous clerical work
Wilma	28	1	M.I.	Posting sheets, keypunch and verify, petty cash custodian, miscellaneous clerical work

Early in 1974, Mayberry installed a management production audit (MPA) system. Basically, this was a system designed to report production data to a computer at corporate headquarters and prepare the weekly operating statements. The data for MPA has to be input via punched cards that are transmitted to corporate headquarters over telephone lines twice a day.

The three M.I. clerks check the statements for errors, enter some additional data, duplicate and distribute them. Prior to the installation of MPA, all this work had been done on electric calculators, mostly by the three M.I. clerks, but with some assistance from Shirley.

Before the installation of the MPA system, none of the clerks knew how to operate a keypunch, a verifier, or a transmitter. When the machines arrived, teaching tapes were procured, and all four clerks taught themselves how to operate the machines. They did a very good job, and the MPA installation was completed in a very short time. Coffin and King were jointly responsible for the installation, but, because Coffin had more people working with MPA, he had responsibility for its operation and maintenance.

About six months after the MPA system had been installed and operating satisfactorily, Coffin began to perceive dissension among the four clerks. Some information was given him directly as "Frances did not work in keypunch today when she was supposed to," or "Ruth left early today and I had to do her work," and "Shirley is typing a report for King and she is supposed to read the pick clocks." Some information was passed on from King: "Ruth says that you (Coffin) are favoring Frances on a particular task assignment." Or there would be disagreements between Ruth and Shirley versus Frances. Wilma, a very quiet person, very seldom got into these arguments.

Finally, Coffin and King had a meeting to attempt to work out a solution. Both agreed that production was satisfactory, quality was about par, and the rest of the plant had few complaints about assistance from the front office. It was agreed that the major problem was that the four clerks did not get along with each other very well.

QUESTIONS

1. What is the problem?
2. What are the most promising approaches to coping with the problem?
3. Develop a plan of action to implement the preferred approach.

CHAPTER **15**

ORGANIZATIONAL CLIMATE AND ORGANIZATIONAL EFFECTIVENESS

LEARNING OBJECTIVES

When you finish this chapter you should be able to:

- *Describe how organization climate may be experienced differently by its members.*
- *Recall several studies that show different organizations have distinguishable climates.*
- *Explain how organization climate has been shown to influence employee behavior.*
- *Summarize why traditional approaches to measuring organizational effectiveness are limited.*
- *Describe five models of organizational effectiveness.*

In this chapter we will be examining two concepts—climate and effectiveness—that are relatively new in the empirical study of organizations. At the outset we must note that both terms are difficult to define and that their impact upon organizations is not clear. Organization climate and effectiveness are complex factors that may be used to describe organizations, but the characteristics and interdependence of the dimensions comprising climate and effectiveness are not clearly understood. Despite these difficulties, the student of organization behavior must be aware of the current status of our knowledge in these areas of management and the implications for the management of human resources.

ORGANIZATION CLIMATE

Probably everyone has been associated in varying degrees with several organizations over some period of time. Whether fraternities, sororities, or businesses, you may have observed that they were different from one another in numerous ways. Even the classes that you attend may vary considerably and influence you consciously or unconsciously. Such differences are partially due to the climate or "atmosphere" of the organization. Have you ever concluded that the climate of one class was more conducive to learning than that experienced in another class? Similar observations and studies have resulted in definitions of organization climate. In this chapter we will define organization climate as[1]

1. a relatively enduring quality of the internal environment,
2. experienced by its members,
3. influencing their behavior,
4. describable in terms of a set of characteristics or attributes, and
5. distinguishing one organization from others.

Although "climate" denotes the internal characteristics of an organization, the climate is partially a product of the environment. As an open system, the organization is invariably influenced by numerous cultural, economic, political, and technological factors. Furthermore, these factors are different for each organization. To pull together some of the external factors and internal aspects of an organization that collectively produce a given climate, Figure 15-1 presents some of the determining variables.

According to one proposal, five aspects of an organization play a particularly important role in determining an organization's climate: size and shape, leadership patterns, communication patterns, the organization's goals, and decision-making procedures.[2] Four of these five factors in organization climate are included as management dimensions in the internal environment as shown in Figure 15-1.

Figure 15-1

An Overview of Factors Contributing to Organization Climate

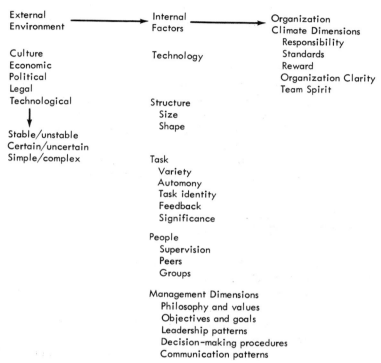

External Environment → Internal Factors → Organization Climate Dimensions
- Responsibility
- Standards
- Reward
- Organization Clarity
- Team Spirit

Culture
Economic
Political
Legal
Technological

↓

Stable/unstable
Certain/uncertain
Simple/complex

Technology

Structure
  Size
  Shape

Task
  Variety
  Automony
  Task identity
  Feedback
  Significance

People
  Supervision
  Peers
  Groups

Management Dimensions
  Philosophy and values
  Objectives and goals
  Leadership patterns
  Decision-making procedures
  Communication patterns

DIMENSIONS OF ORGANIZATION CLIMATE

One of the most difficult aspects of defining the organization climate is the determination of what variables to use in defining the climate. Most measures of climate focus upon particular aspects of the work environment, but the aspects singled out tend to vary from one study to another. An agreement upon the dimensions of organization climate and their definition remains one of the most pressing concerns by organization researchers. An intensive examination of the literature has revealed four common factors in the study of organization climate.[3]

1. Individual autonomy: The individual's freedom to exercise his or her responsibility, independence, and initiative.

459

2. Degree of structure imposed upon the position: The degree to which objectives of the job and methods for accomplishing it are established and communicated.

3. Reward orientation: The degree to which the organization rewards individuals for hard work or achievement.

4. Consideration, warmth, and support: The support and stimulation received from one's superior.

Researchers have measured climate by having employees indicate the extent to which various statements characterize their work situation. Given the item, ''The philosophy of our management emphasizes the human factors, how people feel, etc.,'' the employee may respond definitely agree, inclined to agree, inclined to disagree, or definitely disagree with the statement. In responding to numerous such items, the employee gives his or her perception of the organization's climate. The responses of all employees are factor analyzed to identify the dimensions or characteristics of the climate.

ORGANIZATION CLIMATE: EXPERIENCED BY ITS MEMBERS

In our overall view of climate shown in Figure 15-1, we noted environmental influences and the ingredients of the work environment that individually and collectively interact to produce a ''climate.'' However, it is imperative to note that climate is a function of how one perceives it; it is not an objective reality. This observation takes us back to Chapter 2 where we examined perception and noted that each individual perceives things differently. Personal characteristics such as needs, values, and attitudes, products of each person's individual, and unique developmental history influence one's perception of various aspects of the work environment. The individual's needs, incentives, and expectancies are *satisfied* or *frustrated* by his or her perception of the work environment. Such experienced motivation tends to lead to behavioral outcomes—absenteeism, accidents, quality of work, quantity of work, and turnover. The whole process we have just described may be depicted as follows:

Work Environment or Climate → Personal Perception of Climate → Motivation → Behavioral Outcomes

For the student of organization behavior, this diagram is a reminder that it is not the ''objective'' reality of the organization climate but how the individual perceives the climate that is important. The manager cannot assume that he or she has been instrumental in creating a ''healthy'' or ''satisfying'' climate; the manager must try to ascertain how the employees view the climate.

Multiple Climates in an Organization

One study found two substantially different perceptions of climate in a small, rapidly growing, single-office consulting firm that was five years old.[4] The organization had grown from 12 to 180 employees preceding the study and was involved mainly in social science studies under contract to various governmental agencies. Two groups of professional employees were selected for study and comparison. The first group consisted of the nineteen employees who had been with the organization for over three years; this group was designated as first generation. A second group, labeled second generation, consisted of twenty employees chosen randomly from sixty employees who had been with the organization for six months to two years. There were no statistically significant differences in the groups on marital status, sex, or educational level. Age, hierarchical level, and personality dimensions also did not significantly relate to the quality of individual–organization relationship. Data on the quality of the individual–organization relationship were gathered by conducting a relatively nondirective interview with each employee and resulted in 264 statements. These statements were then grouped into twenty-five comment categories and a scoring format subsequently developed that summated the difference between the positive and negative comments by each individual. The differences in comments by the first and second generation are shown in Table 15-1. The balance between the positive and negative comments for both first and second generation was significant at the .01 level; that is, a difference of this amount could happen by chance only in one out of a hundred times and is therefore due to basic differences.

Table 15-1

Total Positive and Negative Comments

Generation	Positive	Negative	Balance*
First	19.1	11.3	7.8
Second	15.6	20.3	− 4.8

*Difference significant at .01 level.
Source: H. Russell Johnson, "A New Conceptualization of Source of Organizational Climate," *Administrative Science Quarterly*, Vol. 21, March 1976, p. 97.

The analysis dividing the positive and negative comments into twenty-five comment categories is shown in Table 15-2. As the table shows, first-hand generation employees expressed significantly more positive perceptions than did second-generation employees on eleven of the twenty-five categories. In other words, early joiners of the organization indicated that they had established and maintained a different, more positive relationship within the firm than did newer employees. The only exception was commitment to organization in which second-generation employees were most positive in their perceptions. The author notes, however, that their

Table 15-2

Net Positive and Negative Comments According to Generation

Comment Categories	Generation	
	First	Second
Commitment to organization	2.3	6.1**
Organization climate	2.3	−1.5*
Evaluation of own performance	3.0	.4*
Personal goals and strategies	2.8	.5
Structure, systems, and practices	−1.6	−5.5*
Organization goals and incentives	1.6	−.5*
Quality of product	.3	−3.8***
Style of top management	−1.7	−2.9
Superior–subordinate relations	−1.0	−5.6**
Organizational role expectations	1.1	−.5
Individual role expectations	2.5	−1.1*
Changes in formal systems	.3	−.2***
Changes in formal climate	.1	−.2
Organizational changes	2.9	−1.4**
Support for initiative	4.5	2.4
Reward systems	−.06	−2.0
Participation in decisions	−.6	−.3
Pressure on job	−.4	−2.7**
Social atmosphere	.4	−.3
Sales orientation	.5	−1.1*
Congruence of individual and organizational expectations	−.2	−2.0
Dependence on superior	.3	1.0
Bad faith in individual– organization relationship	.0	−1.5
Commitment to type of work performed	.8	1.2
Desire for promotion	−.1	−.1

*$p < .05$.
**$p < .025$
***$p < .01$.

All negative numbers indicate negative net effects.

Source: H. Russell Johnson, "A New Conceptualization of Source of Organizational Climate," *Administrative Science Quarterly*, 21, (March 1976), p. 98.

professions of general commitments were often combined with negative comments about specific aspects of the organization and speculates that they were defenses against guilt associated with their negative comments.

In explaining the generational difference in perception of the individual–organization relationship, it was noted that the rapid growth in size had been accompanied by dramatic changes in central issues about the relationship between the organization and its environment, changes in the internal climate, and changes in performance of the organization's primary task. Growth of the organization was also accompanied by changes in its structure and working relationships in the direction of greater task specialization, formalization of roles, formal systems of information and control to rationalize planning, and performance evaluation of both teams and individuals. These changes tended to produce changes in organizational climate as perceived by the employees. First-generation employees were vaguely aware of the changes in the formal organization, but, by maintaining and utilizing access to the informal system, they had almost totally avoided the impact of the changes on their own relationships in the organization. The informal system remained as adaptive as it had been because they all, including top management, personally preferred that type of system and because it continued to perform effectively for them.

On the other hand, second-generation employees were not working for the organization when the informal system was the only system and consequently did not have access to and/or skills in utilizing the informal arrangements to facilitate pursuit of their objectives. To these employees, the formal systems and climate were the basis for their relationship with the organization. The second generation was aware of the existence of the informal systems, but their awareness was as vague or imprecise as was the first generation's awareness of the formal system and climate.[5]

> Perhaps the most obvious implication of the data is that each generation group perceived a different climate within the organization. That experienced by first-generation members was flexible, strongly oriented toward individuality and interpersonal relationships, nonauthoritarian, and generally concerned with integration of individual and organizational goals. Second-generation members perceived a climate that was more rigid and procedural, had a more hierarchically based influence and authority system, was more impersonal, and placed greater emphasis on organizational goals. Therefore . . . the conclusion follows that the small organization studied had two climates.

To the manager of organization behavior, the possibiilty of multiple climates indicates the need for caution in examining and/or utilizing climate data. Before reading too much into overall or organization-wide measures, each relatively homogenous subunit must be examined separately. Understanding and potential remedial measures can reasonably begin only at a subsystem or subunit level.

Climate and Organization Level

Another study demonstrated how the perception of organization climate is peculiar to the individual and his or her position or role in the organization by examining the psychological perception of climate of 1,039 managerial-level personnel from four organizations that had been separated into three groups or echelons—top, middle, and lower.[6] These three levels of management were compared on their perception of the following climate factors.

1. Clarity and efficiency of structure: The degee to which organizational policies and guidelines are clearly defined; responsibility is assigned; methods and procedures are kept current; and decisions are timely and appropriate.
2. Hindrance: The extent to which inefficient work procedures and administrative trivia interfere with successful completion of tasks.
3. Rewards: The extent to which employees feel that rewards are adequate and fair and that sufficient opportunities exist for growth and advancement.
4. Esprit: The degree to which employees express feelings of pride, loyalty, cooperation, and friendliness in their work activities.
5. Management trust and consideration: The degree to which management places trust and confidence in subordinates by allowing them sufficient latitude in their work, also in the encouragement of innovation.
6. Challenge and risk: The extent to which policies and practices encourage high standards of work performance and reasonable risk taking among employees.

An analysis of the three levels of management disclosed that there were significant differences for four of the six climate factors. The climate factors of structure and challenge/risk were not significantly different between the management levels, but climate varied significantly on the hindrance, rewards, esprit, and trust/consideration dimensions. The same results were found when the four organizations were studied as separate entities. The authors concluded that climate is perceived differently by top, middle, and lower levels of management.

ORGANIZATION CLIMATE: DISTINGUISHING ONE ORGANIZATION FROM ANOTHER

Does the climate of one organization differ from that of another? One would reasonably expect to observe differences in climate especially when the external environments and internal environments vary from one another. As we have already discovered, even subunits within the same organization may have their own unique climates. However, we need to look closely at the climate dimensions on which organizations differ and learn why they do so. Several studies will be examined to explore climate differences between organizations.

Dynamic versus Static Organizations

Pritchard and Karasick tested the validity of their climate measure by comparing the cimates of two firms having a clear-cut difference in value orientations,[7] as such organizations would be expected to have markedly different organizational climates. Company A was a national franchising chain that was highly achievement oriented, expansion minded, aggressive, dynamic, and democratic, and skilled in handling operating problems. There were forty-six managers included in the study who were employed in one of the five regional offices located around the country. The managers were from different vertical levels and functional areas. Company B was a manufacturing company that was low in achievement orientation, conservative, less dynamic, centralized, and paternalistic. The thirty managers from this company were considered to be representative of the managers employed by company B. The eleven dimensions used were as follows.

1. Autonomy: Degree of freedom that managers have in day-to-day operating decisions such as when to work, when not to work, and how to solve job problems.
2. Conflict versus cooperation: Degree to which managers either compete with each other or work together in getting things done and in the allocation of scarce resources such as materials, clerical help, and so on.
3. Social relations: Degree to which the organization has a friendly and warm social atmosphere.
4. Structure: Degree to which the organization specifies the methods and procedures used to accomplish tasks; the degree to which the organization likes to specify and codify and write things down in a very explicit form.
5. Level of rewards: Degree to which managers are well rewarded; this includes salary, fringe benefits, and other status symbols.
6. Performance–reward dependency: Extent to which the reward system (salary, promotions, fringe benefits, etc.) is fair and appropriate; degree to which these rewards are based on worth, ability, and past performance rather than on luck, whom you know, how well a manager can manipulate people, and so on.
7. Motivation to achieve: Degree to which the organization attempts to excel; the strength of its desire to be number one. A high rating reflects a lack of complacency even in the face of good profits, growth, and the like.

8. Status polarization: Degree to which there are definite physical distinctions (e.g., special parking places and office decorations) as well as psychological distinctions (informal social boundaries, treatment of the subordinates as inferior, etc.) between managerial levels in the organization.

9. Flexibility and innovation: Willingness to try new procedures and experiment with change that is not really necessary due to some potential crisis situation but rather to improving a situation or process that may currently be working satisfactorily.

10. Decision centralization: Extent to which the organization delegates the responsibility for making decisions, either as widely as possible or centralizing it as much as possible. Decentralization includes the idea of shared authority in decision making.

11. Supportiveness: Degree to which the organization is interested in and is willing to support its managers in both job- and nonjob-related matters —the organization's degree of interest in the welfare of its managers.

Using seven of these eleven climate dimensions, the researchers hypothesized that company A (achievement oriented, dynamic) would be higher on the climate dimensions of "motivation to achieve," "flexibility and innovation," and "performance–reward dependency" but lower on "social relations," "decision centralization," "structure," and "status polarization" when compared with company B (conservative, static). Table 15-3 presents the results of comparing the two climates: the data tend to support the hypothesis.

Table 15-3

Climate Scores for Company A versus Company B

Climate Dimensions	Mean Company A	Company B	T Test
Achievement	31.1	28.0	3.87**
Flexibility and innovation	21.6	20.0	2.03*
Performance–reward dependency	18.7	16.9	2.99**
Social relations	21.7	20.8	1.30
Decision centralization	15.6	17.4	2.09*
Structure	19.5	18.5	.93
Status polarization	11.9	13.5	2.12*

*$p < .05$.
**$p < .01$.

Source: Robert D. Pritchard and Bernard W. Karasick, "The Effects of Organizational Climate on Managerial Job Performance and Job Satisfaction," *Organizational Behavior and Human Performance*, 9, (February 1973), p. 137.

Using a T-test to determine if the climate differences of the two companies were significant or due to chance, it was found that, of the seven predictions made, five were significant and two were insignificant. Only on the "social relations" and "structure" dimensions were the differences between the two firms not as predicted. One can conclude that these two organizations with different value orientations produced different climates.

A Tale of Two Bureaucracies

In the quest for validation of their organizational climate measuring instrument, Payne and Pheysey also compared two organizations.[8] Aston was a subsidiary of a large international corporation and engaged in small-batch production. The organization had many rules, regulations, and standard procedures and also a centralized authority structure. The Carrs organization manufactured motor vehicles and was very similar to Aston on three main structural variables: structuring of activities, concentration of authority, and percentage of nonproduction personnel. Table 15-4 gives

Table 15-4

Dimensions of Organization for Two Contrasted Organizations*

Features	Carrs	Aston
Contextual		
Number of employees	2,913	350
Degree of integration of production technology	61	68
Woodward classification of technology	Mass production (VII)	Small batch (IV)
Degree of dependence on other organizations	54	69
Structural		
Degree of structuring	62	59
Concentration of authority	50	48
Percentage of nonproduction personnel	65	65
Ratio of workers to supervisors	57	38
Number of job levels in the hierarchy	66	33

*Other than number of employees and the Woodward technology classification, scores are standard scores based on a sample of fifty-two organizations: mean and standard deviation of the standard scores is 50 and 15, respectively.

Source: R. L. Payne and D. C. Pheysey, "G. G. Stern's Organizational Climate Index: A Reconceptualization and Application to Business Organizations," *Organizational Behavior and Human Performance,* Vol. 6, (January 1971), p. 91.

these and other details for comparing the two companies. The essential difference between the two organizations is that Carrs is more than eight times as large as Aston. The researchers concluded, "In simple terms, we might say we have a small manufacturing bureaucracy and a rather large manufacturing bureaucracy."[9]

Reasoning from other research studies, the investigators expected that a large bureaucracy, particularly one with a high ratio of workers to supervisors and a tall management hierarchy such as Carrs, would find it difficult to create a climate in which employees would feel that the organization was progressive and in control of its affairs, close to their supervisors, and free to use their own initiative. Furthermore, due to the high number of employees, the large bureaucracy would find it difficult to create such good communications and interpersonal relations, so that the alienating effects of bureaucratic rules could not be countered by good interpersonal relations as could be created in a small company. Consequently, the researchers predicted that Carrs would be higher on the leaders' psychological distance scale and lower on management concern for employee involvement, sociability, task orientation, industriousness, and administrative efficiency than the Aston firm. All the predictions were supported. Carrs did score significantly different from Aston on all the predicted climate scales. Aston, although a small bureaucracy, had created a climate that was more open minded, yet concerned with rules and efficient administration, while being very concerned with the intellectual, scientific, and technical aspects of its work. The researchers concluded that "Because of its small size, Aston seems to have achieved all the benefits of the rationality of the bureaucratic system and few, if any, of the costs."[10]

ORGANIZATION CLIMATE: INFLUENCES EMPLOYEE BEHAVIOR

As noted, the organizational climate interacts with personal individual characteristics such as abilities, needs, and values and subsequently influences behavior. As one would expect, the behavioral outcomes of interest to managers of organizations are absenteeism, accidents, job performance, turnover, and even job satisfaction. Studies of organization climate have focused on the relationship between climate and behavioral outcomes.

We will examine two studies conducted in laboratories simulating industrial firms that used climate dimensions as independent variables; that is, climate was varied or changed, and its subsequent impact on behavior, the dependent variable, was studied.

Consistent and Inconsistent Climates

One study had 260 managers work through an in-basket test.[11] Two climate dimensions were varied: one pertained to rules and the other to supervision. The effects of rules were studied in two climate settings, innovative (few rules) and highly structured (rules oriented). The effect of supervision was also examined in two climate settings—close supervision and loose supervision. Consequently, different combinations could be structured to create different climates. The dependent variable was the predictability of in-basket performance as determined by tests and biographical data. This can be visualized as climate (varied) leads to in-basket performance (predicted). Several conclusions of this study were very impressive. (1) Predictability of performance was higher under the innovative climate. (2) Performance was more predictable for those managers who worked in a consistent climate (innovation and loose supervision or rules and close supervision) than for those who performed in an inconsistent climate (innovation and close supervision or rules and loose supervision). (3) Managers employed different work methods under different climate conditions. For example, under the climate conditions permitting more freedom, administrators dealt more directly with peers, whereas, in the restrictive climates, they tended to work through more formal channels. In summary, the experimental laboratory study definitely showed climate to influence behavior.

Three Faces of Climate

Litwin and Stringer designed a laboratory simulation to study the influence of leadership style and organization climate on the motivation and behavior of organizations.[12] Three simulated business organizations were created, each with fifteen members plus a president who was a member of the research staff conducting the study. The presidents were instructed regarding the leadership style that they were to maintain throughout the experiment. The work for each firm involved the production of miniature models of radar towers and radar-controlled guns of various kinds from "erector set" parts. A typical product was comprised of from thirty to fifty parts. Each business had three major tasks and three corresponding functional departments: production, product development, and accounting. The businesses were responsible to a simulated government agency, which released specifications for the products and product changes and also requested bids on product orders of various sizes. Although each business started with the same product line, additions to and shifts in the product line were required. The simulated government agency utilized a cost-plus control procedure, and the presidents were responsible for the preparation of detailed accounting statements showing material usage, labor efficiency, productivity, and contract by contract performance.

The fifteen subjects assigned to each business included thirteen men and two women. All were hired to participate in the study. The three business groups were matched on age, college major, work experience, need for achievement, need for affiliation, need for power, and personality profiles.

The experiment was conducted over a two-week period, comprising eight actual days of organization life; the work day averaged about six hours. Data collected daily were used to provide feedback to the presidents indicating to what extent they were achieving the intended leadership styles. Some of the results utilizing leadership style, climate, and motivation aroused are shown in Table 15-5.

A close examination of Table 15-5 reveals that three distinct leadership styles were created, and each produced a different organization climate. In the experiment, observation, interview, and questionnaire data were used to study the climate. The questionnaire tapped the following climate dimensions: structure, responsibility, risk, reward, warmth and support, and conflict. The most descriptive climate dimensions for each organization are shown in Table 15-5 under the heading of climate. The climates were designated as power and authoritarian for organization A, affiliation and democratic for organization B, and achieving and goal directed for organization C. Each climate was effective in arousing its own unique need, or motive, as seen in the motivation column of Table 15–5.

Some readers may be inclined at this point to say, "So what, the bottom line is production." Table 15-6 gives the impact that climate had upon performance and also satisfaction.

Organization C, with its achievement and goal-directed climate outperformed its two competitors in introducing new products, cutting material cost substantially, and generating the highest profits. Organization A (power and authoritarian) enjoyed the best "quality" reputation because it never attempted to "cut corners" and was conservative in its bidding. However, it was not able to innovate and was inflexible when confronted with changing market demand. Organization B (affiliative and democratic) had the poorest profit showing but enjoyed a good "quality" image and was able to innovate. Its bids were generally competitive with those of the other organizations, but it was unprofitable because it supported an extremely high (unfavorable) labor variance.

Several conclusions drawn are relevant to understanding organization climates: (1) Distinct organizational climates can be created by varying leadership styles. (2) Once created, these climates seem to have significant, often dramatic, effects on motivation and correspondingly on performance and job satisfaction. Each of the three experimentally induced climates aroused a different motivation pattern.

Table 15-5

Leadership Style, Climate, and Motivation of Three Simulated Business Firms

Leadership Style	Climate	Motivation
Organization A Maintain order Exercise authority and control Criticize poor performance Criticize deviation from rules Stress conservation Avoid deep involvement	Power and authoritarian: high structure, low responsibility, low reward, low warmth and support	High level of power motivation
Organization B Maintain informality Avoid individual punishment Give general positive rewards Create friendly relationships Create relaxed atmosphere Stress cooperation Avoid conflict Create personal relationships with subordinates	Affiliative and democratic: high warmth and support, high reward	High level of affiliation motivation
Organization C Maintain informality Set high standards for individuals and organization Give rewards, praise, promotion Reward excellent performance Give individual and organizational support Stress cooperation in work Tolerate personal and task-related conflict Stress moderate risk, create organization pride, stress challenge and excitement of work	Achieving and goal directed: high responsibility, high risk, high reward, high warmth and support	High level of achievement motivation

Source: Adapted from George H. Litwin, "Climate and Motivation: An Experimental Study," in Renato Tagiuri and George H. Litwin, eds., *Organizational Climate,* (Boston: Division of Research, Graduate School of Business Administration, Harvard University, 1968), pp. 178.

Table 15-6

Effects of Climate on Performance
and Satisfaction

	Organization		
	A	B	C
Performance			
Profit (loss)	$7.70	$(5.30)	$72.30
% Profit margin (loss)	.81%	(0.08%)	11.7%
Number of new products developed	4	6	8
Materials savings innovations	$0.00	$25.10	$43.80
Units rejected by government	0	1	4
Satisfaction	low	high	high
	3.2	6.2	5.8

Source: George H. Litwin, "Climate and Motivation: An Experimental Study," in Renato Tagiuri and George H. Litwin, eds. *Organizational Climate* (Boston: Division of Research, Graduate School of Business Administration, Harvard University, 1968), p. 178.

An Examination of Two Field Studies

The two previous studies of the impact of climate upon behavior or performance were conducted in a laboratory setting, which is ideal for controlling and measuring experimental variables. However, when one moves out into the real world, experimental controls become extremely difficult. Consequently, one may ask whether the climate–behavior linkage obtained in somewhat idealized setting are to be found in the field, that is, in business, industry, and government. With such a purpose in mind, we will examine several studies conducted in organizational settings.

The multifaceted study of Pritchard and Karasick to which we referred previously also examined the relationship of climate measures to satisfaction and job performance.[13] Managers from a national franchising chain and a manufacturing firm were the subjects of the investigation. The climate dimensions used in this study were defined on page 465. Job satisfaction was measured by the Minnesota satisfaction questionnaire, a twenty-item scale that gives a global or single index of satisfaction. The items included various aspects on the job such as security, working conditions, and advancement opportunities. Job performance consisted of a rating given by a management consultant based upon interviews with each manager's superior(s) and on the basis of performance. Job satisfaction and performance were correlated with the climate dimensions; the results are shown in Table 15–7.

Table 15-7

Correlations between Climate Factors
and Individual Satisfaction and Performance

Climate Factor	Satisfaction	Performance
Autonomy	.11	.05
Conflict versus cooperation	.48**	.16
Social relations	.51**	−.07
Structure	.32**	−.07
Level of rewards	.66**	.24*
Performance–reward dependency	.50**	.14
Achievement	.65**	.25*
Status polarization	−.39**	−.14
Flexibility and innovation	.42**	.08
Decision centralization	−.39**	−.04
Supportiveness	.52**	−.04

$*p < .05.$
$**p < .01.$

Source: Robert D. Pritchard and Bernard W. Karasick, "The Effects of Organizational Climate on Managerial Job Performance and Job Satisfaction," *Organizational Behavior and Human Performance* 9 (February 1973), p. 139.

Of the eleven climate dimensions, ten were significantly related to job satisfaction. The dimensions most highly related to satisfaction were achievement (.65), level of rewards (.66), social relations (.51), performance–reward dependency (.50), and supportiveness (.52). It is interesting to note that satisfaction was negatively associated with status polarization (i.e., physical and psychological distinctions between managerial levels) and also decision centralization. There were small positive correlations between two climate dimensions: level of rewards and achievement and ratings of individual job performance. In summary, climate seemed to be strongly related to individual satisfaction but much less related to individual performance.

Another study also explored the climate–job satisfaction and climate–job performance relationship.[14] The research was conducted at a major midwestern medical complex and included 961 registered nurses, licensed practical nurses, nurses' aids, technologists, therapists, dietitians, technicians, and clerical and janitorial personnel. The climate questionnaire was taken from the Litwin and Stringer measuring instrument with certain questions reworded very slightly to fit the medical environment. The modified questionnaire was factor analyzed to determine independent climate dimensions. The six factors are as follows:

1. Feeling toward other people: Perception of co-workers and others in the organization.
2. Feeling toward management and/or organization.
3. Policy and promotion clarity: The clarity of promotion policy and the opportunity for promotion as well as the clarity of organizational policies, organization structure, and job satisfaction.
4. Job pressure and standards: Perception of pressure on the job and the emphasis placed on high job standards by management.
5. Openness of upward communication: The communication between employees and management, the willingness of managers to accept and act on subordinates' ideas, the career counseling of subordinates by management.
6. Risk in decision making: The degree of risk concomitant with management decision making.

The job description index questionnaire was employed to obtain measures of satisfaction in five areas: work, supervision, co-workers, promotion, and pay. Job performance was determined by supervisory rating of each employee.

Table 15-8 shows the correlations of the organization climate factors with the five measures of satisfaction (the JDI scales) and performance. Examination discloses that the climate factors of feeling toward people, feeling toward management, and policy and promotional clarity are all positively correlated with each of the given job satisfaction scales. On the other hand, job pressure and standards are negatively correlated to all the satisfaction measures. The risk factor shows substantially lower, but significant, relationships with the measures of job satisfaction. When we look at the correlations between all climate factors and job performance, we find that they are all significant, because of the large sample size, but generally low. In summary, the relationships among the climate factors, job satisfaction, and job performance are very significant.

The two studies are typical of many undertaken in the area of organizational climate in several respects. Job satisfaction is usually found to be highly related to climate dimensions. If the climate is perceived as supportive and consistent with one's needs and values, job satisfaction tends to be high. One conclusion from the analysis of climate satisfaction studies is that "organizational climate is related to job satisfaction in terms of interpersonal relations, group cohesiveness, task-involvement, and the like."[15] On

Table 15-8

Correlations of the Organizational Climate Factors with the Job Description Index Scales and Performance Evaluation*

Organizational Climate Factors	Job Satisfaction (JDI)					Perform-ance
	Work	Super-vision	Co-workers	Promotion	Pay	
1. Feeling toward other people	.45	.53	.46	.40	.25	.24
2. Feeling toward management	.28	.42	.23	.35	.13	.09
3. Policy and promotion clarity	.25	.39	.23	.48	.17	.09
4. Job pressure and standards	−.15	−.23	−.10	−.04	−.13	−.11
5. Openness of upward communication	.31	.45	.24	.44	.20	.16
6. Risk in decision making	.13	.17	.09	.15	.08	.10

*All correlations are significant between the .02 and .001 levels except the one underlined.

Source: William R. La Follette and Henry P. Sims, Jr., "Is Satisfaction Redundant with Organizational Climate?" *Organizational Behavior and Human Performance,* Vol. 13, April 1975, p. 267.

the other hand, climate–performance linkages, while definitely related, tend to be lower. The failure to demonstrate a closer connection between climate dimensions and performance may be due to the low validity and reliability of the performance measures themselves. Also, job performance is a function of many dimensions, and the concept of a single criterion of a global nature, like supervisory ratings, may be unrealistic.

Finally, the practice of combining the perceptions of all subjects to obtain an overall or single climate measure may lower the climate–performance relationship. A single climate score for an organization fails to reflect the great diversity found in the work environments of different subunits. An example of this was noted in the study that found two distinct climates being perceived by first- and second-generation employees. Aggregated or overall measures of climate in this study would have been meaningless. In the Pritchard and Karasick study, a discrepancy was found in the results between analyses made with individuals and analyses made with subunits.[16]

When all subjects were combined, weak relationships between climate and performance resulted, but fairly high relationships emerged when groups of subjects (subunits) were examined. While the original summation of all individuals consisted of persons from two companies in this study, the divergence in work environment may well be equally as great within a single organization. Consequently, one may wonder if the summation of all data into a composite score does not result in the loss of both the causes and effects of distinct multiple climates within an organization.

Summary

Organization climate has been considered as a quality of an organization's internal environment that is experienced and influences the behavior of its members. The behavioral implications are evident in that an individual's expectations are frustrated or satisfied by his or her perceived environment and may affect absenteeism, turnover, quantity and quality of work, and so on. Climate is a product of numerous environmental and internal organizational factors that are subject to some degree of control or influence by management.

While the characteristics or dimensions of climate vary from one investigation to another, there are common dimensions of climate throughout many of these studies. It is quite evident from the foregoing material that the concept of climate is not as precise and operational as one would desire. However, climate is an important construct for the student of organization behavior and/or managers.

On the basis of the investigations and writings on organization climate, the following conclusions appear justified:

1. Organizations of any size or complexity may have multiple climates, and each relatively homogenous subunit should be examined separately and remedial measures tailored to that unit, if needed.
2. The organization climate is perceived differently by top, middle and lower levels of management. This is another way of partitioning an organization into different homogenous groups.
3. There is sufficient evidence to conclude that organizations do have climates that differ from one another.
4. The laboratory and field studies of the "organizations" previously surveyed indicate that climate variables influence the predictability of performance, motivation, satisfaction, and performance.

ORGANIZATION EFFECTIVENESS

We have just examined organization climate as a potentially useful concept to the manager or student of organization behavior but lacking the consistency and precision one might desire. As we move to a consideration of organization effectiveness, the student should be aware that this area has the same characteristics. Nonetheless, one will find it profitable to become intimately acquainted with the concept of organizational effectiveness. Consequently, we will try to develop a general definition of effectiveness, examine some of the criteria and models used to access effectiveness, and finally explore the relevance of this concept to the manager.

The previous examination of organization climate implicitly and explicitly indicated that this concept should be related to organizational effectiveness or some aspect of effectiveness. Similar parallels of determinants are depicted in the diagram following.

The external environment impacts upon the internal environment, which in essence sets the stage for organization climate and effectiveness. Furthermore, these two factors—climate and effectiveness—would appear related to one another. A favorable climate would be expected to influence the effectiveness of individuals, groups, and eventually the total organization. Finally, an effective organization would be characterized by a definite climate, certainly different from an ineffective one.

The effectiveness of organizations have frequently been defined in terms of singular or multiple goal achievement. Goals or objectives are stated as criteria for success, and then the organization evaluates its performance or efficiency as the extent to which such predetermined goals were attained. For example, an organization may have as its goals for next year to increase return on investment by 7 percent or increase sales volume to 100,000 units, reduce production cost by 3 percent, and so on. The greater the degree of goal achievement, the more effective the organization. A goal achievement concept of organization effectiveness at all managerial levels is well documented in management and organizational literature. Such goals are widely used because they

1. are often easily quantified measures,
2. correspond closely to available accounting information,
3. represent the overt reasons for the organization's existence,
4. are easily communicated, and
5. provide guideposts or standards to assess performance and grant rewards.

While managers obviously use performance goals as indicators of efficiency, the limitations of such measures are being perceived. Both managers and researchers are seeking additional and more valid efficiency measures.

VIEWPOINTS OF EFFECTIVENESS CRITERIA

The criteria of effectiveness can be examined from different points of view.[17] The focus may be

macro or micro
univariate or multivariate
static or dynamic
limited or universal

Management researchers have directed their attention to organization-wide (macro) efficiency indicators such as profit or productivity in some investigations. Other studies have focused upon micro measurements such as individual performance.

The criterion variable selected as indicative of effectiveness may be a single measure (univariate) or multivariate (i.e., based upon a number of criteria). A review of various effective measures utilized by researchers identified the most widely used univariate efficiency measures.[18] These were (1) overall performance, as measured by employee or supervisory ratings; (2) productivity, as measured by actual output data; (3) employee satisfaction, as measured by self-report questionnaires; (4) profit, or rate of return, as based upon accounting data; (5) withdrawal, as shown by turnover and absenteeism data. However, it is difficult to defend the use of single measures as comprehensive or adequate criteria of organizational effectiveness. For example, profit may not reflect less cost per unit of product attributable to efficiency but simply what consumers will pay, lack of competition, or, in some instances, outright luck. The more recent and sophisticated models are multivariate.

Effectiveness models also differ in the extent to which generalizations may be drawn by others. Some models purport to be universal in that they are relevant to any organization, whatever its nature. Models of this variety are so general that they are of little value to managers or even some researchers. Other models, however, utilize efficiency criteria that are contingent or dependent upon the specific group of organizations being studied (i.e., their unique properties).

Finally, criteria measures may be static or dynamic. If static, the measures reflect past levels of activity and, as such, "look backward." In other words, such efficiency measures are a post mortem and evaluate past performance. Since it is questionable as to whether or not an organization can be judged successful only on the basis of past achievements, attention is now given to the dynamic characteristics of performance. Such considerations focus on those activities necessary to remaining viable in the future.

MULTIVARIATE EFFECTIVENESS MODELS

A very meaningful approach to the study of effectiveness consists of using several variables and determining how they jointly influence organizational success. Such integrative approaches are generally more comprehensive and attempt to account for more of the variability in effectiveness.

The results of one study of seventeen multiple variable models to ascertain what criteria of effectiveness were most frequently used are shown in Table 15-9.[19] The author concluded from his comparison of these multivariate models that there was a definite lack of consensus as to what constitutes a useful and valid set of effectiveness measures. An examination of the evaluation crtieria in Table 15-9 indicates adaptability—flexibility was mentioned or used most often, followed by productivity, and then satisfaction. However, only adaptability and flexibility were utilized in more than half the models surveyed. Rather than conclude that attempts to measure organizational effectiveness are fruitless, the author believes that the effectiveness concept is so complex that more flexible, comprehensive indicators are required.

Table 15-9

Frequency of Occurrence of Evaluation Criteria in Seventeen Models of Organizational Effectiveness

Evaluation Criteria	Number of Times Mentioned
Adaptability and flexibility	10
Productivity	6
Satisfaction	5
Profitability	3
Resource acquisition	3
Absence of strain	2
Control over environment	2
Development	2
Efficiency	2
Employee retention	2
Growth	2
Integration	2
Open communications	2
Survival	2
All other criteria	1

Source: Richard M. Steers, "Problems on the Measurement of Organizational Effectiveness," *Administrative Science Quarterly*, Vol. 20, December 1975, p. 549.

An Adaptability–Coping Approach

An increasing amount of emphasis is being placed upon a system's capacity to survive, adapt, maintain itself, and grow. Static or historical performance goals such as profits or productivity do not adequately convey an ability or capacity to cope effectively in the near future. One researcher has developed an analogy between the concept of mental health and organization efficiency.[20] Given that organizations are open systems coping with various environments, the most significant characteristic for understanding effectiveness is adaptability and problem solving. These characteristics also are criteria for evaluating mental health. The author proposed the following three criteria for organizational health.

1. Adaptability: The ability to solve problems and react flexibly to changing internal and external demands (i.e., learning through experience).
2. A sense of identity: The knowledge by the organization of what its goals are and what it is to do (i.e., its mission and role).
3. Reality testing: The ability to search out, accurately perceive, and correctly interpret the environment.

These activities are basic to accurate problem solving.

However, the question remains as to how an organization can cope with its environment, obtain and process information, and appropriately alter its operations. One author proposes maintaining effectiveness through an adaptive–coping cycle consisting of six stages.[21]

1. Sensing a change in some part of the internal or external environment.
2. Importing the relevant information about the change into those parts of the organization that can act upon it.
3. Changing production or conversion processes inside the organization according to the information obtained.
4. Stabilizing internal changes while reducing or managing undesirable by-products.
5. Exporting new products, service , and so on, which are more in line with the originally perceived changes in the environment and the degree of integration of the internal environment.
6. Obtaining feedback on the success of the change through further sensing of the state of the external environment and the degree of integration of the internal environment.

The coping cycle is especially relevant to criteria of adaptability and reality testing as proposed for organizational health. The organization is able to maintain and improve its effectiveness in response to either internal or external changes.

A Time-Effectiveness Model

A model of organizational effectiveness has been developed that not only combines several measures or criteria but also adds a new element—time—that enables one to speak of effectiveness in the short, intermediate, and long run.[22] Different effectiveness criteria are relevant at varying time intervals and point to the ultimate requirement of survival. The model is illustrated in Figure 15-2.

Figure 15-2

Criteria of Organizational Effectiveness

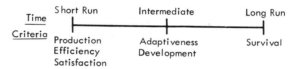

Source: James L. Gibson, John M. Ivancevich, and James H. Donnelly, Jr., *Organizations: Behavior, Structure, and Processes,* 3rd ed (Dallas: Business Publications, Inc. 1979), p. 30. ©1979 by Business Publications, Inc.

As seen, the short-run indicators include production, efficiency, and satisfaction measures. The criteria termed intermediate include adaptation and development. Finally, survival is the ultimate or long-run measure of organizational effectiveness.

The meanings of the measures incorporated in the model are outlined briefly here.

1. Production: The ability of the organization to produce the quality of output that the environment demands. Measures include profit, sales, market share, students graduated, patients released, clients served, and so on.

2. Efficiency: The ratio of outputs to inputs. Measures include rate of return on capital, unit cost, waste, downtime, cost per patient, and so on.

3. Satisfaction: The benefits received by employees. Measures include employee attitudes, turnover, absenteeism, tardiness, and grievances.

4. Adaptiveness: The extent to which the organization can and does respond to internally and externally induced changes. There are no specific and concrete measures, but appropriate policies and procedures can facilitate adaptiveness.

5. Development: The investment an organization makes in itself by means of training programs for managerial and nonmanagerial personnel.

The use of time in this model means that an organization may be evaluated as effective in terms of production, satisfaction, and efficiency criteria but ineffective in terms of adaptiveness or development or perhaps both. Survival would be questionable. An optimal balance of an organization's performance over time is crucial and also among the criteria within a given time period. Therefore, it is necessary for the manager to recognize the need for determining potential relationships between different time effectiveness criteria prior to implementing policies designed to affect such criteria.

A Production–Adaptation Model

One effectiveness model has production and adaptation components. The approach is based upon the reasoning that effective organizations produce more and higher-quality outputs and adapt more effectively to environmental and internal problems than do less effective ones. Consequently, organizational effectiveness is defined as "the ability of an organization to mobilize its centers of power for action—production and adaptation."[23] Using these two effectiveness measures the following criteria were developed.

A. Productivity
   1. Quantity of the product
   2. Quality of the product
   3. Efficiency with which the product is produced
B. Adaptability
   1. Early warning detection
      a. anticipating problem in advance and developing satisfactory and timely solutions
      b. staying abreast of new technologies and methods applicable to the organization
   2. Behavioral adaptation
      a. prompt acceptance of solutions
      b. prevalent acceptance of solutions
C. Flexibility
   1. Organizing centers of power to cope with temporarily unpredictable overloads of work

These definitions and measures of effectiveness were intended to be as free of goal orientation as possible and to focus on the effectiveness of *work processes*. This approach avoids the arbitrariness of selecting managerial goals or those found in corporate charters, goals that may be vague, not universally accepted, or perhaps goals that mask the real objectives of the organization. The effectiveness model tends to be universal in that nearly all organizations produce something, no matter how intangible, and also tend to require some degree of adaptability and flexibility for survival.

By using questions that permit five degrees of response or agreement, each of the effectiveness criteria is measured. The questions are presented to provide more insight into each criterion.[24]

Production: Quantity

Thinking now of the various things produced by the people you know in your division, how much are they producing?

Production: Quality

How good would you say is the quality of the products or services produced by the people you know in your division?

Production: Efficiency

Do the people in your division seem to get maximum output from the resources (money, people, equipment, etc.) they have available? That is, how efficiently do they do their work?

Adaptation: Anticipating Problems and Solving Them Satisfactorily

How good a job is done by the people in your division in anticipating problems that may come up in the future and preventing them from occurring or minimizing their effects?

Adaptation: Awareness of Potential Solutions

From time to time newer ways are discovered to organize work, and newer equipment and techniques are found with which to do the work. How good a job do the people in your division do at keeping up with those changes that could affect the way they do their work?

Adaptation: Promptness of Adjustment

When changes are made in the routines or equipment, how quickly do the people in your division accept and adjust to these changes?

Adaptation: Prevalence of Adjustment

What proportion of the people in your division readily accept and adjust to these changes?

Flexibility

From time to time emergencies arise, such as crash programs, schedules moved ahead, or a breakdown in the flow of work. When these emergencies occur, they cause work overloads for many people. Some work groups cope with these emergencies more readily and successfully than do others. How good a job do the people in your division do at coping with these situations?

These questions provide the basis for the computation of three indexes and an overall effectiveness index. The productivity index is determined by combining the scores of three production questions and determining the average of all eight items. The correlations and measures of relationship among the indexes demonstrated that they measured three different, but related, organizational processes. Four federal governmental agencies and a mental institution were studied utilizing the effectiveness instrument. The results indicated that it was a valid measure.

Midrange Effectiveness Criteria

As we have seen, the ultimate criteria of organizational effectiveness often refer to long-run goal achievement or even survival. Such criteria are usually stated in broad terms and are difficult to define in terms of specific measures. Managers therefore develop various levels of midrange criteria that are easier to measure and, because of their relationship to the ultimate criterion of suvival, can be used in the short-run assessment of effectiveness. Reasoning along such lines, one researcher compiled 114 characteristics of organizations that are considered measures of organizational effectiveness.[25] These measures were then subjected to factor analysis that grouped them into twenty-four dimensions considered basic to the general concept of effectiveness. These dimensions are shown in Table 15-10.

Managers of 283 organizations completed a questionnaire evaluating their organizations on each of the criteria. Additionally, an overall measure of effectiveness was obtained by having each manager indicate on a nine-point scale where his or her organization stood on effectiveness. By relating the twenty-four midrange criteria to the overall effectiveness measure, it was found that 58 percent of the variance in judgment of overall effectiveness was explained. However, it was found that four of the effectiveness dimensions accounted for practically the same amount of variance. Using these four measures, an effectiveness model for general business was obtained as shown below; the numbers reflect the relative importance of each criterion.

Organizational effectiveness equals

(.24) productivity-support-utilization,
+ (.22) planning,
+ (.16) reliability,
+ (.12) initiative.

The dominant dimension in this model is productivity–support–utilization, a complex of characteristics. Although these concepts are separable, measures of them were so closely related that they were treated as a single dimension.

Table 15-10

Dimensions of Organizational Effectiveness

Dimension

Flexibility: Willingly tries out new ideas and suggestions, ready to tackle unusual problems.

Development: Personnel participate in training and development activities; high level of personnel competence and skill.

Cohesion: Lack of complaints and grievances; conflict among cliques within the organization.

Democratic supervision: Subordinate participation in work decisions.

Reliability: Meets objectives without necessity of follow-up and checking.

Selectivity: Doesn't accept marginal employees rejected by other organizations.

Diversity: Wide range of job responsibilities and personnel abilities within the organization.

Delegation: High degree of delegation by supervisors.

Bargaining: Rarely bargains with other organizations for favors and cooperation.

Emphasis on results: Results, output, and performance emphasized, not procedures.

Staffing: Personnel flexibility among assignments; development for promotion from within the organization.

Coordination: Coordinates and schedules activities with other organizations, utilizes staff assistance

Decentralization: Work and procedural decisions delegated to lowest levels.

Understanding: Organization philosophy, policy, directives understood and accepted by all.

Conflict: Little conflict with other organization units about authority or failure to meet responsibilities.

Personnel planning: Performance not disrupted by personnel absences, turnover, lost time.

Supervisory support: Supervisors support their subordinates.

Planning: Operations planned and scheduled to avoid lost time; little time spent on minor crises.

Cooperation: Operations scheduled and coordinated with other organizations; rarely fails to meet responsibilities.

Productivity-support-stabilization: Efficient performance; mutual support and respect of supervisors and subordinates; utilization of personnel skills and abilities.

Communication: Free flow of work information and communications within the organization

Turnover: Little turnover from inability to do the job.

Initiation: Initiates improvements in work methods and operations.

Supervisory control: Supervisors in control of progress of work.

Source: Thomas A. Mahoney and William Weitzel, "Management Models of Organizational Effectiveness," *Administrative Science Quarterly*, XIV, (September 1969), p. 358.

Using the approach of utilizing closely related dimensions, the following expanded model was developed (Figure 15-3). The model of general business can be viewed as consisting of a hierarchy of criteria with overall effectiveness as the ultimate criterion. The high-order criteria are productivity, planning, initiation, and reliable performance. Finally, the low-order criteria of cohesion, supervisory control, and the like tend to reflect the characteristics of the organization climate.

Figure 15-3

General Business Model

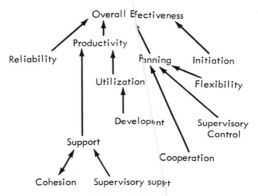

Source: Thomas A. Mahoney and William Weitzel, Management Models of Organizational Effectiveness," *Administrative Science Quarterly*, 14 (Seember 1969), p. 359.

One may raise the question of whether different organizations will have different efficiency dimensions since the general business model is based upon a very heterogeneous sample of organizations. To determine the dimensions for a particular type of organization, the same analysis was performed on a homogeneous sample of 103 st units within four research and development organizations. Three dimensions—reliability, cooperation, and development—comprised the prima contributions to overall effectiveness. The expanded research model is own in Figure 15-4.

The dimensions for research and development organizations are quite different from those observed in the general business model. Reliability is the only dimension appearing on both models; the R&D organizations place more emphasis on cooperation and development. While both groups looked at the same set of midrange criteria, they agned different degrees of importance to their contribution toward overall organizational effectiveness. Each group of managers employed different models of organizational effectiveness criteria for judging organizational uni

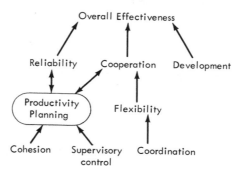

Figure 15-4

Research and Development Model

Source: Thomas A. Mahoney and William Weitzel, "Managerial Models of Organizational Effectiveness," *Administrative Science Quarterly*, 14, (September 1969), p. 359.

Levels of Analysis

Many models of effectiveness deal exclusively with organization-wide measures and ignore other potential levels of analysis. One author concludes, "if we are to make meaningful recommendations to managers about effectiveness—models of organizational effectiveness must be developed which attempt to specify or at least account for the relationships between individual processes and organizational behavior."[26] Since little has been done on this critical problem, a model paralleling the three levels of organizational behavior around which your text is organized may be helpful. Lawless has developed such a three-tier approach and much of what follows is based upon his model.[27]

The three levels of effectiveness are seen as related to one another and may be depicted as follows:

Effectiveness is not a matter of luck, but the result of people, as individuals, accomplishing something. One does not find effective groups or organizations without effective individuals. However, what reflects effectiveness at each level? How is effectiveness to be measured?

For individual effectiveness, there are usually measures of personal output and numerous characteristics that may be measured by personnel and supervisory rating schemes. Effectiveness factors will be dependent upon the individual job or role in the organization. At the group level, effectiveness measures may take the form of group productivity, group morale, adaptability, flexibility, and the like. Finally, at the organization-wide level many of the criteria may be like the ones previously examined—production, satisfaction, efficiency, and adaptiveness. Some of these criteria, depending upon the organization, may also be quite appropriate at both the group and individual level. The three levels of effectiveness could appear as those shown in Figure 15-5.

Figure 15-5

Three Levels of Effectiveness

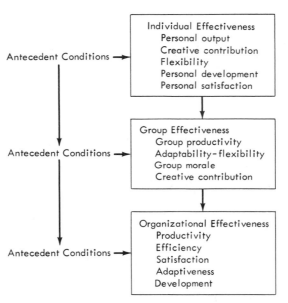

Source: David J. Lawless, EFFECTIVE MANAGEMENT: Social Psychological Approach, ©1972, p. 394. Adapted by permission of Prentice-Hall, Inc., Englewood Cliffs, New Jersey.

While effectiveness measures indicate what one might like to find in an organization, group, or individual, the manager is especially concerned about the antecedents or causal factors of effectiveness. With some insight into such contributing factors, one could manage more effectively so as to enhance effectiveness at all levels. This text has tried to examine some of the antecedents to the three levels of effectiveness under the control of the manager. Can you reconstruct some of these?

Coping adequately with the antecedent conditions at each of the three levels might well constitute a measure of managerial efficiency that, in turn, is a determinant of overall organizational efficiency.

Summary

The goal achievement approach to effectiveness is used at all managerial levels in modern, well-managed organizations. However, managers and researchers are seeking additional and more valid efficiency measures. Rather than utilizing one criterion as indicative of effectiveness, such as profit, several variables are used. An increasing amount of research effort is being directed to discover how a system's capacity to adapt and maintain itself are related to its survival. Internal processes that collectively add up to organizational effectiveness are being examined. Since survival is a long-run criterion, attention is being given to short-run and intermediate indicators of effectiveness that point to the likelihood of long-run survival. The time dimension stimulates a balanced evaluation of various performance measures rather than the sacrifice of intermediate measures to short-term expediency.

Just as differing time frame measures of effectiveness point to survival, so do effectiveness measures at the individual and group levels point to organizational effectiveness. Much of the material in previous chapters has been given to exploring the antecedent conditions that increase the probability of effectiveness at the individual, group, and organizational level.

Although logic would dictate a strong relationship between organization climate and organization effectiveness, little research has been conducted in this area. The first section of this chapter on organization climate demonstrated a positive and significant relationship between several climate dimensions and measures of satisfaction and productivity, both effectiveness measures. The student of organization behavior must wait for badly needed refinements in the area of climate and effectiveness and also an adequate effort to examine the potential link between these two concepts.

QUESTIONS FOR STUDY AND DISCUSSION

1. What does organization climate mean to you? Can you describe the external and internal factors that may influence an organization's climate?

2. Since the organization climate is whatever a person perceives it to be rather than objective reality, why should anyone be concerned about it?

3. Have you been associated with organizations (or classes) having different climates? If so, what seemed to account for the difference? Which did you prefer? Why?

4. How would you create an achievement–goal-directed climate? What behaviors would you expect in this climate?

5. How are job satisfaction and performance related to organization climate? What are some of the difficulties in drawing conclusions about these relationships?

6. There are several ways of viewing organization effectiveness. Which do you prefer? Why?

7. Why is an adaptability–coping approach to effectiveness an improvement over traditionally used measures of profit and/or productivity?

8. What does the time effectiveness model contribute to an evaluation of organizational effectiveness?

9. What is meant by midrange effectiveness criteria? Are they likely to differ from one kind of organization to another? Why?

10. In the "three levels of effectiveness" model, effectiveness may be promoted by antecedent conditions. What conditions do you think will contribute to the effectiveness of each level: individual, group, organization?

NOTES

[1]Tagiuri, Renato, "The Concept of Organizational Climate," in Renato Tagiuri and George H. Litwin, eds., *Organizational Climate* (Boston: Division of Research, Graduate School of Business Administration, Harvard University, 1968), pp. 25, 26.

[2]*Ibid.,* p. 29.

[3]Campbell, J., M. Dunnette, E. Lawler, and K. Weick, *Managerial Behavior, Performance, and Effectiveness* (New York: McGraw-Hill, 1970), p. 393.

[4]Johnson, Russell H., "A New Conceptualization of Source of Organizational Climate," *Administrative Science Quarterly,* 21 (March 1976), pp. 95–103.

[5]*Ibid.,* p. 101.

[6]Gavin, James F. and John G. Howe, "Psychological Climate: Some Theoretical and Empirical Considerations," *Behavioral Science* 20 (1975): 228–240.

[7]Pritchard, Robert D. and Bernard W. Karasick, "The Effects of Organizational Climate on Managerial Job Performance and Job Satisfaction," *Organizational Behavior and Human Performance* 9 (1973): 126–146.

[8]Payne, R. L. and D. C. Pheysey, "G. G. Stern's Organizational Climate Index: A Reconceptualization and Application to Business Organizations," *Organizational Behavior and Human Performance* 6 (1971): 77–98.

[9]*Ibid.,* p. 90.

[10]*Ibid.,* p. 93.

[11]Fredericksen, N., "Some Effects of Organizational Climates and Administrative Performance," Research Memorandum RM-66-21 (Educational Testing Service, 1966).

[12]Litwin, George H., "Climate and Motivation: An Experimental Study," in Tagiuri and Litwin, *op. cit.,* pp. 169–189.

[13]Pritchard and Karasick, *op. cit.,* pp. 138–139.

[14]LaFollette, William R. and Henry P. Sims, Jr., "Is Satisfaction Redundant with Organizational Climate?" *Organizational Behavior and Human Performance* 13 (1975): 257–278.

[15]Hellriegel, Don and John W. Slocum, Jr., "Organizational Cimate: Measures, Research and Contingencies," *Academy of Management Journal* 17 (June 1974): 263. See also Woodman, Richard and Donald C. King, "Organization Climate: Science or Folklore," *Academy of Management Review,* 3, No. 4, (Oct., 1978), pp. 816–826.

[16]Pritchard and Karasick, *op. cit.,* p. 142.

[17]Steers, Richard M., "Problems in the Measurement of Organizational Effectiveness," *Administrative Science Quarterly* 20 (December 1975): 546–558. See also Kilmann, Ralph

H. and Richard P. Herden, ''Towards A Systematic Methodology For Evaluating The Impact of Interventions on Organizational Effectiveness,'' *Academy of Management Review,* 1, No. 3, (July 1976), pp. 87–98.

[18]Campbell, John P., ''Research into the Nature of Organizational Effectiveness: An Endangered Species?'' Working paper, University of Minnesota. Noted in Steers, *op. cit.*

[19]Steers, *op. cit.,* p. 549.

[20]Schein, Edgar H., *Organizational Psychology,* 2nd ed. (Englewood Cliffs, N.J.: Prentice-Hall, 1970), p. 118.

[21]*Ibid.,* pp. 120–121.

[22]Gibson, James L., John M. Ivancevich, and James H. Donnelly, Jr., *Organizations,* 3rd ed. (Dallas: Business Publications, 1979), pp. 29–32.

[23]Mott, Paul E., *The Characteristics of Effective Organizations* (New York: Harper and Row, 1972), p. 17.

[24]*Ibid.,* pp. 22–24.

[25]Mahoney, Thomas A. and William Weitzel, ''Managerial Models of Organizational Effectiveness,'' *Administrative Science Quarterly* 14 (September 1969): 357–365.

[26]Steers, *op. cit.,* p. 554.

[27]Lawless, David J., *Effective Management* (Englewood Cliffs, N.J.: Prentice-Hall, 1972), pp. 391–399.

cases cases cases

Case Study: A Group Climate

A GROUP WITH PROBLEMS

Tom Baker was group supervisor for Controls Maintenance (CM), which consisted of some forty-seven hourly wage employees. The unit was divided into two sections and a rotating shift. Their purpose was to maintain, repair, troubleshoot, and install electrical, electronic, and pneumatic control facilities that required working closely with the Manufacturing Division.

The CM unit had been formed by combining the former Electrical and Instrument Maintenance groups when it had become apparent to plant management that the complexity of modern controls equipment created many jurisdictional arguments that detracted from the continuity of operations. An attempt by a local unit of an international union to represent the members of the former Electrical group had been defeated prior to combining the two groups.

The hourly wage employees of the newly formed CM organization had not reacted well to the change. No additional pay had been granted for the new job. Cross-training of electrical and instrument backgrounds was given, but many former Instrument group employees were not interested in electrical work, and some hourly wage leaders seemed convinced that the CM combination was made to defeat further attempts to unionize.

Tom Baker had been transferred from the Manufacturing Division. He was convinced that tighter discipline was needed and instructed his two section supervisors to engage in more formal (written) discipline to reduce the number of maintenance errors leading to losses in production. The section supervisors were hesitant to dictate disciplinary action to their crew supervisors because the hourly employees considered formal discipline nonconstructive and a threat to their jobs. Also the crew supervisors did not want to provide an issue that could rally the ever-present undercurrent for union representation. (A partial organization chart follows.)

Figure 1

A Partial Organization Chart

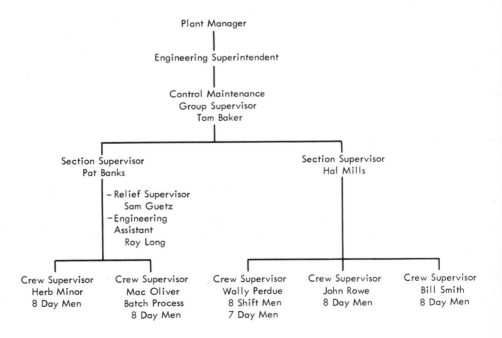

During a period when the relief supervisor was managing the batch-process crew, one of the maintenance employees, Ted Moore, had accepted controller settings from a manufacturing engineer, adjusted the controller, and left the job without further checks. The controller later malfunctioned and caused a loss in production. Tom Baker viewed Moore's action as a serious breach of good maintenance practice and insisted that formal discipline be applied. Sam Guetz, relief supervisor, had a talk with Ted Moore and entered a formal complaint in his record. The complaint stated that a CM mechanic should determine the optimum controller settings himself and be personally assured that the process was properly controlled before departing the job.

Moore felt that he had been treated unfairly, and he drew up a formal grievance in the presence of the personnel manager. In presenting his grievance to Pat Banks, section supervisor, he maintained two points: (1) formal discipline was excessive for the offense, and (2) it was common practice to accept controller settings from Manufacturing and that this method was approved by Mac Oliver, the crew supervisor.

When he returned from vacation, Mac Oliver confirmed that he did agree to acceptance of controller settings from Manufacturing. He went on to say, "We encourage a close working relationship with Manufacturing. The men know what is required, and I trust them to do it. I don't believe in looking over their shoulders all day."

Banks reported his findings to Tom Baker and advised that the formal complaint be withdrawn.

Baker said, "Pat, I'm concerned that Mac has not set proper standards for crew performance. There seems to be a reluctance on his part to use formal discipline. I've also noticed that his crew takes prolonged breaks and I've seen a few jobs with unnecessary workers. I'd like you to devise a development program for Mac, to encourage him to gain control of his crew."

The grievance was honored and the formal complaint withdrawn. Some of the men made offhand remarks to crew supervisors that Baker was attempting to pass out formal discipline "like they do in Manufacturing."

Business faltered in 1974 and plant management sought to reduce costs. Several layoffs were necessary. Five junior employees of CM group were sent back to Manufacturing and CM was forced to maintain output and services with fewer people. Moves were made to reduce two-worker jobs and to limit breaks.

A union petition for representation was presented to plant management. It was challenged in a hearing, but an election was set. While fighting the union issue, CM management identified many of its employees as pro-union or pro-company. The greatest pro-union support existed in the batch-process crew and the shift mechanics. The union was defeated by a narrow margin.

THE REORGANIZATION

Hal Mills, section supervisor, had long been concerned with the problems of the shift mechanics. They thought of themselves as "red-headed step-children." They complained of insufficient tools and spare parts. One shift mechanic had filed a grievance for a change in the shift operation.

Hal Mills reasoned that a change in first-line supervisors was necessary because Wally Perdue had too many men to supervise and the shift mechanics needed a crew supervisor who could devote attention to their problems. He convinced Tom Baker that the change in supervision should be made.

It was a time of supervisory change. Sam Guetz, relief supervisor, resigned. Pat Banks was transferred to Manufacturing, and Herb Minor was promoted from first line to take his place.

Tom Baker called a meeting of his two section supervisors, Herb Minor and Hal Mills, to discuss the planned changes in first line: "As you know, I've been concerned with Mac's performance in the batch-process crew and would like to evaluate him in a new position. In addition Hal advises that Wally Perdue has been ineffective in handling the shift mechanics. Since the relief supervisor slot is open, I think we should assign Mac Oliver to relief and let him administer the shift operation. What are your feelings?" Herb Minor spoke up, "I don't see how we can weaken the batch-process area by taking Mac out of there. I'm new in my job and I'm going to need support until I can get established." Baker replied, "I've considered that and I believe that Roy Long, our engineering assistant, has supervisory potential and he has been working closely with that crew for three years. He also has done some short-term relief work. He knows the area and I think the workers would accept him." Herb said, "Well, I don't know, Roy is a little difficult to understand when he talks to you, although he is a very energetic worker." Hal Mills interjected, "I don't think we have much choice. The shift mechanics have been the source of most of our pro-union agitation. We must get them under effective supervisory control. Wally can't handle them with his work load. We can consider promoting from the work crews. Tom Rogers said, "We went through that when Sam Guetz quit. Management will not consider an hourly wage person for a supervisory position. We either use Roy or make no move." The decision to assign Roy Long as batch-process crew supervisor was reached.

As several problems had been uncovered during the union campaign, the engineering superintendent, Tom Baker's boss, elected to institute programs to incease crew effectiveness thereby hoping to raise morale and prevent a future bid by the union. Each crew supervisor was asked to keep the workers busy with challenging work, limit breaks, and start training programs for the least effective employees. There was no formal plan. Each crew supervisor was to use methods best suited to his operation.

In his first report to Tom Baker and Herb Minor, Roy Long outlined some surprising observations: "These people are used to working as buddies. When I assigned one of them a job, he went and got his buddy to go along. I reminded them that I was assigning one man. On another occasion, I asked one of them to do a rush job, and he said that he would get to it in a few minutes. It seems that I'm constantly forced to break up little groups in conversation. One of them even told me about a certain job that "We don't do it that way over here." I'm convinced that Ted Moore is a leader in the crew attitude. You know he was pro-union in the last campaign. I recommend that we move a few people to break up this snake's nest."

At the conclusion of the report, Tom Baker said that he didn't know that things were that bad in the batch-process crew.

LEADERSHIP DIFFICULTIES

In the meantime, John Rowe, crew supervisor, came to see Hal Mills. "Hal, I think you should know that some of the workers in the batch-process crew have been talking to my people about Roy Long. For the most part they say that Roy is always hounding them and asking questions about their job progress. They say that they can't understand him. He waves his arms and makes facial expressions and doesn't say what he means. They say he doesn't believe in two-worker jobs and bothers them when on break or at lunch. They say he doesn't trust them, and he already has had a run-in with someone at whom he was shouting in the office."

"Hal, I'm sure you remember our previous conversations. At that time we didn't think that Roy was supervisory material, and you know that the men resented his pro-company stand when he was a hourly wage worker in the first union campaign. I'm sure that you and Tom Baker had your reasons for promoting him. I sure hope it works out for Roy's sake."

The following week, the entire batch-process crew scheduled an after-hours meeting with the personnel manager. In the meeting, the crew presented a list of complaints about Roy Long. Some men stated that they would seek transfers to another group if Long wasn't removed from his position. Crew reaction of this nature had not occurred in the plant since the first union campaign, and the plant manager was quite disturbed. He requested that Tom Baker and personnel get together and straighten out the situation.

Tom Baker decided that, since the workers had chosen to bypass Herb Minor, their crew supervisor, in presenting their complaints to personnel, he would request Herb to interview each worker individually and get all the facts together. This tactic followed a cooling-off period of three days. Herb made a point to listen and not to debate the worker's observations. A few of the interviews were summarized by him as follows:

"He talks to us like children. Working adults need to be treated like adults. He constantly asks, are you done? He can't communicate. Gets messed up in his instructions. I don't want to hurt Roy. I worked with him when he was engineering assistant. We had a good relationship then, but he can't continue as a supervisor."

"Roy doesn't believe in two-worker jobs. He bugs us about the job when we are at lunch. He appears very nervous as a supervisor—was much happier as an engineering assistant."

"Long got started off wrong. He had an explosive situation with Howell, and we all could hear shouting behind the door. I'm not a leader in this movement. Everyone is opposed to change. This could be part of our problem. We always put out 150 percent for Mac Oliver. It seems like Mac was demoted."

"One reason we went to personnel on this is because we asked their help when Roy was doing some relief supervising. Personnel told us to give him another chance then. I've never seen this type of problem in twenty years of service."

"I've heard him criticize another mechanic in my presence. Someone told him that this practice was wrong. He doesn't do it anymore."

"We told Tom Baker that Roy Long would never make a supervisor back when he was filling in on relief supervising, but Baker apparently won't listen. How many mistakes does he have to make before he realizes that he's not infallible?"

"We're tired of training supervisors. We need someone we can respect. Someone to get an answer from. Roy is good as an engineering assistant, but he hasn't got instrument experience. A lot of men will probably request a transfer from his crew."

"I haven't been in this crew long. I think I can get along with anybody. I know Roy personally and am used to his mannerisms. Like when he checks on whether you're done with a job—just his way of keeping up. There is an awful lot of confusion in the crew."

In the meantime, Hal Mills had been discussing the problem with some of his first-line supervisors to get their evaluation.

"Some of my men say that the actions of the batch-process crew are disgusting. They think that Roy Long has tried to force the people to work, and they're not used to that."

"You know that the workers can run off a supervisor anytime they want. I know of three who lost their jobs in the first union campaign, and we know damned well why Chuck White was transferred to another plant during this past campaign. We crew supervisors wonder when we're ever going to get any backing from management."

Tom Rogers called Herb Minor and Hal Mills together to outline a plan to correct the batch-process crew problem.

QUESTIONS

1. Evaluate the CM groups on the following climate dimensions:

A. Clarity and efficiency of structure: The degree to which organizational policies and guidelines are clearly defined; responsibility is assigned; methods and procedures are kept current; and decisions are timely and appropriate.

Good __ __ __ __ __ Poor
      5 4 3 2 1

B. Hindrance: The extent to which inefficient work procedures and administrative trivia interfere with successful completion of tasks.

Low __ __ __ __ __ High
    5 4 3 2 1

C. Rewards: The extent to which employees feel that rewards are adequate and fair and that sufficient opportunities exist for growth and advancement.

Fair __ __ __ __ __ Poor
    5 4 3 2 1

D. Esprit: The degree to which employees express feelings of pride, loyalty, cooperation, and friendliness in their work activities.

High __ __ __ __ __ Low
    5 4 3 2 1

E. Management trust and consideration: The degree to which management places trust and confidence in subordinates by allowing them sufficient latitude in their work, also in the encouragement of innovation.

High __ __ __ __ __ Low
    5 4 3 2 1

F. Challenge and risk: The extent to which policies and practices encourage high standards of work performance and reasonable risk taking among employees.

High __ __ __ __ __ Low
    5 4 3 2 1

2. What conclusions do you draw from the evaluation of climate?
3. Evaluate Tom Baker's leadership.
4. Evaluate Roy Long's leadership. To what extent do you think he is trying to live up to management's expectations?
5. How has leadership contributed to the climate of the CM group?
6. What other factors are affecting the climate?
7. What would you do to change this climate? Outline your plan of action.

cases cases cases

Case Study: A Change in Climate and Effectiveness

AN ELITE DEPARTMENT

The Engineering Department of the Mellon Machine Company was generally considered to be the elite department of the plant (see the partial organization chart of the company). Each product engineer was assigned one or more projects. These projects consisted of the redesign and improvement of existing tools or the design and development of new tools for the product line. For the new tools, the marketing department provided some guidance in the form of specifications for power output, functional requirements, size, and optional equipment. Also, competitive lines were closely examined for any worthwhile innovations that might be used. In addition to the assigned projects, the product engineers were also given assignments for designing specials for customers. A special usually consisted of some slight modification to an existing product to allow it to perform a particular function for the customer.

Figure 1

A Partial Organization Chart

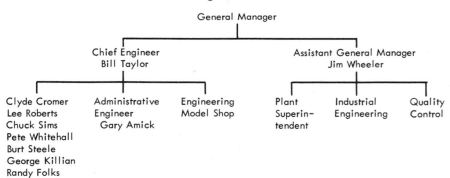

The product engineer was responsible for keeping each of his projects up to date and within the specified budget for the project. Due to work on specials, customer problems, or other work that interfered with the engineer's time, some of the assigned projects would fall behind schedule. This usually created no problems, and the project could be rescheduled.

If an engineer ran into a difficult problem on a project, he was always welcome to consult the chief engineer, Bill Taylor, who seemed to enjoy getting involved in the technical aspects of the projects and helping the engineers work out the more difficult problems. If the engineer had a project going smoothly, Taylor seldom saw any reason to get involved with it. He appeared to have confidence in the engineers' judgment and decision-making capabilities. He was pretty much willing to let the engineer run his own project with a minimum of direct supervision.

After the design work and model testing for a project was completed, Industrial Engineering would prepare a preliminary cost estimate of the proposed new tool. Industrial Engineering would also consult the product engineer at this time for possible design changes that would allow the parts to be more easily and economically manufactured.

Using Industrial Engineering's cost estimates and Marketing's sales forecast figures, a decision would be made by headquarters on whether or not to put the new tool in production.

If it was decided to put the new tool into production, the Engineering Department would release the parts drawings for the required tooling to be made up. These drawings had usually been made up before the first models were built, and most of the drawings were made by detail draftsmen under the supervision of the product engineer. Usually, the only drafting work done by the engineer was that amount necessary in the original design of the tool.

Once production of the tool was started, the engineer was expected to be available to consult with assembly, manufacturing, or quality control on any problems that might arise during the production start-up. The engineers were always quite willing to go out in the shop and work with whatever department was having problems with a new tool. Along these same lines, engineering was usually consulted when problems occurred with assembly of older model tools in production. Sometimes the problems were caused by incorrectly manufactured parts and at other times by an engineering design that needed to be corrected. Engineering was usually depended upon to solve this type of problem in the shop. The problems due to incorrectly made parts were often due to improper design of tooling fixtures by the Industrial Engineering Department.

Under Bill Taylor, the engineers seemed to be quite pleased with their work. Lee Roberts remarked, "I believe this is one of the best places I have ever worked. Bill really gives us interesting projects, and I get the feeling that he will always back us up if headquarters or anyone else should question any of our projects or design work." Clyde Cromer said, "Bill is really a great guy to work for. I feel like I always know where he stands and what he expects from me."

PROBLEMS IN THE ECONOMY AND IN MARKETING

Sales for the company continued to climb, and in 1972 a record sales mark was attained. As the economy began to slump in 1973, the sales of machine tools fell off quite sharply. In the spring of 1974, the company began to lay off hourly employees as well as some salaried personnel. In the Engineering Department, both draftsmen, the product designer, two model makers, and the secretary were let go.

Naturally, the turn of events created an air of uneasiness among the engineers. As time passed, sales leveled off at a lower level and no further layoffs occurred. Engineers were now required to do their own drafting work and make minor engineering changes that were formerly handled by the draftsmen under the supervision of the engineers. However, this did not seem to create too much of a problem or draw too many complaints from the engineers.

In the fall of 1974, it became apparent that one of the competing manufacturers was having a fair amount of success with a new line of low-cost tools. With the economic slump of 1973, tool manufacturers began to compete on price to get sales. As several other competitors introduced low-cost product lines on the market, the company decided to bring out a low-cost line of tools. This was accomplished in the early part of 1975.

It was the general opinion around the Engineering Department that the Marketing Department did not give adequate guidance to Engineering in deciding what new tools or product lines should be introduced. It seemed that the company always played a waiting game to see what the competition would do. Bill Taylor had often complained to his manager at headquarters about this. He also indicated that the sales personnel did not have adequate technical training, and as a result their technical knowledge of the product line was too limited.

NEW LEADERSHIP

To provide a stronger, more aggressive marketing policy, Bill Taylor was promoted to a position of tool applications and product manager. At this time Jim Wheeler was moved from assistant general manager to Bill Taylor's position of chief engineer. Wheeler had held the positions of either chief engineer or director of engineering for twenty-five years prior to becoming an assistant general manager. The position of assistant general manager was eliminated. Bill Taylor moved into the assistant general manager's office at the front of the plant, and Jim Wheeler moved into the chief engineer's office.

Upon moving into his new office, one of the first things that Jim Wheeler did was have the engineers rearrange the empty drafting tables that were located in the open area of the room. There was also some rearranging of file cabinets and other office furniture. The rearrangement did not appear to serve any functional purpose, and it seemed like a waste of time to the engineers involved in moving the furniture.

Several months later Chuck Sims complained that Jim Wheeler appeared to be upset about not having a copy of a letter that Chuck had written to a customer concerning a tool application. He said that Jim told him he wanted to receive copies of any correspondence between engineers and customers.

Near the end of the summer, one of the engineers received some sample castings from a foundry. These castings showed a design change that had been made by an engineer. Jim Wheeler had previously agreed to making the change. Since the sample castings met engineering specifications, the engineer had informed Purchasing that it was all right to order a production run of the castings. Gary Amick, administrative engineer, later told the engineer that Mr. Wheeler had wanted to see the sample castings and that it might be a good idea to show them to him. Wheeler said that he always liked to see things such as the sample castings even though there were no problems involved. It was now becoming clear to the engineers that Jim wanted to be in on every detail of the projects.

One day while working on a prototype in the engineering laboratory, Lee Roberts said, "What's going on around here anyway? Last week I discussed with Jim some changes I wanted to try on this new motor. Today I went in to show him the results, and I don't think he even remembered that we had talked about it before." Burt Steele remarked, "Things sure have changed since Jim took over Engineering. We don't have anyone to stand up for us anymore." Pete Whitehall said, "Two days ago he gave me a project to work on. I went in his office this morning to ask him a question about something, and he asked me if I was working on any assigned project. He seemed surprised when I told him he had just given me an assigned project two days before that was not due to be completed for another month." George Killian stated, "Maybe he is trying to keep up with the details so much that he doesn't have time for the big items."

In the late fall, two of the engineers were discussing their annual performance appraisals.

Chuck: Lee, did you ever get your performance appraisal?
Lee: Finally. It was about six weeks late though. Also I thought maybe Bill would be in on it, but he wasn't.
Chuck: That's right. We really haven't been under Jim for much more than half a year. All in all, though, my appraisal was pretty good.
Lee: Mine was all right, but I've had better ones under Bill.

At the beginning of 1975, a cost reduction and standards program was initiated. This was largely the responsibility of the Industrial Engineering Department. At this time Jim Wheeler talked to the engineers in a meeting and said that engineering management at headquarters expected all projects to be on schedule and within the stated budget. He said there would have to be a real good reason for any deviation.

As the standards and cost reduction program was put into effect, the drafting load in engineering became a good deal heavier. Changes to engineering drawings were done only by engineering. A fairly larger amount of the cost-reduction program required changing existing engineering drawings or making new ones. Industrial engineering would send their change requests through Jim Wheeler or Greg Amick, administrative engineer, who would in turn assign the request to an engineer. They often requested that the changes be made as soon as possible.

One day as the engineers were sitting at their lunch tables, Lee Roberts said, "I don't have any assigned projects that I'm working on right now. All I have been doing is what amounts to drafting work for I.E." George Killian said, "Me too. Jim brought in a big stack of drawings yesterday and said that they (I.E.) were in a hurry to have some changes made." Chuck Sims added, "It seems like a waste of time and money to me to have engineers doing plain drafting work when we could be working on new projects."

Burt Steele remarked that even Gary Amick had been out on one of the vacant drawing boards doing some drafting. Randy Folks said, "It doesn't seem to matter what any other department wants. They can usually get the request through Jim, and then we wind up having to do the job. We do things requested by Marketing, I.E., and Manufacturing that we never had to worry about before. I think that Jim is trying to make a good impression on the other department managers and is not looking out for us." Lee said, "He is always bugging me about some small detail on a project. He makes suggestions on the way he wants things done, but, when it comes to help on the big problems, I don't think he is as good technically as Bill." Chuck added, "I've been thinking about looking around for another job, but there isn't much demand for engineers right now."

QUESTIONS

1. What changes in climate have taken place in the engineering group?

2. Evaluate the Mellon Machinery Company using the time effectiveness model. What predictions do you make about the company?

3. Evaluate the company's using the adaptability–coping approach. What is your conclusion?

4. Evaluate the company on the basis of the "three levels of effectiveness" model. What antecedent conditions would you initiate or change at each level to improve effectiveness?

index